EP Fourth Reader
Days 91-180

EP Reader Series

Volume 4

Second Edition

CONTENTS

ACKNOWLEDGEMENTS

Thank you to Abigail Baia for her beautiful cover art.

Welcome to Easy Peasy All-in-One Homeschool's Fourth Reader Days 91-180

We hope you enjoy curling up with this book of books.

This is the first half of Easy Peasy's offline version of its assignments for the second half of Reading 4. The novels and poetry included are found in the public domain and have been gathered here along with each day's assignment directions. There are differences between this course and the online version because some reading assignments are not found in the public domain and had to be replaced.

In addition to the readings, online lessons and activities from Easy Peasy's website have been replaced with offline versions found in this book.

It is noted when children could use online vocabulary games for review, but there alternative options for review.

This is only the second half of the course, Days 91-180. The rest of the course is in EP Fourth Reader Days 1-90.

Day 91

1. Read the second part of chapter ten of *The Railway Children*.
2. Tell someone about the chapter.

Mother put her head out of the window, and it wasn't half a minute after that she was in the garden kneeling by the side of Peter, who never for an instant ceased to squeal.

"What happened, Bobbie?" Mother asked.

"It was the rake," said Phyllis. "Peter was pulling at it, so was Bobbie, and she let go and he went over."

"Stop that noise, Peter," said Mother. "Come. Stop at once."

Peter used up what breath he had left in a last squeal and stopped.

"Now," said Mother, "are you hurt?"

"If he was really hurt, he wouldn't make such a fuss," said Bobbie, still trembling with fury; "he's not a coward!"

"I think my foot's broken off, that's all," said Peter, huffily, and sat up. Then he turned quite white. Mother put her arm round him.

"He is hurt," she said; "he's fainted. Here, Bobbie, sit down and take his head on your lap."

Then Mother undid Peter's boots. As she took the right one off, something dripped from his foot on to the ground. It was red blood. And when the stocking came off there were three red wounds in Peter's foot and ankle, where the teeth of the rake had bitten him, and his foot was covered with red smears.

"Run for water--a basinful," said Mother, and Phyllis ran. She upset most of the water out of the basin in her haste, and had to fetch more in a jug.

Peter did not open his eyes again till Mother had tied her handkerchief round his foot, and she and Bobbie had carried him in and laid him on the brown wooden settle in the dining-room. By this time Phyllis was halfway to the Doctor's.

Mother sat by Peter and bathed his foot and talked to him, and Bobbie went out and got tea ready, and put on the kettle.

"It's all I can do," she told herself. "Oh, suppose Peter should die, or be a helpless cripple for life, or have to walk with crutches, or wear a boot with a sole like a log of wood!"

She stood by the back door reflecting on these gloomy possibilities, her eyes fixed on the water-butt.

"I wish I'd never been born," she said, and she said it out loud.

1

"Why, lawk a mercy, what's that for?" asked a voice, and Perks stood before her with a wooden trug basket full of green-leaved things and soft, loose earth.

"Oh, it's you," she said. "Peter's hurt his foot with a rake--three great gaping wounds, like soldiers get. And it was partly my fault."

"That it wasn't, I'll go bail," said Perks. "Doctor seen him?"

"Phyllis has gone for the Doctor."

"He'll be all right; you see if he isn't," said Perks. "Why, my father's second cousin had a hay-fork run into him, right into his inside, and he was right as ever in a few weeks, all except his being a bit weak in the head afterwards, and they did say that it was along of his getting a touch of the sun in the hay-field, and not the fork at all. I remember him well. A kind-'earted chap, but soft, as you might say."

Bobbie tried to let herself be cheered by this heartening reminiscence.

"Well," said Perks, "you won't want to be bothered with gardening just this minute, I dare say. You show me where your garden is, and I'll pop the bits of stuff in for you. And I'll hang about, if I may make so free, to see the Doctor as he comes out and hear what he says. You cheer up, Missie. I lay a pound he ain't hurt, not to speak of."

But he was. The Doctor came and looked at the foot and bandaged it beautifully, and said that Peter must not put it to the ground for at least a week.

"He won't be lame, or have to wear crutches or a lump on his foot, will he?" whispered Bobbie, breathlessly, at the door.

"My aunt! No!" said Dr. Forrest; "he'll be as nimble as ever on his pins in a fortnight. Don't you worry, little Mother Goose."

It was when Mother had gone to the gate with the Doctor to take his last instructions and Phyllis was filling the kettle for tea, that Peter and Bobbie found themselves alone.

"He says you won't be lame or anything," said Bobbie.

"Oh, course I shan't, silly," said Peter, very much relieved all the same.

"Oh, Peter, I am so sorry," said Bobbie, after a pause.

"That's all right," said Peter, gruffly.

"It was all my fault," said Bobbie.

"Rot," said Peter.

"If we hadn't quarrelled, it wouldn't have happened. I knew it was wrong to quarrel. I wanted to say so, but somehow I couldn't."

"Don't drivel," said Peter. "I shouldn't have stopped if you had said it. Not likely. And besides, us rowing hadn't anything to do with it. I might have caught my foot in the hoe, or taken off my fingers in the chaff-cutting machine or blown my nose off with fireworks. It would have been hurt just the same whether we'd been rowing or not."

"But I knew it was wrong to quarrel," said Bobbie, in tears, "and now you're hurt and--"

"Now look here," said Peter, firmly, "you just dry up. If you're not careful, you'll turn into a beastly little Sunday-school prig, so I tell you."

"I don't mean to be a prig. But it's so hard not to be when you're really trying to be good."

(The Gentle Reader may perhaps have suffered from this difficulty.)

"Not it," said Peter; "it's a jolly good thing it wasn't you was hurt. I'm glad it was me. There! If it had been you, you'd have been lying on the sofa looking like a suffering angel and being the light of the anxious household and all that. And I couldn't have stood it."

"No, I shouldn't," said Bobbie.

"Yes, you would," said Peter.

"I tell you I shouldn't."

"I tell you you would."

"Oh, children," said Mother's voice at the door. "Quarrelling again? Already?"

"We aren't quarrelling--not really," said Peter. "I wish you wouldn't think it's rows every time we don't agree!" When Mother had gone out again, Bobbie broke out:--

"Peter, I am sorry you're hurt. But you are a beast to say I'm a prig."

"Well," said Peter unexpectedly, "perhaps I am. You did say I wasn't a coward, even when you were in such a wax. The only thing is--don't you be a prig, that's all. You keep your eyes open and if you feel priggishness coming on just stop in time. See?"

"Yes," said Bobbie, "I see."

"Then let's call it Pax," said Peter, magnanimously: "bury the hatchet in the fathoms of the past. Shake hands on it. I say, Bobbie, old chap, I am tired."

He was tired for many days after that, and the settle seemed hard and uncomfortable in spite of all the pillows and bolsters and soft folded rugs. It was terrible not to be able to go out. They moved the settle to the window, and from there Peter could see the smoke of the trains winding along the valley. But he could not see the trains.

At first Bobbie found it quite hard to be as nice to him as she wanted to be, for fear he should think her priggish. But that soon wore off, and both she and Phyllis were, as he observed, jolly good sorts. Mother sat with him when his sisters were out. And the words, "he's not a coward," made Peter determined not to make any fuss about the pain in his foot, though it was rather bad, especially at night.

Praise helps people very much, sometimes.

There were visitors, too. Mrs. Perks came up to ask how he was, and so did the Station Master, and several of the village people. But the time went slowly, slowly.

"I do wish there was something to read," said Peter. "I've read all our books fifty times over."

"I'll go to the Doctor's," said Phyllis; "he's sure to have some."

"Only about how to be ill, and about people's nasty insides, I expect," said Peter.

"Perks has a whole heap of Magazines that came out of trains when people are tired of them," said Bobbie. "I'll run down and ask him."

So the girls went their two ways.

Bobbie found Perks busy cleaning lamps.

"And how's the young gent?" said he.

"Better, thanks," said Bobbie, "but he's most frightfully bored. I came to ask if you'd got any Magazines you could lend him."

"There, now," said Perks, regretfully, rubbing his ear with a black and oily lump of cotton waste, "why didn't I think of that, now? I was trying to think of something as 'ud amuse him only this morning, and I couldn't think of anything better than a guinea-pig. And a young chap I know's going to fetch that over for him this tea-time."

"How lovely! A real live guinea! He will be pleased. But he'd like the Magazines as well."

"That's just it," said Perks. "I've just sent the pick of 'em to Snigson's boy--him what's just getting over the pewmonia. But I've lots of illustrated papers left."

He turned to the pile of papers in the corner and took up a heap six inches thick.

"There!" he said. "I'll just slip a bit of string and a bit of paper round 'em."

He pulled an old newspaper from the pile and spread it on the table, and made a neat parcel of it.

"There," said he, "there's lots of pictures, and if he likes to mess 'em about with his paint-box, or coloured chalks or what not, why, let him. I don't want 'em."

"You're a dear," said Bobbie, took the parcel, and started. The papers were heavy, and when she had to wait at the level-crossing while a train went by, she rested the parcel on the top of the gate. And idly she looked at the printing on the paper that the parcel was wrapped in.

Suddenly she clutched the parcel tighter and bent her head over it. It seemed like some horrible dream. She read on--the bottom of the column was torn off--she could read no farther.

She never remembered how she got home. But she went on tiptoe to her room and locked the door. Then she undid the parcel and read that printed column again, sitting on the edge of her bed, her hands and feet icy cold and her face burning. When she had read all there was, she drew a long, uneven breath.

"So now I know," she said.

What she had read was headed, 'End of the Trial. Verdict. Sentence.'

The name of the man who had been tried was the name of her Father. The verdict was 'Guilty.' And the sentence was 'Five years' Penal Servitude.'

"Oh, Daddy," she whispered, crushing the paper hard, "it's not true--I don't believe it. You never did it! Never, never, never!"

There was a hammering on the door.

"What is it?" said Bobbie.

"It's me," said the voice of Phyllis; "tea's ready, and a boy's brought Peter a guinea-pig. Come along down."

And Bobbie had to.

Day 92

1. Read the first part of chapter eleven of *The Railway Children*.
2. What was Father arrested for? What happened at his trial? (Answers)
3. Do the children think he is innocent? Do you?

Bobbie knew the secret now. A sheet of old newspaper wrapped round a parcel--just a little chance like that--had given the secret to her. And she had to go down to tea and pretend that there was nothing the matter. The pretence was bravely made, but it wasn't very successful.

For when she came in, everyone looked up from tea and saw her pink- lidded eyes and her pale face with red tear-blotches on it.

"My darling," cried Mother, jumping up from the tea-tray, "whatever is the matter?"

"My head aches, rather," said Bobbie. And indeed it did.

"Has anything gone wrong?" Mother asked.

"I'm all right, really," said Bobbie, and she telegraphed to her Mother from her swollen eyes this brief, imploring message--"Not before the others!"

Tea was not a cheerful meal. Peter was so distressed by the obvious fact that something horrid had happened to Bobbie that he limited his speech to repeating, "More bread and butter, please," at startlingly short intervals. Phyllis stroked her sister's hand under the table to express sympathy, and knocked her cup over as she did it. Fetching a cloth and wiping up the spilt milk helped Bobbie a little. But she thought that tea would never end. Yet at last it did end, as all things do at last, and when Mother took out the tray, Bobbie followed her.

"She's gone to own up," said Phyllis to Peter; "I wonder what she's done."

"Broken something, I suppose," said Peter, "but she needn't be so silly over it. Mother never rows for accidents. Listen! Yes, they're going upstairs. She's taking Mother up to show her--the water-jug with storks on it, I expect it is."

Bobbie, in the kitchen, had caught hold of Mother's hand as she set down the tea-things.

"What is it?" Mother asked.

But Bobbie only said, "Come upstairs, come up where nobody can hear us."

When she had got Mother alone in her room she locked the door and then stood quite still, and quite without words.

All through tea she had been thinking of what to say; she had decided that "I know all," or "All is known to me," or "The terrible secret is a secret no longer," would be the proper thing. But now that she and her Mother and that awful sheet of newspaper were alone in the room together, she found that she could say nothing.

Suddenly she went to Mother and put her arms round her and began to cry again. And still she could find no words, only, "Oh, Mammy, oh, Mammy, oh, Mammy," over and over again.

Mother held her very close and waited.

Suddenly Bobbie broke away from her and went to her bed. From under her mattress she pulled out the paper she had hidden there, and held it out, pointing to her Father's name with a finger that shook.

"Oh, Bobbie," Mother cried, when one little quick look had shown her what it was, "you don't believe it? You don't believe Daddy did it?"

6

"No," Bobbie almost shouted. She had stopped crying.

"That's all right," said Mother. "It's not true. And they've shut him up in prison, but he's done nothing wrong. He's good and noble and honourable, and he belongs to us. We have to think of that, and be proud of him, and wait."

Again Bobbie clung to her Mother, and again only one word came to her, but now that word was "Daddy," and "Oh, Daddy, oh, Daddy, oh, Daddy!" again and again.

"Why didn't you tell me, Mammy?" she asked presently.

"Are you going to tell the others?" Mother asked.

"No."

"Why?"

"Because--"

"Exactly," said Mother; "so you understand why I didn't tell you. We two must help each other to be brave."

"Yes," said Bobbie; "Mother, will it make you more unhappy if you tell me all about it? I want to understand."

So then, sitting cuddled up close to her Mother, Bobbie heard "all about it." She heard how those men, who had asked to see Father on that remembered last night when the Engine was being mended, had come to arrest him, charging him with selling State secrets to the Russians--with being, in fact, a spy and a traitor. She heard about the trial, and about the evidence--letters, found in Father's desk at the office, letters that convinced the jury that Father was guilty.

"Oh, how could they look at him and believe it!" cried Bobbie; "and how could any one do such a thing!"

"Someone did it," said Mother, "and all the evidence was against Father. Those letters--"

"Yes. How did the letters get into his desk?"

"Someone put them there. And the person who put them there was the person who was really guilty."

"He must be feeling pretty awful all this time," said Bobbie, thoughtfully.

"I don't believe he had any feelings," Mother said hotly; "he couldn't have done a thing like that if he had."

"Perhaps he just shoved the letters into the desk to hide them when he thought he was going to be found out. Why don't you tell the lawyers, or someone, that it must have been that person? There wasn't anyone that would have hurt Father on purpose, was there?"

"I don't know--I don't know. The man under him who got Daddy's place when he--when the awful thing happened--he was always jealous of your Father because Daddy was so clever and everyone thought such a lot of him. And Daddy never quite trusted that man."

"Couldn't we explain all that to someone?"

"Nobody will listen," said Mother, very bitterly, "nobody at all. Do you suppose I've not tried everything? No, my dearest, there's nothing to be done. All we can do, you and I and Daddy, is to be brave, and patient, and--" she spoke very softly--"to pray, Bobbie, dear."

"Mother, you've got very thin," said Bobbie, abruptly.

"A little, perhaps."

"And oh," said Bobbie, "I do think you're the bravest person in the world as well as the nicest!"

"We won't talk of all this any more, will we, dear?" said Mother; "we must bear it and be brave. And, darling, try not to think of it. Try to be cheerful, and to amuse yourself and the others. It's much easier for me if you can be a little bit happy and enjoy things. Wash your poor little round face, and let's go out into the garden for a bit."

The other two were very gentle and kind to Bobbie. And they did not ask her what was the matter. This was Peter's idea, and he had drilled Phyllis, who would have asked a hundred questions if she had been left to herself.

A week later Bobbie managed to get away alone. And once more she wrote a letter. And once more it was to the old gentleman.

"My dear Friend," she said, "you see what is in this paper. It is not true. Father never did it. Mother says someone put the papers in Father's desk, and she says the man under him that got Father's place afterwards was jealous of Father, and Father suspected him a long time. But nobody listens to a word she says, but you are so good and clever, and you found out about the Russian gentleman's wife directly. Can't you find out who did the treason because he wasn't Father upon my honor; he is an Englishman and uncapable to do such things, and then they would let Father out of prison. It is dreadful, and Mother is getting so thin. She told us once to pray for all prisoners and captives. I see now. Oh, do help me--there is only just Mother and me know, and we can't do anything. Peter and Phil don't know. I'll pray for you twice every day as long as I live if you'll only try--just try to find out. Think if it was your Daddy, what you would feel. Oh, do, do, do help me.

With love I remain Your affectionately little friend,

Roberta.

P.S. Mother would send her kind regards if she knew I am writing-- but it is no use telling her I am, in case you can't do anything. But I know you will. Bobbie with best love."

She cut the account of her Father's trial out of the newspaper with Mother's big cutting-out scissors, and put it in the envelope with her letter.

Then she took it down to the station, going out the back way and round by the road, so that the others should not see her and offer to come with her, and she gave the letter to the Station Master to give to the old gentleman next morning.

"Where have you been?" shouted Peter, from the top of the yard wall where he and Phyllis were.

"To the station, of course," said Bobbie; "give us a hand, Pete."

She set her foot on the lock of the yard door. Peter reached down a hand.

"What on earth?" she asked as she reached the wall-top--for Phyllis and Peter were very muddy. A lump of wet clay lay between them on the wall, they had each a slip of slate in a very dirty hand, and behind Peter, out of the reach of accidents, were several strange rounded objects rather like very fat sausages, hollow, but closed up at one end.

"It's nests," said Peter, "swallows' nests. We're going to dry them in the oven and hang them up with string under the eaves of the coach-house."

"Yes," said Phyllis; "and then we're going to save up all the wool and hair we can get, and in the spring we'll line them, and then how pleased the swallows will be!"

"I've often thought people don't do nearly enough for dumb animals," said Peter with an air of virtue. "I do think people might have thought of making nests for poor little swallows before this."

"Oh," said Bobbie, vaguely, "if everybody thought of everything, there'd be nothing left for anybody else to think about."

"Look at the nests--aren't they pretty?" said Phyllis, reaching across Peter to grasp a nest.

"Look out, Phil, you goat," said her brother. But it was too late; her strong little fingers had crushed the nest.

"There now," said Peter.

"Never mind," said Bobbie.

"It is one of my own," said Phyllis, "so you needn't jaw, Peter. Yes, we've put our initial names on the ones we've done, so that the swallows will know who they've got to be so grateful to and fond of."

"Swallows can't read, silly," said Peter.

"Silly yourself," retorted Phyllis; "how do you know?"

"Who thought of making the nests, anyhow?" shouted Peter.

"I did," screamed Phyllis.

"Nya," rejoined Peter, "you only thought of making hay ones and sticking them in the ivy for the sparrows, and they'd have been sopping long before egg-laying time. It was me said clay and swallows."

"I don't care what you said."

"Look," said Bobbie, "I've made the nest all right again. Give me the bit of stick to mark your initial name on it. But how can you? Your letter and Peter's are the same. P. for Peter, P. for Phyllis."

"I put F. for Phyllis," said the child of that name. "That's how it sounds. The swallows wouldn't spell Phyllis with a P., I'm certain-sure."

"They can't spell at all," Peter was still insisting.

"Then why do you see them always on Christmas cards and valentines with letters round their necks? How would they know where to go if they couldn't read?"

"That's only in pictures. You never saw one really with letters round its neck."

"Well, I have a pigeon, then; at least Daddy told me they did. Only it was under their wings and not round their necks, but it comes to the same thing, and--"

"I say," interrupted Bobbie, "there's to be a paperchase to-morrow."

"Who?" Peter asked.

"Grammar School. Perks thinks the hare will go along by the line at first. We might go along the cutting. You can see a long way from there."

The paperchase was found to be a more amusing subject of conversation than the reading powers of swallows. Bobbie had hoped it might be. And next morning Mother let them take their lunch and go out for the day to see the paperchase.

"If we go to the cutting," said Peter, "we shall see the workmen, even if we miss the paperchase."

Of course it had taken some time to get the line clear from the rocks and earth and trees that had fallen on it when the great landslip happened. That was the occasion, you will remember, when the three children saved the train from being wrecked by waving six little red-flannel-petticoat flags. It is always interesting to watch people working, especially when they work with such interesting things as spades and picks and shovels and planks and barrows, when they have cindery red fires in iron pots with round holes in them, and red lamps hanging near the works at night. Of course the children were never out at night; but once, at dusk, when Peter had got out of his bedroom skylight on to the roof, he had seen the red lamp shining far away at the edge of the cutting. The children had often been down to watch the work, and this day the interest of picks and spades, and barrows being wheeled along planks, completely put the paperchase out of their heads, so that they quite jumped when a voice just behind them panted, "Let me pass, please." It was the hare--a big-boned, loose-limbed boy, with dark hair lying flat on a very damp forehead. The bag of torn paper under his arm was fastened across one shoulder by a strap. The children stood back. The hare ran along the line, and the workmen leaned on their picks to watch him. He ran on steadily and disappeared into the mouth of the tunnel.

Day 93

1. Read the second part of chapter eleven of *The Railway Children*.
2. Tell someone about the chapter.

"That's against the by-laws," said the foreman.

"Why worry?" said the oldest workman; "live and let live's what I always say. Ain't you never been young yourself, Mr. Bates?"

"I ought to report him," said the foreman.

"Why spoil sport's what I always say."

"Passengers are forbidden to cross the line on any pretence," murmured the foreman, doubtfully.

"He ain't no passenger," said one of the workmen.

"Nor 'e ain't crossed the line, not where we could see 'im do it," said another.

"Nor yet 'e ain't made no pretences," said a third.

"And," said the oldest workman, "'e's outer sight now. What the eye don't see the 'art needn't take no notice of's what I always say."

11

And now, following the track of the hare by the little white blots of scattered paper, came the hounds. There were thirty of them, and they all came down the steep, ladder-like steps by ones and twos and threes and sixes and sevens. Bobbie and Phyllis and Peter counted them as they passed. The foremost ones hesitated a moment at the foot of the ladder, then their eyes caught the gleam of scattered whiteness along the line and they turned towards the tunnel, and, by ones and twos and threes and sixes and sevens, disappeared in the dark mouth of it. The last one, in a red jersey, seemed to be extinguished by the darkness like a candle that is blown out.

"They don't know what they're in for," said the foreman; "it isn't so easy running in the dark. The tunnel takes two or three turns."

"They'll take a long time to get through, you think?" Peter asked.

"An hour or more, I shouldn't wonder."

"Then let's cut across the top and see them come out at the other end," said Peter; "we shall get there long before they do."

The counsel seemed good, and they went.

They climbed the steep steps from which they had picked the wild cherry blossom for the grave of the little wild rabbit, and reaching the top of the cutting, set their faces towards the hill through which the tunnel was cut. It was stiff work.

"It's like Alps," said Bobbie, breathlessly.

"Or Andes," said Peter.

"It's like Himmy what's its names?" gasped Phyllis. "Mount Everlasting. Do let's stop."

"Stick to it," panted Peter; "you'll get your second wind in a minute."

Phyllis consented to stick to it--and on they went, running when the turf was smooth and the slope easy, climbing over stones, helping themselves up rocks by the branches of trees, creeping through narrow openings between tree trunks and rocks, and so on and on, up and up, till at last they stood on the very top of the hill where they had so often wished to be.

"Halt!" cried Peter, and threw himself flat on the grass. For the very top of the hill was a smooth, turfed table-land, dotted with mossy rocks and little mountain-ash trees.

The girls also threw themselves down flat.

"Plenty of time," Peter panted; "the rest's all down hill."

When they were rested enough to sit up and look round them, Bobbie cried:--

"Oh, look!"

"What at?" said Phyllis.

"The view," said Bobbie.

"I hate views," said Phyllis, "don't you, Peter?"

"Let's get on," said Peter.

"But this isn't like a view they take you to in carriages when you're at the seaside, all sea and sand and bare hills. It's like the 'coloured counties' in one of Mother's poetry books."

"It's not so dusty," said Peter; "look at the Aqueduct straddling slap across the valley like a giant centipede, and then the towns sticking their church spires up out of the trees like pens out of an inkstand. I think it's more like

"There could he see the banners
 Of twelve fair cities shine."

"I love it," said Bobbie; "it's worth the climb."

"The paperchase is worth the climb," said Phyllis, "if we don't lose it. Let's get on. It's all down hill now."

"I said that ten minutes ago," said Peter.

"Well, I've said it now," said Phyllis; "come on."

"Loads of time," said Peter. And there was. For when they had got down to a level with the top of the tunnel's mouth--they were a couple of hundred yards out of their reckoning and had to creep along the face of the hill--there was no sign of the hare or the hounds.

"They've gone long ago, of course," said Phyllis, as they leaned on the brick parapet above the tunnel.

"I don't think so," said Bobbie, "but even if they had, it's ripping here, and we shall see the trains come out of the tunnel like dragons out of lairs. We've never seen that from the top side before."

"No more we have," said Phyllis, partially appeased.

It was really a most exciting place to be in. The top of the tunnel seemed ever so much farther from the line than they had expected, and it was like being on a bridge, but a bridge overgrown with bushes and creepers and grass and wild-flowers.

"I know the paperchase has gone long ago," said Phyllis every two minutes, and she hardly knew whether she was pleased or disappointed when Peter, leaning over the parapet, suddenly cried:--

"Look out. Here he comes!"

They all leaned over the sun-warmed brick wall in time to see the hare, going very slowly, come out from the shadow of the tunnel.

"There, now," said Peter, "what did I tell you? Now for the hounds!"

Very soon came the hounds--by ones and twos and threes and sixes and sevens--and they also were going slowly and seemed very tired. Two or three who lagged far behind came out long after the others.

"There," said Bobbie, "that's all--now what shall we do?"

"Go along into the tulgy wood over there and have lunch," said Phyllis; "we can see them for miles from up here."

"Not yet," said Peter. "That's not the last. There's the one in the red jersey to come yet. Let's see the last of them come out."

But though they waited and waited and waited, the boy in the red jersey did not appear.

"Oh, let's have lunch," said Phyllis; "I've got a pain in my front with being so hungry. You must have missed seeing the red-jerseyed one when he came out with the others--"

But Bobbie and Peter agreed that he had not come out with the others.

"Let's get down to the tunnel mouth," said Peter; "then perhaps we shall see him coming along from the inside. I expect he felt spun-chuck, and rested in one of the manholes. You stay up here and watch, Bob, and when I signal from below, you come down. We might miss seeing him on the way down, with all these trees."

So the others climbed down and Bobbie waited till they signalled to her from the line below. And then she, too, scrambled down the roundabout slippery path among roots and moss till she stepped out between two dogwood trees and joined the others on the line. And still there was no sign of the hound with the red jersey.

"Oh, do, do let's have something to eat," wailed Phyllis. "I shall die if you don't, and then you'll be sorry."

"Give her the sandwiches, for goodness' sake, and stop her silly mouth," said Peter, not quite unkindly. "Look here," he added, turning to Bobbie, "perhaps we'd better have one each, too. We may need all our strength. Not more than one, though. There's no time."

"What?" asked Bobbie, her mouth already full, for she was just as hungry as Phyllis.

"Don't you see," replied Peter, impressively, "that red-jerseyed hound has had an accident--that's what it is. Perhaps even as we speak he's lying with his head on the metals, an unresisting prey to any passing express--"

"Oh, don't try to talk like a book," cried Bobbie, bolting what was left of her sandwich; "come on. Phil, keep close behind me, and if a train comes, stand flat against the tunnel wall and hold your petticoats close to you."

"Give me one more sandwich," pleaded Phyllis, "and I will."

"I'm going first," said Peter; "it was my idea," and he went.

Of course you know what going into a tunnel is like? The engine gives a scream and then suddenly the noise of the running, rattling train changes and grows different and much louder. Grown-up people pull up the windows and hold them by the strap. The railway carriage suddenly grows like night--with lamps, of course, unless you are in a slow local train, in which case lamps are not always provided. Then by and by the darkness outside the carriage window is touched by puffs of cloudy whiteness, then you see a blue light on the walls of the tunnel, then the sound of the moving train changes once more, and you are out in the good open air again, and grown-ups let the straps go. The windows, all dim with the yellow breath of the tunnel, rattle down into their places, and you see once more the dip and catch of the telegraph wires beside the line, and the straight-cut hawthorn hedges with the tiny baby trees growing up out of them every thirty yards.

All this, of course, is what a tunnel means when you are in a train. But everything is quite different when you walk into a tunnel on your own feet, and tread on shifting, sliding stones and gravel on a path that curves downwards from the shining metals to the wall. Then you see slimy, oozy trickles of water running down the inside of the tunnel, and you notice that the bricks are not red or brown, as they are at the tunnel's mouth, but dull, sticky, sickly green. Your voice, when you speak, is quite changed from what it was out in the sunshine, and it is a long time before the tunnel is quite dark.

It was not yet quite dark in the tunnel when Phyllis caught at Bobbie's skirt, ripping out half a yard of gathers, but no one noticed this at the time.

"I want to go back," she said, "I don't like it. It'll be pitch dark in a minute. I won't go on in the dark. I don't care what you say, I won't."

"Don't be a silly cuckoo," said Peter; "I've got a candle end and matches, and--what's that?"

"That" was a low, humming sound on the railway line, a trembling of the wires beside it, a buzzing, humming sound that grew louder and louder as they listened.

"It's a train," said Bobbie.

"Which line?"

"Let me go back," cried Phyllis, struggling to get away from the hand by which Bobbie held her.

"Don't be a coward," said Bobbie; "it's quite safe. Stand back."

15

"Come on," shouted Peter, who was a few yards ahead. "Quick! Manhole!"

The roar of the advancing train was now louder than the noise you hear when your head is under water in the bath and both taps are running, and you are kicking with your heels against the bath's tin sides. But Peter had shouted for all he was worth, and Bobbie heard him. She dragged Phyllis along to the manhole. Phyllis, of course, stumbled over the wires and grazed both her legs. But they dragged her in, and all three stood in the dark, damp, arched recess while the train roared louder and louder. It seemed as if it would deafen them. And, in the distance, they could see its eyes of fire growing bigger and brighter every instant.

"It is a dragon--I always knew it was--it takes its own shape in here, in the dark," shouted Phyllis. But nobody heard her. You see the train was shouting, too, and its voice was bigger than hers.

And now, with a rush and a roar and a rattle and a long dazzling flash of lighted carriage windows, a smell of smoke, and blast of hot air, the train hurtled by, clanging and jangling and echoing in the vaulted roof of the tunnel. Phyllis and Bobbie clung to each other. Even Peter caught hold of Bobbie's arm, "in case she should be frightened," as he explained afterwards.

And now, slowly and gradually, the tail-lights grew smaller and smaller, and so did the noise, till with one last whiz the train got itself out of the tunnel, and silence settled again on its damp walls and dripping roof.

"Oh!" said the children, all together in a whisper.

Peter was lighting the candle end with a hand that trembled.

"Come on," he said; but he had to clear his throat before he could speak in his natural voice.

"Oh," said Phyllis, "if the red-jerseyed one was in the way of the train!"

"We've got to go and see," said Peter.

"Couldn't we go and send someone from the station?" said Phyllis.

"Would you rather wait here for us?" asked Bobbie, severely, and of course that settled the question.

So the three went on into the deeper darkness of the tunnel. Peter led, holding his candle end high to light the way. The grease ran down his fingers, and some of it right up his sleeve. He found a long streak from wrist to elbow when he went to bed that night.

It was not more than a hundred and fifty yards from the spot where they had stood while the train went by that Peter stood still, shouted "Hullo," and then went on much quicker than before. When the others caught him up, he stopped. And he stopped within a yard of what they had come into the tunnel to look for. Phyllis saw a gleam of red, and shut her eyes tight. There, by the curved, pebbly down line, was the red-jerseyed hound. His back was against the wall, his arms hung limply by his sides, and his eyes were shut.

"Was the red, blood? Is he all killed?" asked Phyllis, screwing her eyelids more tightly together.

"Killed? Nonsense!" said Peter. "There's nothing red about him except his jersey. He's only fainted. What on earth are we to do?"

"Can we move him?" asked Bobbie.

"I don't know; he's a big chap."

"Suppose we bathe his forehead with water. No, I know we haven't any, but milk's just as wet. There's a whole bottle."

"Yes," said Peter, "and they rub people's hands, I believe."

"They burn feathers, I know," said Phyllis.

"What's the good of saying that when we haven't any feathers?"

"As it happens," said Phyllis, in a tone of exasperated triumph, "I've got a shuttlecock in my pocket. So there!"

And now Peter rubbed the hands of the red-jerseyed one. Bobbie burned the feathers of the shuttlecock one by one under his nose, Phyllis splashed warmish milk on his forehead, and all three kept on saying as fast and as earnestly as they could: "Oh, look up, speak to me! For my sake, speak!"

Day 94

  1. Read the first part of chapter twelve of *The Railway Children*.
  2. Tell someone about the chapter.

"Oh, look up! Speak to me! For my sake, speak!" The children said the words over and over again to the unconscious hound in a red jersey, who sat with closed eyes and pale face against the side of the tunnel.

"Wet his ears with milk," said Bobbie. "I know they do it to people that faint--with eau-de-Cologne. But I expect milk's just as good."

So they wetted his ears, and some of the milk ran down his neck under the red jersey. It was very dark in the tunnel. The candle end Peter had carried, and which now burned on a flat stone, gave hardly any light at all.

"Oh, do look up," said Phyllis. "For my sake! I believe he's dead."

"For my sake," repeated Bobbie. "No, he isn't."

"For any sake," said Peter; "come out of it." And he shook the sufferer by the arm.

And then the boy in the red jersey sighed, and opened his eyes, and shut them again and said in a very small voice, "Chuck it."

"Oh, he's not dead," said Phyllis. "I knew he wasn't," and she began to cry.

"What's up? I'm all right," said the boy.

"Drink this," said Peter, firmly, thrusting the nose of the milk bottle into the boy's mouth. The boy struggled, and some of the milk was upset before he could get his mouth free to say:--

"What is it?"

"It's milk," said Peter. "Fear not, you are in the hands of friends. Phil, you stop bleating this minute."

"Do drink it," said Bobbie, gently; "it'll do you good."

So he drank. And the three stood by without speaking to him.

"Let him be a minute," Peter whispered; "he'll be all right as soon as the milk begins to run like fire through his veins."

He was.

"I'm better now," he announced. "I remember all about it." He tried to move, but the movement ended in a groan. "Bother! I believe I've broken my leg," he said.

"Did you tumble down?" asked Phyllis, sniffing.

"Of course not--I'm not a kiddie," said the boy, indignantly; "it was one of those beastly wires tripped me up, and when I tried to get up again I couldn't stand, so I sat down. Gee whillikins! it does hurt, though. How did you get here?"

"We saw you all go into the tunnel and then we went across the hill to see you all come out. And the others did--all but you, and you didn't. So we are a rescue party," said Peter, with pride.

"You've got some pluck, I will say," remarked the boy.

"Oh, that's nothing," said Peter, with modesty. "Do you think you could walk if we helped you?"

"I could try," said the boy.

He did try. But he could only stand on one foot; the other dragged in a very nasty way.

"Here, let me sit down. I feel like dying," said the boy. "Let go of me--let go, quick--" He lay down and closed his eyes. The others looked at each other by the dim light of the little candle.

"What on earth!" said Peter.

"Look here," said Bobbie, quickly, "you must go and get help. Go to the nearest house."

"Yes, that's the only thing," said Peter. "Come on."

"If you take his feet and Phil and I take his head, we could carry him to the manhole."

They did it. It was perhaps as well for the sufferer that he had fainted again.

"Now," said Bobbie, "I'll stay with him. You take the longest bit of candle, and, oh--be quick, for this bit won't burn long."

"I don't think Mother would like me leaving you," said Peter, doubtfully. "Let me stay, and you and Phil go."

"No, no," said Bobbie, "you and Phil go--and lend me your knife. I'll try to get his boot off before he wakes up again."

"I hope it's all right what we're doing," said Peter.

"Of course it's right," said Bobbie, impatiently. "What else would you do? Leave him here all alone because it's dark? Nonsense. Hurry up, that's all."

So they hurried up.

Bobbie watched their dark figures and the little light of the little candle with an odd feeling of having come to the end of everything. She knew now, she thought, what nuns who were bricked up alive in convent walls felt like. Suddenly she gave herself a little shake.

"Don't be a silly little girl," she said. She was always very angry when anyone else called her a little girl, even if the adjective that went first was not "silly" but "nice" or "good" or "clever." And it was only when she was very angry with herself that she allowed Roberta to use that expression to Bobbie.

She fixed the little candle end on a broken brick near the red- jerseyed boy's feet. Then she opened Peter's knife. It was always hard to manage--a halfpenny was generally needed to get it open at all. This time Bobbie somehow got it open with her thumbnail. She broke the nail, and it hurt horribly. Then she cut the boy's bootlace, and got the boot off. She tried to pull off his stocking, but his leg was dreadfully swollen, and it did not seem to be the proper shape. So she cut the stocking down, very slowly and carefully. It was a brown, knitted stocking, and she wondered who had knitted it, and whether it was the boy's mother, and whether she was feeling anxious about him, and how she would feel when he was brought home with his leg broken. When Bobbie had got the stocking off and saw the poor leg, she felt as though the tunnel was growing darker, and the ground felt unsteady, and nothing seemed quite real.

"Silly little girl!" said Roberta to Bobbie, and felt better.

"The poor leg," she told herself; "it ought to have a cushion--ah!"

She remembered the day when she and Phyllis had torn up their red flannel petticoats to make danger signals to stop the train and prevent an accident. Her flannel petticoat to-day was white, but it would be quite as soft as a red one. She took it off.

"Oh, what useful things flannel petticoats are!" she said; "the man who invented them ought to have a statue directed to him." And she said it aloud, because it seemed that any voice, even her own, would be a comfort in that darkness.

"What ought to be directed? Who to?" asked the boy, suddenly and very feebly.

"Oh," said Bobbie, "now you're better! Hold your teeth and don't let it hurt too much. Now!"

She had folded the petticoat, and lifting his leg laid it on the cushion of folded flannel.

"Don't faint again, please don't," said Bobbie, as he groaned. She hastily wetted her handkerchief with milk and spread it over the poor leg.

"Oh, that hurts," cried the boy, shrinking. "Oh--no, it doesn't--it's nice, really."

"What's your name?" said Bobbie.

"Jim."

"Mine's Bobbie."

"But you're a girl, aren't you?"

"Yes, my long name's Roberta."

"I say--Bobbie."

"Yes?"

"Wasn't there some more of you just now?"

"Yes, Peter and Phil--that's my brother and sister. They've gone to get someone to carry you out."

"What rum names. All boys'."

"Yes--I wish I was a boy, don't you?"

"I think you're all right as you are."

"I didn't mean that--I meant don't you wish you were a boy, but of course you are without wishing."

"You're just as brave as a boy. Why didn't you go with the others?"

"Somebody had to stay with you," said Bobbie.

"Tell you what, Bobbie," said Jim, "you're a brick. Shake." He reached out a red-jerseyed arm and Bobbie squeezed his hand.

"I won't shake it," she explained, "because it would shake you, and that would shake your poor leg, and that would hurt. Have you got a hanky?"

"I don't expect I have." He felt in his pocket. "Yes, I have. What for?"

She took it and wetted it with milk and put it on his forehead.

"That's jolly," he said; "what is it?"

"Milk," said Bobbie. "We haven't any water--"

"You're a jolly good little nurse," said Jim.

"I do it for Mother sometimes," said Bobbie--"not milk, of course, but scent, or vinegar and water. I say, I must put the candle out now, because there mayn't be enough of the other one to get you out by."

"By George," said he, "you think of everything."

Bobbie blew. Out went the candle. You have no idea how black-velvety the darkness was.

"I say, Bobbie," said a voice through the blackness, "aren't you afraid of the dark?"

"Not--not very, that is--"

"Let's hold hands," said the boy, and it was really rather good of him, because he was like most boys of his age and hated all material tokens of affection, such as kissing and holding of hands. He called all such things "pawings," and detested them.

The darkness was more bearable to Bobbie now that her hand was held in the large rough hand of the red-jerseyed sufferer; and he, holding her little smooth hot paw, was surprised to find that he did not mind it so much as he expected. She tried to talk, to amuse him, and "take his mind off" his sufferings, but it is very difficult to go on talking in the dark, and presently they found themselves in a silence, only broken now and then by a--

"You all right, Bobbie?"

or an--

"I'm afraid it's hurting you most awfully, Jim. I am so sorry."

And it was very cold.

*   *   *   *   *   *

Peter and Phyllis tramped down the long way of the tunnel towards daylight, the candle-grease dripping over Peter's fingers. There were no accidents unless you count Phyllis's catching her frock on a wire, and tearing a long, jagged slit in it, and tripping over her bootlace when it came undone, or going down on her hands and knees, all four of which were grazed.

"There's no end to this tunnel," said Phyllis--and indeed it did seem very very long.

"Stick to it," said Peter; "everything has an end, and you get to it if you only keep all on."

Which is quite true, if you come to think of it, and a useful thing to remember in seasons of trouble--such as measles, arithmetic, impositions, and those times when you are in disgrace, and feel as though no one would ever love you again, and you could never--never again--love anybody.

Day 95

1. Read the second part of chapter twelve of *The Railway Children*.
2. Tell someone about the chapter.

"Hurray," said Peter, suddenly, "there's the end of the tunnel--looks just like a pin-hole in a bit of black paper, doesn't it?"

The pin-hole got larger--blue lights lay along the sides of the tunnel. The children could see the gravel way that lay in front of them; the air grew warmer and sweeter. Another twenty steps and they were out in the good glad sunshine with the green trees on both sides.

Phyllis drew a long breath.

"I'll never go into a tunnel again as long as ever I live," said she, "not if there are twenty hundred thousand millions hounds inside with red jerseys and their legs broken."

"Don't be a silly cuckoo," said Peter, as usual. "You'd have to."

"I think it was very brave and good of me," said Phyllis.

"Not it," said Peter; "you didn't go because you were brave, but because Bobbie and I aren't skunks. Now where's the nearest house, I wonder? You can't see anything here for the trees."

"There's a roof over there," said Phyllis, pointing down the line.

22

"That's the signal-box," said Peter, "and you know you're not allowed to speak to signalmen on duty. It's wrong."

"I'm not near so afraid of doing wrong as I was of going into that tunnel," said Phyllis. "Come on," and she started to run along the line. So Peter ran, too.

It was very hot in the sunshine, and both children were hot and breathless by the time they stopped, and bending their heads back to look up at the open windows of the signal-box, shouted "Hi!" as loud as their breathless state allowed. But no one answered. The signal-box stood quiet as an empty nursery, and the handrail of its steps was hot to the hands of the children as they climbed softly up. They peeped in at the open door. The signalman was sitting on a chair tilted back against the wall. His head leaned sideways, and his mouth was open. He was fast asleep.

"My hat!" cried Peter; "wake up!" And he cried it in a terrible voice, for he knew that if a signalman sleeps on duty, he risks losing his situation, let alone all the other dreadful risks to trains which expect him to tell them when it is safe for them to go their ways.

The signalman never moved. Then Peter sprang to him and shook him. And slowly, yawning and stretching, the man awoke. But the moment he was awake he leapt to his feet, put his hands to his head "like a mad maniac," as Phyllis said afterwards, and shouted:--

"Oh, my heavens--what's o'clock?"

"Twelve thirteen," said Peter, and indeed it was by the white-faced, round-faced clock on the wall of the signal-box.

The man looked at the clock, sprang to the levers, and wrenched them this way and that. An electric bell tingled--the wires and cranks creaked, and the man threw himself into a chair. He was very pale, and the sweat stood on his forehead "like large dewdrops on a white cabbage," as Phyllis remarked later. He was trembling, too; the children could see his big hairy hands shake from side to side, "with quite extra-sized trembles," to use the subsequent words of Peter. He drew long breaths. Then suddenly he cried, "Thank God, thank God you come in when you did--oh, thank God!" and his shoulders began to heave and his face grew red again, and he hid it in those large hairy hands of his.

"Oh, don't cry--don't," said Phyllis, "it's all right now," and she patted him on one big, broad shoulder, while Peter conscientiously thumped the other.

But the signalman seemed quite broken down, and the children had to pat him and thump him for quite a long time before he found his handkerchief--a red one with mauve and white horseshoes on it--and mopped his face and spoke. During this patting and thumping interval a train thundered by.

"I'm downright shamed, that I am," were the words of the big signalman when he had stopped crying; "snivelling like a kid." Then suddenly he seemed to get cross. "And what was you doing up here, anyway?" he said; "you know it ain't allowed."

"Yes," said Phyllis, "we knew it was wrong--but I wasn't afraid of doing wrong, and so it turned out right. You aren't sorry we came."

"Lor' love you--if you hadn't 'a' come--" he stopped and then went on. "It's a disgrace, so it is, sleeping on duty. If it was to come to be known--even as it is, when no harm's come of it."

"It won't come to be known," said Peter; "we aren't sneaks. All the same, you oughtn't to sleep on duty--it's dangerous."

"Tell me something I don't know," said the man, "but I can't help it. I know'd well enough just how it 'ud be. But I couldn't get off. They couldn't get no one to take on my duty. I tell you I ain't had ten minutes' sleep this last five days. My little chap's ill--pewmonia, the Doctor says--and there's no one but me and 'is little sister to do for him. That's where it is. The gell must 'ave her sleep. Dangerous? Yes, I believe you. Now go and split on me if you like."

"Of course we won't," said Peter, indignantly, but Phyllis ignored the whole of the signalman's speech, except the first six words.

"You asked us," she said, "to tell you something you don't know. Well, I will. There's a boy in the tunnel over there with a red jersey and his leg broken."

"What did he want to go into the blooming tunnel for, then?" said the man.

"Don't you be so cross," said Phyllis, kindly. "we haven't done anything wrong except coming and waking you up, and that was right, as it happens."

Then Peter told how the boy came to be in the tunnel.

"Well," said the man, "I don't see as I can do anything. I can't leave the box."

"You might tell us where to go after someone who isn't in a box, though," said Phyllis.

"There's Brigden's farm over yonder--where you see the smoke a-coming up through the trees," said the man, more and more grumpy, as Phyllis noticed.

"Well, good-bye, then," said Peter.

But the man said, "Wait a minute." He put his hand in his pocket and brought out some money--a lot of pennies and one or two shillings and sixpences and half-a-crown. He picked out two shillings and held them out.

"Here," he said. "I'll give you this to hold your tongues about what's taken place to-day."

There was a short, unpleasant pause. Then:--

"You are a nasty man, though, aren't you?" said Phyllis.

Peter took a step forward and knocked the man's hand up, so that the shillings leapt out of it and rolled on the floor.

"If anything could make me sneak, that would!" he said. "Come, Phil," and marched out of the signal-box with flaming cheeks.

Phyllis hesitated. Then she took the hand, still held out stupidly, that the shillings had been in.

"I forgive you," she said, "even if Peter doesn't. You're not in your proper senses, or you'd never have done that. I know want of sleep sends people mad. Mother told me. I hope your little boy will soon be better, and--"

"Come on, Phil," cried Peter, eagerly.

"I give you my sacred honour-word we'll never tell anyone. Kiss and be friends," said Phyllis, feeling how noble it was of her to try to make up a quarrel in which she was not to blame.

The signalman stooped and kissed her.

"I do believe I'm a bit off my head, Sissy," he said. "Now run along home to Mother. I didn't mean to put you about--there."

So Phil left the hot signal-box and followed Peter across the fields to the farm.

When the farm men, led by Peter and Phyllis and carrying a hurdle covered with horse-cloths, reached the manhole in the tunnel, Bobbie was fast asleep and so was Jim. Worn out with the pain, the Doctor said afterwards.

"Where does he live?" the bailiff from the farm asked, when Jim had been lifted on to the hurdle.

"In Northumberland," answered Bobbie.

"I'm at school at Maidbridge," said Jim. "I suppose I've got to get back there, somehow."

"Seems to me the Doctor ought to have a look in first," said the bailiff.

"Oh, bring him up to our house," said Bobbie. "It's only a little way by the road. I'm sure Mother would say we ought to."

"Will your Ma like you bringing home strangers with broken legs?"

"She took the poor Russian home herself," said Bobbie. "I know she'd say we ought."

"All right," said the bailiff, "you ought to know what your Ma 'ud like. I wouldn't take it upon me to fetch him up to our place without I asked the Missus first, and they call me the Master, too."

"Are you sure your Mother won't mind?" whispered Jim.

"Certain," said Bobbie.

"Then we're to take him up to Three Chimneys?" said the bailiff.

"Of course," said Peter.

"Then my lad shall nip up to Doctor's on his bike, and tell him to come down there. Now, lads, lift him quiet and steady. One, two, three!"

*　　*　　*　　*　　*　　*

Thus it happened that Mother, writing away for dear life at a story about a Duchess, a designing villain, a secret passage, and a missing will, dropped her pen as her work-room door burst open, and turned to see Bobbie hatless and red with running.

"Oh, Mother," she cried, "do come down. We found a hound in a red jersey in the tunnel, and he's broken his leg and they're bringing him home."

"They ought to take him to the vet," said Mother, with a worried frown; "I really can't have a lame dog here."

"He's not a dog, really--he's a boy," said Bobbie, between laughing and choking.

"Then he ought to be taken home to his mother."

"His mother's dead," said Bobbie, "and his father's in Northumberland. Oh, Mother, you will be nice to him? I told him I was sure you'd want us to bring him home. You always want to help everybody."

Mother smiled, but she sighed, too. It is nice that your children should believe you willing to open house and heart to any and every one who needs help. But it is rather embarrassing sometimes, too, when they act on their belief.

"Oh, well," said Mother, "we must make the best of it."

When Jim was carried in, dreadfully white and with set lips whose red had faded to a horrid bluey violet colour, Mother said:--

"I am glad you brought him here. Now, Jim, let's get you comfortable in bed before the Doctor comes!"

And Jim, looking at her kind eyes, felt a little, warm, comforting flush of new courage.

"It'll hurt rather, won't it?" he said. "I don't mean to be a coward. You won't think I'm a coward if I faint again, will you? I really and truly don't do it on purpose. And I do hate to give you all this trouble."

"Don't you worry," said Mother; "it's you that have the trouble, you poor dear--not us."

And she kissed him just as if he had been Peter. "We love to have you here--don't we, Bobbie?"

"Yes," said Bobbie--and she saw by her Mother's face how right she had been to bring home the wounded hound in the red jersey.

Day 96

1. Read the first part of chapter thirteen of *The Railway Children*.
2. Tell someone what's happening in the book.

Mother did not get back to her writing all that day, for the red- jerseyed hound whom the children had brought to Three Chimneys had to be put to bed. And then the Doctor came, and hurt him most horribly. Mother was with him all through it, and that made it a little better than it would have been, but "bad was the best," as Mrs. Viney said.

The children sat in the parlour downstairs and heard the sound of the Doctor's boots going backwards and forwards over the bedroom floor. And once or twice there was a groan.

"It's horrible," said Bobbie. "Oh, I wish Dr. Forrest would make haste. Oh, poor Jim!"

"It is horrible," said Peter, "but it's very exciting. I wish Doctors weren't so stuck-up about who they'll have in the room when they're doing things. I should most awfully like to see a leg set. I believe the bones crunch like anything."

"Don't!" said the two girls at once.

"Rubbish!" said Peter. "How are you going to be Red Cross Nurses, like you were talking of coming home, if you can't even stand hearing me say about bones crunching? You'd have to hear them crunch on the field of battle--and be steeped in gore up to the elbows as likely as not, and--"

"Stop it!" cried Bobbie, with a white face; "you don't know how funny you're making me feel."

"Me, too," said Phyllis, whose face was pink.

"Cowards!" said Peter.

27

"I'm not," said Bobbie. "I helped Mother with your rake-wounded foot, and so did Phil--you know we did."

"Well, then!" said Peter. "Now look here. It would be a jolly good thing for you if I were to talk to you every day for half an hour about broken bones and people's insides, so as to get you used to it."

A chair was moved above.

"Listen," said Peter, "that's the bone crunching."

"I do wish you wouldn't," said Phyllis. "Bobbie doesn't like it."

"I'll tell you what they do," said Peter. I can't think what made him so horrid. Perhaps it was because he had been so very nice and kind all the earlier part of the day, and now he had to have a change. This is called reaction. One notices it now and then in oneself. Sometimes when one has been extra good for a longer time than usual, one is suddenly attacked by a violent fit of not being good at all. "I'll tell you what they do," said Peter; "they strap the broken man down so that he can't resist or interfere with their doctorish designs, and then someone holds his head, and someone holds his leg--the broken one, and pulls it till the bones fit in--with a crunch, mind you! Then they strap it up and--let's play at bone-setting!"

"Oh, no!" said Phyllis.

But Bobbie said suddenly: "All right--let's! I'll be the doctor, and Phil can be the nurse. You can be the broken boner; we can get at your legs more easily, because you don't wear petticoats."

"I'll get the splints and bandages," said Peter; "you get the couch of suffering ready."

The ropes that had tied up the boxes that had come from home were all in a wooden packing-case in the cellar. When Peter brought in a trailing tangle of them, and two boards for splints, Phyllis was excitedly giggling.

"Now, then," he said, and lay down on the settle, groaning most grievously.

"Not so loud!" said Bobbie, beginning to wind the rope round him and the settle. "You pull, Phil."

"Not so tight," moaned Peter. "You'll break my other leg."

Bobbie worked on in silence, winding more and more rope round him.

"That's enough," said Peter. "I can't move at all. Oh, my poor leg!" He groaned again.

"Sure you can't move?" asked Bobbie, in a rather strange tone.

"Quite sure," replied Peter. "Shall we play it's bleeding freely or not?" he asked cheerfully.

"You can play what you like," said Bobbie, sternly, folding her arms and looking down at him where he lay all wound round and round with cord. "Phil and I are going away. And we shan't untie you till you promise never, never to talk to us about blood and wounds unless we say you may. Come, Phil!"

"You beast!" said Peter, writhing. "I'll never promise, never. I'll yell, and Mother will come."

"Do," said Bobbie, "and tell her why we tied you up! Come on, Phil. No, I'm not a beast, Peter. But you wouldn't stop when we asked you and--"

"Yah," said Peter, "it wasn't even your own idea. You got it out of Stalky!"

Bobbie and Phil, retiring in silent dignity, were met at the door by the Doctor. He came in rubbing his hands and looking pleased with himself.

"Well," he said, "that job's done. It's a nice clean fracture, and it'll go on all right, I've no doubt. Plucky young chap, too--hullo! what's all this?"

His eye had fallen on Peter who lay mousy-still in his bonds on the settle.

"Playing at prisoners, eh?" he said; but his eyebrows had gone up a little. Somehow he had not thought that Bobbie would be playing while in the room above someone was having a broken bone set.

"Oh, no!" said Bobbie, "not at prisoners. We were playing at setting bones. Peter's the broken boner, and I was the doctor."

The Doctor frowned.

"Then I must say," he said, and he said it rather sternly, "that's it's a very heartless game. Haven't you enough imagination even to faintly picture what's been going on upstairs? That poor chap, with the drops of sweat on his forehead, and biting his lips so as not to cry out, and every touch on his leg agony and--"

"You ought to be tied up," said Phyllis; "you're as bad as--"

"Hush," said Bobbie; "I'm sorry, but we weren't heartless, really."

"I was, I suppose," said Peter, crossly. "All right, Bobbie, don't you go on being noble and screening me, because I jolly well won't have it. It was only that I kept on talking about blood and wounds. I wanted to train them for Red Cross Nurses. And I wouldn't stop when they asked me."

"Well?" said Dr. Forrest, sitting down.

"Well--then I said, 'Let's play at setting bones.' It was all rot. I knew Bobbie wouldn't. I only said it to tease her. And then when she said 'yes,' of course I had to go through with it. And they tied me up. They got it out of Stalky. And I think it's a beastly shame."

He managed to writhe over and hide his face against the wooden back of the settle.

"I didn't think that anyone would know but us," said Bobbie, indignantly answering Peter's unspoken reproach. "I never thought of your coming in. And hearing about blood and wounds does really make me feel most awfully funny. It was only a joke our tying him up. Let me untie you, Pete."

"I don't care if you never untie me," said Peter; "and if that's your idea of a joke--"

"If I were you," said the Doctor, though really he did not quite know what to say, "I should be untied before your Mother comes down. You don't want to worry her just now, do you?"

"I don't promise anything about not saying about wounds, mind," said Peter, in very surly tones, as Bobbie and Phyllis began to untie the knots.

"I'm very sorry, Pete," Bobbie whispered, leaning close to him as she fumbled with the big knot under the settle; "but if you only knew how sick you made me feel."

"You've made me feel pretty sick, I can tell you," Peter rejoined. Then he shook off the loose cords, and stood up.

"I looked in," said Dr. Forrest, "to see if one of you would come along to the surgery. There are some things that your Mother will want at once, and I've given my man a day off to go and see the circus; will you come, Peter?"

Peter went without a word or a look to his sisters.

The two walked in silence up to the gate that led from the Three Chimneys field to the road. Then Peter said:--

"Let me carry your bag. I say, it is heavy--what's in it?"

"Oh, knives and lancets and different instruments for hurting people. And the ether bottle. I had to give him ether, you know-- the agony was so intense."

Peter was silent.

"Tell me all about how you found that chap," said Dr. Forrest.

Peter told. And then Dr. Forrest told him stories of brave rescues; he was a most interesting man to talk to, as Peter had often remarked.

Then in the surgery Peter had a better chance than he had ever had of examining the Doctor's balance, and his microscope, and his scales and measuring glasses. When all the things were ready that Peter was to take back, the Doctor said suddenly:--

"You'll excuse my shoving my oar in, won't you? But I should like to say something to you."

"Now for a rowing," thought Peter, who had been wondering how it was that he had escaped one.

"Something scientific," added the Doctor.

"Yes," said Peter, fiddling with the fossil ammonite that the Doctor used for a paper-weight.

"Well then, you see. Boys and girls are only little men and women. And we are much harder and hardier than they are--" (Peter liked the "we." Perhaps the Doctor had known he would.)--"and much stronger, and things that hurt them don't hurt us. You know you mustn't hit a girl--"

"I should think not, indeed," muttered Peter, indignantly.

"Not even if she's your own sister. That's because girls are so much softer and weaker than we are; they have to be, you know," he added, "because if they weren't, it wouldn't be nice for the babies. And that's why all the animals are so good to the mother animals. They never fight them, you know."

"I know," said Peter, interested; "two buck rabbits will fight all day if you let them, but they won't hurt a doe."

"No; and quite wild beasts--lions and elephants--they're immensely gentle with the female beasts. And we've got to be, too."

"I see," said Peter.

"And their hearts are soft, too," the Doctor went on, "and things that we shouldn't think anything of hurt them dreadfully. So that a man has to be very careful, not only of his fists, but of his words. They're awfully brave, you know," he went on. "Think of Bobbie waiting alone in the tunnel with that poor chap. It's an odd thing--the softer and more easily hurt a woman is the better she can screw herself up to do what has to be done. I've seen some brave women--your Mother's one," he ended abruptly.

"Yes," said Peter.

"Well, that's all. Excuse my mentioning it. But nobody knows everything without being told. And you see what I mean, don't you?"

"Yes," said Peter. "I'm sorry. There!"

"Of course you are! People always are--directly they understand. Everyone ought to be taught these scientific facts. So long!"

They shook hands heartily. When Peter came home, his sisters looked at him doubtfully.

"It's Pax," said Peter, dumping down the basket on the table. "Dr. Forrest has been talking scientific to me. No, it's no use my telling you what he said; you wouldn't understand. But it all comes to you girls being poor, soft, weak, frightened things like rabbits, so us men have just got to put up with them. He said you were female beasts. Shall I take this up to Mother, or will you?"

"I know what boys are," said Phyllis, with flaming cheeks; "they're just the nastiest,

rudest-"

"They're very brave," said Bobbie, "sometimes."

"Ah, you mean the chap upstairs? I see. Go ahead, Phil--I shall put up with you whatever you say because you're a poor, weak, frightened, soft--"

"Not if I pull your hair you won't," said Phyllis, springing at him.

"He said 'Pax,'" said Bobbie, pulling her away. "Don't you see," she whispered as Peter picked up the basket and stalked out with it, "he's sorry, really, only he won't say so? Let's say we're sorry."

"It's so goody goody," said Phyllis, doubtfully; "he said we were female beasts, and soft and frightened--"

"Then let's show him we're not frightened of him thinking us goody goody," said Bobbie; "and we're not any more beasts than he is."

And when Peter came back, still with his chin in the air, Bobbie said:--

"We're sorry we tied you up, Pete."

"I thought you would be," said Peter, very stiff and superior.

This was hard to bear. But--

"Well, so we are," said Bobbie. "Now let honour be satisfied on both sides."

"I did call it Pax," said Peter, in an injured tone.

"Then let it be Pax," said Bobbie. "Come on, Phil, let's get the tea. Pete, you might lay the cloth."

"I say," said Phyllis, when peace was really restored, which was not till they were washing up the cups after tea, "Dr. Forrest didn't really say we were female beasts, did he?"

"Yes," said Peter, firmly, "but I think he meant we men were wild beasts, too."

"How funny of him!" said Phyllis, breaking a cup.

Day 97

1. Read the second part of chapter thirteen of *The Railway Children*.
2. Tell someone about the chapter.

"May I come in, Mother?" Peter was at the door of Mother's writing room, where Mother sat at her table with two candles in front of her. Their flames looked orange and violet against the clear grey blue of the sky where already a few stars were twinkling.

"Yes, dear," said Mother, absently, "anything wrong?" She wrote a few more words and then laid down her pen and began to fold up what she had written. "I was just writing to Jim's grandfather. He lives near here, you know."

"Yes, you said so at tea. That's what I want to say. Must you write to him, Mother? Couldn't we keep Jim, and not say anything to his people till he's well? It would be such a surprise for them."

"Well, yes," said Mother, laughing, "I think it would."

"You see," Peter went on, "of course the girls are all right and all that--I'm not saying anything against them. But I should like it if I had another chap to talk to sometimes."

"Yes," said Mother, "I know it's dull for you, dear. But I can't help it. Next year perhaps I can send you to school--you'd like that, wouldn't you?"

"I do miss the other chaps, rather," Peter confessed; "but if Jim could stay after his leg was well, we could have awful larks."

"I've no doubt of it," said Mother. "Well--perhaps he could, but you know, dear, we're not rich. I can't afford to get him everything he'll want. And he must have a nurse."

"Can't you nurse him, Mother? You do nurse people so beautifully."

"That's a pretty compliment, Pete--but I can't do nursing and my writing as well. That's the worst of it."

"Then you must send the letter to his grandfather?"

"Of course--and to his schoolmaster, too. We telegraphed to them both, but I must write as well. They'll be most dreadfully anxious."

"I say, Mother, why can't his grandfather pay for a nurse?" Peter suggested. "That would be ripping. I expect the old boy's rolling in money. Grandfathers in books always are."

"Well, this one isn't in a book," said Mother, "so we mustn't expect him to roll much."

"I say," said Peter, musingly, "wouldn't it be jolly if we all were in a book, and you were writing it? Then you could make all sorts of jolly things happen, and make Jim's legs get well at once and be all right to-morrow, and Father come home soon and--"

"Do you miss your Father very much?" Mother asked, rather coldly, Peter thought.

"Awfully," said Peter, briefly.

Mother was enveloping and addressing the second letter.

"You see," Peter went on slowly, "you see, it's not only him being Father, but now he's away there's no other man in the house but me--that's why I want Jim to stay so frightfully much. Wouldn't you like to be writing that book with us all in it, Mother, and make Daddy come home soon?"

Peter's Mother put her arm round him suddenly, and hugged him in silence for a minute. Then she said:--

"Don't you think it's rather nice to think that we're in a book that God's writing? If I were writing the book, I might make mistakes. But God knows how to make the story end just right--in the way that's best for us."

"Do you really believe that, Mother?" Peter asked quietly.

"Yes," she said, "I do believe it--almost always--except when I'm so sad that I can't believe anything. But even when I can't believe it, I know it's true--and I try to believe. You don't know how I try, Peter. Now take the letters to the post, and don't let's be sad any more. Courage, courage! That's the finest of all the virtues! I dare say Jim will be here for two or three weeks yet."

For what was left of the evening Peter was so angelic that Bobbie feared he was going to be ill. She was quite relieved in the morning to find him plaiting Phyllis's hair on to the back of her chair in quite his old manner.

It was soon after breakfast that a knock came at the door. The children were hard at work cleaning the brass candlesticks in honour of Jim's visit.

"That'll be the Doctor," said Mother; "I'll go. Shut the kitchen door--you're not fit to be seen."

But it wasn't the Doctor. They knew that by the voice and by the sound of the boots that went upstairs. They did not recognise the sound of the boots, but everyone was certain that they had heard the voice before.

There was a longish interval. The boots and the voice did not come down again.

"Who can it possibly be?" they kept on asking themselves and each other.

"Perhaps," said Peter at last, "Dr. Forrest has been attacked by highwaymen and left for dead, and this is the man he's telegraphed for to take his place. Mrs. Viney said he had a local tenant to do his work when he went for a holiday, didn't you, Mrs. Viney?"

"I did so, my dear," said Mrs. Viney from the back kitchen.

"He's fallen down in a fit, more likely, said Phyllis, "all human aid despaired of. And this is his man come to break the news to Mother."

"Nonsense!" said Peter, briskly; "Mother wouldn't have taken the man up into Jim's bedroom. Why should she? Listen--the door's opening. Now they'll come down. I'll open the door a crack."

He did.

"It's not listening," he replied indignantly to Bobbie's scandalised remarks; "nobody in their senses would talk secrets on the stairs. And Mother can't have secrets to talk with Dr. Forrest's stable-man--and you said it was him."

"Bobbie," called Mother's voice.

They opened the kitchen door, and Mother leaned over the stair railing.

"Jim's grandfather has come," she said; "wash your hands and faces and then you can see him. He wants to see you!" The bedroom door shut again.

"There now!" said Peter; "fancy us not even thinking of that! Let's have some hot water, Mrs. Viney. I'm as black as your hat."

The three were indeed dirty, for the stuff you clean brass candlesticks with is very far from cleaning to the cleaner.

They were still busy with soap and flannel when they heard the boots and the voice come down the stairs and go into the dining-room. And when they were clean, though still damp--because it takes such a long time to dry your hands properly, and they were very impatient to see the grandfather--they filed into the dining-room.

Mother was sitting in the window-seat, and in the leather-covered armchair that Father always used to sit in at the other house sat--

THEIR OWN OLD GENTLEMAN!

"Well, I never did," said Peter, even before he said, "How do you do?" He was, as he explained afterwards, too surprised even to remember that there was such a thing as politeness--much less to practise it.

"It's our own old gentleman!" said Phyllis.

"Oh, it's you!" said Bobbie. And then they remembered themselves and their manners and said, "How do you do?" very nicely.

"This is Jim's grandfather, Mr. --" said Mother, naming the old gentleman's name.

"How splendid!" said Peter; "that's just exactly like a book, isn't it, Mother?"

"It is, rather," said Mother, smiling; "things do happen in real life that are rather like books, sometimes."

"I am so awfully glad it is you," said Phyllis; "when you think of the tons of old gentlemen there are in the world--it might have been almost anyone."

"I say, though," said Peter, "you're not going to take Jim away, though, are you?"

"Not at present," said the old gentleman. "Your Mother has most kindly consented to let him stay here. I thought of sending a nurse, but your Mother is good enough to say that she will nurse him herself."

"But what about her writing?" said Peter, before anyone could stop him. "There won't be anything for him to eat if Mother doesn't write."

"That's all right," said Mother, hastily.

The old gentleman looked very kindly at Mother.

"I see," he said, "you trust your children, and confide in them."

"Of course," said Mother.

"Then I may tell them of our little arrangement," he said. "Your Mother, my dears, has consented to give up writing for a little while and to become a Matron of my Hospital."

"Oh!" said Phyllis, blankly; "and shall we have to go away from Three Chimneys and the Railway and everything?"

"No, no, darling," said Mother, hurriedly.

"The Hospital is called Three Chimneys Hospital," said the old gentleman, "and my unlucky Jim's the only patient, and I hope he'll continue to be so. Your Mother will be Matron, and there'll be a hospital staff of a housemaid and a cook--till Jim's well."

"And then will Mother go on writing again?" asked Peter.

"We shall see," said the old gentleman, with a slight, swift glance at Bobbie; "perhaps something nice may happen and she won't have to."

"I love my writing," said Mother, very quickly.

"I know," said the old gentleman; "don't be afraid that I'm going to try to interfere. But one never knows. Very wonderful and beautiful things do happen, don't they? And we live most of our lives in the hope of them. I may come again to see the boy?"

"Surely," said Mother, "and I don't know how to thank you for making it possible for me to nurse him. Dear boy!"

"He kept calling Mother, Mother, in the night," said Phyllis. "I woke up twice and heard him."

"He didn't mean me," said Mother, in a low voice to the old gentleman; "that's why I wanted so much to keep him."

The old gentleman rose.

"I'm so glad," said Peter, "that you're going to keep him, Mother."

"Take care of your Mother, my dears," said the old gentleman. "She's a woman in a million."

"Yes, isn't she?" whispered Bobbie.

"God bless her," said the old gentleman, taking both Mother's hands, "God bless her! Ay, and she shall be blessed. Dear me, where's my hat? Will Bobbie come with me to the gate?"

At the gate he stopped and said:--

"You're a good child, my dear--I got your letter. But it wasn't needed. When I read about your Father's case in the papers at the time, I had my doubts. And ever since I've known who you were, I've been trying to find out things. I haven't done very much yet. But I have hopes, my dear--I have hopes."

"Oh!" said Bobbie, choking a little.

"Yes--I may say great hopes. But keep your secret a little longer. Wouldn't do to upset your Mother with a false hope, would it?"

"Oh, but it isn't false!" said Bobbie; "I know you can do it. I knew you could when I wrote. It isn't a false hope, is it?"

"No," he said, "I don't think it's a false hope, or I wouldn't have told you. And I think you deserve to be told that there is a hope."

"And you don't think Father did it, do you? Oh, say you don't think he did."

"My dear," he said, "I'm perfectly certain he didn't."

If it was a false hope, it was none the less a very radiant one that lay warm at Bobbie's heart, and through the days that followed lighted her little face as a Japanese lantern is lighted by the candle within.

Day 98

    1.   Read the first part of chapter fourteen of *The Railway Children*.
Vocabulary

    2.   Write synonyms for each of the following words. (Remember: synonyms are words with similar meaning.)
        • conflict, result, pleasure, crafty, terrifying, anxious, envy, inquire, dismay, dispute, clad

Life at the Three Chimneys was never quite the same again after the old gentleman came to see his grandson. Although they now knew his name, the children never spoke of him by it--at any rate, when they were by themselves. To them he was always the old gentleman, and I think he had better be the old gentleman to us, too. It wouldn't make him seem any more real to you, would it, if I were to tell you that his name was Snooks or Jenkins (which it wasn't)?--and, after all, I must be allowed to keep one secret. It's the only one; I have told you everything else, except what I am going to tell you in this chapter, which is the last. At least, of course, I haven't told you everything. If I were to do that, the book would never come to an end, and that would be a pity, wouldn't it?

Well, as I was saying, life at Three Chimneys was never quite the same again. The cook and the housemaid were very nice (I don't mind telling you their names--they were Clara and Ethelwyn), but they told Mother they did not seem to want Mrs. Viney, and that she was an old muddler. So Mrs. Viney came only two days a week to do washing and ironing. Then Clara and Ethelwyn said they could do the work all right if they weren't interfered with, and that meant that the children no longer got the tea and cleared it away and washed up the tea-things and dusted the rooms.

This would have left quite a blank in their lives, although they had often pretended to themselves and to each other that they hated housework. But now that Mother had no writing and no housework to do, she had time for lessons. And lessons the children had to do. However nice the person who is teaching you may be, lessons are lessons all the world over, and at their best are worse fun than peeling potatoes or lighting a fire.

On the other hand, if Mother now had time for lessons, she also had time for play, and to make up little rhymes for the children as she used to do. She had not had much time for rhymes since she came to Three Chimneys.

There was one very odd thing about these lessons. Whatever the children were doing, they always wanted to be doing something else. When Peter was doing his Latin, he thought it would be nice to be learning History like Bobbie. Bobbie would have preferred Arithmetic, which was what Phyllis happened to be doing, and Phyllis of course thought Latin much the most interesting kind of lesson. And so on.

So, one day, when they sat down to lessons, each of them found a little rhyme at its place. I put the rhymes in to show you that their Mother really did understand a little how children feel about things, and also the kind of words they use, which is the case with very few grown-up people. I suppose most grown-ups have very bad memories, and have forgotten how they felt when they were little. Of course, the verses are supposed to be spoken by the children.

PETER

I once thought Caesar easy pap--
  How very soft I must have been!
When they start Caesar with a chap
  He little know what that will mean.
Oh, verbs are silly stupid things.
I'd rather learn the dates of kings!

BOBBIE

The worst of all my lesson things
  Is learning who succeeded who
In all the rows of queens and kings,
  With dates to everything they do:
With dates enough to make you sick;--
I wish it was Arithmetic!

PHYLLIS

Such pounds and pounds of apples fill
  My slate--what is the price you'd spend?
You scratch the figures out until
  You cry upon the dividend.
I'd break the slate and scream for joy
If I did Latin like a boy!

This kind of thing, of course, made lessons much jollier. It is something to know that the person who is teaching you sees that it is not all plain sailing for you, and does not think that it is just your stupidness that makes you not know your lessons till you've learned them!

Then as Jim's leg got better it was very pleasant to go up and sit with him and hear tales about his school life and the other boys. There was one boy, named Parr, of whom Jim seemed to have formed the lowest possible opinion, and another boy named Wigsby Minor, for whose views Jim had a great respect. Also there were three brothers named Paley, and the youngest was called Paley Terts, and was much given to fighting.

Peter drank in all this with deep joy, and Mother seemed to have listened with some interest, for one day she gave Jim a sheet of paper on which she had written a rhyme about Parr, bringing in Paley and Wigsby by name in a most wonderful way, as well as all the reasons Jim had for not liking Parr, and Wigsby's wise opinion on the matter. Jim was immensely pleased. He had never had a rhyme written expressly for him before. He read it till he knew it by heart and then he sent it to Wigsby, who liked it almost as much as Jim did. Perhaps you may like it, too.

THE NEW BOY

His name is Parr: he says that he
Is given bread and milk for tea.
He says his father killed a bear.
He says his mother cuts his hair.

He wears galoshes when it's wet.
I've heard his people call him "Pet"!
He has no proper sense of shame;
He told the chaps his Christian name.

He cannot wicket-keep at all,
He's frightened of a cricket ball.
He reads indoors for hours and hours.
He knows the names of beastly flowers.

He says his French just like Mossoo--
A beastly stuck-up thing to do--
He won't keep cave, shirks his turn
And says he came to school to learn!

He won't play football, says it hurts;
He wouldn't fight with Paley Terts;

40

He couldn't whistle if he tried,
And when we laughed at him he cried!

Now Wigsby Minor says that Parr
Is only like all new boys are.
I know when I first came to school
I wasn't such a jolly fool!

Jim could never understand how Mother could have been clever enough to do it. To the others it seemed nice, but natural. You see they had always been used to having a mother who could write verses just like the way people talk, even to the shocking expression at the end of the rhyme, which was Jim's very own.

Jim taught Peter to play chess and draughts and dominoes, and altogether it was a nice quiet time.

Only Jim's leg got better and better, and a general feeling began to spring up among Bobbie, Peter, and Phyllis that something ought to be done to amuse him; not just games, but something really handsome. But it was extraordinarily difficult to think of anything.

"It's no good," said Peter, when all of them had thought and thought till their heads felt quite heavy and swollen; "if we can't think of anything to amuse him, we just can't, and there's an end of it. Perhaps something will just happen of its own accord that he'll like."

"Things do happen by themselves sometimes, without your making them," said Phyllis, rather as though, usually, everything that happened in the world was her doing.

"I wish something would happen," said Bobbie, dreamily, "something wonderful."

And something wonderful did happen exactly four days after she had said this. I wish I could say it was three days after, because in fairy tales it is always three days after that things happen. But this is not a fairy story, and besides, it really was four and not three, and I am nothing if not strictly truthful.

They seemed to be hardly Railway children at all in those days, and as the days went on each had an uneasy feeling about this which Phyllis expressed one day.

"I wonder if the Railway misses us," she said, plaintively. "We never go to see it now."

"It seems ungrateful," said Bobbie; "we loved it so when we hadn't anyone else to play with."

"Perks is always coming up to ask after Jim," said Peter, "and the signalman's little boy is better. He told me so."

"I didn't mean the people," explained Phyllis; "I meant the dear Railway itself."

"The thing I don't like," said Bobbie, on this fourth day, which was a Tuesday, "is our having stopped waving to the 9.15 and sending our love to Father by it."

"Let's begin again," said Phyllis. And they did.

Somehow the change of everything that was made by having servants in the house and Mother not doing any writing, made the time seem extremely long since that strange morning at the beginning of things, when they had got up so early and burnt the bottom out of the kettle and had apple pie for breakfast and first seen the Railway.

It was September now, and the turf on the slope to the Railway was dry and crisp. Little long grass spikes stood up like bits of gold wire, frail blue harebells trembled on their tough, slender stalks, Gipsy roses opened wide and flat their lilac-coloured discs, and the golden stars of St. John's Wort shone at the edges of the pool that lay halfway to the Railway. Bobbie gathered a generous handful of the flowers and thought how pretty they would look lying on the green-and-pink blanket of silk-waste that now covered Jim's poor broken leg.

"Hurry up," said Peter, "or we shall miss the 9.15!"

"I can't hurry more than I am doing," said Phyllis. "Oh, bother it! My bootlace has come undone again!"

"When you're married," said Peter, "your bootlace will come undone going up the church aisle, and your man that you're going to get married to will tumble over it and smash his nose in on the ornamented pavement; and then you'll say you won't marry him, and you'll have to be an old maid."

"I shan't," said Phyllis. "I'd much rather marry a man with his nose smashed in than not marry anybody."

"It would be horrid to marry a man with a smashed nose, all the same," went on Bobbie. "He wouldn't be able to smell the flowers at the wedding. Wouldn't that be awful!"

"Bother the flowers at the wedding!" cried Peter. "Look! the signal's down. We must run!"

They ran. And once more they waved their handkerchiefs, without at all minding whether the handkerchiefs were clean or not, to the 9.15.

"Take our love to Father!" cried Bobbie. And the others, too, shouted:--

"Take our love to Father!"

The old gentleman waved from his first-class carriage window. Quite violently he waved. And there was nothing odd in that, for he always had waved. But what was really remarkable was that from every window handkerchiefs fluttered, newspapers signalled, hands waved wildly. The train swept by with a rustle and roar, the little pebbles jumped and danced under it as it passed, and the children were left looking at each other.

"Well!" said Peter.

"Well!" said Bobbie.

"Well!" said Phyllis.

"Whatever on earth does that mean?" asked Peter, but he did not expect any answer.

"I don't know," said Bobbie. "Perhaps the old gentleman told the people at his station to look out for us and wave. He knew we should like it!"

Day 99

1. Read the second part of chapter fourteen of *The Railway Children*.
2. What happens at the end of the book?

Now, curiously enough, this was just what had happened. The old gentleman, who was very well known and respected at his particular station, had got there early that morning, and he had waited at the door where the young man stands holding the interesting machine that clips the tickets, and he had said something to every single passenger who passed through that door. And after nodding to what the old gentleman had said--and the nods expressed every shade of surprise, interest, doubt, cheerful pleasure, and grumpy agreement--each passenger had gone on to the platform and read one certain part of his newspaper. And when the passengers got into the train, they had told the other passengers who were already there what the old gentleman had said, and then the other passengers had also looked at their newspapers and seemed very astonished and, mostly, pleased. Then, when the train passed the fence where the three children were, newspapers and hands and handkerchiefs were waved madly, till all that side of the train was fluttery with white like the pictures of the King's Coronation in the biograph at Maskelyne and Cook's. To the children it almost seemed as though the train itself was alive, and was at last responding to the love that they had given it so freely and so long.

"It is most extraordinarily rum!" said Peter.

"Most stronery!" echoed Phyllis.

But Bobbie said, "Don't you think the old gentleman's waves seemed more significating than usual?"

"No," said the others.

"I do," said Bobbie. "I thought he was trying to explain something to us with his newspaper."

"Explain what?" asked Peter, not unnaturally.

"I don't know," Bobbie answered, "but I do feel most awfully funny. I feel just exactly as if something was going to happen."

"What is going to happen," said Peter, "is that Phyllis's stocking is going to come down."

This was but too true. The suspender had given way in the agitation of the waves to the 9.15. Bobbie's handkerchief served as first aid to the injured, and they all went home.

Lessons were more than usually difficult to Bobbie that day. Indeed, she disgraced herself so deeply over a quite simple sum about the division of 48 pounds of meat and 36 pounds of bread among 144 hungry children that Mother looked at her anxiously.

"Don't you feel quite well, dear?" she asked.

"I don't know," was Bobbie's unexpected answer. "I don't know how I feel. It isn't that I'm lazy. Mother, will you let me off lessons to-day? I feel as if I wanted to be quite alone by myself."

"Yes, of course I'll let you off," said Mother; "but--"

Bobbie dropped her slate. It cracked just across the little green mark that is so useful for drawing patterns round, and it was never the same slate again. Without waiting to pick it up she bolted. Mother caught her in the hall feeling blindly among the waterproofs and umbrellas for her garden hat.

"What is it, my sweetheart?" said Mother. "You don't feel ill, do you?"

"I don't know," Bobbie answered, a little breathlessly, "but I want to be by myself and see if my head really is all silly and my inside all squirmy-twisty."

"Hadn't you better lie down?" Mother said, stroking her hair back from her forehead.

"I'd be more alive in the garden, I think," said Bobbie.

But she could not stay in the garden. The hollyhocks and the asters and the late roses all seemed to be waiting for something to happen. It was one of those still, shiny autumn days, when everything does seem to be waiting.

Bobbie could not wait.

"I'll go down to the station," she said, "and talk to Perks and ask about the signalman's little boy."

So she went down. On the way she passed the old lady from the Post-office, who gave her a kiss and a hug, but, rather to Bobbie's surprise, no words except:--

"God bless you, love--" and, after a pause, "run along--do."

The draper's boy, who had sometimes been a little less than civil and a little more than contemptuous, now touched his cap, and uttered the remarkable words:--

"'Morning, Miss, I'm sure--"

The blacksmith, coming along with an open newspaper in his hand, was even more strange in his manner. He grinned broadly, though, as a rule, he was a man not given to smiles, and waved the newspaper long before he came up to her. And as he passed her, he said, in answer to her "Good morning":--

"Good morning to you, Missie, and many of them! I wish you joy, that I do!"

"Oh!" said Bobbie to herself, and her heart quickened its beats, "something is going to happen! I know it is--everyone is so odd, like people are in dreams."

The Station Master wrung her hand warmly. In fact he worked it up and down like a pump-handle. But he gave her no reason for this unusually enthusiastic greeting. He only said:--

"The 11.54's a bit late, Miss--the extra luggage this holiday time," and went away very quickly into that inner Temple of his into which even Bobbie dared not follow him.

Perks was not to be seen, and Bobbie shared the solitude of the platform with the Station Cat. This tortoiseshell lady, usually of a retiring disposition, came to-day to rub herself against the brown stockings of Bobbie with arched back, waving tail, and reverberating purrs.

"Dear me!" said Bobbie, stooping to stroke her, "how very kind everybody is to-day--even you, Pussy!"

Perks did not appear until the 11.54 was signalled, and then he, like everybody else that morning, had a newspaper in his hand.

"Hullo!" he said, "'ere you are. Well, if this is the train, it'll be smart work! Well, God bless you, my dear! I see it in the paper, and I don't think I was ever so glad of anything in all my born days!" He looked at Bobbie a moment, then said, "One I must have, Miss, and no offence, I know, on a day like this 'ere!" and with that he kissed her, first on one cheek and then on the other.

"You ain't offended, are you?" he asked anxiously. "I ain't took too great a liberty? On a day like this, you know--"

"No, no," said Bobbie, "of course it's not a liberty, dear Mr. Perks; we love you quite as much as if you were an uncle of ours--but--on a day like what?"

"Like this 'ere!" said Perks. "Don't I tell you I see it in the paper?"

"Saw what in the paper?" asked Bobbie, but already the 11.54 was steaming into the station and the Station Master was looking at all the places where Perks was not and ought to have been.

Bobbie was left standing alone, the Station Cat watching her from under the bench with friendly golden eyes.

Of course you know already exactly what was going to happen. Bobbie was not so clever. She had the vague, confused, expectant feeling that comes to one's heart in dreams. What her heart expected I can't tell--perhaps the very thing that you and I know was going to happen--but her mind expected nothing; it was almost blank, and felt nothing but tiredness and stupidness and an empty feeling, like your body has when you have been a long walk and it is very far indeed past your proper dinner-time.

Only three people got out of the 11.54. The first was a countryman with two baskety boxes full of live chickens who stuck their russet heads out anxiously through the wicker bars; the second was Miss Peckitt, the grocer's wife's cousin, with a tin box and three brown-paper parcels; and the third--

"Oh! my Daddy, my Daddy!" That scream went like a knife into the heart of everyone in the train, and people put their heads out of the windows to see a tall pale man with lips set in a thin close line, and a little girl clinging to him with arms and legs, while his arms went tightly round her.

*   *   *   *   *   *

"I knew something wonderful was going to happen," said Bobbie, as they went up the road, "but I didn't think it was going to be this. Oh, my Daddy, my Daddy!"

"Then didn't Mother get my letter?" Father asked.

"There weren't any letters this morning. Oh! Daddy! it is really you, isn't it?"

The clasp of a hand she had not forgotten assured her that it was. "You must go in by yourself, Bobbie, and tell Mother quite quietly that it's all right. They've caught the man who did it. Everyone knows now that it wasn't your Daddy."

"I always knew it wasn't," said Bobbie. "Me and Mother and our old gentleman."

"Yes," he said, "it's all his doing. Mother wrote and told me you had found out. And she told me what you'd been to her. My own little girl!" They stopped a minute then.

And now I see them crossing the field. Bobbie goes into the house, trying to keep her eyes from speaking before her lips have found the right words to "tell Mother quite quietly" that the sorrow and the struggle and the parting are over and done, and that Father has come home.

I see Father walking in the garden, waiting--waiting. He is looking at the flowers, and each flower is a miracle to eyes that all these months of Spring and Summer have seen only flagstones and gravel and a little grudging grass. But his eyes keep turning towards the house. And presently he leaves the garden and goes to stand outside the nearest door. It is the back door, and across the yard the swallows are circling. They are getting ready to fly away from cold winds and keen frost to the land where it is always summer. They are the same swallows that the children built the little clay nests for.

Now the house door opens. Bobbie's voice calls:--

"Come in, Daddy; come in!"

He goes in and the door is shut. I think we will not open the door or follow him. I think that just now we are not wanted there. I think it will be best for us to go quickly and quietly away. At the end of the field, among the thin gold spikes of grass and the harebells and Gipsy roses and St. John's Wort, we may just take one last look, over our shoulders, at the white house where neither we nor anyone else is wanted now.

Day 100

1. What were your favorite things about *The Railway Children*? What didn't you like about it?
2. Write about the book. Tell the author, the title, the main characters, what happened (in a short summary), and if you can, what you think is something the story taught you. You could also include what you liked and didn't like about the book.

Day 101

1. Read chapter 1 of *A Little Princess*. (To all you boys out there, I'm sorry, but you got to read about all the brothers on the island. Get over the title and enjoy the book.)
2. What's the setting of the story? What's the set up for the plot? (That means how does the story get started.)

SARA

ONCE on a dark winter's day, when the yellow fog hung so thick and heavy in the streets of London that the lamps were lighted and the shop windows blazed with gas as they do at night, an odd-looking little girl sat in a cab with her father and was driven rather slowly through the big thoroughfares.

She sat with her feet tucked under her, and leaned against her father, who held her in his arm, as she stared out of the window at the passing people with a queer old-fashioned thoughtfulness in her big eyes.

She was such a little girl that one did not expect to see such a look on her small face. It would have been an old look for a child of twelve, and Sara Crewe was only seven. The fact was, however, that she was always dreaming and thinking odd things and could not herself remember any time when she had not been thinking things about grown-up people and the world they belonged to. She felt as if she had lived a long, long time.

At this moment she was remembering the voyage she had just made from Bombay with her father, Captain Crewe. She was thinking of the big ship, of the Lascars passing silently to and fro on it, of the children playing about on the hot deck, and of some young officers' wives who used to try to make her talk to them and laugh at the things she said.

Principally, she was thinking of what a queer thing it was that at one time one was in India in the blazing sun, and then in the middle of the ocean, and then driving in a strange vehicle through strange streets where the day was as dark as the night. She found this so puzzling that she moved closer to her father.

"Papa," she said in a low, mysterious little voice which was almost a whisper, "papa."

"What is it, darling?" Captain Crewe answered, holding her closer and looking down into her face. "What is Sara thinking of?"

"Is this the place?" Sara whispered, cuddling still closer to him. "Is it, papa?"

"Yes, little Sara, it is. We have reached it at last." And though she was only seven years old, she knew that he felt sad when he said it.

It seemed to her many years since he had begun to prepare her mind for "the place," as she always called it. Her mother had died when she was born, so she had never known or missed her. Her young, handsome, rich, petting father seemed to be the only relation she had in the world. They had always played together and been fond of each other. She only knew he was rich because she had heard people say so when they thought she was not listening, and she had also heard them say that when she grew up she would be rich, too. She did not know all that being rich meant. She had always lived in a beautiful bungalow, and had been used to seeing many servants who made salaams to her and called her "Missee Sahib," and gave her her own way in everything. She had had toys and pets and an ayah who worshipped her, and she had gradually learned that people who were rich had these things. That, however, was all she knew about it.

During her short life only one thing had troubled her, and that thing was "the place" she was to be taken to some day. The climate of India was very bad for children, and as soon as possible they were sent away from it--generally to England and to school. She had seen other children go away, and had heard their fathers and mothers talk about the letters they received from them. She had known that she would be obliged to go also, and though sometimes her father's stories of the voyage and the new country had attracted her, she had been troubled by the thought that he could not stay with her.

"Couldn't you go to that place with me, papa?" she had asked when she was five years old. "Couldn't you go to school, too? I would help you with your lessons."

"But you will not have to stay for a very long time, little Sara," he had always said. "You will go to a nice house where there will be a lot of little girls, and you will play together, and I will send you plenty of books, and you will grow so fast that it will seem scarcely a year before you are big enough and clever enough to come back and take care of papa."

She had liked to think of that. To keep the house for her father; to ride with him, and sit at the head of his table when he had dinner parties; to talk to him and read his books--that would be what she would like most in the world, and if one must go away to "the place" in England to attain it, she must make up her mind to go. She did not care very much for other little girls, but if she had plenty of books she could console herself. She liked books more than anything else, and was, in fact, always inventing stories of beautiful things and telling them to herself. Sometimes she had told them to her father, and he had liked them as much as she did.

"Well, papa," she said softly, "if we are here I suppose we must be resigned."

He laughed at her old-fashioned speech and kissed her. He was really not at all resigned himself, though he knew he must keep that a secret. His quaint little Sara had been a great companion to him, and he felt he should be a lonely fellow when, on his return to India, he went into his bungalow knowing he need not expect to see the small figure in its white frock come forward to meet him. So he held her very closely in his arms as the cab rolled into the big, dull square in which stood the house which was their destination.

It was a big, dull, brick house, exactly like all the others in its row, but that on the front door there shone a brass plate on which was engraved in black letters:

Miss Minchin,

Select Seminary for Young Ladies.

"Here we are, Sara," said Captain Crewe, making his voice sound as cheerful as possible. Then he lifted her out of the cab and they mounted the steps and rang the bell. Sara often thought afterward that the house was somehow exactly like Miss Minchin. It was respectable and well furnished, but everything in it was ugly; and the very armchairs seemed to have hard bones in them. In the hall everything was hard and polished--even the red cheeks of the moon face on the tall clock in the corner had a severe varnished look. The drawing room into which they were ushered was covered by a carpet with a square pattern upon it, the chairs were square, and a heavy marble timepiece stood upon the heavy marble mantel.

As she sat down in one of the stiff mahogany chairs, Sara cast one of her quick looks about her.

"I don't like it, papa," she said. "But then I dare say soldiers--even brave ones--don't really like going into battle."

Captain Crewe laughed outright at this. He was young and full of fun, and he never tired of hearing Sara's queer speeches.

"Oh, little Sara," he said. "What shall I do when I have no one to say solemn things to me? No one else is as solemn as you are."

"But why do solemn things make you laugh so?" inquired Sara.

"Because you are such fun when you say them," he answered, laughing still more. And then suddenly he swept her into his arms and kissed her very hard, stopping laughing all at once and looking almost as if tears had come into his eyes.

It was just then that Miss Minchin entered the room. She was very like her house, Sara felt: tall and dull, and respectable and ugly. She had large, cold, fishy eyes, and a large, cold, fishy smile. It spread itself into a very large smile when she saw Sara and Captain Crewe. She had heard a great many desirable things of the young soldier from the lady who had recommended her school to him. Among other things, she had heard that he was a rich father who was willing to spend a great deal of money on his little daughter.

"It will be a great privilege to have charge of such a beautiful and promising child, Captain Crewe," she said, taking Sara's hand and stroking it. "Lady Meredith has told me of her unusual cleverness. A clever child is a great treasure in an establishment like mine."

Sara stood quietly, with her eyes fixed upon Miss Minchin's face. She was thinking something odd, as usual.

"Why does she say I am a beautiful child?" she was thinking. "I am not beautiful at all. Colonel Grange's little girl, Isobel, is beautiful. She has dimples and rose-colored cheeks, and long hair the color of gold. I have short black hair and green eyes; besides which, I am a thin child and not fair in the least. I am one of the ugliest children I ever saw. She is beginning by telling a story."

She was mistaken, however, in thinking she was an ugly child. She was not in the least like Isobel Grange, who had been the beauty of the regiment, but she had an odd charm of her own. She was a slim, supple creature, rather tall for her age, and had an intense, attractive little face. Her hair was heavy and quite black and only curled at the tips; her eyes were greenish gray, it is true, but they were big, wonderful eyes with long, black lashes, and though she herself did not like the color of them, many other people did. Still she was very firm in her belief that she was an ugly little girl, and she was not at all elated by Miss Minchin's flattery.

"I should be telling a story if I said she was beautiful," she thought; "and I should know I was telling a story. I believe I am as ugly as she is--in my way. What did she say that for?"

After she had known Miss Minchin longer she learned why she had said it. She discovered that she said the same thing to each papa and mamma who brought a child to her school.

Sara stood near her father and listened while he and Miss Minchin talked. She had been brought to the seminary because Lady Meredith's two little girls had been educated there, and Captain Crewe had a great respect for Lady Meredith's experience. Sara was to be what was known as "a parlor boarder," and she was to enjoy even greater privileges than parlor boarders usually did. She was to have a pretty bedroom and sitting room of her own; she was to have a pony and a carriage, and a maid to take the place of the ayah who had been her nurse in India.

"I am not in the least anxious about her education," Captain Crewe said, with his gay laugh, as he held Sara's hand and patted it. "The difficulty will be to keep her from learning too fast and too much. She is always sitting with her little nose burrowing into books. She doesn't read them, Miss Minchin; she gobbles them up as if she were a little wolf instead of a little girl. She is always starving for new books to gobble, and she wants grown-up books--great, big, fat ones--French and German as well as English--history and biography and poets, and all sorts of things. Drag her away from her books when she reads too much. Make her ride her pony in the Row or go out and buy a new doll. She ought to play more with dolls."

"Papa," said Sara, "you see, if I went out and bought a new doll every few days I should have more than I could be fond of. Dolls ought to be intimate friends. Emily is going to be my intimate friend."

Captain Crewe looked at Miss Minchin and Miss Minchin looked at Captain Crewe.

"Who is Emily?" she inquired.

"Tell her, Sara," Captain Crewe said, smiling.

Sara's green-gray eyes looked very solemn and quite soft as she answered.

"She is a doll I haven't got yet," she said. "She is a doll papa is going to buy for me. We are going out together to find her. I have called her Emily. She is going to be my friend when papa is gone. I want her to talk to about him."

Miss Minchin's large, fishy smile became very flattering indeed.

"What an original child!" she said. "What a darling little creature!"

"Yes," said Captain Crewe, drawing Sara close. "She is a darling little creature. Take great care of her for me, Miss Minchin."

Sara stayed with her father at his hotel for several days; in fact, she remained with him until he sailed away again to India. They went out and visited many big shops together, and bought a great many things. They bought, indeed, a great many more things than Sara needed; but Captain Crewe was a rash, innocent young man and wanted his little girl to have everything she admired and everything he admired himself, so between them they collected a wardrobe much too grand for a child of seven. There were velvet dresses trimmed with costly furs, and lace dresses, and embroidered ones, and hats with great, soft ostrich feathers, and ermine coats and muffs, and boxes of tiny gloves and handkerchiefs and silk stockings in such abundant supplies that the polite young women behind the counters whispered to each other that the odd little girl with the big, solemn eyes must be at least some foreign princess--perhaps the little daughter of an Indian rajah.

And at last they found Emily, but they went to a number of toy shops and looked at a great many dolls before they discovered her.

"I want her to look as if she wasn't a doll really," Sara said. "I want her to look as if she listens when I talk to her. The trouble with dolls, papa"--and she put her head on one side and reflected as she said it--"the trouble with dolls is that they never seem to hear." So they looked at big ones and little ones at dolls with black eyes and dolls with blue--at dolls with brown curls and dolls with golden braids, dolls dressed and dolls undressed.

"You see," Sara said when they were examining one who had no clothes. "If, when I find her, she has no frocks, we can take her to a dressmaker and have her things made to fit. They will fit better if they are tried on."

After a number of disappointments they decided to walk and look in at the shop windows and let the cab follow them. They had passed two or three places without even going in, when, as they were approaching a shop which was really not a very large one, Sara suddenly started and clutched her father's arm.

"Oh, papa!" she cried. "There is Emily!"

A flush had risen to her face and there was an expression in her green-gray eyes as if she had just recognized someone she was intimate with and fond of.

"She is actually waiting there for us!" she said. "Let us go in to her."

"Dear me," said Captain Crewe, "I feel as if we ought to have someone to introduce us."

"You must introduce me and I will introduce you," said Sara. "But I knew her the minute I saw her--so perhaps she knew me, too."

Perhaps she had known her. She had certainly a very intelligent expression in her eyes when Sara took her in her arms. She was a large doll, but not too large to carry about easily; she had naturally curling golden-brown hair, which hung like a mantle about her, and her eyes were a deep, clear, gray-blue, with soft, thick eyelashes which were real eyelashes and not mere painted lines.

"Of course," said Sara, looking into her face as she held her on her knee, "of course papa, this is Emily."

So Emily was bought and actually taken to a children's outfitter's shop and measured for a wardrobe as grand as Sara's own. She had lace frocks, too, and velvet and muslin ones, and hats and coats and beautiful lace-trimmed underclothes, and gloves and handkerchiefs and furs.

"I should like her always to look as if she was a child with a good mother," said Sara. "I'm her mother, though I am going to make a companion of her."

Captain Crewe would really have enjoyed the shopping tremendously, but that a sad thought kept tugging at his heart. This all meant that he was going to be separated from his beloved, quaint little comrade.

He got out of his bed in the middle of that night and went and stood looking down at Sara, who lay asleep with Emily in her arms. Her black hair was spread out on the pillow and Emily's golden-brown hair mingled with it, both of them had lace-ruffled nightgowns, and both had long eyelashes which lay and curled up on their cheeks. Emily looked so like a real child that Captain Crewe felt glad she was there. He drew a big sigh and pulled his mustache with a boyish expression.

"Heigh-ho, little Sara!" he said to himself "I don't believe you know how much your daddy will miss you."

The next day he took her to Miss Minchin's and left her there. He was to sail away the next morning. He explained to Miss Minchin that his solicitors, Messrs. Barrow & Skipworth, had charge of his affairs in England and would give her any advice she wanted, and that they would pay the bills she sent in for Sara's expenses. He would write to Sara twice a week, and she was to be given every pleasure she asked for.

"She is a sensible little thing, and she never wants anything it isn't safe to give her," he said.

Then he went with Sara into her little sitting room and they bade each other good-by. Sara sat on his knee and held the lapels of his coat in her small hands, and looked long and hard at his face.

"Are you learning me by heart, little Sara?" he said, stroking her hair.

"No," she answered. "I know you by heart. You are inside my heart." And they put their arms round each other and kissed as if they would never let each other go.

When the cab drove away from the door, Sara was sitting on the floor of her sitting room, with her hands under her chin and her eyes following it until it had turned the corner of the square. Emily was sitting by her, and she looked after it, too. When Miss Minchin sent her sister, Miss Amelia, to see what the child was doing, she found she could not open the door.

"I have locked it," said a queer, polite little voice from inside. "I want to be quite by myself, if you please."

Miss Amelia was fat and dumpy, and stood very much in awe of her sister. She was really the better-natured person of the two, but she never disobeyed Miss Minchin. She went downstairs again, looking almost alarmed.

"I never saw such a funny, old-fashioned child, sister," she said. "She has locked herself in, and she is not making the least particle of noise."

"It is much better than if she kicked and screamed, as some of them do," Miss Minchin answered. "I expected that a child as much spoiled as she is would set the whole house in an uproar. If ever a child was given her own way in everything, she is."

"I've been opening her trunks and putting her things away," said Miss Amelia. "I never saw anything like them--sable and ermine on her coats, and real Valenciennes lace on her underclothing. You have seen some of her clothes. What do you think of them?"

"I think they are perfectly ridiculous," replied Miss Minchin, sharply; "but they will look very well at the head of the line when we take the schoolchildren to church on Sunday. She has been provided for as if she were a little princess."

And upstairs in the locked room Sara and Emily sat on the floor and stared at the corner round which the cab had disappeared, while Captain Crewe looked backward, waving and kissing his hand as if he could not bear to stop.

Day 102

1.   Read chapter 2 of *A Little Princess* and tell someone about the chapter.
2.   Is Sarah good at French? (Answers)

A FRENCH LESSON

WHEN Sara entered the school-room the next morning everybody looked at her with wide, interested eyes. By that time every pupil—from Lavinia Herbert, who was nearly thirteen and felt quite grown up, to Lottie Legh, who was only just four and the baby of the school—had heard a great deal about her. They knew very certainly that she was Miss Minchin's show pupil and was considered a credit to the establishment. One or two of them had even caught a glimpse of her French maid, Mariette, who had arrived the evening before. Lavinia had managed to pass Sara's room when the door was open, and had seen Mariette opening a box which had arrived late from some shop.

"It was full of petticoats with lace frills on them—frills and frills," she whispered to her friend Jessie as she bent over her geography. "I saw her shaking them out. I heard Miss Minchin say to Miss Amelia that her clothes were so grand that they were ridiculous for a child. My mamma says that children should be dressed simply. She has got one of those petticoats on now. I saw it when she sat down."

"She has silk stockings on!" whispered Jessie, bending over her geography also. "And what little feet! I never saw such little feet."

"Oh," sniffed Lavinia, spitefully, "that is the way her slippers are made. My mamma says that even big feet can be made to look small if you have a clever shoemaker. I don't think she is pretty at all. Her eyes are such a queer color."

"She isn't pretty as other pretty people are," said Jessie, stealing a glance across the room; "but she makes you want to look at her again. She has tremendously long eyelashes, but her eyes are almost green."

Sara was sitting quietly in her seat, waiting to be told what to do. She had been placed near Miss Minchin's desk. She was not abashed at all by the many pairs of eyes watching her. She was interested and looked back quietly at the children who looked at her. She wondered what they were thinking of, and if they liked Miss Minchin, and if they cared for their lessons, and if any of them had a papa at all like her own. She had had a long talk with Emily about her papa that morning.

"He is on the sea now, Emily," she had said. "We must be very great friends to each other and tell each other things. Emily, look at me. You have the nicest eyes I ever saw—but I wish you could speak."

She was a child full of imaginings and whimsical thoughts, and one of her fancies was that there would be a great deal of comfort in even pretending that Emily was alive and really heard and understood. After Mariette had dressed her in her dark-blue school-room frock and tied her hair with a dark-blue ribbon, she went to Emily, who sat in a chair of her own, and gave her a book.

"You can read that while I am downstairs," she said; and, seeing Mariette looking at her curiously, she spoke to her with a serious little face.

"What I believe about dolls," she said, "is that they can do things they will not let us know about. Perhaps, really, Emily can read and talk and walk, but she will only do it when people are out of the room. That is her secret. You see, if people knew that dolls could do things, they would make them work. So, perhaps, they have promised each other to keep it a secret. If you stay in the room, Emily will just sit there and stare; but if you go out, she will begin to read, perhaps, or go and look out of the window. Then if she heard either of us coming, she would just run back and jump into her chair and pretend she had been there all the time."

"Comme elle est drôle!" Mariette said to herself, and when she went downstairs she told the head housemaid about it. But she had already begun to like this odd little girl who had such an intelligent small face and such perfect manners. She had taken care of children before who were not so polite. Sara was a very fine little person, and had a gentle, appreciative way of saying, "If you please, Mariette," "Thank you, Mariette," which was very charming. Mariette told the head housemaid that she thanked her as if she was thanking a lady.

"Elle a l'air d'une princesse, cette petite," she said. Indeed, she was very much pleased with her new little mistress and liked her place greatly.

After Sara had sat in her seat in the school-room for a few minutes, being looked at by the pupils, Miss Minchin rapped in a dignified manner upon her desk.

"Young ladies," she said, "I wish to introduce you to your new companion." All the little girls rose in their places, and Sara rose also. "I shall expect you all to be very agreeable to Miss Crewe; she has just come to us from a great distance—in fact, from India. As soon as lessons are over you must make each other's acquaintance."

The pupils bowed ceremoniously, and Sara made a little courtesy, and then they sat down and looked at each other again.

"Sara," said Miss Minchin in her school-room manner, "come here to me."

She had taken a book from the desk and was turning over its leaves. Sara went to her politely.

"As your papa has engaged a French maid for you," she began, "I conclude that he wishes you to make a special study of the French language."

Sara felt a little awkward.

"I think he engaged her," she said, "because he—he thought I would like her, Miss Minchin."

"I am afraid," said Miss Minchin, with a slightly sour smile, "that you have been a very spoiled little girl and always imagine that things are done because you like them. My impression is that your papa wished you to learn French."

If Sara had been older or less punctilious about being quite polite to people, she could have explained herself in a very few words. But, as it was, she felt a flush rising on her cheeks. Miss Minchin was a very severe and imposing person, and she seemed so absolutely sure that Sara knew nothing whatever of French that she felt as if it would be almost rude to correct her. The truth was that Sara could not remember the time when she had not seemed to know French. Her father had often spoken it to her when she had been a baby. Her mother had been a French woman, and Captain Crewe had loved her language, so it happened that Sara had always heard and been familiar with it.

"I—I have never really learned French, but—but—" she began, trying shyly to make herself clear.

One of Miss Minchin's chief secret annoyances was that she did not speak French herself, and was desirous of concealing the irritating fact. She, therefore, had no intention of discussing the matter and laying herself open to innocent questioning by a new little pupil.

"That is enough," she said with polite tartness. "If you have not learned, you must begin at once. The French master, Monsieur Dufarge, will be here in a few minutes. Take this book and look at it until he arrives."

Sara's cheeks felt warm. She went back to her seat and opened the book. She looked at the first page with a grave face. She knew it would be rude to smile, and she was very determined not to be rude. But it was very odd to find herself expected to study a page which told her that "le père" meant "the father," and "la mère" meant "the mother."

Miss Minchin glanced toward her scrutinizingly.

"You look rather cross, Sara," she said. "I am sorry you do not like the idea of learning French."

"I am very fond of it," answered Sara, thinking she would try again; "but—"

"You must not say 'but' when you are told to do things," said Miss Minchin. "Look at your book again."

And Sara did so, and did not smile, even when she found that "le fils" meant "the son," and "le frère" meant "the brother."

"When Monsieur Dufarge comes," she thought, "I can make him understand."

Monsieur Dufarge arrived very shortly afterward. He was a very nice, intelligent, middle-aged Frenchman, and he looked interested when his eyes fell upon Sara trying politely to seem absorbed in her little book of phrases.

"Is this a new pupil for me, madame?" he said to Miss Minchin. "I hope that is my good fortune."

"Her papa—Captain Crewe—is very anxious that she should begin the language. But I am afraid she has a childish prejudice against it. She does not seem to wish to learn," said Miss Minchin.

"I am sorry of that, mademoiselle," he said kindly to Sara. "Perhaps, when we begin to study together, I may show you that it is a charming tongue."

Little Sara rose in her seat. She was beginning to feel rather desperate, as if she were almost in disgrace. She looked up into Monsieur Dufarge's face with her big, green-gray eyes, and they were quite innocently appealing. She knew that he would understand as soon as she spoke. She began to explain quite simply in pretty and fluent French. Madame had not understood. She had not learned French exactly—not out of books—but her papa and other people had always spoken it to her, and she had read it and written it as she had read and written English. Her papa loved it, and she loved it because he did. Her dear mamma, who had died when she was born, had been French. She would be glad to learn anything monsieur would teach her, but what she had tried to explain to madame was that she already knew the words in this book—and she held out the little book of phrases.

When she began to speak Miss Minchin started quite violently and sat staring at her over her eye-glasses, almost indignantly, until she had finished. Monsieur Dufarge began to smile, and his smile was one of great pleasure. To hear this pretty childish voice speaking his own language so simply and charmingly made him feel almost as if he were in his native land—which in dark, foggy days in London sometimes seemed worlds away. When she had finished, he took the phrase book from her, with a look almost affectionate. But he spoke to Miss Minchin.

"Ah, madame," he said, "there is not much I can teach her. She has not learned French; she is French. Her accent is exquisite."

"You ought to have told me," exclaimed Miss Minchin, much mortified, turning to Sara.

"I—I tried," said Sara. "I—I suppose I did not begin right."

Miss Minchin knew she had tried, and that it had not been her fault that she was not allowed to explain. And when she saw that the pupils had been listening and that Lavinia and Jessie were giggling behind their French grammars, she felt infuriated.

"Silence, young ladies!" she said severely, rapping upon the desk. "Silence at once!"

And she began from that minute to feel rather a grudge against her show pupil.

Day 103

1.   Read chapter 3 of *A Little Princess* and tell someone about the chapter.
2.   Tell someone about the chapter. Who's Ermengarde?

ERMENGARDE

ON that first morning, when Sara sat at Miss Minchin's side, aware that the whole school-room was devoting itself to observing her, she had noticed very soon one little girl, about her own age, who looked at her very hard with a pair of light, rather dull, blue eyes. She was a fat child who did not look as if she were in the least clever, but she had a good-naturedly pouting mouth. Her flaxen hair was braided in a tight pigtail, tied with a ribbon, and she had pulled this pigtail around her neck, and was biting the end of the ribbon, resting her elbows on the desk, as she stared wonderingly at the new pupil. When Monsieur Dufarge began to speak to Sara, she looked a little frightened; and when Sara stepped forward and, looking at him with the innocent, appealing eyes, answered him, without any warning, in French, the fat little girl gave a startled jump, and grew quite red in her awed amazement. Having wept hopeless tears for weeks in her efforts to remember that "la mère" meant "the mother," and "le père," "the father,"—when one spoke sensible English—it was almost too much for her suddenly to find herself listening to a child her own age who seemed not only quite familiar with these words, but apparently knew any number of others, and could mix them up with verbs as if they were mere trifles.

She stared so hard and bit the ribbon on her pigtail so fast that she attracted the attention of Miss Minchin, who, feeling extremely cross at the moment, immediately pounced upon her.

"Miss St. John!" she exclaimed severely. "What do you mean by such conduct? Remove your elbows! Take your ribbon out of your mouth! Sit up at once!"

Upon which Miss St. John gave another jump, and when Lavinia and Jessie tittered she became redder than ever—so red, indeed, that she almost looked as if tears were coming into her poor, dull, childish eyes; and Sara saw her and was so sorry for her that she began rather to like her and want to be her friend. It was a way of hers always to want to spring into any fray in which someone was made uncomfortable or unhappy.

"If Sara had been a boy and lived a few centuries ago," her father used to say, "she would have gone about the country with her sword drawn, rescuing and defending everyone in distress. She always wants to fight when she sees people in trouble."

So she took rather a fancy to fat, slow, little Miss St. John, and kept glancing toward her through the morning. She saw that lessons were no easy matter to her, and that there was no danger of her ever being spoiled by being treated as a show pupil. Her French lesson was a pathetic thing. Her pronunciation made even Monsieur Dufarge smile in spite of himself, and Lavinia and Jessie and the more fortunate girls either giggled or looked at her in wondering disdain. But Sara did not laugh. She tried to look as if she did not hear when Miss St. John called "le bon pain," "lee bong pang." She had a fine, hot little temper of her own, and it made her feel rather savage when she heard the titters and saw the poor, stupid, distressed child's face.

"It isn't funny, really," she said between her teeth, as she bent over her book. "They ought not to laugh."

When lessons were over and the pupils gathered together in groups to talk, Sara looked for Miss St. John, and finding her bundled rather disconsolately in a window-seat, she walked over to her and spoke. She only said the kind of thing little girls always say to each other by way of beginning an acquaintance, but there was something friendly about Sara, and people always felt it.

"What is your name?" she said.

To explain Miss St. John's amazement one must recall that a new pupil is, for a short time, a somewhat uncertain thing; and of this new pupil the entire school had talked the night before until it fell asleep quite exhausted by excitement and contradictory stories. A new pupil with a carriage and a pony and a maid, and a voyage from India to discuss, was not an ordinary acquaintance.

"My name's Ermengarde St. John," she answered.

"Mine is Sara Crewe," said Sara. "Yours is very pretty. It sounds like a story book."

"Do you like it?" fluttered Ermengarde. "I—I like yours."

Miss St. John's chief trouble in life was that she had a clever father. Sometimes this seemed to her a dreadful calamity. If you have a father who knows everything, who speaks seven or eight languages, and has thousands of volumes which he has apparently learned by heart, he frequently expects you to be familiar with the contents of your lesson books at least; and it is not improbable that he will feel you ought to be able to remember a few incidents of history and to write a French exercise. Ermengarde was a severe trial to Mr. St. John. He could not understand how a child of his could be a notably and unmistakably dull creature who never shone in anything.

"Good heavens!" he had said more than once, as he stared at her, "there are times when I think she is as stupid as her Aunt Eliza!"

If her Aunt Eliza had been slow to learn and quick to forget a thing entirely when she had learned it, Ermengarde was strikingly like her. She was the monumental dunce of the school, and it could not be denied.

"She must be made to learn," her father said to Miss Minchin.

Consequently Ermengarde spent the greater part of her life in disgrace or in tears. She learned things and forgot them; or, if she remembered them, she did not understand them. So it was natural that, having made Sara's acquaintance, she should sit and stare at her with profound admiration.

"You can speak French, can't you?" she said respectfully.

Sara got on to the window-seat, which was a big, deep one, and, tucking up her feet, sat with her hands clasped round her knees.

"I can speak it because I have heard it all my life," she answered. "You could speak it if you had always heard it."

"Oh, no, I couldn't," said Ermengarde. "I never could speak it!"

"Why?" inquired Sara, curiously.

Ermengarde shook her head so that the pigtail wobbled.

"You heard me just now," she said. "I'm always like that. I can't say the words. They're so queer."

She paused a moment, and then added with a touch of awe in her voice:

"You are clever, aren't you?"

Sara looked out of the window into the dingy square, where the sparrows were hopping and twittering on the wet, iron railings and the sooty branches of the trees. She reflected a few moments. She had heard it said very often that she was "clever," and she wondered if she was—and if she was, how it had happened.

"I don't know," she said. "I can't tell." Then, seeing a mournful look on the round, chubby face, she gave a little laugh and changed the subject.

"Would you like to see Emily?" she inquired.

"Who is Emily?" Ermengarde asked, just as Miss Minchin had done.

"Come up to my room and see," said Sara, holding out her hand.

They jumped down from the window-seat together, and went up-stairs.

"Is it true," Ermengarde whispered, as they went through the hall—"is it true that you have a play-room all to yourself?"

"Yes," Sara answered. "Papa asked Miss Minchin to let me have one, because—well, it was because when I play I make up stories and tell them to myself, and I don't like people to hear me. It spoils it if I think people listen."

They had reached the passage leading to Sara's room by this time, and Ermengarde stopped short, staring, and quite losing her breath.

"You make up stories!" she gasped. "Can you do that—as well as speak French? Can you?"

Sara looked at her in simple surprise.

"Why, anyone can make up things," she said. "Have you never tried?"

She put her hand warningly on Ermengarde's.

"Let us go very quietly to the door," she whispered, "and then I will open it quite suddenly; perhaps we may catch her."

She was half laughing, but there was a touch of mysterious hope in her eyes which fascinated Ermengarde, though she had not the remotest idea what it meant, or whom it was she wanted to "catch," or why she wanted to catch her. Whatsoever she meant, Ermengarde was sure it was something delightfully exciting. So, quite thrilled with expectation, she followed her on tiptoe along the passage. They made not the least noise until they reached the door. Then Sara suddenly turned the handle, and threw it wide open. Its opening revealed the room quite neat and quiet, a fire gently burning in the grate, and a wonderful doll sitting in a chair by it, apparently reading a book.

"Oh, she got back to her seat before we could see her!" Sara claimed. "Of course they always do. They are as quick as lightning."

Ermengarde looked from her to the doll and back again.

"Can she—walk?" she asked breathlessly.

"Yes," answered Sara. "At least I believe she can. At least I pretend I believe she can. And that makes it seem as if it were true. Have you never pretended things?"

"No," said Ermengarde. "Never. I—tell me about it."

She was so bewitched by this odd, new companion that she actually stared at Sara instead of at Emily—notwithstanding that Emily was the most attractive doll person she had ever seen.

"Let us sit down," said Sara, "and I will tell you. It's so easy that when you begin you can't stop. You just go on and on doing it always. And it's beautiful. Emily, you must listen. This is Ermengarde St. John, Emily. Ermengarde, this is Emily. Would you like to hold her?"

"Oh, may I?" said Ermengarde. "May I, really? She is beautiful!" And Emily was put into her arms.

Never in her dull, short life had Miss St. John dreamed of such an hour as the one she spent with the queer new pupil before they heard the lunch-bell ring and were obliged to go down-stairs.

Sara sat upon the hearth-rug and told her strange things. She sat rather huddled up, and her green eyes shone and her cheeks flushed. She told stories of the voyage, and stories of India; but what fascinated Ermengarde the most was her fancy about the dolls who walked and talked, and who could do anything they chose when the human beings were out of the room, but who must keep their powers a secret and so flew back to their places "like lightning" when people returned to the room.

"We couldn't do it," said Sara, seriously. "You see, it's a kind of magic."

Once, when she was relating the story of the search for Emily, Ermengarde saw her face suddenly change. A cloud seemed to pass over it and put out the light in her shining eyes. She drew her breath in so sharply that it made a funny, sad little sound, and then she shut her lips and held them tightly closed, as if she was determined either to do or not to do something. Ermengarde had an idea that if she had been like any other little girl, she might have suddenly burst out sobbing and crying. But she did not.

"Have you a—a pain?" Ermengarde ventured.

"Yes," Sara answered, after a moment's silence. "But it is not in my body." Then she added something in a low voice which she tried to keep quite steady, and it was this: "Do you love your father more than anything else in all the whole world?"

Ermengarde's mouth fell open a little. She knew that it would be far from behaving like a respectable child at a select seminary to say that it had never occurred to you that you could love your father, that you would do anything desperate to avoid being left alone in his society for ten minutes. She was, indeed, greatly embarrassed.

"I—I scarcely ever see him," she stammered. "He is always in the library—reading things."

"I love mine more than all the world ten times over," Sara said. "That is what my pain is. He has gone away."

She put her head quietly down on her little, huddled-up knees, and sat very still for a few minutes.

"She's going to cry out loud," thought Ermengarde, fearfully.

But she did not. Her short, black locks tumbled about her ears, and she sat still. Then she spoke without lifting her head.

"I promised him I would bear it," she said. "And I will. You have to bear things. Think what soldiers bear! Papa is a soldier. If there was a war he would have to bear marching and thirstiness and, perhaps, deep wounds. And he would never say a word—not one word."

Ermengarde could only gaze at her, but she felt that she was beginning to adore her. She was so wonderful and different from anyone else.

Presently, she lifted her face and shook back her black locks, with a queer little smile.

"If I go on talking and talking," she said, "and telling you things about pretending, I shall bear it better. You don't forget, but you bear it better."

Ermengarde did not know why a lump came into her throat and her eyes felt as if tears were in them.

"Lavinia and Jessie are 'best friends,' " she said rather huskily. "I wish we could be 'best friends.' Would you have me for yours? You're clever, and I'm the stupidest child in the school, but I—oh, I do so like you!"

"I'm glad of that," said Sara. "It makes you thankful when you are liked. Yes. We will be friends. And I'll tell you what"—a sudden gleam lighting her face—"I can help you with your French lessons."

Day 104

1. Read chapter 4 of *A Little Princess*.
2. The second paragraph of this chapter sets up the point of the book. Reread the second paragraph. The first paragraph starts the chapter. There is a little space between each paragraph. The second paragraph begins, "Things happen…"
3. What is Sara's question? (Answers)
4. What do you think? Do do you think true character shows in trial?
5. What does the Bible say about trial and testing?
    - Deuteronomy 8:2 says that God tests people to know what's in their hearts.
6. Are trials good? Useful? Necessary? Explain your answer to a parent.

Vocabulary

1. Suffixes are what is added onto the end of a word, like "est" on happiest.
2. Add a suffix to change the meanings of these words. Here are some examples: library-librarian, attain-attainable
3. Say the words out loud if you are stuck and try different endings on them until something makes sense! Do your best. (Answers)

    - great, forget, excite, annoy, affection, private, free, depend, lion, child

LOTTIE

IF Sara had been a different kind of child, the life she led at Miss Minchin's Select Seminary for the next ten years would not have been at all good for her. She was treated more as if she were a distinguished guest at the establishment than as if she were a mere little girl. If she had been a self-opinionated, domineering child, she might have become disagreeable enough to be unbearable through being so much indulged and flattered. If she had been an indolent child, she would have learned nothing. Privately Miss Minchin disliked her, but she was far too worldly a woman to do or say anything which might make such a desirable pupil wish to leave her school. She knew quite well that if Sara wrote to her papa to tell him she was uncomfortable or unhappy, Captain Crewe would remove her at once. Miss Minchin's opinion was that if a child were continually praised and never forbidden to do what she liked, she would be sure to be fond of the place where she was so treated. Accordingly, Sara was praised for her quickness at her lessons, for her good manners, for her amiability to her fellow-pupils, for her generosity if she gave sixpence to a beggar out of her full little purse; the simplest thing she did was treated as if it were a virtue, and if she had not had a disposition and a clever little brain, she might have been a very self-satisfied young person. But the clever little brain told her a great many sensible and true things about herself and her circumstances, and now and then she talked these things over to Ermengarde as time went on.

"Things happen to people by accident," she used to say. "A lot of nice accidents have happened to me. It just happened that I always liked lessons and books, and could remember things when I learned them. It just happened that I was born with a father who was beautiful and nice and clever, and could give me everything I liked. Perhaps I have not really a good temper at all, but if you have everything you want and everyone is kind to you, how can you help but be good-tempered? I don't know"—looking quite serious— "how I shall ever find out whether I am really a nice child or a horrid one. Perhaps I'm a hideous child, and no one will ever know, just because I never have any trials."

"Lavinia has no trials," said Ermengarde, stolidly, "and she is horrid enough."

Sara rubbed the end of her little nose reflectively, as she thought the matter over.

"Well," she said at last, "perhaps—perhaps that is because Lavinia is growing." This was the result of a charitable recollection of having heard Miss Amelia say that Lavinia was growing so fast that she believed it affected her health and temper.

Lavinia, in fact, was spiteful. She was inordinately jealous of Sara. Until the new pupil's arrival, she had felt herself the leader in the school. She had led because she was capable of making herself extremely disagreeable if the others did not follow her. She domineered over the little children, and assumed grand airs with those big enough to be her companions. She was rather pretty, and had been the best-dressed pupil in the procession when the Select

Seminary walked out two by two, until Sara's velvet coats and sable muffs appeared, combined with drooping ostrich feathers, and were led by Miss Minchin at the head of the line. This, at the beginning, had been bitter enough; but as time went on it became apparent that Sara was a leader, too, and not because she could make herself disagreeable, but because she never did.

"There's one thing about Sara Crewe," Jessie had enraged her "best friend" by saying honestly, "she's never 'grand' about herself the least bit, and you know she might be, Lavvie. I believe I couldn't help being—just a little—if I had so many fine things and was made such a fuss over. It's disgusting, the way Miss Minchin shows her off when parents come."

"'Dear Sara must come into the drawing room and talk to Mrs. Musgrave about India,'" mimicked Lavinia, in her most highly flavored imitation of Miss Minchin. "'Dear Sara must speak French to Lady Pitkin. Her accent is so perfect.' She didn't learn her French at the Seminary, at any rate. And there's nothing so clever in her knowing it. She says herself she didn't learn it at all. She just picked it up, because she always heard her papa speak it. And, as to her papa, there is nothing so grand in being an Indian officer."

"Well," said Jessie, slowly, "he's killed tigers. He killed the one in the skin Sara has in her room. That's why she likes it so. She lies on it and strokes its head, and talks to it as if it was a cat."

"She's always doing something silly," snapped Lavinia. "My mamma says that way of hers of pretending things is silly. She says she will grow up eccentric."

It was quite true that Sara was never "grand." She was a friendly little soul, and shared her privileges and belongings with a free hand. The little ones, who were accustomed to being disdained and ordered out of the way by mature ladies aged ten and twelve, were never made to cry by this most envied of them all. She was a motherly young person, and when people fell down and scraped their knees, she ran and helped them up and patted them, or found in her pocket a bonbon or some other article of a soothing nature. She never pushed them out of her way or alluded to their years as a humiliation and a blot upon their small characters.

"If you are four you are four," she said severely to Lavinia on an occasion of her having—it must be confessed—slapped Lottie and called her "a brat;" "but you will be five next year, and six the year after that. And," opening large, convicting eyes, "it only takes sixteen years to make you twenty."

"Dear me!" said Lavinia, "how we can calculate!" In fact, it was not to be denied that sixteen and four made twenty—and twenty was an age the most daring were scarcely bold enough to dream of.

So the younger children adored Sara. More than once she had been known to have a tea-party, made up of these despised ones, in her own room. And Emily had been played with, and Emily's own tea-service used—the one with cups which held quite a lot of much-sweetened weak tea and had blue flowers on them. No one had seen such a very real doll's tea set before. From that afternoon Sara was regarded as a goddess and a queen by the entire alphabet class.

Lottie Legh worshipped her to such an extent that if Sara had not been a motherly person, she would have found her tiresome. Lottie had been sent to school by a rather flighty young papa who could not imagine what else to do with her. Her young mother had died, and as the child had been treated like a favorite doll or a very spoiled pet monkey or lap-dog ever since the first hour of her life, she was a very appalling little creature. When she wanted anything or did not want anything she wept and howled; and, as she always wanted the things she could not have, and did not want the things that were best for her, her shrill little voice was usually to be heard uplifted in wails in one part of the house or another.

Her strongest weapon was that in some mysterious way she had found out that a very small girl who had lost her mother was a person who ought to be pitied and made much of. She had probably heard some grown-up people talking her over in the early days, after her mother's death. So it became her habit to make great use of this knowledge.

The first time Sara took her in charge was one morning when, on passing a sitting-room, she heard both Miss Minchin and Miss Amelia trying to suppress the angry wails of some child who, evidently, refused to be silenced. She refused so strenuously indeed that Miss Minchin was obliged to almost shout—in a stately and severe manner—to make herself heard.

"What is she crying for?" she almost yelled.

"Oh—oh—oh!" Sara heard; "I haven't got any mam—ma-a!"

"Oh, Lottie!" screamed Miss Amelia. "Do stop, darling! Don't cry! Please don't!"

"Oh! oh! oh!" Lottie howled tempestuously. "Haven't—got—any—mam—ma-a!"

"She ought to be whipped," Miss Minchin proclaimed. "You shall be whipped, you naughty child!"

Lottie wailed more loudly than ever. Miss Amelia began to cry. Miss Minchin's voice rose until it almost thundered, then suddenly she sprang up from her chair in impotent indignation and flounced out of the room, leaving Miss Amelia to arrange the matter.

Sara had paused in the hall, wondering if she ought to go into the room, because she had recently begun a friendly acquaintance with Lottie and might be able to quiet her. When

Miss Minchin came out and saw her, she looked rather annoyed. She realized that her voice, as heard from inside the room, could not have sounded either dignified or amiable.

"Oh, Sara!" she exclaimed, endeavoring to produce a suitable smile.

"I stopped," explained Sara, "because I knew it was Lottie—and I thought, perhaps—just perhaps, I could make her be quiet. May I try, Miss Minchin?"

"If you can. You are a clever child," answered Miss Minchin, drawing in her mouth sharply. Then, seeing that Sara looked slightly chilled by her asperity, she changed her manner. "But you are clever in everything," she said in her approving way. "I dare say you can manage her. Go in." And she left her.

When Sara entered the room, Lottie was lying upon the floor, screaming and kicking her small fat legs violently, and Miss Amelia was bending over her in consternation and despair, looking quite red and damp with heat. Lottie had always found, when in her own nursery at home, that kicking and screaming would always be quieted by any means she insisted on. Poor plump Miss Amelia was trying first one method, and then another.

"Poor darling," she said one moment, "I know you haven't any mamma, poor—" Then in quite another tone: "If you don't stop, Lottie, I will shake you. Poor little angel! There—there! You wicked, bad, detestable child, I will smack you! I will!"

Sara went to them quietly. She did not know at all what she was going to do, but she had a vague inward conviction that it would be better not to say such different kinds of things quite so helplessly and excitedly.

"Miss Amelia," she said in a low voice, "Miss Minchin says I may try to make her stop—may I?"

Miss Amelia turned and looked at her hopelessly. "Oh, do you think you can?" she gasped.

"I don't know whether I can," answered Sara, still in her half-whisper; "but I will try."

Miss Amelia stumbled up from her knees with a heavy sigh, and Lottie's fat little legs kicked as hard as ever.

"If you will steal out of the room," said Sara, "I will stay with her."

"Oh, Sara!" almost whimpered Miss Amelia. "We never had such a dreadful child before. I don't believe we can keep her."

But she crept out of the room, and was very much relieved to find an excuse for doing it.

Sara stood by the howling furious child for a few moments, and looked down at her without saying anything. Then she sat down flat on the floor beside her and waited. Except for Lottie's angry screams, the room was quite quiet. This was a new state of affairs for little Miss Legh, who was accustomed, when she screamed, to hear other people protest and implore and command and coax by turns. To lie and kick and shriek, and find the only person near you not seeming to mind in the least, attracted her attention. She opened her tight-shut streaming eyes to see who this person was. And it was only another little girl. But it was the one who owned Emily and all the nice things. And she was looking at her steadily and as if she was merely thinking. Having paused for a few seconds to find this out, Lottie thought she must begin again, but the quiet of the room and of Sara's odd, interested face made her first howl rather half-hearted.

"I—haven't—any—ma—ma—ma-a!" she announced; but her voice was not so strong.

Sara looked at her still more steadily, but with a sort of understanding in her eyes.

"Neither have I," she said.

This was so unexpected that it was astounding. Lottie actually dropped her legs, gave a wriggle, and lay and stared. A new idea will stop a crying child when nothing else will. Also it was true that while Lottie disliked Miss Minchin, who was cross, and Miss Amelia, who was foolishly indulgent, she rather liked Sara, little as she knew her. She did not want to give up her grievance, but her thoughts were distracted from it, so she wriggled again, and, after a sulky sob, said:

"Where is she?"

Sara paused a moment. Because she had been told that her mamma was in heaven, she had thought a great deal about the matter, and her thoughts had not been quite like those of other people.

"She went to heaven," she said. "But I am sure she comes out sometimes to see me—though I don't see her. So does yours. Perhaps they can both see us now. Perhaps they are both in this room."

Lottie sat bolt upright, and looked about her. She was a pretty, little, curly-headed creature, and her round eyes were like wet forget-me-nots. If her mamma had seen her during the last half-hour, she might not have thought her the kind of child who ought to be related to an angel.

Sara went on talking. Perhaps some people might think that what she said was rather like a fairy story, but it was all so real to her own imagination that Lottie began to listen in spite of herself. She had been told that her mamma had wings and a crown, and she had been shown pictures of ladies in beautiful white night-gowns, who were said to be angels. But Sara seemed to be telling a real story about a lovely country where real people were.

"There are fields and fields of flowers," she said, forgetting herself, as usual, when she began, and talking rather as if she were in a dream—"fields and fields of lilies—and when the soft wind blows over them it wafts the scent of them into the air—and everybody always breathes it, because the soft wind is always blowing. And little children run about in the lily fields and gather armfuls of them, and laugh and make little wreaths. And the streets are shining. And no one is ever tired, however far they walk. They can float anywhere they like. And there are walls made of pearl and gold all round the city, but they are low enough for the people to go and lean on them, and look down on to the earth and smile, and send beautiful messages."

Whatsoever story she had begun to tell, Lottie would, no doubt, have stopped crying, and been fascinated into listening; but there was no denying that this story was prettier than most others. She dragged herself close to Sara, and drank in every word until the end came—far too soon. When it did come, she was so sorry that she put up her lip ominously.

"I want to go there," she cried. "I—haven't any mamma in this school."

Sara saw the danger signal, and came out of her dream. She took hold of the chubby hand and pulled her close to her side with a coaxing little laugh.

"I will be your mamma," she said. "We will play that you are my little girl. And Emily shall be your sister."

Lottie's dimples all began to show themselves.

"Shall she?" she said.

"Yes," answered Sara, jumping to her feet. "Let us go and tell her. And then I will wash your face and brush your hair."

To which Lottie agreed quite cheerfully, and trotted out of the room and up-stairs with her, without seeming even to remember that the whole of the last hour's tragedy had been caused by the fact that she had refused to be washed and brushed for lunch and Miss Minchin had been called in to use her majestic authority.

And from that time Sara was an adopted mother.

Day 105

1.   Read chapter 5 of *A Little Princess*.
2.   Tell someone about the chapter.
3.   Who is Becky?

BECKY

OF COURSE the greatest power Sara possessed and the one which gained her even more followers than her luxuries and the fact that she was "the show pupil," the power that Lavinia and certain other girls were most envious of, and at the same time most fascinated by in spite of themselves, was her power of telling stories and of making everything she talked about seem like a story, whether it was one or not.

Anyone who has been at school with a teller of stories knows what the wonder means— how he or she is followed about and besought in a whisper to relate romances; how groups gather round and hang on the outskirts of the favored party in the hope of being allowed to join in and listen. Sara not only could tell stories, but she adored telling them. When she sat or stood in the midst of a circle and began to invent wonderful things, her green eyes grew big and shining, her cheeks flushed, and, without knowing that she was doing it, she began to act and made what she told lovely or alarming by the raising or dropping of her voice, the bend and sway of her slim body, and the dramatic movement of her hands. She forgot that she was talking to listening children; she saw and lived with the fairy folk, or the kings and queens and beautiful ladies, whose adventures she was narrating. Sometimes when she had finished her story, she was quite out of breath with excitement, and would lay her hand on her thin, little, quick-rising chest, and half laugh as if at herself.

"When I am telling it," she would say, "it doesn't seem as if it was only made up. It seems more real than you are—more real than the school-room. I feel as if I were all the people in the story—one after the other. It is queer."

She had been at Miss Minchin's school about two years when, one foggy winter's afternoon, as she was getting out of her carriage, comfortably wrapped up in her warmest velvets and furs and looking very much grander than she knew, she caught sight, as she crossed the pavement, of a dingy little figure standing on the area steps, and stretching its neck so that its wide-open eyes might peer at her through the railings. Something in the eagerness and timidity of the smudgy face made her look at it, and when she looked she smiled because it was her way to smile at people.

But the owner of the smudgy face and the wide-open eyes evidently was afraid that she ought not to have been caught looking at pupils of importance. She dodged out of sight like a Jack-in-the-box and scurried back into the kitchen, disappearing so suddenly that if she had not been such a poor, little forlorn thing, Sara would have laughed in spite of herself. That very evening, as Sara was sitting in the midst of a group of listeners in a corner of the school-room telling one of her stories, the very same figure timidly entered the room, carrying a coal-box much too heavy for her, and knelt down upon the hearth-rug to replenish the fire and sweep up the ashes.

She was cleaner than she had been when she peeped through the area railings, but she looked just as frightened. She was evidently afraid to look at the children or seem to be listening. She put on pieces of coal cautiously with her fingers so that she might make no disturbing noise, and she swept about the fire-irons very softly. But Sara saw in two minutes that she was deeply interested in what was going on, and that she was doing her work slowly in the hope of catching a word here and there. And realizing this, she raised her voice and spoke more clearly.

"The Mermaids swam softly about in the crystal-green water, and dragged after them a fishing-net woven of deep-sea pearls," she said. "The Princess sat on the white rock and watched them."

It was a wonderful story about a princess who was loved by a prince merman, and went to live with him in shining caves under the sea.

The small drudge before the grate swept the hearth once and then swept it again. Having done it twice, she did it three times; and, as she was doing it the third time, the sound of the story so lured her to listen that she fell under the spell and actually forgot that she had no right to listen at all, and also forgot everything else. She sat down upon her heels as she knelt on the hearth-rug, and the brush hung idly in her fingers. The voice of the story-teller went on and drew her with it into winding grottos under the sea, glowing with soft, clear blue light, and paved with pure golden sands. Strange sea flowers and grasses waved about her, and far away faint singing and music echoed.

The hearth-brush fell from the work-roughened hand, and Lavinia Herbert looked round.

"That girl has been listening," she said.

The culprit snatched up her brush, and scrambled to her feet. She caught at the coal-box and simply scuttled out of the room like a frightened rabbit.

Sara felt rather hot-tempered.

"I knew she was listening," she said. "Why shouldn't she?"

Lavinia tossed her head with great elegance.

"Well," she remarked, "I do not know whether your mamma would like you to tell stories to servant girls, but I know my mamma wouldn't like me to do it."

"My mamma!" said Sara, looking odd. "I don't believe she would mind in the least. She knows that stories belong to everybody."

"I thought," retorted Lavinia, in severe recollection, "that your mamma was dead. How can she know things?"

"Do you think she doesn't know things?" said Sara, in her stern little voice. Sometimes she had a rather stern little voice.

"Sara's mamma knows everything," piped in Lottie. "So does my mamma—'cept Sara is my mamma at Miss Minchin's—my other one knows everything. The streets are shining, and there are fields and fields of lilies, and everybody gathers them. Sara tells me when she puts me to bed."

"You wicked thing," said Lavinia, turning on Sara; "making fairy stories about heaven."

"There are much more splendid stories in Revelation," returned Sara. "Just look and see! How do you know mine are fairy stories? But I can tell you"—with a fine bit of unheavenly temper—"you will never find out whether they are or not if you're not kinder to people than you are now. Come along, Lottie." And she marched out of the room, rather hoping that she might see the little servant again somewhere, but she found no trace of her when she got into the hall.

"Who is that little girl who makes the fires?" she asked Mariette that night.

Mariette broke forth into a flow of description.

Ah, indeed, Mademoiselle Sara might well ask. She was a forlorn little thing who had just taken the place of scullery-maid— though, as to being scullery-maid, she was everything else besides. She blacked boots and grates, and carried heavy coal-scuttles up and down stairs, and scrubbed floors and cleaned windows, and was ordered about by everybody. She was fourteen years old, but was so stunted in growth that she looked about twelve. In truth, Mariette was sorry for her. She was so timid that if one chanced to speak to her it appeared as if her poor, frightened eyes would jump out of her head.

"What is her name?" asked Sara, who had sat by the table, with her chin on her hands, as she listened absorbedly to the recital.

Her name was Becky. Mariette heard everyone below-stairs calling, "Becky, do this," and "Becky, do that," every five minutes in the day.

Sara sat and looked into the fire, reflecting on Becky for some time after Mariette left her. She made up a story of which Becky was the ill-used heroine. She thought she looked as if she had never had quite enough to eat. Her very eyes were hungry. She hoped she should see her again, but though she caught sight of her carrying things up or down stairs on several occasions, she always seemed in such a hurry and so afraid of being seen that it was impossible to speak to her.

But a few weeks later, on another foggy afternoon, when she entered her sitting-room she found herself confronting a rather pathetic picture. In her own special and pet easy-chair before the bright fire, Becky—with a coal smudge on her nose and several on her apron, with her poor little cap hanging half off her head, and an empty coal-box on the floor near her—sat fast asleep, tired out beyond even the endurance of her hard-working young body. She had been sent up to put the bedrooms in order for the evening. There were a great many of them, and she had been running about all day. Sara's rooms she had saved until the last. They were not like the other rooms, which were plain and bare. Ordinary pupils were expected to be satisfied with mere necessaries. Sara's comfortable sitting-room seemed a bower of luxury to the scullery-maid, though it was, in fact, merely a nice, bright little room. But there were pictures and books in it, and curious things from India; there was a sofa and the low, soft chair; Emily sat in a chair of her own, with the air of a presiding goddess, and there was always a glowing fire and a polished grate. Becky saved it until the end of her afternoon's work, because it rested her to go into it, and she always hoped to snatch a few minutes to sit down in the soft chair and look about her, and think about the wonderful good fortune of the child who owned such surroundings and who went out on the cold days in beautiful hats and coats one tried to catch a glimpse of through the area railing.

On this afternoon, when she had sat down, the sensation of relief to her short, aching legs had been so wonderful and delightful that it had seemed to soothe her whole body, and the glow of warmth and comfort from the fire had crept over her like a spell, until, as she looked at the red coals, a tired, slow smile stole over her smudged face, her head nodded forward without her being aware of it, her eyes drooped, and she fell fast asleep. She had really been only about ten minutes in the room when Sara entered, but she was in as deep a sleep as if she had been, like the Sleeping Beauty, slumbering for a hundred years. But she did not look—poor Becky!—like a Sleeping Beauty at all. She looked only like an ugly, stunted, worn-out little scullery drudge.

Sara seemed as much unlike her as if she were a creature from another world.

On this particular afternoon she had been taking her dancing-lesson, and the afternoon on which the dancing-master appeared was rather a grand occasion at the seminary, though it occurred every week. The pupils were attired in their prettiest frocks, and as Sara danced particularly well, she was very much brought forward, and Mariette was requested to make her as diaphanous and fine as possible.

To-day a frock the color of a rose had been put on her, and Mariette had bought some real buds and made her a wreath to wear on her black locks. She had been learning a new, delightful dance in which she had been skimming and flying about the room, like a large rose-colored butterfly, and the enjoyment and exercise had brought a brilliant, happy glow into her face.

When she entered the room, she floated in with a few of the butterfly steps—and there sat Becky, nodding her cap sideways off her head.

"Oh!" cried Sara, softly, when she saw her. "That poor thing!"

It did not occur to her to feel cross at finding her pet chair occupied by the small, dingy figure. To tell the truth, she was quite glad to find it there. When the ill-used heroine of her story wakened, she could talk to her. She crept toward her quietly, and stood looking at her. Becky gave a little snore.

"I wish she'd waken herself," Sara said. "I don't like to waken her. But Miss Minchin would be cross if she found out. I'll just wait a few minutes."

She took a seat on the edge of the table, and sat swinging her slim, rose-colored legs, and wondering what it would be best to do. Miss Amelia might come in at any moment, and if she did, Becky would be sure to be scolded.

"But she is so tired," she thought. "She is so tired!" A piece of flaming coal ended her perplexity for her that very moment. It broke off from a large lump and fell on to the fender. Becky started, and opened her eyes with a frightened gasp. She did not know she had fallen asleep. She had only sat down for one moment and felt the beautiful glow—and here she found herself staring in wild alarm at the wonderful pupil, who sat perched quite near her, like a rose-colored fairy, with interested eyes.

She sprang up and clutched at her cap. She felt it dangling over her ear, and tried wildly to put it straight. Oh, she had got herself into trouble now with a vengeance! To have impudently fallen asleep on such a young lady's chair! She would be turned out of doors without wages.

She made a sound like a big breathless sob.

"Oh, miss! Oh, miss!" she stuttered. "I arst yer pardon, miss! Oh, I do, miss!"

Sara jumped down, and came quite close to her.

"Don't be frightened," she said, quite as if she had been speaking to a little girl like herself. "It doesn't matter the least bit."

"I didn't go to do it, miss," protested Becky. "It was the warm fire—an' me bein' so tired. It—it wasn't impertinence!"

Sara broke into a friendly little laugh, and put her hand on her shoulder.

"You were tired," she said; "you could not help it. You are not really awake yet."

How poor Becky stared at her! In fact, she had never heard such a nice, friendly sound in anyone's voice before. She was used to being ordered about and scolded, and having her ears boxed. And this one—in her rose-colored dancing afternoon splendor—was looking at her as if she were not a culprit at all—as if she had a right to be tired—even to fall asleep! The touch of the soft, slim little paw on her shoulder was the most amazing thing she had ever known.

"Ain't—ain't yer angry, miss?" she gasped. "Ain't yer goin' to tell the missus?"

"No," cried out Sara. "Of course I'm not."

The woeful fright in the coal-smutted face made her suddenly so sorry that she could scarcely bear it. One of her queer thoughts rushed into her mind. She put her hand against Becky's cheek.

"Why," she said, "we are just the same—I am only a little girl like you. It's just an accident that I am not you, and you are not me!"

Becky did not understand in the least. Her mind could not grasp such amazing thoughts, and "an accident" meant to her a calamity in which some one was run over or fell off a ladder and was carried to "the 'orspital."

"A' accident, miss," she fluttered respectfully. "Is it?"

"Yes," Sara answered, and she looked at her dreamily for a moment. But the next she spoke in a different tone. She realized that Becky did not know what she meant.

"Have you done your work?" she asked. "Dare you stay here a few minutes?"

Becky lost her breath again.

"Here, miss? Me?"

Sara ran to the door, opened it, and looked out and listened.

"No one is anywhere about," she explained. "If your bedrooms are finished, perhaps you might stay a tiny while. I thought—perhaps—you might like a piece of cake."

The next ten minutes seemed to Becky like a sort of delirium. Sara opened a cupboard, and gave her a thick slice of cake. She seemed to rejoice when it was devoured in hungry bites. She talked and asked questions, and laughed until Becky's fears actually began to calm themselves, and she once or twice gathered boldness enough to ask a question or so herself, daring as she felt it to be.

"Is that—" she ventured, looking longingly at the rose-colored frock. And she asked it almost in a whisper. "Is that there your best?"

"It is one of my dancing-frocks," answered Sara. "I like it, don't you?"

For a few seconds Becky was almost speechless with admiration. Then she said in an awed voice:

"Onct I see a princess. I was standin' in the street with the crowd outside Covin' Garden, watchin' the swells go inter the operer. An' there was one everyone stared at most. They ses to each other, 'That's the princess.' She was a growed-up young lady, but she was pink all over—gownd an' cloak, an' flowers an' all. I called her to mind the minnit I see you, sittin' there on the table, miss. You looked like her."

"I've often thought," said Sara, in her reflecting voice, "that I should like to be a princess; I wonder what it feels like. I believe I will begin pretending I am one."

Becky stared at her admiringly, and, as before, did not understand her in the least. She watched her with a sort of adoration. Very soon Sara left her reflections and turned to her with a new question.

"Becky," she said, "weren't you listening to that story?"

"Yes, miss," confessed Becky, a little alarmed again. "I knowed I hadn't orter, but it was that beautiful I—I couldn't help it."

"I liked you to listen to it," said Sara. "If you tell stories, you like nothing so much as to tell them to people who want to listen. I don't know why it is. Would you like to hear the rest?"

Becky lost her breath again.

"Me hear it?" she cried. "Like as if I was a pupil, miss! All about the Prince—and the little white Merbabies swimming about laughing—with stars in their hair?"

Sara nodded.

"You haven't time to hear it now, I'm afraid," she said; "but if you will tell me just what time you come to do my rooms, I will try to be here and tell you a bit of it every day until it is finished. It's a lovely long one—and I'm always putting new bits to it."

"Then," breathed Becky, devoutly, "I wouldn't mind how heavy the coal-boxes was—or what the cook done to me, if—if I might have that to think of."

"You may," said Sara. "I'll tell it all to you."

When Becky went down-stairs, she was not the same Becky who had staggered up, loaded down by the weight of the coal-scuttle. She had an extra piece of cake in her pocket, and she had been fed and warmed, but not only by cake and fire. Something else had warmed and fed her, and the something else was Sara.

When she was gone Sara sat on her favorite perch on the end of her table. Her feet were on a chair, her elbows on her knees, and her chin in her hands.

"If I was a princess—a real princess," she murmured, "I could scatter largess to the populace. But even if I am only a pretend princess, I can invent little things to do for people. Things like this. She was just as happy as if it was largess. I'll pretend that to do things people like is scattering largess. I've scattered largess."

Day 106

1. Read chapter 6 of *A Little Princess*.
2. Tell someone what happened in the chapter.

Vocabulary

1. Decide whether the word pairs are synonyms or antonyms. (Answers)
   - ancient – modern, admire – respect, abundant – scarce, compromise – negotiate, dismay – distress, alert – inattentive, anticipate – expect, creative – unimaginative, clumsy – graceful, strife – conflict

THE DIAMOND-MINES

NOT very long after this a very exciting thing happened. Not only Sara, but the entire school, found it exciting, and made it the chief subject of conversation for weeks after it occurred. In one of his letters Captain Crewe told a most interesting story. A friend who had been at school with him when he was a boy had unexpectedly come to see him in India. He was the owner of a large tract of land upon which diamonds had been found, and he was engaged in developing the mines. If all went as was confidently expected, he would become possessed of such wealth as it made one dizzy to think of; and because he was fond of the friend of his school-days, he had given him an opportunity to share in this enormous fortune by becoming a partner in his scheme. This, at least, was what Sara gathered from his letters. It is true that any other business scheme, however magnificent, would have had but small attraction for her or for the school-room; but "diamond mines" sounded so like the "Arabian Nights" that no one could be indifferent. Sara thought them enchanting, and painted pictures, for Ermengarde and Lottie, of labyrinthine passages in the bowels of the earth, where sparkling stones studded the walls and roofs and ceilings, and strange, dark men dug them out with heavy picks. Ermengarde delighted in the story, and Lottie insisted on its being retold to her every evening. Lavinia was very spiteful about it, and told Jessie that she didn't believe such things as diamond-mines existed.

"My mamma has a diamond ring which cost forty pounds," she said. "And it is not a big one, either. If there were mines full of diamonds, people would be so rich it would be ridiculous."

"Perhaps Sara will be so rich that she will be ridiculous," giggled Jessie.

"She's ridiculous without being rich," Lavinia sniffed.

"I believe you hate her," said Jessie.

"No, I don't," snapped Lavinia. "But I don't believe in mines full of diamonds."

"Well, people have to get them from somewhere," said Jessie. "Lavinia," with a new giggle, "what do you think Gertrude says?"

"I don't know, I'm sure; and I don't care if it's something more about that everlasting Sara."

"Well, it is. One of her 'pretends' is that she is a princess. She plays it all the time—even in school. She says it makes her learn her lessons better. She wants Ermengarde to be one, too, but Ermengarde says she is too fat."

"She is too fat," said Lavinia. "And Sara is too thin."

Naturally, Jessie giggled again.

"She says it has nothing to do with what you look like, or what you have. It has only to do with what you think of, and what you do." "I suppose she thinks she could be a princess if she was a beggar," said Lavinia. "Let us begin to call her Your Royal Highness."

Lessons for the day were over, and they were sitting before the school-room fire, enjoying the time they liked best. It was the time when Miss Minchin and Miss Amelia were taking their tea in the sitting-room sacred to themselves. At this hour a great deal of talking was done, and a great many secrets changed hands, particularly if the younger pupils behaved themselves well, and did not squabble or run about noisily, which it must be confessed they usually did. When they made an uproar the older girls usually interfered with scoldings and shakes. They were expected to keep order, and there was danger that if they did not, Miss Minchin or Miss Amelia would appear and put an end to festivities. Even as Lavinia spoke the door opened and Sara entered with Lottie, whose habit was to trot everywhere after her like a little dog.

"There she is, with that horrid child!" exclaimed Lavinia in a whisper. "If she's so fond of her, why doesn't she keep her in her own room? She will begin howling about something in five minutes."

It happened that Lottie had been seized with a sudden desire to play in the school-room, and had begged her adopted parent to come with her. She joined a group of little ones who were playing in a corner. Sara curled herself up in the window-seat, opened a book, and began to read. It was a book about the French Revolution, and she was soon lost in a harrowing picture of the prisoners in the Bastille—men who had spent so many years in dungeons that when they were dragged out by those who rescued them, their long, gray hair and beards almost hid their faces, and they had forgotten that an outside world existed at all, and were like beings in a dream.

She was so far away from the school-room that it was not agreeable to be dragged back suddenly by a howl from Lottie. Never did she find anything so difficult as to keep herself from losing her temper when she was suddenly disturbed while absorbed in a book. People who are fond of books know the feeling of irritation which sweeps over them at such a moment. The temptation to be unreasonable and snappish is one not easy to manage.

"It makes me feel as if someone had hit me," Sara had told Ermengarde once in confidence. "And as if I want to hit back. I have to remember things quickly to keep from saying something ill-tempered."

She had to remember things quickly when she laid her book on the window-seat and jumped down from her comfortable corner.

Lottie had been sliding across the school-room floor, and, having first irritated Lavinia and Jessie by making a noise, had ended by falling down and hurting her fat knee. She was screaming and dancing up and down in the midst of a group of friends and enemies, who were alternately coaxing and scolding her.

"Stop this minute, you cry-baby! Stop this minute!" Lavinia commanded.

"I'm not a cry-baby—I'm not!" wailed Lottie. "Sara, Sa—ra!"

"If she doesn't stop, Miss Minchin will hear her," cried Jessie. "Lottie darling, I'll give you a penny!"

"I don't want your penny," sobbed Lottie; and she looked down at the fat knee, and, seeing a drop of blood on it, burst forth again.

Sara flew across the room and, kneeling down, put her arms round her.

"Now, Lottie," she said. "Now, Lottie, you promised Sara."

"She said I was a cry-baby," wept Lottie.

Sara patted her, but spoke in the steady voice Lottie knew.

"But if you cry, you will be one, Lottie pet. You promised."

Lottie remembered that she had promised, but she preferred to lift up her voice.

"I haven't any mamma," she proclaimed. "I haven't—a bit—of mamma."

"Yes, you have," said Sara, cheerfully. "Have you forgotten? Don't you know that Sara is your mamma? Don't you want Sara for your mamma?"

Lottie cuddled up to her with a consoled sniff.

"Come and sit in the window-seat with me," Sara went on, "and I'll whisper a story to you."

"Will you?" whimpered Lottie. "Will you—tell me—about the diamond-mines?"

"The diamond-mines?" broke out Lavinia. "Nasty, little spoiled thing, I should like to slap her!"

Sara got up quickly on her feet. It must be remembered that she had been very deeply absorbed in the book about the Bastille, and she had had to recall several things rapidly when she realized that she must go and take care of her adopted child. She was not an angel, and she was not fond of Lavinia.

"Well," she said, with some fire, "I should like to slap you—but I don't want to slap you!" restraining herself. "At least I both want to slap you—and I should like to slap you—but I won't slap you. We are not little gutter children. We are both old enough to know better."

Here was Lavinia's opportunity.

"Ah, yes, your Royal Highness," she said. "We are princesses, I believe. At least one of us is. The school ought to be very fashionable now Miss Minchin has a princess for a pupil."

Sara started toward her. She looked as if she were going to box her ears. Perhaps she was. Her trick of pretending things was the joy of her life. She never spoke of it to girls she was not fond of. Her new "pretend" about being a princess was very near to her heart, and she was shy and sensitive about it. She had meant it to be rather a secret, and here was Lavinia deriding it before nearly all the school. She felt the blood rush up into her face and tingle in her ears. She only just saved herself. If you were a princess, you did not fly into rages. Her hand dropped, and she stood quite still a moment. When she spoke it was in a quiet, steady voice; she held her head up, and everybody listened to her.

"It's true," she said. "Sometimes I do pretend I am a princess. I pretend I am a princess, so that I can try and behave like one."

Lavinia could not think of exactly the right thing to say. Several times she had found that she could not think of a satisfactory reply when she was dealing with Sara. The reason of this was that, somehow, the rest always seemed to be vaguely in sympathy with her opponent. She saw now that they were pricking up their ears interestedly. The truth was, they liked princesses, and they all hoped they might hear something more definite about this one, and drew nearer Sara accordingly.

Lavinia could only invent one remark, and it fell rather flat.

"Dear me!" she said, "I hope, when you ascend the throne, you won't forget us."

"I won't," said Sara, and she did not utter another word, but stood quite still, and stared at her steadily as she saw her take Jessie's arm and turn away.

After this, the girls who were jealous of her used to speak of her as "Princess Sara" whenever they wished to be particularly disdainful, and those who were fond of her gave her the name among themselves as a term of affection. No one called her "Princess" instead of "Sara," but her adorers were much pleased with the picturesqueness and grandeur of the title, and Miss Minchin, hearing of it, mentioned it more than once to visiting parents, feeling that it rather suggested a sort of royal boarding school.

To Becky it seemed the most appropriate thing in the world. The acquaintance begun on the foggy afternoon when she had jumped up terrified from her sleep in the comfortable chair, had ripened and grown, though it must be confessed that Miss Minchin and Miss Amelia knew very little about it. They were aware that Sara was "kind" to the scullery-maid, but they knew nothing of certain delightful moments snatched perilously when, the up-stairs rooms being set in order with lightning rapidity, Sara's sitting-room was reached, and the heavy coal-box set down with a sigh of joy. At such times stories were told by instalments, things of a satisfying nature were either produced and eaten or hastily tucked into pockets to be disposed of at night, when Becky went up-stairs to her attic to bed.

"But I has to eat 'em careful, miss," she said once; " 'cos if I leaves crumbs the rats come out to get 'em."

"Rats!" exclaimed Sara, in horror. "Are there rats there?"

"Lots of 'em, miss," Becky answered in quite a matter-of-fact manner. "There mostly is rats an' mice in attics. You gets used to the noise they makes scuttling about. I've got so I don't mind 'em s' long as they don't run over my piller."

"Ugh!" said Sara.

"You gets used to anythin' after a bit," said Becky. "You have to, miss, if you're born a scullery-maid. I'd rather have rats than cockroaches."

"So would I," said Sara; "I suppose you might make friends with a rat in time, but I don't believe I should like to make friends with a cockroach."

Sometimes Becky did not dare to spend more than a few minutes in the bright, warm room, and when this was the case perhaps only a few words could be exchanged, and a small purchase slipped into the old-fashioned pocket Becky carried under her dress skirt, tied round her waist with a band of tape. The search for and discovery of satisfying things to eat which could be packed into small compass, added a new interest to Sara's existence. When she drove or walked out, she used to look into shop windows eagerly. The first time it occurred to her to bring home two or three little meat-pies, she felt that she had hit upon a discovery. When she exhibited them, Becky's eyes quite sparkled.

"Oh, miss!" she murmured. "Them will be nice an' fillin'.' It's fillin'ness that's best. Sponge cake's a 'evingly thing, but it melts away like—if you understand, miss. These'll just stay in yer stummick."

"Well," hesitated Sara, "I don't think it would be good if they stayed always, but I do believe they will be satisfying."

They were satisfying—and so were beef sandwiches, bought at a cook-shop—and so were rolls and Bologna sausage. In time, Becky began to lose her hungry, tired feeling, and the coal-box did not seem so unbearably heavy.

However heavy it was, and whatsoever the temper of the cook, and the hardness of the work heaped upon her shoulders, she had always the chance of the afternoon to look forward to—the chance that Miss Sara would be able to be in her sitting-room. In fact, the mere seeing of Miss Sara would have been enough without meat-pies. If there was time only for a few words, they were always friendly, merry words that put heart into one; and if there was time for more, then there was an instalment of a story to be told, or some other thing one remembered afterward and sometimes lay awake in one's bed in the attic to think over. Sara—who was only doing what she unconsciously liked better than anything else, Nature having made her for a giver—had not the least idea what she meant to poor Becky, and how wonderful a benefactor she seemed. If Nature has made you for a giver, your hands are born open, and so is your heart; and though there may be times when your hands are empty, your heart is always full, and you can give things out of that—warm things, kind things, sweet things—help and comfort and laughter—and sometimes gay, kind laughter is the best help of all.

Becky had scarcely known what laughter was through all her poor, little hard-driven life. Sara made her laugh, and laughed with her; and, though neither of them quite knew it, the laughter was as "fillin' " as the meat-pies.

A few weeks before Sara's eleventh birthday a letter came to her from her father, which did not seem to be written in such boyish high spirits as usual. He was not very well, and was evidently overweighted by the business connected with the diamond-mines.

"You see, little Sara," he wrote, "your daddy is not a businessman at all, and figures and documents bother him. He does not really understand them, and all this seems so enormous. Perhaps, if I was not feverish I should not be awake, tossing about, one half of the night and spend the other half in troublesome dreams. If my little missus were here, I dare say she would give me some solemn, good advice. You would, wouldn't you, little missus?"

One of his many jokes had been to call her his "little missus" because she had such an old-fashioned air.

He had made wonderful preparations for her birthday. Among other things, a new doll had been ordered in Paris, and her wardrobe was to be, indeed, a marvel of splendid perfection. When she had replied to the letter asking her if the doll would be an acceptable present, Sara had been very quaint.

"I am getting very old," she wrote; "you see, I shall never live to have another doll given me. This will be my last doll. There is something solemn about it. If I could write poetry, I am sure a poem about 'A Last Doll' would be very nice. But I cannot write poetry. I have tried, and it made me laugh. It did not sound like Watts or Coleridge or Shakespeare at all. No one could ever take Emily's place, but I should respect the Last Doll very much; and I am sure the school would love it. They all like dolls, though some of the big ones—the almost fifteen ones—pretend they are too grown up."

Captain Crewe had a splitting headache when he read this letter in his bungalow in India. The table before him was heaped with papers and letters which were alarming him and filling him with anxious dread, but he laughed as he had not laughed for weeks.

"Oh," he said, "she's better fun every year she lives. God grant this business may right itself and leave me free to run home and see her. What wouldn't I give to have her little arms round my neck this minute! What wouldn't I give!"

The birthday was to be celebrated by great festivities. The school-room was to be decorated, and there was to be a party. The boxes containing the presents were to be opened with great ceremony, and there was to be a glittering feast spread in Miss Minchin's sacred room. When the day arrived the whole house was in a whirl of excitement. How the morning passed nobody quite knew, because there seemed such preparations to be made. The school-room was being decked with garlands of holly; the desks had been moved away, and red covers had been put on the forms which were arrayed round the room against the wall.

When Sara went into her sitting-room in the morning, she found on the table a small, dumpy package, tied up in a piece of brown paper. She knew it was a present, and she thought she could guess whom it came from. She opened it quite tenderly. It was a square pincushion, made of not quite clean red flannel, and black pins had been stuck carefully into it to form the words, "Menny happy returns."

"Oh!" cried Sara, with a warm feeling in her heart. "What pains she has taken! I like it so, it—it makes me feel sorrowful."

But the next moment she was mystified. On the under side of the pincushion was secured a card, bearing in neat letters the name "Miss Amelia Minchin."

Sara turned it over and over.

"Miss Amelia!" she said to herself. "How can it be!"

And just at that very moment she heard the door being cautiously pushed open and saw Becky peeping round it.

There was an affectionate, happy grin on her face, and she shuffled forward and stood nervously pulling at her fingers.

"Do yer like it, Miss Sara?" she said. "Do yer?"

"Like it?" cried Sara. "You darling Becky, you made it all yourself."

Becky gave a hysteric but joyful sniff, and her eyes looked quite moist with delight.

"It ain't nothin' but flannin, an' the flannin ain't new; but I wanted to give yer somethin' an' I made it of nights. I knew yer could pretend it was satin with diamond pins in. I tried to when I was makin' it. The card, miss," rather doubtfully; " 't warn't wrong of me to pick it up out o' the dust-bin, was it? Miss 'Meliar had throwed it away. I hadn't no card o' my own, an' I knowed it wouldn't be a proper presink if I didn't pin a card on—so I pinned Miss 'Meliar's."

Sara flew at her and hugged her. She could not have told herself or anyone else why there was a lump in her throat.

"Oh, Becky!" she cried out, with a queer little laugh, "I love you, Becky—I do, I do!"

"Oh, miss!" breathed Becky. "Thank yer, miss, kindly; it ain't good enough for that. The—the flannin wasn't new."

Day 107

1.   Read the first part of chapter 7 of *A Little Princess*.
2.   Tell someone what happened in the chapter.

THE DIAMOND-MINES AGAIN

WHEN Sara entered the holly-hung school-room in the afternoon, she did so as the head of a sort of procession. Miss Minchin, in her grandest silk dress, led her by the hand. A man-servant followed, carrying the box containing the Last Doll, a housemaid carried a second box, and Becky brought up the rear, carrying a third and wearing a clean apron and a new cap. Sara would have much preferred to enter in the usual way, but Miss Minchin had sent for her, and, after an interview in her private sitting-room, had expressed her wishes.

"This is not an ordinary occasion," she said. "I do not desire that it should be treated as one."

So Sara was led grandly in and felt shy when, on her entry, the big girls stared at her and touched each other's elbows, and the little ones began to squirm joyously in their seats.

"Silence, young ladies!" said Miss Minchin, at the murmur which arose. "James, place the box on the table and remove the lid. Emma, put yours upon a chair. Becky!" suddenly and severely.

Becky had quite forgotten herself in her excitement, and was grinning at Lottie, who was wriggling with rapturous expectation. She almost dropped her box, the disapproving voice so startled her, and her frightened, bobbing curtsy of apology was so funny that Lavinia and Jessie tittered.

"It is not your place to look at the young ladies," said Miss Minchin. "You forget yourself. Put your box down."

Becky obeyed with alarmed haste and hastily backed toward the door.

"You may leave us," Miss Minchin announced to the servants with a wave of her hand.

Becky stepped aside respectfully to allow the superior servants to pass out first. She could not help casting a longing glance at the box on the table. Something made of blue satin was peeping from between the folds of tissue paper.

"If you please, Miss Minchin," said Sara, suddenly, "mayn't Becky stay?"

It was a bold thing to do. Miss Minchin was betrayed into something like a slight jump. Then she put her eyeglass up, and gazed at her show pupil disturbedly.

"Becky!" she exclaimed. "My dearest Sara!"

Sara advanced a step toward her.

"I want her because I know she will like to see the presents," she explained. "She is a little girl, too, you know."

Miss Minchin was scandalized. She glanced from one figure to the other.

"My dear Sara," she said, "Becky is the scullery-maid. Scullery-maids—er—are not little girls."

It really had not occurred to her to think of them in that light. Scullery-maids were machines who carried coal-scuttles and made fires.

"But Becky is," said Sara. "And I know she would enjoy herself. Please let her stay—because it is my birthday."

Miss Minchin replied with much dignity:

"As you ask it as a birthday favor—she may stay. Rebecca, thank Miss Sara for her great kindness."

Becky had been backing into the corner, twisting the hem of her apron in delighted suspense. She came forward, bobbing courtesies, but between Sara's eyes and her own there passed a gleam of friendly understanding, while her words tumbled over each other.

"Oh, if you please, miss! I'm that grateful, miss! I did want to see the doll, miss, that I did. Thank you, miss. And thank you, ma'am,"—turning and making an alarmed bob to Miss Minchin—"for letting me take the liberty."

Miss Minchin waved her hand again—this time it was in the direction of the corner near the door.

"Go and stand there," she commanded. "Not too near the young ladies."

Becky went to her place, grinning. She did not care where she was sent, so that she might have the luck of being inside the room, instead of being down-stairs in the scullery, while these delights were going on. She did not even mind when Miss Minchin cleared her throat ominously and spoke again.

"Now, young ladies, I have a few words to say to you," she announced.

"She's going to make a speech," whispered one of the girls. "I wish it was over."

Sara felt rather uncomfortable. As this was her party, it was probable that the speech was about her. It is not agreeable to stand in a school-room and have a speech made about you.

"You are aware, young ladies," the speech began—for it was a speech—"that dear Sara is eleven years old today."

"Dear Sara!" murmured Lavinia.

"Several of you here have also been eleven years old, but Sara's birthdays are rather different from other little girls' birthdays. When she is older she will be heiress to a large fortune, which it will be her duty to spend in a meritorious manner."

"The diamond-mines," giggled Jessie, in a whisper.

Sara did not hear her; but as she stood with her green-gray eyes fixed steadily on Miss Minchin, she felt herself growing rather hot. When Miss Minchin talked about money, she felt somehow that she always hated her—and, of course, it was disrespectful to hate grown-up people.

"When her dear papa, Captain Crewe, brought her from India and gave her into my care," the speech proceeded, "he said to me, in a jesting way, 'I am afraid she will be very rich, Miss Minchin.' My reply was, 'Her education at my seminary, Captain Crewe, shall be such as will adorn the largest fortune.' Sara has become my most accomplished pupil. Her French and her dancing are a credit to the seminary. Her manners—which have caused you to call her Princess Sara—are perfect. Her amiability she exhibits by giving you this afternoon's party. I hope you appreciate her generosity. I wish you to express your appreciation of it by saying aloud all together, 'Thank you, Sara!' "

The entire school-room rose to its feet as it had done the morning Sara remembered so well.

"Thank you, Sara!" it said, and it must be confessed that Lottie jumped up and down. Sara looked rather shy for a moment. She made a curtsy—and it was a very nice one.

"Thank you," she said, "for coming to my party."

"Very pretty, indeed, Sara," approved Miss Minchin. "That is what a real princess does when the populace applauds her. Lavinia"—scathingly—"the sound you just made was extremely like a snort. If you are jealous of your fellow-pupil, I beg you will express your feelings in some more lady-like manner. Now I will leave you to enjoy yourselves."

The instant she had swept out of the room the spell her presence always had upon them was broken. The door had scarcely closed before every seat was empty. The little girls jumped or tumbled out of theirs; the older ones wasted no time in deserting theirs. There was a rush toward the boxes. Sara had bent over one of them with a delighted face.

"These are books, I know," she said.

The little children broke into a rueful murmur, and Ermengarde looked aghast.

"Does your papa send you books for a birthday present?" she exclaimed. "Why, he's as bad as mine. Don't open them, Sara."

"I like them," Sara laughed, but she turned to the biggest box. When she took out the Last Doll it was so magnificent that the children uttered delighted groans of joy, and actually drew back to gaze at it in breathless rapture.

"She is almost as big as Lottie," someone gasped.

Lottie clapped her hands and danced about, giggling.

"She's dressed for the theater," said Lavinia. "Her cloak is lined with ermine."

"Oh!" cried Ermengarde, darting forward, "she has an opera-glass in her hand—a blue-and-gold one!"

"Here is her trunk," said Sara. "Let us open it and look at her things."

She sat down upon the floor and turned the key. The children crowded clamoring around her, as she lifted tray after tray and revealed their contents. Never had the school-room been in such an uproar. There were lace collars and silk stockings and handkerchiefs; there was a jewel-case containing a necklace and a tiara which looked quite as if they were made of real diamonds; there was a long sealskin and muff, there were ball dresses and walking dresses and visiting dresses; there were hats and tea-gowns and fans. Even Lavinia and Jessie forgot that they were too elderly to care for dolls, and uttered exclamations of delight and caught up things to look at them.

"Suppose," Sara said, as she stood by the table, putting a large, black-velvet hat on the impassively smiling owner of all these splendors—"suppose she understands human talk and feels proud of being admired."

"You are always supposing things," said Lavinia, and her air was very superior.

"I know I am," answered Sara, undisturbedly. "I like it. There is nothing so nice as supposing. It's almost like being a fairy. If you suppose anything hard enough it seems as if it were real."

"It's all very well to suppose things if you have everything," said Lavinia. "Could you suppose and pretend if you were a beggar and lived in a garret?"

Sara stopped arranging the Last Doll's ostrich plumes, and looked thoughtful.

"I believe I could," she said. "If one was a beggar, one would have to suppose and pretend all the time. But it mightn't be easy."

She often thought afterward how strange it was that just as she had finished saying this—just at that very moment—Miss Amelia came into the room.

"Sara," she said, "your papa's solicitor, Mr. Barrow, has called to see Miss Minchin, and, as she must talk to him alone and the refreshments are laid in her parlor, you had all better come and have your feast now, so that my sister can have her interview here in the school-room."

Refreshments were not likely to be disdained at any hour, and many pairs of eyes gleamed. Miss Amelia arranged the procession into decorum, and then, with Sara at her side heading it, she led it away, leaving the Last Doll sitting upon a chair with the glories of her wardrobe scattered about her; dresses and coats hung upon chair backs, piles of lace-frilled petticoats lying upon their seats.

Becky, who was not expected to partake of refreshments, had the indiscretion to linger a moment to look at these beauties—it really was an indiscretion.

"Go back to your work, Becky," Miss Amelia had said; but she had stopped to reverently pick up first a muff and then a coat, and while she stood looking at them adoringly, she heard Miss Minchin upon the threshold, and, being smitten with terror at the thought of being accused of taking liberties, she rashly darted under the table, which hid her by its table-cloth.

Miss Minchin came into the room, accompanied by a sharp-featured, dry little gentleman, who looked rather disturbed. Miss Minchin herself also looked rather disturbed, it must be admitted, and she gazed at the dry little gentleman with an irritated and puzzled expression.

She sat down with stiff dignity, and waved him to a chair.

"Pray, be seated, Mr. Barrow," she said.

Mr. Barrow did not sit down at once. His attention seemed attracted by the Last Doll and the things which surrounded her. He settled his eye-glasses and looked at them in nervous disapproval. The Last Doll herself did not seem to mind this in the least. She merely sat upright and returned his gaze indifferently.

"A hundred pounds," Mr. Barrow remarked succinctly. "All expensive material, and made at a Parisian modiste's. He spent money lavishly enough, that young man."

Miss Minchin felt offended. This seemed to be a disparagement of her best patron and was a liberty.

Even solicitors had no right to take liberties.

"I beg your pardon, Mr. Barrow," she said stiffly. "I do not understand."

"Birthday presents," said Mr. Barrow in the same critical manner, "to a child eleven years old! Mad extravagance, I call it."

Miss Minchin drew herself up still more rigidly.

"Captain Crewe is a man of fortune," she said. "The diamond-mines alone—"

Mr. Barrow wheeled round upon her. "Diamond-mines!" he broke out. "There are none! Never were!"

Miss Minchin actually got up from her chair.

"What!" she cried. "What do you mean?"

"At any rate," answered Mr. Barrow, quite snappishly, "it would have been much better if there never had been any."

"Any diamond-mines?" ejaculated Miss Minchin, catching at the back of a chair and feeling as if a splendid dream was fading away from her.

"Diamond-mines spell ruin oftener than they spell wealth," said Mr. Barrow. "When a man is in the hands of a very dear friend and is not a businessman himself, he had better steer clear of the dear friend's diamond-mines, or gold-mines, or any other kind of mines dear friends want his money to put into. The late Captain Crewe—"

Here Miss Minchin stopped him with a gasp.

"The late Captain Crewe!" she cried out; "the late! You don't come to tell me that Captain Crewe is—"

"He's dead, ma'am," Mr. Barrow answered with jerky brusqueness. "Died of jungle fever and business troubles combined. The jungle fever might not have killed him if he had not been driven mad by the business troubles, and the business troubles might not have put an end to him if the jungle fever had not assisted. Captain Crewe is dead!"

Miss Minchin dropped into her chair again. The words he had spoken filled her with alarm.

"What were his business troubles?" she said. "What were they?"

"Diamond-mines," answered Mr. Barrow, "and dear friends—and ruin."

Miss Minchin lost her breath.

"Ruin!" she gasped out.

"Lost every penny. That young man had too much money. The dear friend was mad on the subject of the diamond-mine. He put all his own money into it, and all Captain Crewe's. Then the dear friend ran away—Captain Crewe was already stricken with fever when the news came. The shock was too much for him. He died delirious, raving about his little girl—and didn't leave a penny."

Now Miss Minchin understood, and never had she received such a blow in her life. Her show pupil, her show patron, swept away from the Select Seminary at one blow. She felt as if she had been outraged and robbed, and that Captain Crewe and Sara and Mr. Barrow were equally to blame.

"Do you mean to tell me," she cried out, "that he left nothing! That Sara will have no fortune! That the child is a beggar! That she is left on my hands a little pauper instead of an heiress?"

Mr. Barrow was a shrewd business man, and felt it as well to make his own freedom from responsibility quite clear without any delay.

"She is certainly left a beggar," he replied. "And she is certainly left on your hands, ma'am—as she hasn't a relation in the world that we know of."

Miss Minchin started forward. She looked as if she was going to open the door and rush out of the room to stop the festivities going on joyfully and rather noisily that moment over the refreshments.

"It is monstrous!" she said. "She's in my sitting room at this moment, dressed in silk gauze and lace petticoats, giving a party at my expense."

"She's giving it at your expense, madam, if she's giving it," said Mr. Barrow, calmly. "Barrow & Skipworth are not responsible for anything. There never was a cleaner sweep made of a man's fortune. Captain Crewe died without paying our last bill—and it was a big one."

Miss Minchin turned back from the door in increased indignation. This was worse than anyone could have dreamed of its being.

"That is what has happened to me!" she cried. "I was always so sure of his payments that I went to all sorts of ridiculous expenses for the child. I paid the bills for that ridiculous doll and her ridiculous fantastic wardrobe. The child was to have anything she wanted. She has a carriage and a pony and a maid, and I've paid for all of them since the last cheque came."

Mr. Barrow evidently did not intend to remain to listen to the story of Miss Minchin's grievances after he had made the position of his firm clear and related the mere dry facts. He did not feel any particular sympathy for irate keepers of boarding schools.

"You had better not pay for anything more, ma'am," he remarked, "unless you want to make presents to the young lady. No one will remember you. She hasn't a brass farthing to call her own."

"But what am I to do?" demanded Miss Minchin, as if she felt it entirely his duty to make the matter right. "What am I to do?"

"There isn't anything to do," said Mr. Barrow, folding up his eye-glasses and slipping them into his pocket. "Captain Crewe is dead. The child is left a pauper. Nobody is responsible for her but you."

"I am not responsible for her, and I refuse to be made responsible!"

Miss Minchin became quite white with rage.

Mr. Barrow turned to go.

"I have nothing to do with that, madam," he said uninterestedly. "Barrow & Skipworth are not responsible. Very sorry the thing has happened, of course."

Day 108

　　1.　　　Finish reading chapter 7 of *A Little Princess*.
　　2.　　　Tell someone what happened in the chapter.

"If you think she is to be foisted off on me, you are greatly mistaken," Miss Minchin gasped. "I have been robbed and cheated; I will turn her into the street!"

If she had not been so furious, she would have been too discreet to say quite so much. She saw herself burdened with an extravagantly brought-up child whom she had always resented, and she lost all self-control.

Mr. Barrow undisturbedly moved toward the door.

"I wouldn't do that, madam," he commented; "it wouldn't look well. Unpleasant story to get about in connection with the establishment. Pupil bundled out penniless and without friends."

He was a clever business man, and he knew what he was saying. He also knew that Miss Minchin was a business woman, and would be shrewd enough to see the truth. She could not afford to do a thing which would make people speak of her as cruel and hard-hearted.

"Better keep her and make use of her," he added. "She's a clever child, I believe. You can get a good deal out of her as she grows older."

"I will get a good deal out of her before she grows older!" exclaimed Miss Minchin.

"I am sure you will, ma'am," said Mr. Barrow, with a little sinister smile. "I am sure you will. Good morning!"

He bowed himself out and closed the door, and it must be confessed that Miss Minchin stood for a few moments and glared at it. What he had said was quite true. She knew it. She had absolutely no redress. Her show pupil had melted into nothingness, leaving only a friendless, beggared little girl. Such money as she herself had advanced was lost and could not be regained.

And as she stood there breathless under her sense of injury, there fell upon her ears a burst of gay voices from her own sacred room, which had actually been given up to the feast. She could at least stop this.

But as she started toward the door it was opened by Miss Amelia, who, when she caught sight of the changed, angry face, fell back a step in alarm.

"What is the matter, sister?" she ejaculated.

Miss Minchin's voice was almost fierce when she answered:

"Where is Sara Crewe?"

Miss Amelia was bewildered.

"Sara!" she stammered. "Why, she's with the children in your room, of course."

"Has she a black frock in her sumptuous wardrobe?"—in bitter irony.

"A black frock?" Miss Amelia stammered again. "A black one?"

"She has frocks of every other color. Has she a black one?"

Miss Amelia began to turn pale.

"No—ye-es!" she said. "But it is too short for her. She has only the old black velvet, and she has outgrown it."

"Go and tell her to take off that preposterous pink silk gauze, and put the black one on, whether it is too short or not. She has done with finery!"

Then Miss Amelia began to wring her fat hands and cry.

"Oh, sister!" she sniffed. "Oh, sister! What can have happened?"

Miss Minchin wasted no words.

"Captain Crewe is dead," she said. "He has died without a penny. That spoiled, pampered, fanciful child is left a pauper on my hands."

Miss Amelia sat down quite heavily in the nearest chair.

"Hundreds of pounds have I spent on nonsense for her. And I shall never see a penny of it. Put a stop to this ridiculous party of hers. Go and make her change her frock at once."

"I?" panted Miss Amelia. "M-must I go and tell her now?"

"This moment!" was the fierce answer. "Don't sit staring like a goose. Go!"

Poor Miss Amelia was accustomed to being called a goose. She knew, in fact, that she was rather a goose, and that it was left to geese to do a great many disagreeable things. It was a somewhat embarrassing thing to go into the midst of a room full of delighted children, and tell the giver of the feast that she had suddenly been transformed into a little beggar, and must go upstairs and put on an old black frock which was too small for her. But the thing must be done. This was evidently not the time when questions might be asked.

She rubbed her eyes with her handkerchief until they looked quite red. After which she got up and went out of the room, without venturing to say another word. When her older sister looked and spoke as she had done just now, the wisest course to pursue was to obey orders without any comment. Miss Minchin walked across the room. She spoke to herself aloud without knowing that she was doing it. During the last year the story of the diamond-mines had suggested all sorts of possibilities to her. Even proprietors of seminaries might make fortunes in stocks, with the aid of owners of mines. And now, instead of looking forward to gains, she was left to look back upon losses.

"The Princess Sara, indeed!" she said. "The child has been pampered as if she were a queen."

She was sweeping angrily past the corner table as she said it, and the next moment she started at the sound of a loud, sobbing sniff which issued from under the cover.

"What is that!" she exclaimed angrily. The loud, sobbing sniff was heard again, and she stooped and raised the hanging folds of the table cover.

"How dare you!" she cried out. "How dare you! Come out immediately!"

It was poor Becky who crawled out, and her cap was knocked on one side, and her face was red with repressed crying.

"If you please, 'm—it's me, mum," she explained. "I know I hadn't ought to. But I was lookin' at the doll, mum—an' I was frightened when you come in—an' slipped under the table."

"You have been there all the time, listening," said Miss Minchin.

"No, mum," Becky protested, bobbing courtesies. "Not listenin'—I thought I could slip out without your noticin', but I couldn't an' I had to stay. But I didn't listen, mum—I wouldn't for nothin'. But I couldn't help hearin'."

Suddenly it seemed almost as if she lost all fear of the awful lady before her. She burst into fresh tears.

"Oh, please, 'm," she said; "I dare say you'll give me warnin', mum--but I'm so sorry for poor Miss Sara—I'm so sorry!"

"Leave the room!" ordered Miss Minchin.

Becky courtesied again, the tears openly streaming down her cheeks.

"Yes, 'm; I will, 'm," she said, trembling; "but oh, I just wanted to arst you: Miss Sara— she's been such a rich young lady, an' she's been waited on, 'and and foot; an' what will she do now, mum, without no maid? If—if, oh please, would you let me wait on her after I've done my pots an' kettles? I'd do 'em that quick—if you'd let me wait on her now she's poor. Oh," breaking out afresh, "poor little Miss Sara, mum—that was called a princess."

Somehow, she made Miss Minchin feel more angry than ever. That the very scullery-maid should range herself on the side of this child—whom she realized more fully than ever that she had never liked—was too much. She actually stamped her foot.

"No—certainly not," she said. "She will wait on herself, and on other people, too. Leave the room this instant, or you'll leave your place."

Becky threw her apron over her head and fled. She ran out of the room and down the steps into the scullery, and there she sat down among her pots and kettles, and wept as if her heart would break.

"It's exactly like the ones in the stories," she wailed. "Them pore princess ones that was drove into the world.

* * * * * *

Miss Minchin had never looked quite so still and hard as she did when Sara came to her, a few hours later, in response to a message she had sent her.

Even by that time it seemed to Sara as if the birthday party had either been a dream or a thing which had happened years ago, and had happened in the life of quite another little girl.

Every sign of the festivities had been swept away; the holly had been removed from the school-room walls, and the forms and desks put back into their places. Miss Minchin's sitting-room looked as it always did—all traces of the feast were gone, and Miss Minchin had resumed her usual dress. The pupils had been ordered to lay aside their party frocks;

and this having been done, they had returned to the school-room and huddled together in groups, whispering and talking excitedly.

"Tell Sara to come to my room," Miss Minchin had said to her sister. "And explain to her clearly that I will have no crying or unpleasant scenes."

"Sister," replied Miss Amelia, "she is the strangest child I ever saw. She has actually made no fuss at all. You remember she made none when Captain Crewe went back to India. When I told her what had happened, she just stood quite still and looked at me without making a sound. Her eyes seemed to get bigger and bigger, and she went quite pale. When I had finished, she still stood staring for a few seconds, and then her chin began to shake, and she turned round and ran out of the room and up-stairs. Several of the other children began to cry, but she did not seem to hear them or to be alive to anything but just what I was saying. It made me feel quite queer not to be answered; and when you tell anything sudden and strange, you expect people will say something—whatever it is."

Nobody but Sara herself ever knew what had happened in her room after she had run up-stairs and locked her door. In fact, she herself scarcely remembered anything but that she walked up and down, saying over and over again to herself in a voice which did not seem her own:

"My papa is dead! My papa is dead!"

Once she stopped before Emily, who sat watching her from her chair, and cried out wildly:

"Emily! Do you hear? Do you hear—papa is dead? He is dead in India—thousands of miles away."

When she came into Miss Minchin's sitting room in answer to her summons, her face was white and her eyes had dark rings around them. Her mouth was set as if she did not wish it to reveal what she had suffered and was suffering. She did not look in the least like the rose-colored butterfly child who had flown about from one of her treasures to the other in the decorated school-room. She looked instead a strange, desolate, almost grotesque little figure.

She had put on, without Mariette's help, the cast-aside black-velvet frock. It was too short and tight, and her slender legs looked long and thin, showing themselves from beneath the brief skirt. As she had not found a piece of black ribbon, her short, thick, black hair tumbled loosely about her face and contrasted strongly with its pallor. She held Emily tightly in one arm, and Emily was swathed in a piece of black material.

"Put down your doll," said Miss Minchin. "What do you mean by bringing her here?"

"No," Sara answered. "I will not put her down. She is all I have. My papa gave her to me."

She had always made Miss Minchin feel secretly uncomfortable, and she did so now. She did not speak with rudeness so much as with a cold steadiness with which Miss Minchin felt it difficult to cope—perhaps because she knew she was doing a heartless and inhuman thing.

"You will have no time for dolls in future," she said. "You will have to work and improve yourself and make yourself useful."

Sara kept her big, strange eyes fixed on her, and said not a word.

"Everything will be very different now," Miss Minchin went on. "I suppose Miss Amelia has explained matters to you."

"Yes," answered Sara. "My papa is dead. He left me no money. I am quite poor."

"You are a beggar," said Miss Minchin, her temper rising at the recollection of what all this meant. "It appears that you have no relations and no home, and no one to take care of you."

For a moment the thin, pale little face twitched, but Sara again said nothing.

"What are you staring at?" demanded Miss Minchin, sharply. "Are you so stupid that you cannot understand? I tell you that you are quite alone in the world, and have no one to do anything for you, unless I choose to keep you here out of charity."

"I understand," answered Sara, in a low tone; and there was a sound as if she had gulped down something which rose in her throat. "I understand."

"That doll," cried Miss Minchin, pointing to the splendid birthday gift seated near—"that ridiculous doll, with all her nonsensical, extravagant things—I actually paid the bill for her!"

Sara turned her head toward the chair.

"The Last Doll," she said. "The Last Doll." And her little mournful voice had an odd sound.

"The Last Doll, indeed!" said Miss Minchin. "And she is mine, not yours. Everything you own is mine."

"Please take it away from me, then," said Sara. "I do not want it."

If she had cried and sobbed and seemed frightened, Miss Minchin might almost have had more patience with her. She was a woman who liked to domineer and feel her power, and as she looked at Sara's pale little steadfast face and heard her proud little voice, she quite felt as if her might was being set at naught.

"Don't put on grand airs," she said. "The time for that sort of thing is past. You are not a princess any longer. Your carriage and your pony will be sent away—your maid will be dismissed. You will wear your oldest and plainest clothes—your extravagant ones are no longer suited to your station. You are like Becky—you must work for your living."

To her surprise, a faint gleam of light came into the child's eyes—a shade of relief.

"Can I work?" she said. "If I can work it will not matter so much. What can I do?"

"You can do anything you are told," was the answer. "You are a sharp child, and pick up things readily. If you make yourself useful I may let you stay here. You speak French well, and you can help with the younger children."

"May I?" exclaimed Sara. "Oh, please let me! I know I can teach them. I like them, and they like me."

"Don't talk nonsense about people liking you," said Miss Minchin. "You will have to do more than teach the little ones. You will run errands and help in the kitchen as well as in the school-room. If you don't please me, you will be sent away. Remember that. Now go."

Sara stood still just a moment, looking at her. In her young soul, she was thinking deep and strange things. Then she turned to leave the room.

"Stop!" said Miss Minchin. "Don't you intend to thank me?"

Sara paused, and all the deep, strange thoughts surged up in her breast.

"What for?" she said.

"For my kindness to you," replied Miss Minchin. "For my kindness in giving you a home."

Sara made two or three steps toward her. Her thin little chest heaved up and down, and she spoke in a strange unchildishly fierce way.

"You are not kind," she said. "You are not kind, and it is not a home." And she had turned and run out of the room before Miss Minchin could stop her or do anything but stare after her with stony anger.

She went up the stairs slowly, but panting for breath and she held Emily tightly against her side.

"I wish she could talk," she said to herself. "If she could speak—if she could speak!"

She meant to go to her room and lie down on the tiger-skin, with her cheek upon the great cat's head, and look into the fire and think and think and think. But just before she reached the landing Miss Amelia came out of the door and closed it behind her, and stood before it, looking nervous and awkward. The truth was that she felt secretly ashamed of the thing she had been ordered to do.

"You—you are not to go in there," she said.

"Not go in?" exclaimed Sara, and she fell back a pace.

"That is not your room now," Miss Amelia answered, reddening a little.

Somehow, all at once, Sara understood. She realized that this was the beginning of the change Miss Minchin had spoken of.

"Where is my room?" she asked, hoping very much that her voice did not shake.

"You are to sleep in the attic next to Becky."

Sara knew where it was. Becky had told her about it. She turned, and mounted up two flights of stairs. The last one was narrow, and covered with shabby strips of old carpet. She felt as if she were walking away and leaving far behind her the world in which that other child, who no longer seemed herself, had lived. This child, in her short, tight old frock, climbing the stairs to the attic, was quite a different creature.

When she reached the attic door and opened it, her heart gave a dreary little thump. Then she shut the door and stood against it and looked about her.

Yes, this was another world. The room had a slanting roof and was whitewashed. The whitewash was dingy and had fallen off in places. There was a rusty grate, an old iron bedstead, and a hard bed covered with a faded coverlet. Some pieces of furniture too much worn to be used down-stairs had been sent up. Under the skylight in the roof, which showed nothing but an oblong piece of dull gray sky, there stood an old battered red footstool. Sara went to it and sat down. She seldom cried. She did not cry now. She laid Emily across her knees and put her face down upon her and her arms around her, and sat there, her little black head resting on the black draperies, not saying one word, not making one sound.

And as she sat in this silence there came a low tap at the door—such a low, humble one that she did not at first hear it, and, indeed, was not roused until the door was timidly pushed open and a poor tear-smeared face appeared peeping round it. It was Becky's face, and Becky had been crying furtively for hours and rubbing her eyes with her kitchen apron until she looked strange indeed.

"Oh, miss," she said under her breath. "Might I—would you allow me—jest to come in?"

Sara lifted her head and looked at her. She tried to begin a smile, and somehow she could not. Suddenly—and it was all through the loving mournfulness of Becky's streaming eyes—her face looked more like a child's not so much too old for her years. She held out her hand and gave a little sob.

"Oh, Becky," she said. "I told you we were just the same—only two little girls—just two little girls. You see how true it is. There's no difference now. I'm not a princess anymore."

Becky ran to her and caught her hand, and hugged it to her breast, kneeling beside her and sobbing with love and pain.

"Yes, miss, you are," she cried, and her words were all broken. "Whats'ever 'appens to you—whats'ever—you'd be a princess all the same—an' nothin' couldn't make you nothin' different."

Day 109

1.   Read chapter **8** of *A Little Princess*.
2.   Tell someone what happened in the chapter.

IN THE ATTIC

THE first night she spent in her attic was a thing Sara never forgot. During its passing she lived through a wild, unchildlike woe of which she never spoke to anyone about her. There was no one who would have understood. It was, indeed, well for her that as she lay awake in the darkness her mind was forcibly distracted, now and then, by the strangeness of her surroundings. It was, perhaps, well for her that she was reminded by her small body of material things. If this had not been so, the anguish of her young mind might have been too great for a child to bear. But, really, while the night was passing she scarcely knew that she had a body at all or remembered any other thing than one.

"My papa is dead!" she kept whispering to herself. "My papa is dead!"

It was not until long afterward that she realized that her bed had been so hard that she turned over and over in it to find a place to rest, that the darkness seemed more intense than any she had ever known, and that the wind howled over the roof among the chimneys like something which wailed aloud. Then there was something worse. This was certain scufflings and scratchings and squeakings in the walls and behind the skirting boards. She knew what they meant, because Becky had described them. They meant rats and mice who were either fighting with each other or playing together. Once or twice she even heard sharp-toed feet scurrying across the floor, and she remembered in those after days, when she recalled things, that when first she heard them she started up in bed and sat trembling, and when she lay down again covered her head with the bedclothes.

The change in her life did not come about gradually, but was made all at once.

"She must begin as she is to go on," Miss Minchin said to Miss Amelia. "She must be taught at once what she is to expect."

Mariette had left the house the next morning. The glimpse Sara caught of her sitting-room, as she passed its open door, showed her that everything had been changed. Her ornaments and luxuries had been removed, and a bed had been placed in a corner to transform it into a new pupil's bedroom.

When she went down to breakfast she saw that her seat at Miss Minchin's side was occupied by Lavinia, and Miss Minchin spoke to her coldly.

"You will begin your new duties, Sara," she said, "by taking your seat with the younger children at a smaller table. You must keep them quiet, and see that they behave well and do not waste their food. You ought to have been down earlier. Lottie has already upset her tea."

That was the beginning, and from day to day the duties given to her were added to. She taught the younger children French and heard their other lessons, and these were the least of her labors. It was found that she could be made use of in numberless directions. She could be sent on errands at any time and in all weathers. She could be told to do things other people neglected. The cook and the housemaids took their tone from Miss Minchin, and rather enjoyed ordering about the "young one" who had been made so much fuss over for so long. They were not servants of the best class, and had neither good manners nor good tempers, and it was frequently convenient to have at hand someone on whom blame could be laid.

During the first month or two, Sara thought that her willingness to do things as well as she could, and her silence under reproof, might soften those who drove her so hard. In her proud little heart she wanted them to see that she was trying to earn her living and not accepting charity. But the time came when she saw that no one was softened at all; and the more willing she was to do as she was told, the more domineering and exacting careless housemaids became, and the more ready a scolding cook was to blame her.

If she had been older, Miss Minchin would have given her the bigger girls to teach and saved money by dismissing an instructress; but while she remained and looked like a child, she could be made more useful as a sort of little superior errand girl and maid of all work. An ordinary errand boy would not have been so clever and reliable. Sara could be trusted with difficult commissions and complicated messages. She could even go and pay bills, and she combined with this the ability to dust a room well and to set things in order.

Her own lessons became things of the past. She was taught nothing, and only after long and busy days spent in running here and there at everybody's orders was she grudgingly allowed to go into the deserted school-room, with a pile of old books, and study alone at night.

"If I do not remind myself of the things I have learned, perhaps I may forget them," she said to herself. "I am almost a scullery-maid, and if I am a scullery-maid who knows nothing, I shall be like poor Becky. I wonder if I could quite forget and begin to drop my h's and not remember that Henry the Eighth had six wives."

One of the most curious things in her new existence was her changed position among the pupils. Instead of being a sort of small royal personage among them, she no longer seemed to be one of their number at all. She was kept so constantly at work that she scarcely ever had an opportunity of speaking to any of them, and she could not avoid seeing that Miss Minchin preferred that she should live a life apart from that of the occupants of the school-room.

"I will not have her forming intimacies and talking to the other children," that lady said. "Girls like a grievance, and if she begins to tell romantic stories about herself, she will become an ill-used heroine, and parents will be given a wrong impression. It is better that she should live a separate life—one suited to her circumstances. I am giving her a home, and that is more than she has any right to expect from me."

Sara did not expect much, and was far too proud to try to continue to be intimate with girls who evidently felt rather awkward and uncertain about her. The fact was that Miss Minchin's pupils were a set of dull, matter-of-fact young people. They were accustomed to being rich and comfortable, and as Sara's frocks grew shorter and shabbier and queerer-looking, and it became an established fact that she wore shoes with holes in them and was sent out to buy groceries and carry them through the streets in a basket on her arm when the cook wanted them in a hurry, they felt rather as if, when they spoke to her, they were addressing an under servant.

"To think that she was the girl with the diamond-mines," Lavinia commented. "She does look an object. And she's queerer than ever. I never liked her much, but I can't bear that way she has now of looking at people without speaking—just as if she was finding them out."

"I am," said Sara, promptly, when she heard of this. "That's what I look at some people for. I like to know about them. I think them over afterward."

The truth was that she had saved herself annoyance several times by keeping her eye on Lavinia, who was quite ready to make mischief, and would have been rather pleased to have made it for the ex-show pupil.

Sara never made any mischief herself, or interfered with anyone. She worked like a drudge; she tramped through the wet streets, carrying parcels and baskets; she labored with the childish inattention of the little ones' French lessons; as she became shabbier and more forlorn-looking, she was told that she had better take her meals downstairs; she was treated as if she was nobody's concern, and her heart grew proud and sore, but she never told anyone what she felt.

"Soldiers don't complain," she would say between her small, shut teeth, "I am not going to do it; I will pretend this is part of a war."

But there were hours when her child heart might almost have broken with loneliness but for three people.

The first, it must be owned, was Becky—just Becky. Throughout all that first night spent in the garret, she had felt a vague comfort in knowing that on the other side of the wall in which the rats scuffled and squeaked there was another young human creature. And during the nights that followed the sense of comfort grew. They had little chance to speak to each other during the day. Each had her own tasks to perform, and any attempt at conversation would have been regarded as a tendency to loiter and lose time.

"Don't mind me, miss," Becky whispered during the first morning, "if I don't say nothin' polite. Some un'd be down on us if I did. I means 'please' an' 'thank you' an' 'beg pardon,' but I dassn't to take time to say it."

But before daybreak she used to slip into Sara's attic and button her dress and give her such help as she required before she went down-stairs to light the kitchen fire. And when night came Sara always heard the humble knock at her door which meant that her handmaid was ready to help her again if she was needed. During the first weeks of her grief Sara felt as if she were too stupefied to talk, so it happened that some time passed before they saw each other much or exchanged visits. Becky's heart told her that it was best that people in trouble should be left alone.

The second of the trio of comforters was Ermengarde, but odd things happened before Ermengarde found her place.

When Sara's mind seemed to awaken again to the life about her, she realized that she had forgotten that an Ermengarde lived in the world. The two had always been friends, but Sara had felt as if she were years the older. It could not be contested that Ermengarde was as dull as she was affectionate. She clung to Sara in a simple, helpless way; she brought her lessons to her that she might be helped; she listened to her every word and besieged her with requests for stories. But she had nothing interesting to say herself, and she loathed books of every description. She was, in fact, not a person one would remember when one was caught in the storm of a great trouble, and Sara forgot her.

It had been all the easier to forget her because she had been suddenly called home for a few weeks. When she came back she did not see Sara for a day or two, and when she met her for the first time she encountered her coming down a corridor with her arms full of garments which were to be taken down-stairs to be mended. Sara herself had already been taught to mend them. She looked pale and unlike herself, and she was attired in the queer, outgrown frock whose shortness showed so much thin black leg.

Ermengarde was too slow a girl to be equal to such a situation. She could not think of anything to say. She knew what had happened, but, somehow, she had never imagined Sara could look like this—so odd and poor and almost like a servant. It made her quite miserable, and she could do nothing but break into a short hysterical laugh and exclaim—aimlessly and as if without any meaning:

"Oh, Sara, is that you?"

"Yes," answered Sara, and suddenly a strange thought passed through her mind and made her face flush.

She held the pile of garments in her arms, and her chin rested upon the top of it to keep it steady. Something in the look of her straight-gazing eyes made Ermengarde lose her wits still more. She felt as if Sara had changed into a new kind of girl, and she had never known her before. Perhaps it was because she had suddenly grown poor and had to mend things and work like Becky.

"Oh," she stammered. "How—how are you?"

"I don't know," Sara replied. "How are you?"

"I'm—I'm quite well," said Ermengarde, overwhelmed with shyness. Then spasmodically she thought of something to say which seemed more intimate. "Are you—are you very unhappy?" she said in a rush.

Then Sara was guilty of an injustice. Just at that moment her torn heart swelled within her, and she felt that if anyone was as stupid as that, one had better get away from her.

"What do you think?" she said. "Do you think I am very happy?" And she marched past her without another word.

In course of time she realized that if her wretchedness had not made her forget things, she would have known that poor, dull Ermengarde was not to be blamed for her unready, awkward ways. She was always awkward, and the more she felt, the more stupid she was given to being.

But the sudden thought which had flashed upon her had made her over-sensitive.

"She is like the others," she had thought. "She does not really want to talk to me. She knows no one does."

So for several weeks a barrier stood between them. When they met by chance Sara looked the other way, and Ermengarde felt too stiff and embarrassed to speak. Sometimes they nodded to each other in passing, but there were times when they did not even exchange a greeting.

"If she would rather not talk to me," Sara thought, "I will keep out of her way. Miss Minchin makes that easy enough."

Miss Minchin made it so easy that at last they scarcely saw each other at all. At that time it was noticed that Ermengarde was more stupid than ever, and that she looked listless and unhappy. She used to sit in the window-seat, huddled in a heap, and stare out of the window without speaking. Once Jessie, who was passing, stopped to look at her curiously.

"What are you crying for, Ermengarde?" she asked.

"I'm not crying," answered Ermengarde, in a muffled, unsteady voice.

"You are," said Jessie. "A great big tear just rolled down the bridge of your nose and dropped off at the end of it. And there goes another."

"Well," said Ermengarde, "I'm miserable—and no one need interfere." And she turned her plump back and took out her handkerchief and boldly hid her face in it.

That night, when Sara went to her attic, she was later than usual. She had been kept at work until after the hour at which the pupils went to bed, and after that she had gone to her lessons in the lonely school-room. When she reached the top of the stairs, she was surprised to see a glimmer of light coming from under the attic door.

"Nobody goes there but myself," she thought quickly; "but someone has lighted a candle."

Someone had, indeed, lighted a candle, and it was not burning in the kitchen candlestick she was expected to use, but in one of those belonging to the pupils' bedrooms. The someone was sitting upon the battered footstool, and was dressed in her night-gown and wrapped up in a red shawl. It was Ermengarde.

"Ermengarde!" cried Sara. She was so startled that she was almost frightened. "You will get into trouble."

Ermengarde stumbled up from her footstool. She shuffled across the attic in her bedroom slippers, which were too large for her. Her eyes and nose were pink with crying.

"I know I shall—if I'm found out." she said. "But I don't care—I don't care a bit. Oh, Sara, please tell me. What is the matter? Why don't you like me any more?"

Something in her voice made the familiar lump rise in Sara's throat. It was so affectionate and simple—so like the old Ermengarde who had asked her to be "best friends." It sounded as if she had not meant what she had seemed to mean during these past weeks.

"I do like you," Sara answered. "I thought—you see, everything is different now. I thought you—were different."

Ermengarde opened her wet eyes wide.

"Why, it was you who were different!" she cried. "You didn't want to talk to me. I didn't know what to do. It was you who were different after I came back."

Sara thought a moment. She saw she had made a mistake.

"I am different," she explained, "though not in the way you think. Miss Minchin does not want me to talk to the girls. Most of them don't want to talk to me. I thought—perhaps—you didn't. So I tried to keep out of your way."

"Oh, Sara," Ermengarde almost wailed in her reproachful dismay. And then after one more look they rushed into each other's arms. It must be confessed that Sara's small black head lay for some minutes on the shoulder covered by the red shawl. When Ermengarde had seemed to desert her, she had felt horribly lonely.

Afterward they sat down upon the floor together, Sara clasping her knees with her arms, and Ermengarde rolled up in her shawl. Ermengarde looked at the odd, big-eyed little face adoringly.

"I couldn't bear it any more," she said. "I dare say you could live without me, Sara; but I couldn't live without you. I was nearly dead. So tonight, when I was crying under the bedclothes, I thought all at once of creeping up here and just begging you to let us be friends again."

"You are nicer than I am," said Sara. "I was too proud to try and make friends. You see, now that trials have come, they have shown that I am not a nice child. I was afraid they would. Perhaps"—wrinkling her forehead wisely—"that is what they were sent for."

"I don't see any good in them," said Ermengarde stoutly.

"Neither do I—to speak the truth," admitted Sara, frankly. "But I suppose there might be good in things, even if we don't see it. There might"—doubtfully—"be good in Miss Minchin."

Ermengarde looked round the attic with a rather fearsome curiosity.

"Sara," she said, "do you think you can bear living here?"

Sara looked round also.

"If I pretend it's quite different, I can," she answered; "or if I pretend it is a place in a story."

She spoke slowly. Her imagination was beginning to work for her. It had not worked for her at all since her troubles had come upon her. She had felt as if it had been stunned.

"Other people have lived in worse places. Think of the Count of Monte Cristo in the dungeons of the Château d'If. And think of the people in the Bastille!"

"The Bastille," half whispered Ermengarde, watching her and beginning to be fascinated. She remembered stories of the French Revolution which Sara had been able to fix in her mind by her dramatic relation of them. No one but Sara could have done it.

A well-known glow came into Sara's eyes.

"Yes," she said, hugging her knees, "that will be a good place to pretend about. I am a prisoner in the Bastille. I have been here for years and years—and years; and everybody has forgotten about me. Miss Minchin is the jailer—and Becky"—a sudden light adding itself to the glow in her eyes—"Becky is the prisoner in the next cell."

She turned to Ermengarde, looking quite like the old Sara.

"I shall pretend that," she said; "and it will be a great comfort."

Ermengarde was at once enraptured and awed.

"And will you tell me all about it?" she said. "May I creep up here at night, whenever it is safe, and hear the things you have made up in the day? It will seem as if we were more 'best friends' than ever."

"Yes," answered Sara, nodding. "Adversity tries people, and mine has tried you and proved how nice you are."

Day 110

1.   Read chapter 9 of *A Little Princess*.
2.   Tell someone what happened in the chapter.
3.   Who is Melchisedec?

MELCHISEDEC

THE third person in the trio was Lottie. She was a small thing and did not know what adversity meant, and was much bewildered by the alteration she saw in her young adopted mother. She had heard it rumored that strange things had happened to Sara, but she could not understand why she looked different—why she wore an old black frock and came into the school-room only to teach instead of to sit in her place of honor and learn lessons herself. There had been much whispering among the little ones when it had been discovered that Sara no longer lived in the rooms in which Emily had so long sat in state. Lottie's chief difficulty was that Sara said so little when one asked her questions. At seven mysteries must be made very clear if one is to understand them.

"Are you very poor now, Sara?" she had asked confidentially the first morning her friend took charge of the small French class. "Are you as poor as a beggar?" She thrust a fat hand into the slim one and opened round, tearful eyes. "I don't want you to be as poor as a beggar."

She looked as if she was going to cry. And Sara hurriedly consoled her.

"Beggars have nowhere to live," she said courageously. "I have a place to live in."

"Where do you live?" persisted Lottie. "The new girl sleeps in your room, and it isn't pretty any more."

"I live in another room," said Sara.

"Is it a nice one?" inquired Lottie. "I want to go and see it."

"You must not talk," said Sara. "Miss Minchin is looking at us. She will be angry with me for letting you whisper."

She had found out already that she was to be held accountable for everything which was objected to. If the children were not attentive, if they talked, if they were restless, it was she who would be reproved.

But Lottie was a determined little person. If Sara would not tell her where she lived, she would find out in some other way. She talked to her small companions and hung about the elder girls and listened when they were gossiping; and acting upon certain information they had unconsciously let drop, she started late one afternoon on a voyage of discovery, climbing stairs she had never known the existence of, until she reached the attic floor. There she found two doors near each other, and opening one, she saw her beloved Sara standing upon an old table and looking out of a window.

"Sara!" she cried, aghast. "Mamma Sara!" She was aghast because the attic was so bare and ugly and seemed so far away from all the world. Her short legs had seemed to have been mounting hundreds of stairs.

Sara turned round at the sound of her voice. It was her turn to be aghast. What would happen now? If Lottie began to cry and any one chanced to hear, they were both lost. She jumped down from her table and ran to the child.

"Don't cry and make a noise," she implored. "I shall be scolded if you do, and I have been scolded all day. It's—it's not such a bad room, Lottie."

"Isn't it?" gasped Lottie, and as she looked round it she bit her lip. She was a spoiled child yet, but she was fond enough of her adopted parent to make an effort to control herself for her sake. Then, somehow, it was quite possible that any place in which Sara lived might turn out to be nice. "Why isn't it, Sara?" she almost whispered.

Sara hugged her close and tried to laugh. There was a sort of comfort in the warmth of the plump, childish body. She had had a hard day and had been staring out of the windows with hot eyes.

"You can see all sorts of things you can't see down-stairs," she said.

"What sort of things?" demanded Lottie, with that curiosity Sara could always awaken even in bigger girls.

"Chimneys—quite close to us—with smoke curling up in wreaths and clouds and going up into the sky—and sparrows hopping about and talking to each other just as if they were people—and other attic windows where heads may pop out any minute and you can wonder who they belong to. And it all feels as high up—as if it was another world."

"Oh, let me see it!" cried Lottie. "Lift me up!"

Sara lifted her up, and they stood on the old table together and leaned on the edge of the flat window in the roof, and looked out.

Anyone who has not done this does not know what a different world they saw. The slates spread out on either side of them and slanted down into the rain gutter-pipes. The sparrows, being at home there, twittered and hopped about quite without fear. Two of them perched on the chimney-top nearest and quarrelled with each other fiercely until one pecked the other and drove him away. The garret window next to theirs was shut because the house next door was empty.

"I wish someone lived there," Sara said. "It is so close that if there was a little girl in the attic, we could talk to each other through the windows and climb over to see each other, if we were not afraid of falling."

The sky seemed so much nearer than when one saw it from the street, that Lottie was enchanted. From the attic window, among the chimney-pots, the things which were happening in the world below seemed almost unreal. One scarcely believed in the existence of Miss Minchin and Miss Amelia and the school-room, and the roll of wheels in the square seemed a sound belonging to another existence.

"Oh, Sara!" cried Lottie, cuddling in her guarding arm. "I like this attic—I like it! It is nicer than down-stairs!"

"Look at that sparrow," whispered Sara. "I wish I had some crumbs to throw to him."

"I have some!" came in a little shriek from Lottie. "I have part of a bun in my pocket; I bought it with my penny yesterday, and I saved a bit."

When they threw out a few crumbs the sparrow jumped and flew away to an adjacent chimney-top. He was evidently not accustomed to intimates in attics, and unexpected crumbs startled him. But when Lottie remained quite still and Sara chirped very softly— almost as if she were a sparrow herself—he saw that the thing which had alarmed him represented hospitality, after all. He put his head on one side, and from his perch on the chimney looked down at the crumbs with twinkling eyes. Lottie could scarcely keep still.

"Will he come? Will he come?" she whispered.

"His eyes look as if he would," Sara whispered back. "He is thinking and thinking whether he dare. Yes, he will! Yes, he is coming!"

He flew down and hopped toward the crumbs, but stopped a few inches away from them, putting his head on one side again, as if reflecting on the chances that Sara and Lottie might turn out to be big cats and jump on him. At last his heart told him they were really nicer than they looked, and he hopped nearer and nearer, darted at the biggest crumb with a lightning peck, seized it, and carried it away to the other side of his chimney.

"Now he knows," said Sara. "And he will come back for the others."

He did come back, and even brought a friend, and the friend went away and brought a relative, and among them they made a hearty meal over which they twittered and chattered and exclaimed, stopping every now and then to put their heads on one side and examine Lottie and Sara. Lottie was so delighted that she quite forgot her first shocked impression of the attic. In fact, when she was lifted down from the table and returned to earthly things, as it were, Sara was able to point out to her many beauties in the room which she herself would not have suspected the existence of.

"It is so little and so high above everything," she said, "that it is almost like a nest in a tree. The slanting ceiling is so funny. See, you can scarcely stand up at this end of the room; and when the morning begins to come I can lie in bed and look right up into the sky through that flat window in the roof. It is like a square patch of light. If the sun is going to shine, little pink clouds float about, and I feel as if I could touch them. And if it rains, the drops patter and patter as if they were saying something nice. Then if there are stars, you can lie and try to count how many go into the patch. It takes such a lot. And just look at that tiny, rusty grate in the corner. If it was polished and there was a fire in it, just think how nice it would be. You see, it's really a beautiful little room."

She was walking round the small place, holding Lottie's hand and making gestures which described all the beauties she was making herself see. She quite made Lottie see them, too. Lottie could always believe in the things Sara made pictures of.

"You see," she said, "there could be a thick, soft blue Indian rug on the floor; and in that corner there could be a soft little sofa, with cushions to curl up on; and just over it could be a shelf full of books so that one could reach them easily; and there could be a fur rug before the fire, and hangings on the wall to cover up the whitewash, and pictures. They would have to be little ones, but they could be beautiful; and there could be a lamp with a deep rose-colored shade; and a table in the middle, with things to have tea with; and a little fat copper kettle singing on the hob; and the bed could be quite different. It could be made soft and covered with a lovely silk coverlet. It could be beautiful. And perhaps we could coax the sparrows until we made such friends with them that they would come and peck at the window and ask to be let in."

"Oh, Sara!" cried Lottie. "I should like to live here!"

When Sara had persuaded her to go down-stairs again, and, after setting her on her way, had come back to her attic, she stood in the middle of it and looked about her. The enchantment of her imaginings for Lottie had died away. The bed was hard and covered with its dingy quilt. The whitewashed wall showed its broken patches, the floor was cold and bare, the grate was broken and rusty, and the battered footstool, tilted sideways on its injured leg, the only seat in the room. She sat down on it for a few minutes and let her head drop in her hands. The mere fact that Lottie had come and gone away again made things seem a little worse—just as perhaps prisoners feel a little more desolate after visitors come and go, leaving them behind.

"It's a lonely place," she said. "Sometimes it's the loneliest place in the world."

She was sitting in this way when her attention was attracted by a slight sound near her. She lifted her head to see where it came from, and if she had been a nervous child she would have left her seat on the battered footstool in a great hurry. A large rat was sitting up on his hind quarters and sniffing the air in an interested manner. Some of Lottie's crumbs had dropped upon the floor and their scent had drawn him out of his hole.

He looked so queer and so like a gray-whiskered dwarf or gnome that Sara was rather fascinated. He looked at her with his bright eyes, as if he were asking a question. He was evidently so doubtful that one of the child's queer thoughts came into her mind.

"I dare say it is rather hard to be a rat," she mused. "Nobody likes you. People jump and run away and scream out, 'Oh, a horrid rat!' I shouldn't like people to scream and jump and say, 'Oh, a horrid Sara!' the moment they saw me. And set traps for me, and pretend they were dinner. It's so different to be a sparrow. But nobody asked this rat if he wanted to be a rat when he was made. Nobody said, 'Wouldn't you rather be a sparrow?' "

She had sat so quietly that the rat had begun to take courage. He was very much afraid of her, but perhaps he had a heart like the sparrow and it told him that she was not a thing which pounced. He was very hungry. He had a wife and a large family in the wall, and they had had frightfully bad luck for several days. He had left the children crying bitterly, and felt he would risk a good deal for a few crumbs, so he cautiously dropped upon his feet.

"Come on," said Sara; "I'm not a trap. You can have them, poor thing! Prisoners in the Bastille used to make friends with rats. Suppose I make friends with you."

How it is that animals understand things I do not know, but it is certain that they do understand. Perhaps there is a language which is not made of words and everything in the world understands it. Perhaps there is a soul hidden in everything and it can always speak, without even making a sound, to another soul. But whatsoever was the reason, the rat knew from that moment that he was safe—even though he was a rat. He knew that this young human being sitting on the red footstool would not jump up and terrify him with wild, sharp noises or throw heavy objects at him which, if they did not fall and crush him, would send him limping in his scurry back to his hole. He was really a very nice rat, and did not mean the least harm. When he had stood on his hind legs and sniffed the air, with his bright eyes fixed on Sara, he had hoped that she would understand this, and would not begin by hating him as an enemy. When the mysterious thing which speaks without saying any words told him that she would not, he went softly toward the crumbs and began to eat them. As he did it he glanced every now and then at Sara, just as the sparrows had done, and his expression was so very apologetic that it touched her heart.

She sat and watched him without making any movement. One crumb was very much larger than the others—in fact, it could scarcely be called a crumb. It was evident that he wanted that piece very much, but it lay quite near the footstool and he was still rather timid.

"I believe he wants it to carry to his family in the wall," Sara thought. "If I do not stir at all, perhaps he will come and get it."

She scarcely allowed herself to breathe, she was so deeply interested. The rat shuffled a little nearer and ate a few more crumbs, then he stopped and sniffed delicately, giving a side glance at the occupant of the footstool; then he darted at the piece of bun with something very like the sudden boldness of the sparrow, and the instant he had possession of it fled back to the wall, slipped down a crack in the skirting board, and was gone.

"I knew he wanted it for his children," said Sara. "I do believe I could make friends with him."

A week or so afterward, on one of the rare nights when Ermengarde found it safe to steal up to the attic, when she tapped on the door with the tips of her fingers Sara did not come to her for two or three minutes. There was, indeed, such a silence in the room at first that Ermengarde wondered if she could have fallen asleep. Then, to her surprise, she heard her utter a little, low laugh and speak coaxingly to someone.

"There!" Ermengarde heard her say. "Take it and go home, Melchisedec! Go home to your wife!"

Almost immediately Sara opened the door, and when she did so she found Ermengarde standing with alarmed eyes upon the threshold.

"Who—who are you talking to, Sara?" she gasped out.

Sara drew her in cautiously, but she looked as if something pleased and amused her.

"You must promise not to be frightened—not to scream the least bit, or I can't tell you," she answered.

Ermengarde felt almost inclined to scream on the spot, but managed to control herself. She looked all round the attic and saw no one. And yet Sara had certainly been speaking to someone. She thought of ghosts.

"Is it—something that will frighten me?" she asked timorously.

"Some people are afraid of them," said Sara. "I was at first—but I am not now."

"Was it—a ghost?" quaked Ermengarde.

"No," said Sara, laughing. "It was my rat."

Ermengarde made one bound, and landed in the middle of the little dingy bed. She tucked her feet under her night-gown and the red shawl. She did not scream, but she gasped with fright.

"Oh! Oh!" she cried under her breath. "A rat! A rat!"

"I was afraid you would be frightened," said Sara. "But you needn't be. I am making him tame. He actually knows me and comes out when I call him. Are you too frightened to want to see him?"

The truth was that, as the days had gone on and, with the aid of scraps brought up from the kitchen, her curious friendship had developed, she had gradually forgotten that the timid creature she was becoming familiar with was a mere rat.

At first Ermengarde was too much alarmed to do anything but huddle in a heap upon the bed and tuck up her feet, but the sight of Sara's composed little countenance and the story of Melchisedec's first appearance began at last to rouse her curiosity, and she leaned forward over the edge of the bed and watched Sara go and kneel down by the hole in the skirting board.

"He—he won't run out quickly and jump on the bed, will he?" she said.

"No," answered Sara. "He's as polite as we are. He is just like a person. Now watch!"

She began to make a low, whistling sound—so low and coaxing that it could only have been heard in entire stillness. She did it several times, looking entirely absorbed in it. Ermengarde thought she looked as if she were working a spell. And at last, evidently in response to it, a gray-whiskered, bright-eyed head peeped out of the hole. Sara had some crumbs in her hand. She dropped them, and Melchisedec came quietly forth and ate them. A piece of larger size than the rest he took and carried in the most businesslike manner back to his home.

"You see," said Sara, "that is for his wife and children. He is very nice. He only eats the little bits. After he goes back I can always hear his family squeaking for joy. There are three kinds of squeaks. One kind is the children's, and one is Mrs. Melchisedec's, and one is Melchisedec's own."

Ermengarde began to laugh.

"Oh, Sara!" she said. "You are queer—but you are nice."

"I know I am queer," admitted Sara, cheerfully; "and I try to be nice." She rubbed her forehead with her little brown paw, and a puzzled, tender look came into her face. "Papa always laughed at me," she said; "but I liked it. He thought I was queer, but he liked me to make up things. I—I can't help making up things. If I didn't, I don't believe I could live."

She paused and glanced around the attic. "I'm sure I couldn't live here," she added in a low voice.

Ermengarde was interested, as she always was. "When you talk about things," she said, "they seem as if they grew real. You talk about Melchisedec as if he was a person."

"He is a person," said Sara. "He gets hungry and frightened, just as we do; and he is married and has children. How do we know he doesn't think things, just as we do? His eyes look as if he was a person. That was why I gave him a name."

She sat down on the floor in her favorite attitude, holding her knees.

"Besides," she said, "he is a Bastille rat sent to be my friend. I can always get a bit of bread the cook has thrown away, and it is quite enough to support him."

"Is it the Bastille yet?" asked Ermengarde, eagerly. "Do you always pretend it is the Bastille?"

"Nearly always," answered Sara. "Sometimes I try to pretend it is another kind of place; but the Bastille is generally easiest—particularly when it is cold."

Just at that moment Ermengarde almost jumped off the bed, she was so startled by a sound she heard. It was like two distinct knocks on the wall.

"What is that?" she exclaimed.

Sara got up from the floor and answered quite dramatically:

"It is the prisoner in the next cell."

"Becky!" cried Ermengarde, enraptured.

"Yes," said Sara. "Listen; the two knocks meant, 'Prisoner, are you there?' "

She knocked three times on the wall herself, as if in answer.

"That means, 'Yes, I am here, and all is well.' "

Four knocks came from Becky's side of the wall.

"That means," explained Sara, "'Then, fellow-sufferer, we will sleep in peace. Good night.'"

Ermengarde quite beamed with delight.

"Oh, Sara!" she whispered joyfully. "It is like a story!"

"It is a story," said Sara. "Everything's a story. You are a story— I am a story. Miss Minchin is a story."

And she sat down again and talked until Ermengarde forgot that she was a sort of escaped prisoner herself, and had to be reminded by Sara that she could not remain in the Bastille all night, but must steal noiselessly down-stairs again and creep back into her deserted bed.

Day 111

1.   Read chapter 10 of *A Little Princess* and tell someone about the chapter.
2.   Tell someone about the chapter.

THE INDIAN GENTLEMAN

BUT it was a perilous thing for Ermengarde and Lottie to make pilgrimages to the attic. They could never be quite sure when Sara would be there, and they could scarcely ever be certain that Miss Amelia would not make a tour of inspection through the bedrooms after the pupils were supposed to be asleep. So their visits were rare ones, and Sara lived a strange and lonely life. It was a lonelier life when she was down-stairs than when she was in her attic. She had no one to talk to; and when she was sent out on errands and walked through the streets, a forlorn little figure carrying a basket or a parcel, trying to hold her hat on when the wind was blowing, and feeling the water soak through her shoes when it was raining, she felt as if the crowds hurrying past her made her loneliness greater. When she had been the Princess Sara, driving through the streets in her brougham, or walking, attended by Mariette, the sight of her bright, eager little face and picturesque coats and hats had often caused people to look after her. A happy, beautifully cared for little girl naturally attracts attention. Shabby, poorly dressed children are not rare enough and pretty enough to make people turn around to look at them and smile. No one looked at Sara in these days, and no one seemed to see her as she hurried along the crowded pavements. She had begun to grow very fast, and, as she was dressed only in such clothes as the plainer remnants of her wardrobe would supply, she knew she looked very queer, indeed. All her valuable garments had been disposed of, and such as had been left for her use she was expected to wear so long as she could put them on at all. Sometimes, when she passed a shop window with a mirror in it, she almost laughed outright on catching a glimpse of herself, and sometimes her face went red and she bit her lip and turned away.

In the evening, when she passed houses whose windows were lighted up, she used to look into the warm rooms and amuse herself by imagining things about the people she saw sitting before the fires or about the tables. It always interested her to catch glimpses of rooms before the shutters were closed. There were several families in the square in which Miss Minchin lived, with which she had become quite familiar in a way of her own. The one she liked best she called the Large Family. She called it the Large Family not because the members of it were big—for, indeed, most of them were little—but because there were so many of them. There were eight children in the Large Family, and a stout, rosy mother, and a stout, rosy father, and a stout, rosy grandmother, and any number of servants. The eight children were always either being taken out to walk or to ride in perambulators by comfortable nurses, or they were going to drive with their mamma, or they were flying to the door in the evening to meet their papa and kiss him and dance around him and drag off his overcoat and look in the pockets for packages, or they were crowding about the nursery windows and looking out and pushing each other and laughing—in fact, they were always doing something enjoyable and suited to the tastes of a large family. Sara was quite fond of them, and had given them names out of books—quite romantic names. She called them the Montmorencys when she did not call them the Large Family. The fat, fair baby with the lace cap was Ethelberta Beauchamp Montmorency; the next baby was Violet Cholmondeley Montmorency; the little boy who could just stagger and who had such round legs was Sydney Cecil Vivian Montmorency; and then came Lilian Evangeline Maud Marion, Rosalind Gladys, Guy Clarence, Veronica Eustacia, and Claude Harold Hector.

One evening a very funny thing happened—though, perhaps, in one sense it was not a funny thing at all.

Several of the Montmorencys were evidently going to a children's party, and just as Sara was about to pass the door they were crossing the pavement to get into the carriage which was waiting for them. Veronica Eustacia and Rosalind Gladys, in white-lace frocks and lovely sashes, had just got in, and Guy Clarence, aged five, was following them. He was such a pretty fellow and had such rosy cheeks and blue eyes, and such a darling little round head covered with curls, that Sara forgot her basket and shabby cloak altogether—in fact, forgot everything but that she wanted to look at him for a moment. So she paused and looked.

It was Christmas time, and the Large Family had been hearing many stories about children who were poor and had no mammas and papas to fill their stockings and take them to the pantomime—children who were, in fact, cold and thinly clad and hungry. In the stories, kind people—sometimes little boys and girls with tender hearts—invariably saw the poor children and gave them money or rich gifts, or took them home to beautiful dinners. Guy Clarence had been affected to tears that very afternoon by the reading of such a story, and he had burned with a desire to find such a poor child and give her a certain sixpence he possessed, and thus provide for her for life. An entire sixpence, he was sure, would mean affluence for evermore. As he crossed the strip of red carpet laid across the pavement from the door to the carriage, he had this very sixpence in the pocket of his very short man-o-war trousers; And just as Rosalind Gladys got into the vehicle and jumped on the seat in order to feel the cushions spring under her, he saw Sara standing on the wet pavement in her shabby frock and hat, with her old basket on her arm, looking at him hungrily.

He thought that her eyes looked hungry because she had perhaps had nothing to eat for a long time. He did not know that they looked so because she was hungry for the warm, merry life his home held and his rosy face spoke of, and that she had a hungry wish to snatch him in her arms and kiss him. He only knew that she had big eyes and a thin face and thin legs and a common basket and poor clothes. So he put his hand in his pocket and found his sixpence and walked up to her benignly.

"Here, poor little girl," he said. "Here is a sixpence. I will give it to you."

Sara started, and all at once realized that she looked exactly like poor children she had seen, in her better days, waiting on the pavement to watch her as she got out of her brougham. And she had given them pennies many a time. Her face went red and then it went pale, and for a second she felt as if she could not take the dear little sixpence.

"Oh, no!" she said. "Oh, no, thank you; I mustn't take it, indeed!"

Her voice was so unlike an ordinary street child's voice and her manner was so like the manner of a well-bred little person that Veronica Eustacia (whose real name was Janet) and Rosalind Gladys (who was really called Nora) leaned forward to listen.

But Guy Clarence was not to be thwarted in his benevolence. He thrust the sixpence into her hand.

"Yes, you must take it, poor little girl!" he insisted stoutly. "You can buy things to eat with it. It is a whole sixpence!"

There was something so honest and kind in his face, and he looked so likely to be heartbrokenly disappointed if she did not take it, that Sara knew she must not refuse him. To be as proud as that would be a cruel thing. So she actually put her pride in her pocket, though it must be admitted her cheeks burned.

"Thank you," she said. "You are a kind, kind little darling thing." And as he scrambled joyfully into the carriage she went away, trying to smile, though she caught her breath quickly and her eyes were shining through a mist. She had known that she looked odd and shabby, but until now she had not known that she might be taken for a beggar.

As the Large Family's carriage drove away, the children inside it were talking with interested excitement.

"Oh, Donald," (this was Guy Clarence's name), Janet exclaimed alarmedly, "why did you offer that little girl your sixpence? I'm sure she is not a beggar!"

"She didn't speak like a beggar!" cried Nora. "And her face didn't really look like a beggar's face!"

"Besides, she didn't beg," said Janet. "I was so afraid she might be angry with you. You know, it makes people angry to be taken for beggars when they are not beggars."

"She wasn't angry," said Donald, a trifle dismayed, but still firm. "She laughed a little, and she said I was a kind, kind little darling thing. And I was!"—stoutly. "It was my whole sixpence."

Janet and Nora exchanged glances.

"A beggar girl would never have said that," decided Janet. "She would have said, 'Thank yer kindly, little gentleman—thank yer, sir;' and perhaps she would have bobbed a courtesy."

Sara knew nothing about the fact, but from that time the Large Family was as profoundly interested in her as she was in it. Faces used to appear at the nursery windows when she passed, and many discussions concerning her were held round the fire.

"She is a kind of servant at the seminary," Janet said. "I don't believe she belongs to anybody. I believe she is an orphan. But she is not a beggar, however shabby she looks."

And afterward she was called by all of them, "The-little-girl-who-is-not-a-beggar," which was, of course, rather a long name, and sounded very funny sometimes when the youngest ones said it in a hurry.

Sara managed to bore a hole in the sixpence and hung it on an old bit of narrow ribbon round her neck. Her affection for the Large Family increased—as, indeed, her affection for everything she could love increased. She grew fonder and fonder of Becky, and she used to look forward to the two mornings a week when she went into the school-room to give the little ones their French lesson. Her small pupils loved her, and strove with each other for the privilege of standing close to her and insinuating their small hands into hers. It fed her hungry heart to feel them nestling up to her. She made such friends with the sparrows that when she stood upon the table, put her head and shoulders out of the attic window, and chirped, she heard almost immediately a flutter of wings and answering twitters, and a little flock of dingy town birds appeared and alighted on the slates to talk to her and make much of the crumbs she scattered. With Melchisedec she had become so intimate that he actually brought Mrs. Melchisedec with him sometimes, and now and then one or two of his children. She used to talk to him, and, somehow, he looked quite as if he understood.

There had grown in her mind rather a strange feeling about Emily, who always sat and looked on at everything. It arose in one of her moments of great desolateness. She would have liked to believe or pretend to believe that Emily understood and sympathized with her. She did not like to own to herself that her only companion could feel and hear nothing. She used to put her in a chair sometimes and sit opposite to her on the old red footstool, and stare and pretend about her until her own eyes would grow large with something which was almost like fear—particularly at night when everything was so still, when the only sound in the attic was the occasional sudden scurry and squeak of Melchisedec's family in the wall. One of her "pretends" was that Emily was a kind of good witch who could protect her. Sometimes, after she had stared at her until she was wrought up to the highest pitch of fancifulness, she would ask her questions and find herself almost feeling as if she would presently answer. But she never did.

"As to answering, though," said Sara, trying to console herself, "I don't answer very often. I never answer when I can help it. When people are insulting you, there is nothing so good for them as not to say a word—just to look at them and think. Miss Minchin turns pale with rage when I do it, Miss Amelia looks frightened, and so do the girls. When you will not fly into a passion people know you are stronger than they are, because you are strong enough to hold in your rage, and they are not, and they say stupid things they wish they hadn't said afterward. There's nothing so strong as rage, except what makes you hold it in—that's stronger. It's a good thing not to answer your enemies. I scarcely ever do. Perhaps Emily is more like me than I am like myself. Perhaps she would rather not answer her friends, even. She keeps it all in her heart."

But though she tried to satisfy herself with these arguments, she did not find it easy. When, after a long, hard day, in which she had been sent here and there, sometimes on long errands through wind and cold and rain, she came in wet and hungry, and was sent out again because nobody chose to remember that she was only a child, and that her slim legs might be tired and her small body might be chilled; when she had been given only harsh words and cold, slighting looks for thanks; when the cook had been vulgar and insolent; when Miss Minchin had been in her worst mood, and when she had seen the girls sneering among themselves at her shabbiness—then she was not always able to comfort her sore, proud, desolate heart with fancies when Emily merely sat upright in her old chair and stared.

One of these nights, when she came up to the attic cold and hungry, with a tempest raging in her young breast, Emily's stare seemed so vacant, her sawdust legs and arms so inexpressive, that Sara lost all control over herself. There was nobody but Emily—no one in the world. And there she sat.

"I shall die presently," she said at first.

Emily simply stared.

"I can't bear this," said the poor child, trembling. "I know I shall die. I'm cold; I'm wet; I'm starving to death. I've walked a thousand miles to-day, and they have done nothing but scold me from morning until night. And because I could not find that last thing the cook sent me for, they would not give me any supper. Some men laughed at me because my old shoes made me slip down in the mud. I'm covered with mud now. And they laughed. Do you hear?"

She looked at the staring glass eyes and complacent face, and suddenly a sort of heartbroken rage seized her. She lifted her little savage hand and knocked Emily off the chair, bursting into a passion of sobbing—Sara who never cried.

"You are nothing but a doll!" she cried. "Nothing but a doll—doll—doll! You care for nothing. You are stuffed with sawdust. You never had a heart. Nothing could ever make you feel. You are a doll!" Emily lay on the floor, with her legs ignominiously doubled up over her head, and a new flat place on the end of her nose; but she was calm, even dignified. Sara hid her face in her arms. The rats in the wall began to fight and bite each other and squeak and scramble. Melchisedec was chastising some of his family.

Sara's sobs gradually quieted themselves. It was so unlike her to break down that she was surprised at herself. After a while she raised her face and looked at Emily, who seemed to be gazing at her round the side of one angle, and, somehow, by this time actually with a kind of glassy-eyed sympathy. Sara bent and picked her up. Remorse overtook her. She even smiled at herself a very little smile.

"You can't help being a doll," she said with a resigned sigh, "any more than Lavinia and Jessie can help not having any sense. We are not all made alike. Perhaps you do your sawdust best." And she kissed her and shook her clothes straight, and put her back upon her chair.

She had wished very much that some one would take the empty house next door. She wished it because of the attic window which was so near hers. It seemed as if it would be so nice to see it propped open someday and a head and shoulders rising out of the square aperture.

"If it looked a nice head," she thought, "I might begin by saying, 'Good morning,' and all sorts of things might happen. But, of course, it's not really likely that anyone but under servants would sleep there."

One morning, on turning the corner of the square after a visit to the grocer's, the butcher's, and the baker's, she saw, to her great delight, that during her rather prolonged absence, a van full of furniture had stopped before the next house, the front doors were thrown open, and men in shirt sleeves were going in and out carrying heavy packages and pieces of furniture.

"It's taken!" she said. "It really is taken! Oh, I do hope a nice head will look out of the attic window!"

She would almost have liked to join the group of loiterers who had stopped on the pavement to watch the things carried in. She had an idea that if she could see some of the furniture she could guess something about the people it belonged to.

"Miss Minchin's tables and chairs are just like her," she thought; "I remember thinking that the first minute I saw her, even though I was so little. I told papa afterward, and he laughed and said it was true. I am sure the Large Family have fat, comfortable armchairs and sofas, and I can see that their red-flowery wallpaper is exactly like them. It's warm and cheerful and kind-looking and happy."

She was sent out for parsley to the greengrocer's later in the day, and when she came up the area steps her heart gave quite a quick beat of recognition. Several pieces of furniture had been set out of the van upon the pavement. There was a beautiful table of elaborately wrought teakwood, and some chairs, and a screen covered with rich Oriental embroidery. The sight of them gave her a weird, homesick feeling. She had seen things so like them in India. One of the things Miss Minchin had taken from her was a carved teakwood desk her father had sent her.

"They are beautiful things," she said; "they look as if they ought to belong to a nice person. All the things look rather grand. I suppose it is a rich family."

The vans of furniture came and were unloaded and gave place to others all the day. Several times it so happened that Sara had an opportunity of seeing things carried in. It became plain that she had been right in guessing that the newcomers were people of large means. All the furniture was rich and beautiful, and a great deal of it was Oriental. Wonderful rugs and draperies and ornaments were taken from the vans, many pictures, and books enough for a library. Among other things there was a superb god Buddha in a splendid shrine.

"Someone in the family must have been in India," Sara thought. "They have got used to Indian things and like them. I am glad. I shall feel as if they were friends, even if a head never looks out of the attic window."

When she was taking in the evening's milk for the cook (there was really no odd job she was not called upon to do), she saw something occur which made the situation more interesting than ever. The handsome, rosy man who was the father of the Large Family walked across the square in the most matter-of-fact manner, and ran up the steps of the next-door house. He ran up them as if he felt quite at home and expected to run up and down them many a time in the future. He stayed inside quite a long time, and several times came out and gave directions to the workmen, as if he had a right to do so. It was quite certain that he was in some intimate way connected with the newcomers and was acting for them.

"If the new people have children," Sara speculated, "the Large Family children will be sure to come and play with them, and they might come up into the attic just for fun."

At night, after her work was done, Becky came in to see her fellow prisoner and bring her news.

"It's a' Nindian gentleman that's comin' to live next door, miss," she said. "I don't know whether he's a black gentleman or not, but he's a Nindian one. He's very rich, an' he's ill, an' the gentleman of the Large Family is his lawyer. He's had a lot of trouble, an' it's made him ill an' low in his mind. He worships idols, miss. He's an 'eathen an' bows down to wood an' stone. I seen a' idol bein' carried in for him to worship. Somebody had oughter send him a trac'. You can get a trac' for a penny."

Sara laughed a little.

"I don't believe he worships that idol," she said; "some people like to keep them to look at because they are interesting. My papa had a beautiful one, and he did not worship it."

But Becky was rather inclined to prefer to believe that the new neighbor was "an 'eathen." It sounded so much more romantic than that he should merely be the ordinary kind of gentleman who went to church with a prayer-book. She sat and talked long that night of what he would be like, of what his wife would be like if he had one, and of what his children would be like if they had children. Sara saw that privately she could not help hoping very much that they would all be black, and would wear turbans, and, above all, that—like their parent—they would all be " 'eathens."

"I never lived next door to no 'eathens, miss," she said; "I should like to see what sort o' ways they'd have."

It was several weeks before her curiosity was satisfied, and then it was revealed that the new occupant had neither wife nor children. He was a solitary man with no family at all, and it was evident that he was shattered in health and unhappy in mind.

A carriage drove up one day and stopped before the house. When the footman dismounted from the box and opened the door the gentleman who was the father of the Large Family got out first. After him there descended a nurse in uniform, then came down the steps two men-servants. They came to assist their master, who, when he was helped out of the carriage, proved to be a man with a haggard, distressed face, and a skeleton body wrapped in furs. He was carried up the steps, and the head of the Large Family went with him, looking very anxious. Shortly afterward a doctor's carriage arrived, and the doctor went in—plainly to take care of him.

"There is such a yellow gentleman next door, Sara," Lottie whispered at the French class afterward. "Do you think he is a Chinee? The geography says the Chinee men are yellow."

"No, he is not Chinese," Sara whispered back; "he is very ill. Go on with your exercise, Lottie. 'Non, monsieur. Je n'ai pas le canif de mon oncle.' "

That was the beginning of the story of the Indian gentleman.

Day 112

1.   Read chapter 11 of *A Little Princess*.
2.   Tell someone what happened in this chapter.

RAM DASS

THERE were fine sunsets even in the square, sometimes. One could only see parts of them, however, between the chimneys and over the roofs. From the kitchen windows one could not see them at all, and could only guess that they were going on because the bricks looked warm and the air rosy or yellow for a while, or perhaps one saw a blazing glow strike a particular pane of glass somewhere. There was, however, one place from which one could see all the splendor of them: the piles of red or gold clouds in the west; or the purple ones edged with dazzling brightness; or the little fleecy, floating ones, tinged with rose-color and looking like flights of pink doves scurrying across the blue in a great hurry if there was a wind. The place where one could see all this, and seem at the same time to breathe a purer air, was, of course, the attic window. When the square suddenly seemed to begin to glow in an enchanted way and look wonderful in spite of its sooty trees and railings, Sara knew something was going on in the sky; and when it was at all possible to leave the kitchen without being missed or called back, she invariably stole away and crept up the flights of stairs, and, climbing on the old table, got her head and body as far out of the window as possible. When she had accomplished this, she always drew a long breath and looked all round her. It used to seem as if she had all the sky and the world to herself. No one else ever looked out of the other attics. Generally the skylights were closed; but even if they were propped open to admit air, no one seemed to come near them. And there Sara would stand, sometimes turning her face upward to the blue which seemed so friendly and near— just like a lovely vaulted ceiling—sometimes watching the west and all the wonderful things that happened there: the clouds melting or drifting or waiting softly to be changed pink or crimson or snow-white or purple or pale dove-gray. Sometimes they made islands or great mountains enclosing lakes of deep turquoise-blue, or liquid amber, or chrysoprase-green; sometimes dark headlands jutted into strange, lost seas; sometimes slender strips of wonderful lands joined other wonderful lands together. There were places where it seemed that one could run or climb or stand and wait to see what next was coming—until, perhaps, as it all melted, one could float away. At least it seemed so to Sara, and nothing had ever been quite so beautiful to her as the things she saw as she stood on the table—her body half out of the skylight—the sparrows twittering with sunset softness on the slates. The sparrows always seemed to her to twitter with a sort of subdued softness just when these marvels were going on.

There was such a sunset as this a few days after the Indian gentleman was brought to his new home; and, as it fortunately happened that the afternoon's work was done in the kitchen and nobody had ordered her to go anywhere or perform any task, Sara found it easier than usual to slip away and go up-stairs.

She mounted her table and stood looking out. It was a wonderful moment. There were floods of molten gold covering the west, as if a glorious tide was sweeping over the world. A deep, rich yellow light filled the air; the birds flying across the tops of the houses showed quite black against it.

"It's a Splendid one," said Sara, softly, to herself. "It makes me feel almost afraid—as if something strange was just going to happen. The Splendid ones always make me feel like that."

She suddenly turned her head because she heard a sound a few yards away from her. It was an odd sound like a queer little squeaky chattering. It came from the window of the next attic. Someone had come to look at the sunset as she had. There was a head and a part of a body emerging from the skylight, but it was not the head or body of a little girl or a housemaid; it was the picturesque white-swathed form and dark-faced, gleaming-eyed, white-turbaned head of a native Indian man-servant—"a Lascar," Sara said to herself quickly—and the sound she had heard came from a small monkey he held in his arms as if he were fond of it, and which was snuggling and chattering against his breast.

As Sara looked toward him he looked toward her. The first thing she thought was that his dark face looked sorrowful and homesick. She felt absolutely sure he had come up to look at the sun, because he had seen it so seldom in England that he longed for a sight of it. She looked at him interestedly for a second, and then smiled across the slates. She had learned to know how comforting a smile, even from a stranger, may be.

Hers was evidently a pleasure to him. His whole expression altered, and he showed such gleaming white teeth as he smiled back that it was as if a light had been illuminated in his dusky face. The friendly look in Sara's eyes was always very effective when people felt tired or dull.

It was perhaps in making his salute to her that he loosened his hold on the monkey. He was an impish monkey and always ready for adventure, and it is probable that the sight of a little girl excited him. He suddenly broke loose, jumped on to the slates, ran across them chattering, and actually leaped on to Sara's shoulder, and from there down into her attic room. It made her laugh and delighted her; but she knew he must be restored to his master— if the Lascar was his master—and she wondered how this was to be done. Would he let her catch him, or would he be naughty and refuse to be caught, and perhaps get away and run off over the roofs and be lost? That would not do at all. Perhaps he belonged to the Indian gentleman, and the poor man was fond of him.

She turned to the Lascar, feeling glad that she remembered still some of the Hindustani she had learned when she lived with her father. She could make the man understand. She spoke to him in the language he knew.

"Will he let me catch him?" she asked.

She thought she had never seen more surprise and delight than the dark face expressed when she spoke in the familiar tongue. The truth was that the poor fellow felt as if his gods had intervened, and the kind little voice came from heaven itself. At once Sara saw that he had been accustomed to European children. He poured forth a flood of respectful thanks. He was the servant of Missee Sahib. The monkey was a good monkey and would not bite; but, unfortunately, he was difficult to catch. He would flee from one spot to another, like the lightning. He was disobedient, though not evil. Ram Dass knew him as if he were his child, and Ram Dass he would sometimes obey, but not always. If Missee Sahib would permit Ram Dass, he himself could cross the roof to her room, enter the windows, and regain the unworthy little animal. But he was evidently afraid Sara might think he was taking a great liberty and perhaps would not let him come.

But Sara gave him leave at once.

"Can you get across?" she inquired.

"In a moment," he answered her.

"Then come," she said; "he is flying from side to side of the room as if he was frightened."

Ram Dass slipped through his attic window and crossed to hers as steadily and lightly as if he had walked on roofs all his life. He slipped through the skylight and dropped upon his feet without a sound. Then he turned to Sara and salaamed again. The monkey saw him and uttered a little scream. Ram Dass hastily took the precaution of shutting the skylight, and then went in chase of him. It was not a very long chase. The monkey prolonged it a few minutes evidently for the mere fun of it, but presently he sprang chattering on to Ram Dass's shoulder and sat there chattering and clinging to his neck with a weird little skinny arm.

Ram Dass thanked Sara profoundly. She had seen that his quick native eyes had taken in at a glance all the bare shabbiness of the room, but he spoke to her as if he were speaking to the little daughter of a rajah, and pretended that he observed nothing. He did not presume to remain more than a few moments after he had caught the monkey, and those moments were given to further deep and grateful obeisance to her in return for her indulgence. This little evil one, he said, stroking the monkey, was, in truth, not so evil as he seemed, and his master, who was ill, was sometimes amused by him. He would have been made sad if his favorite had run away and been lost. Then he salaamed once more and got through the skylight and across the slates again with as much agility as the monkey himself had displayed.

When he had gone Sara stood in the middle of her attic and thought of many things his face and his manner had brought back to her. The sight of his native costume and the profound reverence of his manner stirred all her past memories. It seemed a strange thing to remember that she—the drudge whom the cook had said insulting things to an hour ago—had only a few years ago been surrounded by people who all treated her as Ram Dass had treated her; who salaamed when she went by, whose foreheads almost touched the ground when she spoke to them, who were her servants and her slaves. It was like a sort of dream. It was all over, and it could never come back. It certainly seemed that there was no way in which any change could take place. She knew what Miss Minchin intended that her future should be. So long as she was too young to be used as a regular teacher, she would be used as an errand girl and servant and yet expected to remember what she had learned and in some mysterious way to learn more. The greater number of her evenings she was supposed to spend at study, and at various indefinite intervals she was examined and knew she would have been severely admonished if she had not advanced as was expected of her. The truth, indeed, was that Miss Minchin knew that she was too anxious to learn to require teachers. Give her books, and she would devour them and end by knowing them by heart. She might be trusted to be equal to teaching a good deal in the course of a few years. This was what would happen: when she was older she would be expected to drudge in the school-room as she drudged now in various parts of the house; they would be obliged to give her more respectable clothes, but they would be sure to be plain and ugly and to make her look somehow like a servant. That was all there seemed to be to look forward to, and Sara stood quite still for several minutes and thought it over.

Then a thought came back to her which made the color rise in her cheek and a spark light itself in her eyes. She straightened her thin little body and lifted her head.

"Whatever comes," she said, "cannot alter one thing. If I am a princess in rags and tatters, I can be a princess inside. It would be easy to be a princess if I were dressed in cloth of gold, but it is a great deal more of a triumph to be one all the time when no one knows it. There was Marie Antoinette when she was in prison and her throne was gone and she had only a black gown on, and her hair was white, and they insulted her and called her Widow Capet. She was a great deal more like a queen then than when she was so gay and everything was so grand. I like her best then. Those howling mobs of people did not frighten her. She was stronger than they were, even when they cut her head off."

This was not a new thought, but quite an old one, by this time. It had consoled her through many a bitter day, and she had gone about the house with an expression on her face which Miss Minchin could not understand and which was a source of great annoyance to her, as it seemed as if the child were mentally living a life which held her above the rest of the world. It was as if she scarcely heard the rude and acid things said to her; or, if she heard them, did not care for them at all. Sometimes, when she was in the midst of some harsh, domineering speech, Miss Minchin would find the still, unchildish eyes fixed upon her with something like a proud smile in them. At such times she did not know that Sara was saying to herself:

"You don't know that you are saying these things to a princess, and that if I chose I could wave my hand and order you to execution. I only spare you because I am a princess, and you are a poor, stupid, unkind, vulgar old thing, and don't know any better."

This used to interest and amuse her more than anything else; and queer and fanciful as it was, she found comfort in it and it was a good thing for her. While the thought held possession of her, she could not be made rude and malicious by the rudeness and malice of those about her.

"A princess must be polite," she said to herself.

And so when the servants, taking their tone from their mistress, were insolent and ordered her about, she would hold her head erect and reply to them with a quaint civility which often made them stare at her.

"She's got more airs and graces than if she come from Buckingham Palace, that young one," said the cook, chuckling a little sometimes; "I lose my temper with her often enough, but I will say she never forgets her manners. 'If you please, cook'; 'Will you be so kind, cook?' 'I beg your pardon, cook'; 'May I trouble you, cook?' She drops 'em about the kitchen as if they was nothing."

The morning after the interview with Ram Dass and his monkey, Sara was in the school-room with her small pupils. Having finished giving them their lessons, she was putting the French exercise-books together and thinking, as she did it, of the various things royal personages in disguise were called upon to do: Alfred the Great, for instance, burning the cakes and getting his ears boxed by the wife of the neatherd. How frightened she must have been when she found out what she had done. If Miss Minchin should find out that she—Sara, whose toes were almost sticking out of her boots—was a princess—a real one! The look in her eyes was exactly the look which Miss Minchin most disliked. She would not have it; she was quite near her and was so enraged that she actually flew at her and boxed her ears—exactly as the neatherd's wife had boxed King Alfred's. It made Sara start. She wakened from her dream at the shock, and, catching her breath, stood still a second. Then, not knowing she was going to do it, she broke into a little laugh.

"What are you laughing at, you bold, impudent child?" Miss Minchin exclaimed.

It took Sara a few seconds to control herself sufficiently to remember that she was a princess. Her cheeks were red and smarting from the blows she had received.

"I was thinking," she answered.

"Beg my pardon immediately," said Miss Minchin.

Sara hesitated a second before she replied.

"I will beg your pardon for laughing, if it was rude," she said then; "but I won't beg your pardon for thinking."

"What were you thinking?" demanded Miss Minchin. "How dare you think? What were you thinking?"

Jessie tittered, and she and Lavinia nudged each other in unison. All the girls looked up from their books to listen. Really, it always interested them a little when Miss Minchin attacked Sara. Sara always said something queer, and never seemed the least bit frightened. She was not in the least frightened now, though her boxed ears were scarlet and her eyes were as bright as stars.

"I was thinking," she answered grandly and politely, "that you did not know what you were doing."

"That I did not know what I was doing?" Miss Minchin fairly gasped.

"Yes," said Sara, "and I was thinking what would happen if I were a princess and you boxed my ears—what I should do to you. And I was thinking that if I were one, you would never dare to do it, whatever I said or did. And I was thinking how surprised and frightened you would be if you suddenly found out—"

She had the imagined future so clearly before her eyes that she spoke in a manner which had an effect even upon Miss Minchin. It almost seemed for the moment to her narrow, unimaginative mind that there must be some real power hidden behind this candid daring.

"What?" she exclaimed. "Found out what?"

"That I really was a princess," said Sara, "and could do anything—anything I liked."

Every pair of eyes in the room widened to its full limit. Lavinia leaned forward on her seat to look.

"Go to your room," cried Miss Minchin, breathlessly, "this instant! Leave the school-room! Attend to your lessons, young ladies!"

Sara made a little bow.

"Excuse me for laughing if it was impolite," she said, and walked out of the room, leaving Miss Minchin struggling with her rage, and the girls whispering over their books.

"Did you see her? Did you see how queer she looked?" Jessie broke out. "I shouldn't be at all surprised if she did turn out to be something. Suppose she should!"

Day 113

1. Read chapter 12 of *A Little Princess*.
2. Tell someone what happened in the chapter.

THE OTHER SIDE OF THE WALL

WHEN one lives in a row of houses, it is interesting to think of the things which are being done and said on the other side of the wall of the very rooms one is living in. Sara was fond of amusing herself by trying to imagine the things hidden by the wall which divided the Select Seminary from the Indian gentleman's house. She knew that the school-room was next to the Indian gentleman's study, and she hoped that the wall was thick so that the noise made sometimes after lesson hours would not disturb him.

"I am growing quite fond of him," she said to Ermengarde; "I should not like him to be disturbed. I have adopted him for a friend. You can do that with people you never speak to at all. You can just watch them, and think about them and be sorry for them, until they seem almost like relations. I'm quite anxious sometimes when I see the doctor call twice a day."

"I have very few relations," said Ermengarde, reflectively, "and I'm very glad of it. I don't like those I have. My two aunts are always saying, 'Dear me, Ermengarde! You are very fat. You shouldn't eat sweets,' and my uncle is always asking me things like, 'When did Edward the Third ascend the throne?' and, 'Who died of a surfeit of lampreys?' "

Sara laughed.

"People you never speak to can't ask you questions like that," she said; "and I'm sure the Indian gentleman wouldn't even if he was quite intimate with you. I am fond of him."

She had become fond of the Large Family because they looked happy; but she had become fond of the Indian gentleman because he looked unhappy. He had evidently not fully recovered from some very severe illness. In the kitchen—where, of course, the servants, through some mysterious means, knew everything—there was much discussion of his case. He was not an Indian gentleman really, but an Englishman who had lived in India. He had met with great misfortunes which had for a time so imperilled his whole fortune that he had thought himself ruined and disgraced forever. The shock had been so great that he had almost died of brain-fever; and ever since he had been shattered in health, though his fortunes had changed and all his possessions had been restored to him. His trouble and peril had been connected with mines.

"And mines with diamonds in 'em!" said the cook. "No savin's of mine never goes into no mines—particular diamond ones"—with a side glance at Sara. "We all know somethin' of them."

"He felt as my papa felt," Sara thought. "He was ill as my papa was; but he did not die."

So her heart was more drawn to him than before. When she was sent out at night she used sometimes to feel quite glad, because there was always a chance that the curtains of the house next door might not yet be closed and she could look into the warm room and see her adopted friend. When no one was about she used sometimes to stop, and, holding to the iron railings, wish him good night as if he could hear her.

"Perhaps you can feel if you can't hear," was her fancy. "Perhaps kind thoughts reach people somehow, even through windows and doors and walls. Perhaps you feel a little warm and comforted, and don't know why, when I am standing here in the cold and hoping you will get well and happy again. I am so sorry for you," she would whisper in an intense little voice. "I wish you had a 'little missus' who could pet you as I used to pet papa when he had a headache. I should like to be your 'little missus' myself, poor dear! Good night—good night. God bless you!"

She would go away, feeling quite comforted and a little warmer herself. Her sympathy was so strong that it seemed as if it must reach him somehow as he sat alone in his armchair by the fire, nearly always in a great dressing-gown, and nearly always with his forehead resting in his hand as he gazed hopelessly into the fire. He looked to Sara like a man who had a trouble on his mind still, not merely like one whose troubles lay all in the past.

"He always seems as if he were thinking of something that hurts him now," she said to herself, "but he has got his money back and he will get over his brain-fever in time, so he ought not to look like that. I wonder if there is something else."

If there was something else—something even servants did not hear of—she could not help believing that the father of the Large Family knew it—the gentleman she called Mr. Montmorency. Mr. Montmorency went to see him often, and Mrs. Montmorency and all the little Montmorencys went, too, though less often. He seemed particularly fond of the two elder little girls—the Janet and Nora who had been so alarmed when their small brother Donald had given Sara his sixpence. He had, in fact, a very tender place in his heart for all children, and particularly for little girls. Janet and Nora were as fond of him as he was of them, and looked forward with the greatest pleasure to the afternoons when they were allowed to cross the square and make their well-behaved little visits to him. They were extremely decorous little visits because he was an invalid.

"He is a poor thing," said Janet, "and he says we cheer him up. We try to cheer him up very quietly."

Janet was the head of the family, and kept the rest of it in order. It was she who decided when it was discreet to ask the Indian gentleman to tell stories about India, and it was she who saw when he was tired and it was the time to steal quietly away and tell Ram Dass to go to him. They were very fond of Ram Dass. He could have told any number of stories if he had been able to speak anything but Hindustani. The Indian gentleman's real name was Mr. Carrisford, and Janet told Mr. Carrisford about the encounter with the little-girl-who-was-not-a-beggar. He was very much interested, and all the more so when he heard from Ram Dass of the adventure of the monkey on the roof. Ram Dass made for him a very clear picture of the attic and its desolateness—of the bare floor and broken plaster, the rusty, empty grate, and the hard, narrow bed.

"Carmichael," he said to the father of the Large Family, after he had heard this description, "I wonder how many of the attics in this square are like that one, and how many wretched little servant girls sleep on such beds, while I toss on my down pillows, loaded and harassed by wealth that is, most of it—not mine."

"My dear fellow," Mr. Carmichael answered cheerily, "the sooner you cease tormenting yourself the better it will be for you. If you possessed all the wealth of all the Indies, you could not set right all the discomforts in the world, and if you began to refurnish all the attics in this square, there would still remain all the attics in all the other squares and streets to put in order. And there you are!"

Mr. Carrisford sat and bit his nails as he looked into the glowing bed of coals in the grate.

"Do you suppose," he said slowly, after a pause—"do you think it is possible that the other child—the child I never cease thinking of, I believe—could be—could possibly be reduced to any such condition as the poor little soul next door?"

Mr. Carmichael looked at him uneasily. He knew that the worst thing the man could do for himself, for his reason and his health, was to begin to think in the particular way of this particular subject.

"If the child at Madame Pascal's school in Paris was the one you are in search of," he answered soothingly, "she would seem to be in the hands of people who can afford to take care of her. They adopted her because she had been the favorite companion of their little daughter who died. They had no other children, and Madame Pascal said that they were extremely well-to-do Russians."

"And the wretched woman actually did not know where they had taken her!" exclaimed Mr. Carrisford.

Mr. Carmichael shrugged his shoulders. "She was a shrewd, worldly Frenchwoman, and was evidently only too glad to get the child so comfortably off her hands when the father's death left her totally unprovided for. Women of her type do not trouble themselves about the futures of children who might prove burdens. The adopted parents apparently disappeared and left no trace."

"But you say 'if' the child was the one I am in search of. You say 'if.' We are not sure. There was a difference in the name."

"Madame Pascal pronounced it as if it were Carew instead of Crewe—but that might be merely a matter of pronunciation. The circumstances were curiously similar. An English officer in India had placed his motherless little girl at the school. He had died suddenly after losing his fortune." Mr. Carmichael paused a moment, as if a new thought had occurred to him. "Are you sure the child was left at a school in Paris? Are you sure it was Paris?"

"My dear fellow," broke forth Carrisford, with restless bitterness, "I am sure of nothing. I never saw either the child or her mother. Ralph Crewe and I loved each other as boys, but we had not met since our school-days, until we met in India. I was absorbed in the magnificent promise of the mines. He became absorbed, too. The whole thing was so huge and glittering that we half lost our heads. When we met we scarcely spoke of anything else. I only knew that the child had been sent to school somewhere. I do not even remember, now, how I knew it."

He was beginning to be excited. He always became excited when his still weakened brain was stirred by memories of the catastrophes of the past.

Mr. Carmichael watched him anxiously. It was necessary to ask some questions, but they must be put quietly and with caution.

"But you had reason to think the school was in Paris?"

"Yes," was the answer, "because her mother was a Frenchwoman, and I had heard that she wished her child to be educated in Paris. It seemed only likely that she would be there."

"Yes," Mr. Carmichael said, "it seems more than probable."

The Indian gentleman leaned forward and struck the table with a long, wasted hand.

"Carmichael," he said, "I must find her. If she is alive, she is somewhere. If she is friendless and penniless, it is through my fault. How is a man to get back his nerve with a thing like that on his mind? This sudden change of luck at the mines has made realities of all our most fantastic dreams, and poor Crewe's child may be begging in the street!"

"No, no," said Carmichael. "Try to be calm. Console yourself with the fact that when she is found you have a fortune to hand over to her."

"Why was I not man enough to stand my ground when things looked black?" Carrisford groaned in petulant misery. "I believe I should have stood my ground if I had not been responsible for other people's money as well as my own. Poor Crewe had put into the scheme every penny that he owned. He trusted me—he loved me. And he died thinking I had ruined him—I—Tom Carrisford, who played cricket at Eton with him. What a villain he must have thought me!"

"Don't reproach yourself so bitterly."

"I don't reproach myself because the speculation threatened to fail—I reproach myself for losing my courage. I ran away like a swindler and a thief, because I could not face my best friend and tell him I had ruined him and his child."

The good-hearted father of the Large Family put his hand on his shoulder comfortingly.

"You ran away because your brain had given way under the strain of mental torture," he said. "You were half delirious already. If you had not been you would have stayed and fought it out. You were in a hospital, strapped down in bed, raving with brain-fever, two days after you left the place. Remember that."

Carrisford dropped his forehead in his hands.

"Good God! Yes," he said. "I was driven mad with dread and horror. I had not slept for weeks. The night I staggered out of my house all the air seemed full of hideous things mocking and mouthing at me."

"That is explanation enough in itself," said Mr. Carmichael. "How could a man on the verge of brain-fever judge sanely!"

Carrisford shook his drooping head.

"And when I returned to consciousness poor Crewe was dead—and buried. And I seemed to remember nothing. I did not remember the child for months and months. Even when I began to recall her existence everything seemed in a sort of haze."

He stopped a moment and rubbed his forehead. "It sometimes seems so now when I try to remember. Surely I must sometime have heard Crewe speak of the school she was sent to. Don't you think so?"

"He might not have spoken of it definitely. You never seem even to have heard her real name."

"He used to call her by an odd pet name he had invented. He called her his 'little missus.' But the wretched mines drove everything else out of our heads. We talked of nothing else. If he spoke of the school, I forgot—I forgot. And now I shall never remember."

"Come, come," said Carmichael. "We shall find her yet. We will continue to search for Madame Pascal's good-natured Russians. She seemed to have a vague idea that they lived in Moscow. We will take that as a clue. I will go to Moscow."

"If I were able to travel, I would go with you," said Carrisford; "but I can only sit here wrapped in furs and stare at the fire. And when I look into it I seem to see Crewe's gay young face gazing back at me. He looks as if he were asking me a question. Sometimes I dream of him at night, and he always stands before me and asks the same question in words. Can you guess what he says, Carmichael?"

Mr. Carmichael answered him in a rather low voice.

"Not exactly," he said.

"He always says, 'Tom, old man—Tom—where is the little missus?' "He caught at Carmichael's hand and clung to it. "I must be able to answer him—I must!" he said. "Help me to find her. Help me."

*   *   *   *   *   *

On the other side of the wall Sara was sitting in her garret talking to Melchisedec, who had come out for his evening meal.

"It has been hard to be a princess to-day, Melchisedec," she said. "It has been harder than usual. It gets harder as the weather grows colder and the streets get more sloppy. When Lavinia laughed at my muddy skirt as I passed her in the hall, I thought of something to say all in a flash—and I only just stopped myself in time. You can't sneer back at people like that—if you are a princess. But you have to bite your tongue to hold yourself in. I bit mine. It was a cold afternoon, Melchisedec. And it's a cold night."

Quite suddenly she put her black head down in her arms, as she often did when she was alone.

"Oh, papa," she whispered, "what a long time it seems since I was your 'little missus'!"

This was what happened that day on both sides of the wall.

Day 114

1. Read chapter 13 of *A Little Princess*.
2. Tell someone what happened in this chapter.

ONE OF THE POPULACE

THE winter was a wretched one. There were days on which Sara tramped through snow when she went on her errands; there were worse days when the snow melted and combined itself with mud to form slush; there were others when the fog was so thick that the lamps in the street were lighted all day and London looked as it had looked the afternoon, several years ago, when the cab had driven through the thoroughfares with Sara tucked up on its seat, leaning against her father's shoulder. On such days the windows of the house of the Large Family always looked delightfully cozy and alluring, and the study in which the Indian gentleman sat glowed with warmth and rich color. But the attic was dismal beyond words. There were no longer sunsets or sunrises to look at, and scarcely ever any stars, it seemed to Sara. The clouds hung low over the skylight and were either gray or mud-color, or dropping heavy rain. At four o'clock in the afternoon, even when there was no special fog, the daylight was at an end. If it was necessary to go to her attic for anything, Sara was obliged to light a candle. The women in the kitchen were depressed, and that made them more ill-tempered than ever. Becky was driven like a little slave.

"'Twarn't for you, miss," she said hoarsely to Sara one night when she had crept into the attic—" 'twarn't for you, an' the Bastille, an' bein' the prisoner in the next cell, I should die. That there does seem real now, doesn't it? The missus is more like the head jailer every day she lives. I can jest see them big keys you say she carries. The cook she's like one of the under-jailers. Tell me some more, please, miss—tell me about the subt'ranean passage we've dug under the walls."

"I'll tell you something warmer," shivered Sara. "Get your coverlet and wrap it round you, and I'll get mine, and we will huddle close together on the bed, and I'll tell you about the tropical forest where the Indian gentleman's monkey used to live. When I see him sitting on the table near the window and looking out into the street with that mournful expression, I always feel sure he is thinking about the tropical forest where he used to swing by his tail from cocoanut trees. I wonder who caught him, and if he left a family behind who had depended on him for cocoanuts."

"That is warmer, miss," said Becky, gratefully; "but, someways, even the Bastille is sort of heatin' when you gets to tellin' about it."

"That is because it makes you think of something else," said Sara, wrapping the coverlet round her until only her small dark face was to be seen looking out of it. "I've noticed this. What you have to do with your mind, when your body is miserable, is to make it think of something else."

"Can you do it, miss?" faltered Becky, regarding her with admiring eyes.

Sara knitted her brows a moment.

"Sometimes I can and sometimes I can't," she said stoutly. "But when I can I'm all right. And what I believe is that we always could—if we practised enough. I've been practising a good deal lately, and it's beginning to be easier than it used to be. When things are horrible—just horrible—I think as hard as ever I can of being a princess. I say to myself, 'I am a princess, and I am a fairy one, and because I am a fairy nothing can hurt me or make me uncomfortable.' You don't know how it makes you forget"—with a laugh.

She had many opportunities of making her mind think of something else, and many opportunities of proving to herself whether or not she was a princess. But one of the strongest tests she was ever put to came on a certain dreadful day which, she often thought afterward, would never quite fade out of her memory even in the years to come.

For several days it had rained continuously; the streets were chilly and sloppy and full of dreary, cold mist; there was mud everywhere—sticky London mud—and over everything the pall of drizzle and fog. Of course there were several long and tiresome errands to be done—there always were on days like this—and Sara was sent out again and again, until her shabby clothes were damp through. The absurd old feathers on her forlorn hat were more draggled and absurd than ever, and her downtrodden shoes were so wet that they could not hold any more water. Added to this, she had been deprived of her dinner, because Miss Minchin had chosen to punish her. She was so cold and hungry and tired that her face began to have a pinched look, and now and then some kind-hearted person passing her in the street glanced at her with sudden sympathy. But she did not know that. She hurried on, trying to make her mind think of something else. It was really very necessary. Her way of doing it was to "pretend" and "suppose" with all the strength that was left in her. But really this time it was harder than she had ever found it, and once or twice she thought it almost made her more cold and hungry instead of less so. But she persevered obstinately, and as the muddy water squelched through her broken shoes and the wind seemed trying to drag her thin jacket from her, she talked to herself as she walked, though she did not speak aloud or even move her lips.

"Suppose I had dry clothes on," she thought. "Suppose I had good shoes and a long, thick coat and merino stockings and a whole umbrella. And suppose—suppose—just when I was near a baker's where they sold hot buns, I should find sixpence—which belonged to nobody. Suppose if I did, I should go into the shop and buy six of the hottest buns and eat them all without stopping."

Some very odd things happen in this world sometimes.

It certainly was an odd thing that happened to Sara. She had to cross the street just when she was saying this to herself. The mud was dreadful—she almost had to wade. She picked her way as carefully as she could, but she could not save herself much; only, in picking her way, she had to look down at her feet and the mud, and in looking down—just as she reached the pavement—she saw something shining in the gutter. It was actually a piece of silver—a tiny piece trodden upon by many feet, but still with spirit enough left to shine a little. Not quite a sixpence, but the next thing to it—a fourpenny piece.

In one second it was in her cold little red-and-blue hand.

"Oh," she gasped, "it is true! It is true!"

And then, if you will believe me, she looked straight at the shop directly facing her. And it was a baker's shop, and a cheerful, stout, motherly woman with rosy cheeks was putting into the window a tray of delicious newly baked hot buns, fresh from the oven—large, plump, shiny buns, with currants in them.

It almost made Sara feel faint for a few seconds—the shock, and the sight of the buns, and the delightful odors of warm bread floating up through the baker's cellar window.

She knew she need not hesitate to use the little piece of money. It had evidently been lying in the mud for some time, and its owner was completely lost in the stream of passing people who crowded and jostled each other all day long.

"But I'll go and ask the baker woman if she has lost anything," she said to herself, rather faintly. So she crossed the pavement and put her wet foot on the step. As she did so she saw something that made her stop.

It was a little figure more forlorn even than herself—a little figure which was not much more than a bundle of rags, from which small, bare, red muddy feet peeped out, only because the rags with which their owner was trying to cover them were not long enough. Above the rags appeared a shock head of tangled hair, and a dirty face with big, hollow, hungry eyes.

Sara knew they were hungry eyes the moment she saw them, and she felt a sudden sympathy.

"This," she said to herself, with a little sigh, "is one of the populace—and she is hungrier than I am."

The child—this "one of the populace"—stared up at Sara, and shuffled herself aside a little, so as to give her room to pass. She was used to being made to give room to everybody. She knew that if a policeman chanced to see her he would tell her to "move on."

Sara clutched her little fourpenny piece and hesitated for a few seconds. Then she spoke to her.

"Are you hungry?" she asked.

The child shuffled herself and her rags a little more.

"Ain't I jist?" she said in a hoarse voice. "Jist ain't I?"

"Haven't you had any dinner?" said Sara.

"No dinner,"—more hoarsely still and with more shuffling. "Nor yet no bre'fast—nor yet no supper. No nothin'."

"Since when?" asked Sara.

"Dunno. Never got nothin' today—nowhere. I've axed an' axed."

Just to look at her made Sara more hungry and faint. But those queer little thoughts were at work in her brain, and she was talking to herself, though she was sick at heart.

"If I'm a princess," she was saying—"if I'm a princess—when they were poor and driven from their thrones—they always shared—with the populace—if they met one poorer and hungrier than themselves. They always shared. Buns are a penny each. If it had been sixpence I could have eaten six. It won't be enough for either of us. But it will be better than nothing."

"Wait a minute," she said to the beggar child.

She went into the shop. It was warm and smelled deliciously. The woman was just going to put some more hot buns into the window.

"If you please," said Sara, "have you lost fourpence—a silver fourpence?" And she held the forlorn little piece of money out to her.

The woman looked at it and then at her—at her intense little face and draggled, once fine clothes.

"Bless us! no," she answered. "Did you find it?"

"Yes," said Sara. "In the gutter."

"Keep it, then," said the woman. "It may have been there for a week, and goodness knows who lost it. You could never find out."

"I know that," said Sara, "but I thought I would ask you."

"Not many would," said the woman, looking puzzled and interested and good-natured all at once.

"Do you want to buy something?" she added, as she saw Sara glance at the buns.

"Four buns, if you please," said Sara. "Those at a penny each."

The woman went to the window and put some in a paper bag.

Sara noticed that she put in six.

"I said four, if you please," she explained. "I have only fourpence."

"I'll throw in two for makeweight," said the woman with her good-natured look. "I dare say you can eat them sometime. Aren't you hungry?"

A mist rose before Sara's eyes.

"Yes," she answered. "I am very hungry, and I am much obliged to you for your kindness; and"—she was going to add—"there is a child outside who is hungrier than I am." But just at that moment two or three customers came in at once, and each one seemed in a hurry, so she could only thank the woman again and go out.

The beggar girl was still huddled up in the corner of the step. She looked frightful in her wet and dirty rags. She was staring straight before her with a stupid look of suffering, and Sara saw her suddenly draw the back of her roughened black hand across her eyes to rub away the tears which seemed to have surprised her by forcing their way from under her lids. She was muttering to herself.

Sara opened the paper bag and took out one of the hot buns, which had already warmed her own cold hands a little.

"See," she said, putting the bun in the ragged lap, "this is nice and hot. Eat it, and you will not feel so hungry."

The child started and stared up at her, as if such sudden, amazing good luck almost frightened her; then she snatched up the bun and began to cram it into her mouth with great wolfish bites.

"Oh, my! Oh, my!" Sara heard her say hoarsely, in wild delight. "Oh my!"

Sara took out three more buns and put them down.

The sound in the hoarse, ravenous voice was awful.

"She is hungrier than I am," she said to herself. "She's starving." But her hand trembled when she put down the fourth bun. "I'm not starving," she said—and she put down the fifth.

The little ravening London savage was still snatching and devouring when she turned away. She was too ravenous to give any thanks, even if she had ever been taught politeness— which she had not. She was only a poor little wild animal.

"Good-bye," said Sara.

When she reached the other side of the street she looked back. The child had a bun in each hand and had stopped in the middle of a bite to watch her. Sara gave her a little nod, and the child, after another stare—a curious lingering stare—jerked her shaggy head in response, and until Sara was out of sight she did not take another bite or even finish the one she had begun.

At that moment the baker-woman looked out of her shop window.

"Well, I never!" she exclaimed. "If that young un hasn't given her buns to a beggar child! It wasn't because she didn't want them, either. Well, well, she looked hungry enough. I'd give something to know what she did it for."

She stood behind her window for a few moments and pondered. Then her curiosity got the better of her. She went to the door and spoke to the beggar child.

"Who gave you those buns?" she asked her. The child nodded her head toward Sara's vanishing figure.

"What did she say?" inquired the woman.

"Axed me if I was 'ungry," replied the hoarse voice.

"What did you say?"

"Said I was jist."

"And then she came in and got the buns, and gave them to you, did she?"

The child nodded.

"How many?"

"Five."

The woman thought it over.

"Left just one for herself," she said in a low voice. "And she could have eaten the whole six—I saw it in her eyes."

She looked after the little draggled far-away figure and felt more disturbed in her usually comfortable mind than she had felt for many a day.

"I wish she hadn't gone so quick," she said. "I'm blest if she shouldn't have had a dozen." Then she turned to the child.

"Are you hungry yet?" she said.

"I'm allus hungry," was the answer, "but 't ain't as bad as it was."

"Come in here," said the woman, and she held open the shop door.

The child got up and shuffled in. To be invited into a warm place full of bread seemed an incredible thing. She did not know what was going to happen. She did not care, even.

"Get yourself warm," said the woman, pointing to a fire in the tiny back room. "And look here; when you are hard up for a bit of bread, you can come in here and ask for it. I'm blest if I won't give it to you for that young one's sake."

*　*　*　*　*　*

Sara found some comfort in her remaining bun. At all events, it was very hot, and it was better than nothing. As she walked along she broke off small pieces and ate them slowly to make them last longer.

"Suppose it was a magic bun," she said, "and a bite was as much as a whole dinner. I should be overeating myself if I went on like this."

It was dark when she reached the square where the Select Seminary was situated. The lights in the houses were all lighted. The blinds were not yet drawn in the windows of the room where she nearly always caught glimpses of members of the Large Family. Frequently at this hour she could see the gentleman she called Mr. Montmorency sitting in a big chair, with a small swarm round him, talking, laughing, perching on the arms of his seat or on his knees or leaning against them. This evening the swarm was about him, but he was not seated. On the contrary, there was a good deal of excitement going on. It was evident that a journey was to be taken, and it was Mr. Montmorency who was to take it. A brougham stood before the door, and a big portmanteau had been strapped upon it. The children were dancing about, chattering and hanging on to their father. The pretty rosy mother was standing near him, talking as if she was asking final questions. Sara paused a moment to see the little ones lifted up and kissed and the bigger ones bent over and kissed also.

"I wonder if he will stay away long," she thought. "The portmanteau is rather big. Oh, dear, how they will miss him! I shall miss him myself—even though he doesn't know I am alive."

When the door opened she moved away—remembering the sixpence—but she saw the traveller come out and stand against the background of the warmly-lighted hall, the older children still hovering about him.

"Will Moscow be covered with snow?" said the little girl Janet. "Will there be ice everywhere?"

"Shall you drive in a drosky?" cried another. "Shall you see the Czar?"

"I will write and tell you all about it," he answered, laughing. "And I will send you pictures of muzhiks and things. Run into the house. It is a hideous damp night. I would rather stay with you than go to Moscow. Good night! Good night, duckies! God bless you!" And he ran down the steps and jumped into the brougham.

"If you find the little girl, give her our love," shouted Guy Clarence, jumping up and down on the door mat.

Then they went in and shut the door.

"Did you see," said Janet to Nora, as they went back to the room—"the little-girl-who-is-not-a-beggar was passing? She looked all cold and wet, and I saw her turn her head over her shoulder and look at us. Mamma says her clothes always look as if they had been given her by someone who was quite rich—someone who only let her have them because they were too shabby to wear. The people at the school always send her out on errands on the horridest days and nights there are."

Sara crossed the square to Miss Minchin's area steps, feeling faint and shaky.

"I wonder who the little girl is," she thought—"the little girl he is going to look for."

And she went down the area steps, lugging her basket and finding it very heavy indeed, as the father of the Large Family drove quickly on his way to the station to take the train which was to carry him to Moscow, where he was to make his best efforts to search for the lost little daughter of Captain Crewe.

Day 115

1.   Read chapter 14 of *A Little Princess*.
2.   Tell someone what happened in the chapter.
Vocabulary

1.   Read these sentences from the chapter with your vocabulary words in bold. What do you think is happening? What do you think the words means?
   - He stopped to listen with a **palpitating** heart.
   - He only knew that the men were invading the silence and privacy of the attic; and as the one with the dark face let himself down through the **aperture** with such lightness and **dexterity** that he did not make the slightest sound, Melchisedec turned tail and fled **precipitately** back to his hole.
   - Melchisedec had, in fact, found it rather dull; and when the rain ceased to patter and perfect silence reigned, he decided to come out and **reconnoiter**, though experience taught him that Sara would not return for some time.
2.   After you have made your guesses, read their definitions. (Answers)

WHAT MELCHISEDEC HEARD AND SAW

ON this very afternoon, while Sara was out, a strange thing happened in the attic. Only Melchisedec saw and heard it; and he was so much alarmed and mystified that he scuttled back to his hole and hid there, and really quaked and trembled as he peeped out furtively and with great caution to watch what was going on.

The attic had been very still all the day after Sara had left it in the early morning. The stillness had only been broken by the pattering of the rain upon the slates and the skylight. Melchisedec had, in fact, found it rather dull; and when the rain ceased to patter and perfect silence reigned, he decided to come out and reconnoiter, though experience taught him that Sara would not return for some time. He had been rambling and sniffing about, and had just found a totally unexpected and unexplained crumb left from his last meal, when his attention was attracted by a sound on the roof. He stopped to listen with a palpitating heart. The sound suggested that something was moving on the roof. It was approaching the skylight; it reached the skylight. The skylight was being mysteriously opened. A dark face peered into the attic; then another face appeared behind it, and both looked in with signs of caution and interest. Two men were outside on the roof, and were making silent preparations to enter through the skylight itself. One was Ram Dass and the other was a young man who was the Indian gentleman's secretary; but of course Melchisedec did not know this. He only knew that the men were invading the silence and privacy of the attic; and as the one with the dark face let himself down through the aperture with such lightness and dexterity that he did not make the slightest sound, Melchisedec turned tail and fled precipitately back to his hole. He was frightened to death. He had ceased to be timid with Sara, and knew she would never throw anything but crumbs, and would never make any sound other than the soft, low, coaxing whistling; but strange men were dangerous things to remain near. He lay close and flat near the entrance of his home, just managing to peep through the crack with a bright, alarmed eye. How much he understood of the talk he heard I am not in the least able to say; but, even if he had understood it all, he would probably have remained greatly mystified.

The secretary, who was light and young, slipped through the skylight as noiselessly as Ram Dass had done; and he caught a last glimpse of Melchisedec's vanishing tail.

"Was that a rat?" he asked Ram Dass, in a whisper.

"Yes; a rat, Sahib," answered Ram Dass, also whispering. "There are many in the walls."

"Ugh!" exclaimed the young man. "It is a wonder the child is not terrified of them."

Ram Dass made a gesture with his hands. He also smiled respectfully. He was in his place as the intimate exponent of Sara, though she had only spoken to him once.

"The child is the little friend of all things, Sahib," he answered. "She is not as other children. I see her when she does not see me. I slip across the slates and look at her many nights to see that she is safe. I watch her from my window when she does not know I am near. She stands on the table there and looks out at the sky as if it spoke to her. The sparrows come at her call. The rat she has fed and tamed in her loneliness. The poor slave of the house comes to her for comfort. There is a little child who comes to her in secret; there is one older who worships her and would listen to her forever if she might. This I have seen when I have crept across the roof. By the mistress of the house—who is an evil woman—she is treated like a pariah; but she has the bearing of a child who is of the blood of kings!"

"You seem to know a great deal about her," the secretary said.

"All her life each day I know," answered Ram Dass. "Her going out I know, and her coming in; her sadness and her poor joys; her coldness and her hunger. I know when she is alone until midnight, learning from her books; I know when her secret friends steal to her and she is happier—as children can be, even in the midst of poverty—because they come and she may laugh and talk with them in whispers. If she were ill I should know, and I would come and serve her if it might be done."

"You are sure no one comes near this place but herself, and that she will not return and surprise us. She would be frightened if she found us here, and the Sahib Carrisford's plan would be spoiled."

Ram Dass crossed noiselessly to the door and stood close to it.

"None mount here but herself, Sahib," he said. "She has gone out with her basket and may be gone for hours. If I stand here I can hear any step before it reaches the last flight of the stairs."

The secretary took a pencil and a tablet from his breast pocket.

"Keep your ears open," he said; and he began to walk slowly and softly round the miserable little room, making rapid notes on his tablet as he looked at things.

First he went to the narrow bed. He pressed his hand upon the mattress and uttered an exclamation.

"As hard as a stone," he said. "That will have to be altered some day when she is out. A special journey can be made to bring it across. It cannot be done to-night." He lifted the covering and examined the one thin pillow.

"Coverlet dingy and worn, blanket thin, sheets patched and ragged," he said. "What a bed for a child to sleep in—and in a house which calls itself respectable! There has not been a fire in that grate for many a day," glancing at the rusty fireplace.

"Never since I have seen it," said Ram Dass. "The mistress of the house is not one who remembers that another than herself may be cold."

The secretary was writing quickly on his tablet. He looked up from it as he tore off a leaf and slipped it into his breast pocket.

"It is a strange way of doing the thing," he said. "Who planned it?"

Ram Dass made a modestly apologetic obeisance.

"It is true that the first thought was mine, Sahib," he said; "though it was naught but a fancy. I am fond of this child; we are both lonely. It is her way to relate her visions to her secret friends. Being sad one night, I lay close to the open skylight and listened. The vision she related told what this miserable room might be if it had comforts in it. She seemed to see it as she talked, and she grew cheered and warmed as she spoke. Then she came to this fancy; and the next day, the Sahib being ill and wretched, I told him of the thing to amuse him. It seemed then but a dream, but it pleased the Sahib. To hear of the child's doings gave him entertainment. He became interested in her and asked questions. At last he began to please himself with the thought of making her visions real things."

"You think that it can be done while she sleeps? Suppose she awakened," suggested the secretary; and it was evident that whatsoever the plan referred to was, it had caught and pleased his fancy as well as the Sahib Carrisford's.

"I can move as if my feet were of velvet," Ram Dass replied; "and children sleep soundly— even the unhappy ones. I could have entered this room in the night many times, and without causing her to turn upon her pillow. If the other bearer passes to me the things through the window, I can do all and she will not stir. When she awakens she will think a magician has been here."

He smiled as if his heart warmed under his white robe, and the secretary smiled back at him. "It will be like a story from the Arabian Nights," he said. "Only an Oriental could have planned it. It does not belong to London fogs."

They did not remain very long, to the great relief of Melchisedec, who, as he probably did not comprehend their conversation, felt their movements and whispers ominous. The young secretary seemed interested in everything. He wrote down things about the floor, the fireplace, the broken footstool, the old table, the walls—which last he touched with his hand again and again, seeming much pleased when he found that a number of old nails had been driven in various places.

"You can hang things on them," he said.

Ram Dass smiled mysteriously.

"Yesterday, when she was out," he said, "I entered, bringing with me small, sharp nails which can be pressed into the wall without blows from a hammer. I placed many in the plaster where I may need them. They are ready."

The Indian gentleman's secretary stood still and looked round him as he thrust his tablets back into his pocket.

"I think I have made notes enough; we can go now," he said. "The Sahib Carrisford has a warm heart. It is a thousand pities that he has not found the lost child."

"If he should find her his strength would be restored to him," said Ram Dass. "His God may lead her to him yet."

Then they slipped through the skylight as noiselessly as they had entered it. And, after he was quite sure they had gone, Melchisedec was greatly relieved, and in the course of a few minutes felt it safe to emerge from his hole again and scuffle about in the hope that even such alarming human beings as these might have chanced to carry crumbs in their pockets and drop one or two of them.

Day 116

1.   Read the first part of chapter 15 of *A Little Princess*.
2.   Tell someone what happened in the chapter.

THE MAGIC

WHEN Sara had passed the house next door she had seen Ram Dass closing the shutters, and caught her glimpse of this room also.

"It is a long time since I saw a nice place from the inside," was the thought which crossed her mind.

There was the usual bright fire glowing in the grate, and the Indian gentleman was sitting before it. His head was resting in his hand, and he looked as lonely and unhappy as ever.

"Poor man!" said Sara. "I wonder what you are supposing."

And this was what he was "supposing" at that very moment.

"Suppose," he was thinking, "suppose—even if Carmichael traces the people to Moscow—the little girl they took from Madame Pascal's school in Paris is not the one we are in search of. Suppose she proves to be quite a different child. What steps shall I take next?"

When Sara went into the house she met Miss Minchin, who had come downstairs to scold the cook.

"Where have you wasted your time?" she demanded. "You have been out for hours."

"It was so wet and muddy," Sara answered, "it was hard to walk, because my shoes were so bad and slipped about."

"Make no excuses," said Miss Minchin, "and tell no falsehoods."

Sara went in to the cook. The cook had received a severe lecture and was in a fearful temper as a result. She was only too rejoiced to have someone to vent her rage on, and Sara was a convenience, as usual.

"Why didn't you stay all night?" she snapped.

Sara laid her purchases on the table.

"Here are the things," she said.

The cook looked them over, grumbling. She was in a very savage humor indeed.

"May I have something to eat?" Sara asked rather faintly.

"Tea's over and done with," was the answer. "Did you expect me to keep it hot for you?"

Sara stood silent for a second.

"I had no dinner," she said next, and her voice was quite low. She made it low because she was afraid it would tremble.

"There's some bread in the pantry," said the cook. "That's all you'll get at this time of day."

Sara went and found the bread. It was old and hard and dry. The cook was in too vicious a humor to give her anything to eat with it. It was always safe and easy to vent her spite on Sara. Really, it was hard for the child to climb the three long flights of stairs leading to her attic. She often found them long and steep when she was tired; but to-night it seemed as if she would never reach the top. Several times she was obliged to stop to rest. When she reached the top landing she was glad to see the glimmer of a light coming from under her door. That meant that Ermengarde had managed to creep up to pay her a visit. There was some comfort in that. It was better than to go into the room alone and find it empty and desolate. The mere presence of plump, comfortable Ermengarde, wrapped in her red shawl, would warm it a little.

Yes; there Ermengarde was when she opened the door. She was sitting in the middle of the bed, with her feet tucked safely under her. She had never become intimate with Melchisedec and his family, though they rather fascinated her. When she found herself alone in the attic she always preferred to sit on the bed until Sara arrived. She had, in fact, on this occasion had time to become rather nervous, because Melchisedec had appeared and sniffed about a good deal, and once had made her utter a repressed squeal by sitting up on his hind legs and, while he looked at her, sniffing pointedly in her direction.

"Oh, Sara," she cried out, "I am glad you have come. Melchy would sniff about so. I tried to coax him to go back, but he wouldn't for such a long time. I like him, you know; but it does frighten me when he sniffs right at me. Do you think he ever would jump?"

"No," answered Sara.

Ermengarde crawled forward on the bed to look at her.

"You do look tired, Sara," she said; "you are quite pale."

"I am tired," said Sara, dropping on to the lopsided footstool. "Oh, there's Melchisedec, poor thing. He's come to ask for his supper."

Melchisedec had come out of his hole as if he had been listening for her footstep. Sara was quite sure he knew it. He came forward with an affectionate, expectant expression as Sara put her hand in her pocket and turned it inside out, shaking her head.

"I'm very sorry," she said. "I haven't one crumb left. Go home, Melchisedec, and tell your wife there was nothing in my pocket. I'm afraid I forgot because the cook and Miss Minchin were so cross."

Melchisedec seemed to understand. He shuffled resignedly, if not contentedly, back to his home.

"I did not expect to see you tonight, Ermie," Sara said.

Ermengarde hugged herself in the red shawl.

"Miss Amelia has gone out to spend the night with her old aunt," she explained. "No one else ever comes and looks into the bedrooms after we are in bed. I could stay here until morning if I wanted to."

She pointed toward the table under the skylight. Sara had not looked toward it as she came in. A number of books were piled upon it. Ermengarde's gesture was a dejected one.

"Papa has sent me some more books, Sara," she said. "There they are."

Sara looked round and got up at once. She ran to the table, and picking up the top volume, turned over its leaves quickly. For the moment she forgot her discomforts.

"Ah," she cried out, "how beautiful! Carlyle's 'French Revolution.' I have so wanted to read that!"

"I haven't," said Ermengarde. "And papa will be so cross if I don't. He'll expect me to know all about it when I go home for the holidays. What shall I do?"

Sara stopped turning over the leaves and looked at her with an excited flush on her cheeks.

"Look here," she cried, "if you'll lend me these books, I'll read them—and tell you everything that's in them afterward—and I'll tell it so that you will remember it, too."

"Oh, goodness!" exclaimed Ermengarde. "Do you think you can?"

"I know I can," Sara answered. "The little ones always remember what I tell them."

"Sara," said Ermengarde, hope gleaming in her round face, "if you'll do that, and make me remember, I'll—I'll give you anything."

"I don't want you to give me anything," said Sara. "I want your books—I want them!" And her eyes grew big, and her chest heaved.

"Take them, then," said Ermengarde. "I wish I wanted them—but I don't. I'm not clever, and my father is, and he thinks I ought to be."

Sara was opening one book after the other. "What are you going to tell your father?" she asked, a slight doubt dawning in her mind.

"Oh, he needn't know," answered Ermengarde. "He'll think I've read them."

Sara put down her book and shook her head slowly. "That's almost like telling lies," she said. "And lies—well, you see, they are not only wicked—they're vulgar. Sometimes"—

148

reflectively—"I've thought perhaps I might do something wicked—I might suddenly fly into a rage and kill Miss Minchin, you know, when she was ill-treating me—but I couldn't be vulgar. Why can't you tell your father I read them?"

"He wants me to read them," said Ermengarde, a little discouraged by this unexpected turn of affairs.

"He wants you to know what is in them," said Sara. "And if I can tell it to you in an easy way and make you remember it, I should think he would like that."

"He'll like it if I learn anything in any way," said rueful Ermengarde. "You would if you were my father."

"It's not your fault that—" began Sara. She pulled herself up and stopped rather suddenly. She had been going to say, "It's not your fault that you are stupid."

"That what?" Ermengarde asked.

"That you can't learn things quickly," amended Sara. "If you can't, you can't. If I can— why, I can; that's all."

She always felt very tender of Ermengarde, and tried not to let her feel too strongly the difference between being able to learn anything at once, and not being able to learn anything at all. As she looked at her plump face, one of her wise, old-fashioned thoughts came to her.

"Perhaps," she said, "to be able to learn things quickly isn't everything. To be kind is worth a great deal to other people. If Miss Minchin knew everything on earth and was like what she is now, she'd still be a detestable thing, and everybody would hate her. Lots of clever people have done harm and have been wicked. Look at Robespierre—"

She stopped and examined Ermengarde's countenance, which was beginning to look bewildered. "Don't you remember?" she demanded. "I told you about him not long ago. I believe you've forgotten."

"Well, I don't remember all of it," admitted Ermengarde.

"Well, you wait a minute," said Sara, "and I'll take off my wet things and wrap myself in the coverlet and tell you over again."

She took off her hat and coat and hung them on a nail against the wall, and she changed her wet shoes for an old pair of slippers. Then she jumped on the bed, and drawing the coverlet about her shoulders, sat with her arms round her knees. "Now, listen," she said.

She plunged into the gory records of the French Revolution, and told such stories of it that Ermengarde's eyes grew round with alarm and she held her breath. But though she was rather terrified, there was a delightful thrill in listening, and she was not likely to forget Robespierre again, or to have any doubts about the Princesse de Lamballe.

"You know they put her head on a pike and danced round it," Sara explained. "And she had beautiful floating blonde hair; and when I think of her, I never see her head on her body, but always on a pike, with those furious people dancing and howling."

It was agreed that Mr. St. John was to be told the plan they had made, and for the present the books were to be left in the attic.

"Now let's tell each other things," said Sara. "How are you getting on with your French lessons?"

"Ever so much better since the last time I came up here and you explained the conjugations. Miss Minchin could not understand why I did my exercises so well that first morning."

Sara laughed a little and hugged her knees.

"She doesn't understand why Lottie is doing her sums so well," she said; "but it is because she creeps up here, too, and I help her." She glanced round the room. "The attic would be rather nice—if it wasn't so dreadful," she said, laughing again. "It's a good place to pretend in."

The truth was that Ermengarde did not know anything of the sometimes almost unbearable side of life in the attic and she had not a sufficiently vivid imagination to depict it for herself. On the rare occasions that she could reach Sara's room she only saw the side of it which was made exciting by things which were "pretended" and stories which were told. Her visits partook of the character of adventures; and though sometimes Sara looked rather pale, and it was not to be denied that she had grown very thin, her proud little spirit would not admit of complaints. She had never confessed that at times she was almost ravenous with hunger, as she was to-night. She was growing rapidly, and her constant walking and running about would have given her a keen appetite even if she had had abundant and regular meals of a much more nourishing nature than the unappetizing, inferior food snatched at such odd times as suited the kitchen convenience. She was growing used to a certain gnawing feeling in her young stomach.

"I suppose soldiers feel like this when they are on a long and weary march," she often said to herself. She liked the sound of the phrase, "long and weary march." It made her feel rather like a soldier. She had also a quaint sense of being a hostess in the attic.

"If I lived in a castle," she argued, "and Ermengarde was the lady of another castle, and came to see me, with knights and squires and vassals riding with her, and pennons flying; when I heard the clarions sounding outside the drawbridge I should go down to receive her, and I should spread feasts in the banquet-hall and call in minstrels to sing and play and relate romances. When she comes into the attic I can't spread feasts, but I can tell stories, and not let her know disagreeable things. I dare say poor chatelaines had to do that in time of famine, when their lands had been pillaged." She was a proud, brave little chatelaine, and dispensed generously the one hospitality she could offer—the dreams she dreamed— the visions she saw—the imaginings which were her joy and comfort.

So, as they sat together, Ermengarde did not know that she was faint as well as ravenous, and that while she talked she now and then wondered if her hunger would let her sleep when she was left alone. She felt as if she had never been quite so hungry before.

"I wish I was as thin as you, Sara," Ermengarde said suddenly. "I believe you are thinner than you used to be. Your eyes look so big, and look at the sharp little bones sticking out of your elbow!"

Sara pulled down her sleeve, which had pushed itself up.

"I always was a thin child," she said bravely, "and I always had big green eyes."

"I love your queer eyes," said Ermengarde, looking into them with affectionate admiration. "They always look as if they saw such a long way. I love them—and I love them to be green—though they look black generally."

"They are cat's eyes," laughed Sara; "but I can't see in the dark with them—because I have tried, and I couldn't—I wish I could."

It was just at this minute that something happened at the skylight which neither of them saw. If either of them had chanced to turn and look, she would have been startled by the sight of a dark face which peered cautiously into the room and disappeared as quickly and almost as silently as it had appeared. Not quite as silently, however. Sara, who had keen ears, suddenly turned a little and looked up at the roof.

"That didn't sound like Melchisedec," she said. "It wasn't scratchy enough."

"What?" said Ermengarde, a little startled.

"Didn't you think you heard something?" asked Sara.

"N-no," Ermengarde faltered. "Did you?"

"Perhaps I didn't," said Sara; "but I thought I did. It sounded as if something was on the slates—something that dragged softly."

"What could it be?" said Ermengarde. "Could it be—robbers?"

"No," Sara began cheerfully. "There is nothing to steal—"

She broke off in the middle of her words. They both heard the sound that checked her. It was not on the slates, but on the stairs below, and it was Miss Minchin's angry voice. Sara sprang off the bed, and put out the candle.

"She is scolding Becky," she whispered, as she stood in the darkness. "She is making her cry."

"Will she come in here?" Ermengarde whispered back, panic-stricken.

"No. She will think I am in bed. Don't stir."

It was very seldom that Miss Minchin mounted the last flight of stairs. Sara could only remember that she had done it once before. But now she was angry enough to be coming at least part of the way up, and it sounded as if she was driving Becky before her.

"You impudent, dishonest child!" they heard her say. "Cook tells me she has missed things repeatedly."

" 'T warn't me, mum," said Becky sobbing. "I was 'ungry enough, but 't warn't me—never!"

"You deserve to be sent to prison," said Miss Minchin's voice. "Picking and stealing! Half a meat-pie, indeed!"

" 'T warn't me," wept Becky. "I could 'ave eat a whole un—but I never laid a finger on it."

Miss Minchin was out of breath between temper and mounting the stairs. The meat-pie had been intended for her special late supper. It became apparent that she boxed Becky's ears.

"Don't tell falsehoods," she said. "Go to your room this instant."

Both Sara and Ermengarde heard the slap, and then heard Becky run in her slip-shod shoes up the stairs and into her attic. They heard her door shut, and knew that she threw herself upon her bed.

"I could 'ave e't two of 'em," they heard her cry into her pillow. "An' I never took a bite. 'Twas cook give it to her policeman."

Sara stood in the middle of the room in the darkness. She was clenching her little teeth and opening and shutting fiercely her outstretched hands. She could scarcely stand still, but she dared not move until Miss Minchin had gone down the stairs and all was still.

"The wicked, cruel thing!" she burst forth. "The cook takes things herself and then says Becky steals them. She doesn't! She doesn't! She's so hungry sometimes that she eats crusts out of the ash-barrel!" She pressed her hands hard against her face and burst into passionate little sobs, and Ermengarde, hearing this unusual thing, was overawed by it. Sara was crying! The unconquerable Sara! It seemed to denote something new—some mood she had never known. Suppose—! Suppose—! A new dread possibility presented itself to her kind, slow, little mind all at once. She crept off the bed in the dark and found her way to the table where the candle stood. She struck a match and lit the candle. When she had lighted it, she bent forward and looked at Sara, with her new thought growing to definite fear in her eyes.

"Sara," she said in a timid, almost awe-stricken voice, "are—are—you never told me—I don't want to be rude, but—are you ever hungry?"

It was too much just at that moment. The barrier broke down. Sara lifted her face from her hands.

"Yes," she said in a new passionate way. "Yes, I am. I'm so hungry now that I could almost eat you. And it makes it worse to hear poor Becky. She's hungrier than I am."

Ermengarde gasped.

"Oh! Oh!" she cried woefully; "and I never knew!"

"I didn't want you to know," Sara said. "It would have made me feel like a street beggar. I know I look like a street beggar."

"No, you don't—you don't!" Ermengarde broke in. "Your clothes are a little queer—but you couldn't look like a street beggar. You haven't a street-beggar face."

"A little boy once gave me a sixpence for charity," said Sara, with a short little laugh in spite of herself. "Here it is." And she pulled out the thin ribbon from her neck. "He wouldn't have given me his Christmas sixpence if I hadn't looked as if I needed it."

Somehow the sight of the dear little sixpence was good for both of them. It made them laugh a little, though they both had tears in their eyes.

"Who was he?" asked Ermengarde, looking at it quite as if it had not been a mere ordinary silver sixpence.

"He was a darling little thing going to a party," said Sara. "He was one of the Large Family, the little one with the round legs—the one I call Guy Clarence. I suppose his nursery was crammed with Christmas presents and hampers full of cakes and things, and he could see I had nothing."

Ermengarde gave a little jump backward. The last sentences had recalled something to her troubled mind and given her a sudden inspiration.

"Oh, Sara!" she cried. "What a silly thing I am not to have thought of it!"

"Of what?"

"Something splendid!" said Ermengarde, in an excited hurry. "This very afternoon my nicest aunt sent me a box. It is full of good things. I never touched it, I had so much pudding at dinner, and I was so bothered about papa's books." Her words began to tumble over each other. "It's got cake in it, and little meat-pies, and jam-tarts and buns, and oranges and red-currant wine, and figs and chocolate. I'll creep back to my room and get it this minute, and we'll eat it now."

Sara almost reeled. When one is faint with hunger the mention of food has sometimes a curious effect. She clutched Ermengarde's arm.

"Do you think—you could?" she ejaculated.

"I know I could," answered Ermengarde, and she ran to the door—opened it softly—put her head out into the darkness, and listened. Then she went back to Sara. "The lights are out. Everybody's in bed. I can creep—and creep—and no one will hear."

It was so delightful that they caught each other's hands and a sudden light sprang into Sara's eyes.

"Ermie!" she said. "Let us pretend! Let us pretend it's a party! And oh, won't you invite the prisoner in the next cell?"

"Yes! Yes! Let us knock on the wall now. The jailer won't hear."

Sara went to the wall. Through it she could hear poor Becky crying more softly. She knocked four times.

"That means, 'Come to me through the secret passage under the wall,' she explained. 'I have something to communicate.' "

Five quick knocks answered her.

"She is coming," she said.

Day 117

1.   Finish reading chapter 15 of *A Little Princess*.
2.   Tell someone about the chapter.

Almost immediately the door of the attic opened and Becky appeared. Her eyes were red and her cap was sliding off, and when she caught sight of Ermengarde she began to rub her face nervously with her apron.

"Don't mind me a bit, Becky!" cried Ermengarde.

"Miss Ermengarde has asked you to come in," said Sara, "because she is going to bring a box of good things up here to us."

Becky's cap almost fell off entirely, she broke in with such excitement.

"To eat, miss?" she said. "Things that's good to eat?"

"Yes," answered Sara, "and we are going to pretend a party."

"And you shall have as much as you want to eat," put in Ermengarde. "I'll go this minute!"

She was in such haste that as she tiptoed out of the attic she dropped her red shawl and did not know it had fallen. No one saw it for a minute or so. Becky was too much overpowered by the good luck which had befallen her.

"Oh, miss! oh, miss!" she gasped; "I know it was you that asked her to let me come. It—it makes me cry to think of it." And she went to Sara's side and stood and looked at her worshippingly.

But in Sara's hungry eyes the old light had begun to glow and transform her world for her. Here in the attic—with the cold night outside—with the afternoon in the sloppy streets barely passed—with the memory of the awful unfed look in the beggar child's eyes not yet faded—this simple, cheerful thing had happened like a thing of magic.

She caught her breath.

"Somehow, something always happens," she cried, "just before things get to the very worst. It is as if the Magic did it. If I could only just remember that always. The worst thing never quite comes."

She gave Becky a little cheerful shake.

"No, no! You mustn't cry!" she said. "We must make haste and set the table."

"Set the table, miss?" said Becky, gazing round the room. "What'll we set it with?"

Sara looked round the attic, too.

"There doesn't seem to be much," she answered, half laughing.

That moment she saw something and pounced upon it. It was Ermengarde's red shawl which lay upon the floor.

"Here's the shawl," she cried. "I know she won't mind it. It will make such a nice red table-cloth."

They pulled the old table forward, and threw the shawl over it. Red is a wonderfully kind and comfortable color. It began to make the room look furnished directly.

"How nice a red rug would look on the floor!" exclaimed Sara. "We must pretend there is one!"

Her eye swept the bare boards with a swift glance of admiration. The rug was laid down already.

"How soft and thick it is!" she said, with the little laugh which Becky knew the meaning of; and she raised and set her foot down again delicately, as if she felt something under it.

"Yes, miss," answered Becky, watching her with serious rapture. She was always quite serious.

"What next, now?" said Sara, and she stood still and put her hands over her eyes. "Something will come if I think and wait a little"—in a soft, expectant voice. "The Magic will tell me."

One of her favorite fancies was that on "the outside," as she called it, thoughts were waiting for people to call them. Becky had seen her stand and wait many a time before, and knew that in a few seconds she would uncover an enlightened, laughing face.

In a moment she did.

"There!" she cried. "It has come! I know now! I must look among the things in the old trunk I had when I was a princess."

She flew to its corner and kneeled down. It had not been put in the attic for her benefit, but because there was no room for it elsewhere. Nothing had been left in it but rubbish. But she knew she should find something. The Magic always arranged that kind of thing in one way or another.

In a corner lay a package so insignificant-looking that it had been overlooked, and when she herself had found it she had kept it as a relic. It contained a dozen small white handkerchiefs. She seized them joyfully and ran to the table. She began to arrange them upon the red table-cover, patting and coaxing them into shape with the narrow lace edge curling outward, her Magic working its spells for her as she did it.

"These are the plates," she said. "They are golden plates. These are the richly embroidered napkins. Nuns worked them in convents in Spain."

"Did they, miss?" breathed Becky, her very soul uplifted by the information.

"You must pretend it," said Sara. "If you pretend it enough, you will see them."

"Yes, miss," said Becky; and as Sara returned to the trunk she devoted herself to the effort of accomplishing an end so much to be desired.

Sara turned suddenly to find her standing by the table, looking very queer indeed. She had shut her eyes, and was twisting her face in strange, convulsive contortions, her hands hanging stiffly clenched at her sides. She looked as if she was trying to lift some enormous weight.

"What is the matter, Becky?" Sara cried. "What are you doing?"

Becky opened her eyes with a start.

I was 'a-'pretendin',' miss," she answered a little sheepishly; "I was tryin' to see it like you do. I almost did," with a hopeful grin. "But it takes a lot o' stren'th."

"Perhaps it does if you are not used to it," said Sara, with friendly sympathy; "but you don't know how easy it is when you've done it often. I wouldn't try so hard just at first. It will come to you after a while. I'll just tell you what things are. Look at these."

She held an old summer hat in her hand which she had fished out of the bottom of the trunk. There was a wreath of flowers on it. She pulled the wreath off.

"These are garlands for the feast," she said grandly. "They fill all the air with perfume. There's a mug on the wash-stand, Becky. Oh—and bring the soap dish for a centerpiece."

Becky handed them to her reverently.

"What are they now, miss?" she inquired. "You'd think they was made of crockery—but I know they ain't."

"This is a carven flagon," said Sara, arranging tendrils of the wreath about the mug. "And this"—bending tenderly over the soap dish and heaping it with roses—"is purest alabaster encrusted with gems."

She touched the things gently, a happy smile hovering about her lips which made her look as if she were a creature in a dream.

"My, ain't it lovely!" whispered Becky.

"If we just had something for bonbon dishes," Sara murmured. "There!"—darting to the trunk again. "I remember I saw something this minute."

It was only a bundle of wool wrapped in red and white tissue-paper, but the tissue-paper was soon twisted into the form of little dishes, and was combined with the remaining flowers to ornament the candlestick which was to light the feast. Only the Magic could have made it more than an old table covered with a red shawl and set with rubbish from a long-unopened trunk. But Sara drew back and gazed at it, seeing wonders; and Becky, after staring in delight, spoke with bated breath.

"This 'ere," she suggested, with a glance round the attic—"is it the Bastille now—or has it turned into somethin' different?"

"Oh, yes, yes!" said Sara. "Quite different. It is a banquet-hall!"

"My eye, miss!" ejaculated Becky. "A blanket-'all!" and she turned to view the splendors about her with awed bewilderment.

"A banquet-hall," said Sara. "A vast chamber where feasts are given. It has a vaulted roof, and a minstrels' gallery, and a huge chimney filled with blazing oaken logs, and it is brilliant with waxen tapers twinkling on every side."

"My eye, Miss Sara!" gasped Becky again.

Then the door opened, and Ermengarde came in, rather staggering under the weight of her hamper. She started back with an exclamation of joy. To enter from the chill darkness outside, and find one's self confronted by a totally unanticipated festal board, draped with red, adorned with white napery, and wreathed with flowers, was to feel that the preparations were brilliant indeed.

"Oh, Sara!" she cried out. "You are the cleverest girl I ever saw!"

"Isn't it nice?" said Sara. "They are things out of my old trunk. I asked my Magic, and it told me to go and look."

"But oh, miss," cried Becky, "wait till she's told you what they are! They ain't just—oh, miss, please tell her," appealing to Sara.

So Sara told her, and because her Magic helped her she made her almost see it all: the golden platters—the vaulted spaces—the blazing logs—the twinkling waxen tapers. As the things were taken out of the hamper—the frosted cakes—the fruits—the bonbons and the wine—the feast became a splendid thing.

"It's like a real party!" cried Ermengarde.

"It's like a queen's table," sighed Becky.

Then Ermengarde had a sudden brilliant thought.

"I'll tell you what, Sara," she said. "Pretend you are a princess now and this is a royal feast."

"But it's your feast," said Sara; "you must be the princess, and we will be your maids of honor."

"Oh, I can't," said Ermengarde. "I'm too fat, and I don't know how. You be her."

"Well, if you want me to," said Sara.

But suddenly she thought of something else and ran to the rusty grate.

"There is a lot of paper and rubbish stuffed in here!" she exclaimed. "If we light it, there will be a bright blaze for a few minutes, and we shall feel as if it was a real fire." She struck a match and lighted it up with a great specious glow which illuminated the room.

"By the time it stops blazing," Sara said, "we shall forget about its not being real."

She stood in the dancing glow and smiled.

"Doesn't it look real?" she said. "Now we will begin the party."

She led the way to the table. She waved her hand graciously to Ermengarde and Becky. She was in the midst of her dream.

"Advance, fair damsels," she said in her happy dream-voice, "and be seated at the banquet table. My noble father, the king, who is absent on a long journey, has commanded me to feast you." She turned her head slightly toward the corner of the room. "What, ho! there, minstrels! Strike up with your viols and bassoons. Princesses," she explained rapidly to Ermengarde and Becky, "always had minstrels to play at their feasts. Pretend there is a minstrel gallery up there in the corner. Now we will begin."

They had barely had time to take their pieces of cake into their hands—not one of them had time to do more, when—they all three sprang to their feet and turned pale faces toward the door—listening—listening.

Someone was coming up the stairs. There was no mistake about it. Each of them recognized the angry, mounting tread and knew that the end of all things had come.

"It's—the missus!" choked Becky, and dropped her piece of cake upon the floor.

"Yes," said Sara, her eyes growing shocked and large in her small white face. "Miss Minchin has found us out."

Miss Minchin struck the door open with a blow of her hand. She was pale herself, but it was with rage. She looked from the frightened faces to the banquet-table, and from the banquet-table to the last flicker of the burnt paper in the grate.

"I have been suspecting something of this sort," she exclaimed; "but I did not dream of such audacity. Lavinia was telling the truth."

So they knew that it was Lavinia who had somehow guessed their secret and had betrayed them. Miss Minchin strode over to Becky and boxed her ears for a second time.

"You impudent creature!" she said. "You leave the house in the morning!"

Sara stood quite still, her eyes growing larger, her face paler. Ermengarde burst into tears.

"Oh, don't send her away," she sobbed. "My aunt sent me the hamper. We're—only—having a party."

"So I see," said Miss Minchin, witheringly. "With the Princess Sara at the head of the table." She turned fiercely on Sara. "It is your doing, I know," she cried. "Ermengarde would never have thought of such a thing. You decorated the table, I suppose—with this rubbish." She stamped her foot at Becky. "Go to your attic!" she commanded, and Becky stole away, her face hidden in her apron, her shoulders shaking.

Then it was Sara's turn again.

"I will attend to you to-morrow. You shall have neither breakfast, dinner, nor supper!"

"I have not had either dinner or supper today, Miss Minchin," said Sara, rather faintly.

"Then all the better. You will have something to remember. Don't stand there. Put those things into the hamper again."

She began to sweep them off the table into the hamper herself, and caught sight of Ermengarde's new books.

"And you"—to Ermengarde—"have brought your beautiful new books into this dirty attic. Take them up and go back to bed. You will stay there all day to-morrow, and I shall write to your papa. What would he say if he knew where you are to-night?"

Something she saw in Sara's grave, fixed gaze at this moment made her turn on her fiercely.

"What are you thinking of?" she demanded. "Why do you look at me like that?"

"I was wondering," answered Sara, as she had answered that notable day in the school-room.

"What were you wondering?"

It was very like the scene in the school-room. There was no pertness in Sara's manner. It was only sad and quiet.

"I was wondering," she said in a low voice, "what my papa would say if he knew where I am to-night."

Miss Minchin was infuriated just as she had been before and her anger expressed itself, as before, in an intemperate fashion. She flew at her and shook her.

"You insolent, unmanageable child!" she cried. "How dare you! How dare you!"

She picked up the books, swept the rest of the feast back into the hamper in a jumbled heap, thrust it into Ermengarde's arms, and pushed her before her toward the door.

"I will leave you to wonder," she said. "Go to bed this instant." And she shut the door behind herself and poor stumbling Ermengarde, and left Sara standing quite alone.

The dream was quite at an end. The last spark had died out of the paper in the grate and left only black tinder; the table was left bare, the golden plates and richly embroidered napkins, and the garlands were transformed again into old handkerchiefs, scraps of red and white paper, and discarded artificial flowers all scattered on the floor; the minstrels in the minstrel gallery had stolen away, and the viols and bassoons were still. Emily was sitting with her back against the wall, staring very hard. Sara saw her, and went and picked her up with trembling hands.

"There isn't any banquet left, Emily," she said. "And there isn't any princess. There is nothing left but the prisoners in the Bastille." And she sat down and hid her face.

What would have happened if she had not hidden it just then, and if she had chanced to look up at the skylight at the wrong moment, I do not know—perhaps the end of this chapter might have been quite different—because if she had glanced at the skylight she would certainly have been startled by what she would have seen. She would have seen exactly the same face pressed against the glass and peering in at her as it had peered in earlier in the evening when she had been talking to Ermengarde.

But she did not look up. She sat with her little black head in her arms for some time. She always sat like that when she was trying to bear something in silence. Then she got up and went slowly to the bed.

"I can't pretend anything else—while I am awake," she said. "There wouldn't be any use in trying. If I go to sleep, perhaps a dream will come and pretend for me."

She suddenly felt so tired—perhaps through want of food—that she sat down on the edge of the bed quite weakly.

"Suppose there was a bright fire in the grate, with lots of little dancing flames," she murmured. "Suppose there was a comfortable chair before it—and suppose there was a small table near, with a little hot—hot supper on it. And suppose"—as she drew the thin coverings over her—"suppose this was a beautiful soft bed, with fleecy blankets and large downy pillows. Suppose—suppose—" And her very weariness was good to her, for her eyes closed and she fell fast asleep.

*　　*　　*　　*　　*　　*

She did not know how long she slept. But she had been tired enough to sleep deeply and profoundly—too deeply and soundly to be disturbed by anything, even by the squeaks and scamperings of Melchisedec's entire family, if all his sons and daughters had chosen to come out of their hole to fight and tumble and play.

When she awakened it was rather suddenly, and she did not know that any particular thing had called her out of her sleep. The truth was, however, that it was a sound which had called her back—a real sound—the click of the skylight as it fell in closing after a lithe white figure which slipped through it and crouched down close by upon the slates of the roof—just near enough to see what happened in the attic, but not near enough to be seen.

At first she did not open her eyes. She felt too sleepy and—curiously enough—too warm and comfortable. She was so warm and comfortable, indeed, that she did not believe she was really awake. She never was as warm and cozy as this except in some lovely vision.

"What a nice dream!" she murmured. "I feel quite warm. I—don't—want—to—wake—up."

Of course it was a dream. She felt as if warm, delightful bedclothes were heaped upon her. She could actually feel blankets, and when she put out her hand it touched something exactly like a satin-covered eider-down quilt. She must not awaken from this delight—she must be quite still and make it last.

But she could not—even though she kept her eyes closed tightly, she could not. Something was forcing her to awaken—something in the room. It was a sense of light, and a sound— the sound of a crackling, roaring little fire.

"Oh, I am awakening," she said mournfully. "I can't help it—I can't."

Her eyes opened in spite of herself. And then she actually smiled—for what she saw she had never seen in the attic before, and knew she never should see.

"Oh, I haven't awakened," she whispered, daring to rise on her elbow and look all about her. "I am dreaming yet." She knew it must be a dream, for if she were awake such things could not—could not be.

Do you wonder that she felt sure she had not come back to earth? This is what she saw. In the grate there was a glowing, blazing fire; on the hob was a little brass kettle hissing and boiling; spread upon the floor was a thick, warm crimson rug; before the fire a folding-chair, unfolded, and with cushions on it; by the chair a small folding-table, unfolded, covered with a white cloth, and upon it spread small covered dishes, a cup, a saucer, a tea-pot; on the bed were new warm coverings and a satin-covered down quilt; at the foot a curious wadded silk robe, a pair of quilted slippers, and some books. The room of her dream seemed changed into fairyland—and it was flooded with warm light, for a bright lamp stood on the table covered with a rosy shade.

She sat up, resting on her elbow, and her breathing came short and fast.

"It does not—melt away," she panted. "Oh, I never had such a dream before." She scarcely dared to stir; but at last she pushed the bedclothes aside, and put her feet on the floor with a rapturous smile.

"I am dreaming—I am getting out of bed," she heard her own voice say; and then, as she stood up in the midst of it all, turning slowly from side to side—"I am dreaming it stays— real! I'm dreaming it feels real. It's bewitched—or I'm bewitched. I only think I see it all." Her words began to hurry themselves. "If I can only keep on thinking it," she cried, "I don't care! I don't care!"

She stood panting a moment longer, and then cried out again.

"Oh, it isn't true!" she said. "It can't be true! But oh, how true it seems!"

The blazing fire drew her to it, and she knelt down and held out her hands close to it—so close that the heat made her start back.

"A fire I only dreamed wouldn't be hot," she cried.

She sprang up, touched the table, the dishes, the rug; she went to the bed and touched the blankets. She took up the soft wadded dressing-gown, and suddenly clutched it to her breast and held it to her cheek.

"It's warm. It's soft!" she almost sobbed. "It's real. It must be!"

She threw it over her shoulders, and put her feet into the slippers.

"They are real, too. It's all real!" she cried. "I am not—I am not dreaming!"

She almost staggered to the books and opened the one which lay upon the top. Something was written on the flyleaf—just a few words, and they were these:

"To the little girl in the attic. From a friend."

When she saw that—wasn't it a strange thing for her to do—she put her face down upon the page and burst into tears.

"I don't know who it is," she said; "but somebody cares for me a little. I have a friend."

She took her candle and stole out of her own room and into Becky's, and stood by her bedside.

"Becky, Becky!" she whispered as loudly as she dared. "Wake up!"

When Becky wakened, and she sat upright staring aghast, her face still smudged with traces of tears, beside her stood a little figure in a luxurious wadded robe of crimson silk. The face she saw was a shining, wonderful thing. The Princess Sara—as she remembered her—stood at her very bedside, holding a candle in her hand.

"Come," she said. "Oh, Becky, come!"

Becky was too frightened to speak. She simply got up and followed her, with her mouth and eyes open, and without a word.

And when they crossed the threshold, Sara shut the door gently and drew her into the warm, glowing midst of things which made her brain reel and her hungry senses faint.

"It's true! It's true!" she cried. "I've touched them all. They are as real as we are. The Magic has come and done it, Becky, while we were asleep—the Magic that won't let those worst things ever quite happen."

Day 118

1. Read chapter 16 of *A Little Princess*.
2. Reread this paragraph from the chapter (below). Earlier we noticed how Sara questions whether her true character showed. Was she nice only because she was blessed? Now that she has experienced life from the "other side," how has her character proven?

• "Miss Minchin had expected to see in Sara, when she appeared in the school-room, very much what Lavinia had expected to see. Sara had always been an annoying puzzle to her, because severity never made her cry or look frightened. When she was scolded she stood still and listened politely with a grave face; when she was punished she performed her extra tasks or went without her meals, making no complaint or outward sign of rebellion. The very fact that she never made an impudent answer seemed to Miss Minchin a kind of impudence in itself. But after yesterday's deprivation of meals, the violent scene of last night, the prospect of hunger today, she must surely have broken down. It would be strange indeed if she did not come downstairs with pale cheeks and red eyes and an unhappy, humbled face."

Vocabulary

1. Read these sentences from the chapter with your vocabulary words in bold.
    *   She had seen him that very afternoon, sitting **disconsolately** on a table before a window in the Indian gentleman's house.
    *   Miss Minchin was quite agitated. This was an incident which suggested strange things to her **sordid** mind.
    *   It was, however, just like Sara's singular **obstinate** way.
    *   It is an **impertinence.**
    *   The very fact that she never made an **impudent** answer seemed to Miss Minchin a kind of **impudence** in itself.
    *   It cannot be denied that as they sat before the blazing fire, and ate the nourishing, comfortable food, they felt a kind of **rapturous** awe, and looked into each other's eyes with something like doubt.
2. Decide what you think each word means. Then read their definitions. (Answers)

THE VISITOR

IMAGINE , if you can, what the rest of the evening was like. How they crouched by the fire which blazed and leaped and made so much of itself in the little grate. How they removed the covers of the dishes, and found rich, hot, savory soup, which was a meal in itself, and sandwiches and toast and muffins enough for both of them. The mug from the washstand was used as Becky's tea cup, and the tea was so delicious that it was not necessary to pretend that it was anything but tea. They were warm and full-fed and happy, and it was just like Sara that, having found her strange good fortune real, she should give herself up to the enjoyment of it to the utmost. She had lived such a life of imaginings that she was quite equal to accepting any wonderful thing that happened, and almost to cease, in a short time, to find it bewildering.

"I don't know anyone in the world who could have done it," she said; "but there has been someone. And here we are sitting by their fire—and—and—it's true! And whoever it is—wherever they are—I have a friend, Becky—someone is my friend."

It cannot be denied that as they sat before the blazing fire, and ate the nourishing, comfortable food, they felt a kind of rapturous awe, and looked into each other's eyes with something like doubt.

"Do you think," Becky faltered once, in a whisper, "do you think it could melt away, miss? Hadn't we better be quick?" And she hastily crammed her sandwich into her mouth. If it was only a dream, kitchen manners would be overlooked.

"No, it won't melt away," said Sara. "I am eating this muffin, and I can taste it. You never really eat things in dreams. You only think you are going to eat them. Besides, I keep giving myself pinches; and I touched a hot piece of coal just now, on purpose."

The sleepy comfort which at length almost overpowered them was a heavenly thing. It was the drowsiness of happy, well-fed childhood, and they sat in the fire glow and luxuriated in it until Sara found herself turning to look at her transformed bed.

There were even blankets enough to share with Becky. The narrow couch in the next attic was more comfortable that night than its occupant had ever dreamed that it could be.

As she went out of the room, Becky turned upon the threshold and looked about her with devouring eyes.

"If it ain't here in the mornin', miss," she said, "it's been here tonight, anyways, an' I shan't never forget it." She looked at each particular thing, as if to commit it to memory. "The fire was there," pointing with her finger, "an' the table was before it; an' the lamp was there, an' the light looked rosy red; an' there was a satin cover on your bed, an' a warm rug on the floor, an' everythin' looked beautiful; an' "—she paused a second, and laid her hand on her stomach tenderly—"there was soup an' sandwiches an' muffins—there was." And, with this conviction a reality at least, she went away.

Through the mysterious agency which works in schools and among servants, it was quite well known in the morning that Sara Crewe was in horrible disgrace, that Ermengarde was under punishment, and that Becky would have been packed out of the house before breakfast, but that a scullery maid could not be dispensed with at once. The servants knew that she was allowed to stay because Miss Minchin could not easily find another creature helpless and humble enough to work like a bounden slave for so few shillings a week. The elder girls in the school-room knew that if Miss Minchin did not send Sara away it was for practical reasons of her own.

"She's growing so fast and learning such a lot, somehow," said Jessie to Lavinia, "that she will be given classes soon, and Miss Minchin knows she will have to work for nothing. It was rather nasty of you, Lavvy, to tell about her having fun in the garret. How did you find it out?"

"I got it out of Lottie. She's such a baby she didn't know she was telling me. There was nothing nasty at all in speaking to Miss Minchin. I felt it my duty"—priggishly. "She was being deceitful. And it's ridiculous that she should look so grand, and be made so much of, in her rags and tatters!"

"What were they doing when Miss Minchin caught them?"

"Pretending some silly thing. Ermengarde had taken up her hamper to share with Sara and Becky. She never invites us to share things. Not that I care, but it's rather vulgar of her to share with servant girls in attics. I wonder Miss Minchin didn't turn Sara out—even if she does want her for a teacher."

"If she was turned out where would she go?" inquired Jessie, a trifle anxiously.

"How do I know?" snapped Lavinia. "She'll look rather queer when she comes into the school-room this morning, I should think—after what's happened. She had no dinner yesterday, and she's not to have any today."

Jessie was not as ill-natured as she was silly. She picked up her book with a little jerk.

"Well, I think it's horrid," she said. "They've no right to starve her to death."

When Sara went into the kitchen that morning the cook looked askance at her, and so did the housemaids; but she passed them hurriedly. She had, in fact, overslept herself a little, and as Becky had done the same, neither had had time to see the other, and each had come downstairs in haste.

Sara went into the scullery. Becky was violently scrubbing a kettle, and was actually gurgling a little song in her throat. She looked up with a wildly elated face.

"It was there when I wakened, miss—the blanket," she whispered excitedly. "It was as real as it was last night."

"So was mine," said Sara. "It is all there now—all of it. While I was dressing I ate some of the cold things we left."

"Oh, laws! Oh, laws!" Becky uttered the exclamation in a sort of rapturous groan, and ducked her head over her kettle just in time, as the cook came in from the kitchen.

Miss Minchin had expected to see in Sara, when she appeared in the school-room, very much what Lavinia had expected to see. Sara had always been an annoying puzzle to her, because severity never made her cry or look frightened. When she was scolded she stood still and listened politely with a grave face; when she was punished she performed her extra tasks or went without her meals, making no complaint or outward sign of rebellion. The very fact that she never made an impudent answer seemed to Miss Minchin a kind of impudence in itself. But after yesterday's deprivation of meals, the violent scene of last night, the prospect of hunger today, she must surely have broken down. It would be strange indeed if she did not come downstairs with pale cheeks and red eyes and an unhappy, humbled face.

Miss Minchin saw her for the first time when she entered the school-room to hear the little French class recite its lessons and superintend its exercises. And she came in with a springing step, color in her cheeks, and a smile hovering about the corners of her mouth. It was the most astonishing thing Miss Minchin had ever known. It gave her quite a shock. What was the child made of? What could such a thing mean? She called her at once to her desk.

"You do not look as if you realize that you are in disgrace," she said. "Are you absolutely hardened?"

The truth is that when one is still a child—or even if one is grown up—and has been well fed, and has slept long and softly and warm; when one has gone to sleep in the midst of a fairy story, and has wakened to find it real, one cannot be unhappy or even look as if one were; and one could not, if one tried, keep a glow of joy out of one's eyes. Miss Minchin was almost struck dumb by the look of Sara's eyes when she made her perfectly respectful answer.

"I beg your pardon, Miss Minchin," she said; "I know that I am in disgrace."

"Be good enough not to forget it and look as if you had come into a fortune. It is an impertinence. And remember you are to have no food today."

"Yes, Miss Minchin," Sara answered; but as she turned away her heart leaped with the memory of what yesterday had been. "If the Magic had not saved me just in time," she thought, "how horrible it would have been!"

"She can't be very hungry," whispered Lavinia. "Just look at her. Perhaps she is pretending she has had a good breakfast"—with a spiteful laugh.

"She's different from other people," said Jessie, watching Sara with her class. "Sometimes I'm a bit frightened of her."

"Ridiculous thing!" ejaculated Lavinia.

All through the day the light was in Sara's face, and the color in her cheek. The servants cast puzzled glances at her, and whispered to each other, and Miss Amelia's small blue eyes wore an expression of bewilderment. What such an audacious look of well-being, under august displeasure could mean she could not understand. It was, however, just like Sara's singular obstinate way. She was probably determined to brave the matter out.

One thing Sara had resolved upon, as she thought things over. The wonders which had happened must be kept a secret, if such a thing were possible. If Miss Minchin should choose to mount to the attic again, of course all would be discovered. But it did not seem likely that she would do so for some time at least, unless she was led by suspicion. Ermengarde and Lottie would be watched with such strictness that they would not dare to steal out of their beds again. Ermengarde could be told the story and trusted to keep it secret. If Lottie made any discoveries, she could be bound to secrecy also. Perhaps the Magic itself would help to hide its own marvels.

"But whatever happens," Sara kept saying to herself all day—"whatever happens, somewhere in the world there is a heavenly kind person who is my friend—my friend. If I never know who it is—if I never can even thank him—I shall never feel quite so lonely. Oh, the Magic was good to me!"

If it was possible for weather to be worse than it had been the day before, it was worse this day—wetter, muddier, colder. There were more errands to be done, the cook was more irritable, and, knowing that Sara was in disgrace, she was more savage. But what does anything matter when one's Magic has just proved itself one's friend. Sara's supper of the night before had given her strength, she knew that she should sleep well and warmly, and, even though she had naturally begun to be hungry again before evening, she felt that she could bear it until breakfast-time on the following day, when her meals would surely be given to her again. It was quite late when she was at last allowed to go upstairs. She had been told to go into the school-room and study until ten o'clock, and she had become interested in her work, and remained over her books later.

When she reached the top flight of stairs and stood before the attic door, it must be confessed that her heart beat rather fast.

"Of course it might all have been taken away," she whispered, trying to be brave. "It might only have been lent to me for just that one awful night. But it was lent to me—I had it. It was real."

She pushed the door open and went in. Once inside, she gasped slightly, shut the door, and stood with her back against it looking from side to side.

The Magic had been there again. It actually had, and it had done even more than before. The fire was blazing, in lovely leaping flames, more merrily than ever. A number of new things had been brought into the attic which so altered the look of it that if she had not been past doubting she would have rubbed her eyes. Upon the low table another supper stood—this time with cups and plates for Becky as well as herself; a piece of bright, heavy, strange embroidery covered the battered mantel, and on it some ornaments had been placed. All the bare, ugly things which could be covered with draperies had been concealed and made to look quite pretty. Some odd materials of rich colors had been fastened against the wall with fine, sharp tacks—so sharp that they could be pressed into the wood and plaster without hammering. Some brilliant fans were pinned up, and there were several large cushions, big and substantial enough to use as seats. A wooden box was covered with a rug, and some cushions lay on it, so that it wore quite the air of a sofa.

Sara slowly moved away from the door and simply sat down and looked and looked again.

"It is exactly like something fairy come true," she said. "There isn't the least difference. I feel as if I might wish for anything—diamonds or bags of gold—and they would appear! That wouldn't be any stranger than this. Is this my garret? Am I the same cold, ragged, damp Sara? And to think I used to pretend and pretend and wish there were fairies! The one thing I always wanted was to see a fairy story come true. I am living in a fairy story. I feel as if I might be a fairy myself, and able to turn things into anything else."

She rose and knocked upon the wall for the prisoner in the next cell, and the prisoner came.

When she entered she almost dropped in a heap upon the floor. For a few seconds she quite lost her breath.

"Oh, laws!" she gasped. "Oh, laws, miss!"

"You see," said Sara.

On this night Becky sat on a cushion upon the hearth rug and had a cup and saucer of her own.

When Sara went to bed she found that she had a new thick mattress and big downy pillows. Her old mattress and pillow had been removed to Becky's bedstead, and, consequently, with these additions Becky had been supplied with unheard-of comfort.

"Where does it all come from?" Becky broke forth once. "Laws, who does it, miss?"

"Don't let us even ask", said Sara. "If it were not that I want to say, 'Oh, thank you,' I would rather not know. It makes it more beautiful."

From that time life became more wonderful day by day. The fairy story continued. Almost every day something new was done. Some new comfort or ornament appeared each time Sara opened the door at night, until in a short time the attic was a beautiful little room full of all sorts of odd and luxurious things. The ugly walls were gradually entirely covered with pictures and draperies, ingenious pieces of folding furniture appeared, a bookshelf was hung up and filled with books, new comforts and conveniences appeared one by one, until there seemed nothing left to be desired. When Sara went downstairs in the morning, the remains of the supper were on the table; and when she returned to the attic in the evening, the magician had removed them and left another nice little meal. Miss Minchin was as harsh and insulting as ever, Miss Amelia as peevish, and the servants were as vulgar and rude. Sara was sent on errands in all weathers, and scolded and driven hither and thither; she was scarcely allowed to speak to Ermengarde and Lottie; Lavinia sneered at the increasing shabbiness of her clothes; and the other girls stared curiously at her when she appeared in the school-room. But what did it all matter while she was living in this wonderful mysterious story? It was more romantic and delightful than anything she had ever invented to comfort her starved young soul and save herself from despair. Sometimes, when she was scolded, she could scarcely keep from smiling.

"If you only knew!" she was saying to herself. "If you only knew!"

The comfort and happiness she enjoyed were making her stronger, and she had them always to look forward to. If she came home from her errands wet and tired and hungry, she knew she would soon be warm and well fed after she had climbed the stairs. During the hardest day she could occupy herself blissfully by thinking of what she should see when she opened the attic door, and wondering what new delight had been prepared for her. In a very short time she began to look less thin. Color came into her cheeks, and her eyes did not seem so much too big for her face.

"Sara Crewe looks wonderfully well," Miss Minchin remarked disapprovingly to her sister.

"Yes," answered poor, silly Miss Amelia. "She is absolutely fattening. She was beginning to look like a little starved crow."

"Starved!" exclaimed Miss Minchin, angrily. "There was no reason why she should look starved. She always had plenty to eat!"

"Of—of course," agreed Miss Amelia, humbly, alarmed to find that she had, as usual, said the wrong thing.

"There is something very disagreeable in seeing that sort of thing in a child of her age," said Miss Minchin, with haughty vagueness.

"What—sort of thing?" Miss Amelia ventured.

"It might almost be called defiance," answered Miss Minchin, feeling annoyed because she knew the thing she resented was nothing like defiance, and she did not know what other unpleasant term to use. "The spirit and will of any other child would have been entirely humbled and broken by—by the changes she has had to submit to. But, upon my word, she seems as little subdued as if—as if she were a princess."

"Do you remember," put in the unwise Miss Amelia, "what she said to you that day in the school-room about what you would do if you found out that she was—"

"No, I don't," said Miss Minchin. "Don't talk nonsense." But she remembered very clearly indeed.

Very naturally, even Becky was beginning to look plumper and less frightened. She could not help it. She had her share in the secret fairy story, too. She had two mattresses, two pillows, plenty of bed-covering, and every night a hot supper and a seat on the cushions by the fire. The Bastille had melted away, the prisoners no longer existed. Two comforted children sat in the midst of delights. Sometimes Sara read aloud from her books, sometimes she learned her own lessons, sometimes she sat and looked into the fire and tried to imagine who her friend could be, and wished she could say to him some of the things in her heart.

Then it came about that another wonderful thing happened. A man came to the door and left several parcels. All were addressed in large letters, "To the Little Girl in the right-hand attic."

Sara herself was sent to open the door and take them in. She laid the two largest parcels on the hall table, and was looking at the address, when Miss Minchin came down the stairs and saw her.

"Take the things to the young lady to whom they belong," she said severely. "Don't stand there staring at them."

"They belong to me," answered Sara, quietly.

"To you?" exclaimed Miss Minchin. "What do you mean?"

"I don't know where they come from," said Sara, "but they are addressed to me. I sleep in the right-hand attic. Becky has the other one."

Miss Minchin came to her side and looked at the parcels with an excited expression.

"What is in them?" she demanded.

"I don't know," replied Sara.

"Open them," she ordered.

Sara did as she was told. When the packages were unfolded Miss Minchin's countenance wore suddenly a singular expression. What she saw was pretty and comfortable clothing— clothing of different kinds: shoes, stockings, and gloves, and a warm and beautiful coat. There were even a nice hat and an umbrella. They were all good and expensive things, and on the pocket of the coat was pinned a paper, on which were written these words: "To be worn every day. Will be replaced by others when necessary."

Miss Minchin was quite agitated. This was an incident which suggested strange things to her sordid mind. Could it be that she had made a mistake, after all, and that the neglected child had some powerful though eccentric friend in the background—perhaps some previously unknown relation, who had suddenly traced her whereabouts, and chose to provide for her in this mysterious and fantastic way? Relations were sometimes very odd— particularly rich old bachelor uncles, who did not care for having children near them. A man of that sort might prefer to overlook his young relation's welfare at a distance. Such a person, however, would be sure to be crotchety and hot-tempered enough to be easily offended. It would not be very pleasant if there were such a one, and he should learn all the truth about the thin, shabby clothes, the scant food, and the hard work. She felt very queer indeed, and very uncertain, and she gave a side glance at Sara.

"Well," she said, in a voice such as she had never used since the little girl lost her father, "someone is very kind to you. As the things have been sent, and you are to have new ones when they are worn out, you may as well go and put them on and look respectable. After you are dressed you may come downstairs and learn your lessons in the school-room. You need not go out on any more errands today."

About half an hour afterward, when the school-room door opened and Sara walked in, the entire seminary was struck dumb.

"My word!" ejaculated Jessie, jogging Lavinia's elbow. "Look at the Princess Sara!"

Everybody was looking, and when Lavinia looked she turned quite red.

It was the Princess Sara indeed. At least, since the days when she had been a princess, Sara had never looked as she did now. She did not seem the Sara they had seen come down the back stairs a few hours ago. She was dressed in the kind of frock Lavinia had been used to envying her the possession of. It was deep and warm in color, and beautifully made. Her slender feet looked as they had done when Jessie had admired them, and the hair, whose heavy locks had made her look rather like a Shetland pony when it fell loose about her small, odd face, was tied back with a ribbon.

"Perhaps someone has left her a fortune," Jessie whispered. "I always thought something would happen to her. She's so queer."

"Perhaps the diamond-mines have suddenly appeared again," said Lavinia, scathingly. "Don't please her by staring at her in that way, you silly thing."

"Sara," broke in Miss Minchin's deep voice, "come and sit here."

And while the whole school-room stared and pushed with elbows, and scarcely made any effort to conceal its excited curiosity, Sara went to her old seat of honor, and bent her head over her books.

That night, when she went to her room, after she and Becky had eaten their supper she sat and looked at the fire seriously for a long time.

"Are you making something up in your head, miss?" Becky inquired with respectful softness. When Sara sat in silence and looked into the coals with dreaming eyes it generally meant that she was making a new story. But this time she was not, and she shook her head.

"No," she answered. "I am wondering what I ought to do."

Becky stared—still respectfully. She was filled with something approaching reverence for everything Sara did and said.

"I can't help thinking about my friend," Sara explained. "If he wants to keep himself a secret, it would be rude to try and find out who he is. But I do so want him to know how thankful I am to him—and how happy he has made me. Anyone who is kind wants to know when people have been made happy. They care for that more than for being thanked. I wish—I do wish—"

She stopped short because her eyes at that instant fell upon something standing on a table in a corner. It was something she had found in the room when she came up to it only two days before. It was a little writing-case fitted with paper and envelopes and pens and ink.

"Oh," she exclaimed, "why did I not think of that before?"

She rose and went to the corner and brought the case back to the fire.

"I can write to him," she said joyfully, "and leave it on the table. Then perhaps the person who takes the things away will take it, too. I won't ask him anything. He won't mind my thanking him, I feel sure."

So she wrote a note. This is what she said:

"I hope you will not think it is impolite that I should write this note to you when you wish to keep yourself a secret. Please believe I do not mean to be impolite or try to find out anything at all; only I want to thank you for being so kind to me—so heavenly kind—and making everything like a fairy story. I am so grateful to you, and I am so happy—and so is Becky. Becky feels just as thankful as I do—it is all just as beautiful and wonderful to her as it is to me. We used to be so lonely and cold and hungry, and now—oh, just think what you have done for us! Please let me say just these words. It seems as if I ought to say them. Thank you—thank you—thank you!

"The Little Girl in the Attic."

The next morning she left this on the little table, and in the evening it had been taken away with the other things; so she knew the Magician had received it, and she was happier for the thought. She was reading one of her new books to Becky just before they went to their respective beds, when her attention was attracted by a sound at the skylight. When she looked up from her page she saw that Becky had heard the sound also, as she had turned her head to look and was listening rather nervously.

"Something's there, miss," she whispered.

"Yes," said Sara, slowly. "It sounds—rather like a cat—trying to get in."

She left her chair and went to the skylight. It was a queer little sound she heard—like a soft scratching. She suddenly remembered something and laughed. She remembered a quaint little intruder who had made his way into the attic once before. She had seen him that very afternoon, sitting disconsolately on a table before a window in the Indian gentleman's house.

"Suppose," she whispered in pleased excitement—"just suppose it was the monkey who got away again. Oh, I wish it was!"

She climbed on a chair, very cautiously raised the skylight, and peeped out. It had been snowing all day, and on the snow, quite near her, crouched a tiny, shivering figure, whose small black face wrinkled itself piteously at sight of her.

"It is the monkey," she cried out. "He has crept out of the Lascar's attic, and he saw the light."

Becky ran to her side.

"Are you going to let him in, miss?" she said.

"Yes," Sara answered joyfully. "It's too cold for monkeys to be out. They're delicate. I'll coax him in."

She put a hand out delicately, speaking in a coaxing voice—as she spoke to the sparrows and to Melchisedec—as if she were some friendly little animal herself.

"Come along, monkey darling," she said. "I won't hurt you."

He knew she would not hurt him. He knew it before she laid her soft, caressing little paw on him and drew him towards her. He had felt human love in the slim brown hands of Ram Dass, and he felt it in hers. He let her lift him through the skylight, and when he found himself in her arms he cuddled up to her breast and looked up into her face.

"Nice monkey! Nice monkey!" she crooned, kissing his funny head. "Oh, I do love little animal things."

He was evidently glad to get to the fire, and when she sat down and held him on her knee he looked from her to Becky with mingled interest and appreciation.

"He is plain-looking, miss, ain't he?" said Becky.

"He looks like a very ugly baby," laughed Sara. "I beg your pardon, monkey; but I'm glad you are not a baby. Your mother couldn't be proud of you, and no one would dare to say you looked like any of your relations. Oh, I do like you!"

She leaned back in her chair and reflected.

"Perhaps he's sorry he's so ugly," she said, "and it's always on his mind. I wonder if he has a mind. Monkey, my love, have you a mind?"

But the monkey only put up a tiny paw and scratched his head.

"What shall you do with him?" Becky asked.

"I shall let him sleep with me tonight, and then take him back to the Indian gentleman tomorrow. I am sorry to take you back, monkey; but you must go. You ought to be fondest of your own family; and I'm not a real relation."

And when she went to bed she made him a nest at her feet, and he curled up and slept there as if he were a baby and much pleased with his quarters.

Day 119

1. Read chapter 17 of *A Little Princess*.
2. Tell someone a summary of this chapter.

Vocabulary

1. Read this sentence from the chapter: All three of them incontinently fled from the room and tumbled into the hall. It was in this way they always welcomed their father.
2. Think of a sentence about acting **incontinently**, uncontrolled. Incontinently is an adverb. It describes an action. Use it that way in your sentence. Write it out if you think you'll forget it.

"IT IS THE CHILD!"

THE next afternoon three members of the Large Family sat in the Indian gentleman's library, doing their best to cheer him up. They had been allowed to come in to perform this office because he had specially invited them. He had been living in a state of suspense for some time, and to-day he was waiting for a certain event very anxiously. This event was the return of Mr. Carmichael from Moscow. His stay there had been prolonged from week to week. On his first arrival there, he had not been able satisfactorily to trace the family he had gone in search of. When he felt at last sure that he had found them and had gone to their house, he had been told that they were absent on a journey. His efforts to reach them had been unavailing, so he had decided to remain in Moscow until their return. Mr.

Carrisford sat in his reclining-chair, and Janet sat on the floor beside him. He was very fond of Janet. Nora had found a footstool, and Donald was astride the tiger's head which ornamented the rug made of the animal's skin. It must be owned that he was riding it rather violently.

"Don't chirrup so loud, Donald," Janet said. "When you come to cheer an ill person up you don't cheer him up at the top of your voice. Perhaps cheering up is too loud, Mr. Carrisford?" turning to the Indian gentleman.

But he only patted her shoulder.

"No, it isn't," he answered. "And it keeps me from thinking too much."

"I'm going to be quiet," Donald shouted. "We'll all be as quiet as mice."

"Mice don't make a noise like that," said Janet.

Donald made a bridle of his handkerchief and bounced up and down on the tiger's head.

"A whole lot of mice might," he said cheerfully. "A thousand mice might."

"I don't believe fifty thousand mice would," said Janet, severely; "and we have to be as quiet as one mouse."

Mr. Carrisford laughed and patted her shoulder again.

"Papa won't be very long now," she said. "May we talk about the lost little girl?"

"I don't think I could talk much about anything else just now," the Indian gentleman answered, knitting his forehead with a tired look.

"We like her so much," said Nora. "We call her the little un-fairy princess."

"Why?" the Indian gentleman inquired, because the fancies of the Large Family always made him forget things a little.

It was Janet who answered.

"It is because, though she is not exactly a fairy, she will be so rich when she is found that she will be like a princess in a fairy tale. We called her the fairy princess at first, but it didn't quite suit."

"Is it true," said Nora, "that her papa gave all his money to a friend to put in a mine that had diamonds in it, and then the friend thought he had lost it all and ran away because he felt as if he was a robber?"

"But he wasn't really, you know," put in Janet, hastily.

The Indian gentleman took hold of her hand quickly.

"No, he wasn't really," he said.

"I am sorry for the friend," Janet said; "I can't help it. He didn't mean to do it, and it would break his heart. I am sure it would break his heart."

"You are an understanding little woman, Janet," the Indian gentleman said, and he held her hand close.

"Did you tell Mr. Carrisford," Donald shouted again, "about the little-girl-who-isn't-a-beggar? Did you tell him she has new nice clothes? P'r'aps she's been found by somebody when she was lost."

"There's a cab!" exclaimed Janet. "It's stopping before the door. It is papa!"

They all ran to the windows to look out.

"Yes, it's papa," Donald proclaimed. "But there is no little girl."

All three of them incontinently fled from the room and tumbled into the hall. It was in this way they always welcomed their father. They were to be heard jumping up and down, clapping their hands, and being caught up and kissed.

Mr. Carrisford made an effort to rise and sank back again.

"It is no use," he said. "What a wreck I am!"

Mr. Carmichael's voice approached the door.

"No, children," he was saying; "you may come in after I have talked to Mr. Carrisford. Go and play with Ram Dass."

Then the door opened and he came in. He looked rosier than ever, and brought an atmosphere of freshness and health with him; but his eyes were disappointed and anxious as they met the invalid's look of eager question even as they grasped each other's hands.

"What news?" Mr. Carrisford asked. "The child the Russian people adopted?"

"She is not the child we are looking for," was Mr. Carmichael's answer. "She is much younger than Captain Crewe's little girl. Her name is Emily Carew. I have seen and talked to her. The Russians were able to give me every detail."

How wearied and miserable the Indian gentleman looked! His hand dropped from Mr. Carmichael's.

"Then the search has to be begun over again," he said. "That is all. Please sit down."

Mr. Carmichael took a seat. Somehow, he had gradually grown fond of this unhappy man. He was himself so well and happy, and so surrounded by cheerfulness and love, that desolation and broken health seemed pitifully unbearable things. If there had been the sound of just one gay little high-pitched voice in the house, it would have been so much less forlorn. And that a man should be compelled to carry about in his breast the thought that he had seemed to wrong and desert a child was not a thing one could face.

"Come, come," he said in his cheery voice; "we'll find her yet."

"We must begin at once. No time must be lost," Mr. Carrisford fretted. "Have you any new suggestion to make—any whatsoever?"

Mr. Carmichael felt rather restless, and he rose and began to pace the room with a thoughtful, though uncertain face.

"Well, perhaps," he said. "I don't know what it may be worth. The fact is, an idea occurred to me as I was thinking the thing over in the train on the journey from Dover."

"What was it? If she is alive, she is somewhere."

"Yes; she is somewhere. We have searched the schools in Paris. Let us give up Paris and begin in London. That was my idea— to search London."

"There are schools enough in London," said Mr. Carrisford. Then he slightly started, roused by a recollection. "By the way, there is one next door."

"Then we will begin there. We cannot begin nearer than next door."

"No," said Carrisford. "There is a child there who interests me; but she is not a pupil. And she is a little dark, forlorn creature, as unlike poor Crewe as a child could be."

Perhaps the Magic was at work again at that very moment—the beautiful Magic. It really seemed as if it might be so. What was it that brought Ram Dass into the room—even as his master spoke—salaaming respectfully, but with a scarcely concealed touch of excitement in his dark, flashing eyes?

"Sahib," he said, "the child herself has come—the child the sahib felt pity for. She brings back the monkey who had again run away to her attic under the roof. I have asked that she remain. It was my thought that it would please the sahib to see and speak with her."

"Who is she?" inquired Mr. Carmichael.

"God knows," Mr. Carrrisford answered. "She is the child I spoke of. A little drudge at the school." He waved his hand to Ram Dass, and addressed him. "Yes, I should like to see her. Go and bring her in." Then he turned to Mr. Carmichael. "While you have been away," he explained, "I have been desperate. The days were so dark and long. Ram Dass told me of this child's miseries, and together we invented a romantic plan to help her. I suppose it was a childish thing to do; but it gave me something to plan and think of. Without the help of an agile, soft-footed Oriental like Ram Dass, however, it could not have been done."

Then Sara came into the room. She carried the monkey in her arms, and he evidently did not intend to part from her, if it could be helped. He was clinging to her and chattering, and the interesting excitement of finding herself in the Indian gentleman's room had brought a flush to Sara's cheeks.

"Your monkey ran away again," she said, in her pretty voice. "He came to my garret window last night, and I took him in because it was so cold. I would have brought him back if it had not been so late. I knew you were ill and might not like to be disturbed."

The Indian gentleman's hollow eyes dwelt on her with curious interest.

"That was very thoughtful of you," he said.

Sara looked toward Ram Dass, who stood near the door.

"Shall I give him to the Lascar?" she asked.

"How do you know he is a Lascar?" said the Indian gentleman, smiling a little.

"Oh, I know Lascars," Sara said, handing over the reluctant monkey. "I was born in India."

The Indian gentleman sat upright so suddenly, and with such a change of expression, that she was for a moment quite startled.

"You were born in India," he exclaimed, "were you? Come here." And he held out his hand.

Sara went to him and laid her hand in his, as he seemed to want to take it. She stood still, and her green-gray eyes met his wonderingly. Something seemed to be the matter with him.

"You live next door?" he demanded.

"Yes; I live at Miss Minchin's seminary."

"But you are not one of her pupils?"

A strange little smile hovered about Sara's mouth. She hesitated a moment.

"I don't think I know exactly what I am," she replied.

"Why not?"

"At first I was a pupil, and a parlor boarder; but now—"

"You were a pupil! What are you now?"

The queer little sad smile was on Sara's lips again.

"I sleep in the attic, next to the scullery-maid," she said. "I run errands for the cook—I do anything she tells me; and I teach the little ones their lessons."

"Question her, Carmichael," said Mr. Carrisford, sinking back as if he had lost his strength. "Question her; I cannot."

The big, kind father of the Large Family knew how to question little girls. Sara realized how much practice he had had when he spoke to her in his nice, encouraging voice.

"What do you mean by 'At first,' my child?" he inquired.

"When I was first taken there by my papa."

"Where is your papa?"

"He died," said Sara, very quietly. "He lost all his money and there was none left for me. There was no one to take care of me or to pay Miss Minchin."

"Carmichael!" the Indian gentleman cried out loudly. "Carmichael!"

"We must not frighten her," Mr. Carmichael said aside to him in a quick, low voice; and he added aloud to Sara: "So you were sent up into the attic, and made into a little drudge. That was about it, wasn't it?"

"There was no one to take care of me," said Sara. "There was no money; I belong to nobody."

"How did your father lose his money?" the Indian gentleman broke in breathlessly.

"He did not lose it himself," Sara answered, wondering still more each moment. "He had a friend he was very fond of—he was very fond of him. It was his friend who took his money. He trusted his friend too much."

The Indian gentleman's breath came more quickly.

"The friend might have meant to do no harm," he said. "It might have happened through a mistake."

Sara did not know how unrelenting her quiet young voice sounded as she answered. If she had known, she would surely have tried to soften it for the Indian gentleman's sake.

"The suffering was just as bad for my papa," she said. "It killed him."

"What was your father's name?" the Indian gentleman said. "Tell me."

"His name was Ralph Crewe," Sara answered, feeling startled. "Captain Crewe. He died in India."

The haggard face contracted, and Ram Dass sprang to his master's side.

"Carmichael," the invalid gasped, "it is the child—the child!"

For a moment Sara thought he was going to die. Ram Dass poured out drops from a bottle, and held them to his lips. Sara stood near, trembling a little. She looked in a bewildered way at Mr. Carmichael.

"What child am I?" she faltered.

"He was your father's friend," Mr. Carmichael answered her. "Don't be frightened. We have been looking for you for two years."

Sara put her hand up to her forehead, and her mouth trembled. She spoke as if she were in a dream.

"And I was at Miss Minchin's all the while," she half whispered. "Just on the other side of the wall."

Day 120

1. Read chapter 18 of *A Little Princess*.
2. Tell someone about the chapter.

"I TRIED NOT TO BE"

IT was pretty, comfortable Mrs. Carmichael who explained everything. She was sent for at once, and came across the square to take Sara into her warm arms and make clear to her all that had happened. The excitement of the totally unexpected discovery had been temporarily almost overpowering to Mr. Carrisford in his weak condition.

"Upon my word," he said faintly to Mr. Carmichael, when it was suggested that the little girl should go into another room, "I feel as if I do not want to lose sight of her."

"I will take care of her," Janet said, "and mamma will come in a few minutes." And it was Janet who led her away.

"We're so glad you are found," she said. "You don't know how glad we are that you are found."

Donald stood with his hands in his pockets, and gazed at Sara with reflecting and self-reproachful eyes.

"If I'd just asked what your name was when I gave you my sixpence," he said, "you would have told me it was Sara Crewe, and then you would have been found in a minute."

Then Mrs. Carmichael came in. She looked very much moved, and suddenly took Sara in her arms and kissed her.

"You look bewildered, poor child," she said. "And it is not to be wondered at."

Sara could only think of one thing.

"Was he," she said, with a glance toward the closed door of the library—"was he the wicked friend? Oh, do tell me!"

Mrs. Carmichael was crying as she kissed her again. She felt as if she ought to be kissed very often because she had not been kissed for so long.

"He was not wicked, my dear," she answered. "He did not really lose your papa's money. He only thought he had lost it; and because he loved him so much his grief made him so ill that for a time he was not in his right mind. He almost died of brain fever, and long before he began to recover your poor papa was dead."

"And he did not know where to find me," murmured Sara. "And I was so near." Somehow, she could not forget that she had been so near.

"He believed you were in school in France," Mrs. Carmichael explained. "And he was continually misled by false clues. He has looked for you everywhere. When he saw you pass by, looking so sad and neglected, he did not dream that you were his friend's poor child; but because you were a little girl, too, he was sorry for you, and wanted to make you happier. And he told Ram Dass to climb into your attic window and try to make you comfortable."

Sara gave a start of joy; her whole look changed.

"Did Ram Dass bring the things?" she cried out; "did he tell Ram Dass to do it? Did he make the dream that came true?"

"Yes, my dear—yes! He is kind and good, and he was sorry for you, for little lost Sara Crewe's sake."

The library door opened and Mr. Carmichael appeared, calling Sara to him with a gesture.

"Mr. Carrisford is better already," he said. "He wants you to come to him."

Sara did not wait. When the Indian gentleman looked at her as she entered, he saw that her face was all alight.

She went and stood before his chair, with her hands clasped together against her breast.

"You sent the things to me," she said, in a joyful emotional little voice, "the beautiful, beautiful things? You sent them!"

"Yes, poor, dear child, I did," he answered her. He was weak and broken with long illness and trouble, but he looked at her with the look she remembered in her father's eyes—that look of loving her and wanting to take her in his arms. It made her kneel down by him, just as she used to kneel by her father when they were the dearest friends and lovers in the world.

"Then it is you who are my friend," she said; "it is you who are my friend!" And she dropped her face on his thin hand and kissed it again and again.

"The man will be himself again in three weeks," Mr. Carmichael said aside to his wife. "Look at his face already."

In fact, he did look changed. Here was the "little missus," and he had new things to think of and plan for already. In the first place, there was Miss Minchin. She must be interviewed and told of the change which had taken place in the fortunes of her pupil.

Sara was not to return to the Seminary at all. The Indian gentleman was very determined upon that point. She must remain where she was, and Mr. Carmichael should go and see Miss Minchin himself.

"I am glad I need not go back," said Sara. "She will be very angry. She does not like me; though perhaps it is my fault, because I do not like her."

But, oddly enough, Miss Minchin made it unnecessary for Mr. Carmichael to go to her, by actually coming in search of her pupil herself. She had wanted Sara for something, and on inquiry had heard an astonishing thing. One of the housemaids had seen her steal out of the area with something hidden under her cloak, and had also seen her go up the steps of the next door and enter the house.

"What does she mean!" cried Miss Minchin to Miss Amelia.

"I don't know, I'm sure, sister," answered Miss Amelia. "Unless she has made friends with him because he has lived in India."

"It would be just like her to thrust herself upon him and try to gain his sympathies in some such impertinent fashion," said Miss Minchin. "She must have been in the house for two hours. I will not allow such presumption. I shall go and inquire into the matter, and apologize for her intrusion."

Sara was sitting on a footstool close to Mr. Carrisford's knee, and listening to some of the many things he felt it necessary to try to explain to her, when Ram Dass announced the visitor's arrival.

Sara rose involuntarily, and became rather pale; but Mr. Carrisford saw that she stood quietly, and showed none of the ordinary signs of child terror.

Miss Minchin entered the room with a sternly dignified manner. She was correctly and well dressed, and rigidly polite.

"I am sorry to disturb Mr. Carrisford," she said; "but I have explanations to make. I am Miss Minchin, the proprietress of the Young Ladies' Seminary next door."

The Indian gentleman looked at her for a moment in silent scrutiny. He was a man who had naturally a rather hot temper, and he did not wish it to get too much the better of him.

"So you are Miss Minchin?" he said.

"I am, sir."

"In that case," the Indian gentleman replied, "you have arrived at the right time. My solicitor, Mr. Carmichael, was just on the point of going to see you."

Mr. Carmichael bowed slightly, and Miiss Minchin looked from him to Mr. Carrisford in amazement.

"Your solicitor!" she said. "I do not understand. I have come here as a matter of duty. I have just discovered that you have been intruded upon through the forwardness of one of my pupils—a charity pupil. I came to explain that she intruded without my knowledge." She turned upon Sara. "Go home at once," she commanded indignantly. "You shall be severely punished. Go home at once."

The Indian gentleman drew Sara to his side and patted her hand.

"She is not going."

Miss Minchin felt rather as if she must be losing her senses.

"Not going!" she repeated.

"No," said Mr. Carrisford. "She is not going home—if you give your house that name. Her home for the future will be with me."

Miss Minchin fell back in amazed indignation.

"With you! With you sir! What does this mean?"

"Kindly explain the matter, Carmichael," said the Indian gentleman; "and get it over as quickly as possible." And he made Sara sit down again, and held her hands in his—which was another trick of her papa's.

Then Mr. Carmichael explained—in the quiet, level-toned, steady manner of a man who knew his subject, and all its legal significance, which was a thing Miss Minchin understood as a business woman, and did not enjoy.

"Mr. Carrisford, madam," he said, "was an intimate friend of the late Captain Crewe. He was his partner in certain large investments. The fortune which Captain Crewe supposed he had lost has been recovered, and is now in Mr. Carrisford's hands."

"The fortune!" cried Miss Minchin; and she really lost color as she uttered the exclamation. "Sara's fortune!"

"It will be Sara's fortune," replied Mr. Carmichael, rather coldly. "It is Sara's fortune now, in fact. Certain events have increased it enormously. The diamond-mines have retrieved themselves."

"The diamond-mines!" Miss Minchin gasped out. If this was true, nothing so horrible, she felt, had ever happened to her since she was born.

"The diamond-mines," Mr. Carmichael repeated, and he could not help adding, with a rather sly, unlawyer-like smile, "There are not many princesses, Miss Minchin, who are richer than your little charity pupil, Sara Crewe, will be. Mr. Carrisford has been searching for her for nearly two years; he has found her at last, and he will keep her."

After which he asked Miss Minchin to sit down while he explained matters to her fully, and went into such detail as was necessary to make it quite clear to her that Sara's future was an assured one, and that what had seemed to be lost was to be restored to her tenfold; also, that she had in Mr. Carrisford a guardian as well as a friend.

Miss Minchin was not a clever woman, and in her excitement she was silly enough to make one desperate effort to regain what she could not help seeing she had lost through her worldly folly.

"He found her under my care," she protested. "I have done everything for her. But for me she would have starved in the streets."

Here the Indian gentleman lost his temper.

"As to starving in the streets," he said, "she might have starved more comfortably there than in your attic."

"Captain Crewe left her in my charge," Miss Minchin argued. "She must return to it until she is of age. She can be a parlor-boarder again. She must finish her education. The law will interfere in my behalf."

"Come, come, Miss Minchin," Mr. Carmichael interposed, "the law will do nothing of the sort. If Sara herself wishes to return to you, I dare say Mr. Carrisford might not refuse to allow it. But that rests with Sara."

"Then," said Miss Minchin, "I appeal to Sara. I have not spoiled you, perhaps," she said awkwardly to the little girl; "but you know that your papa was pleased with your progress. And—ahem!—I have always been fond of you."

Sara's green-gray eyes fixed themselves on her with the quiet, clear look Miss Minchin particularly disliked.

"Have you Miss Minchin?" she said; "I did not know that."

Miss Minchin reddened and drew herself up.

"You ought to have known it," said she; "but children, unfortunately, never know what is best for them. Amelia and I always said you were the cleverest child in the school. Will you not do your duty to your poor papa and come home with me?"

Sara took a step toward her and stood still. She was thinking of the day when she had been told that she belonged to nobody, and was in danger of being turned into the street; she was thinking of the cold, hungry hours she had spent alone with Emily and Melchisedec in the attic. She looked Miss Minchin steadily in the face.

"You know why I will not go home with you, Miss Minchin," she said; "you know quite well."

A hot flush showed itself on Miss Minchin's hard, angry face.

"You will never see your companions again," she began. "I will see that Ermengarde and Lottie are kept away—"

Mr. Carmichael stopped her with polite firmness.

"Excuse me," he said; "she will see anyone she wishes to see. The parents of Miss Crewe's fellow-pupils are not likely to refuse her invitations to visit her at her guardian's house. Mr. Carrisford will attend to that."

It must be confessed that even Miss Minchin flinched. This was worse than the eccentric bachelor uncle who might have a peppery temper and be easily offended at the treatment of his niece. A woman of sordid mind could easily believe that most people would not refuse to allow their children to remain friends with a little heiress of diamond-mines. And if Mr. Carrisford chose to tell certain of her patrons how unhappy Sara Crewe had been made, many unpleasant things might happen.

"You have not undertaken an easy charge," she said to the Indian gentleman, as she turned to leave the room; "you will discover that very soon. The child is neither truthful nor grateful. I suppose"—to Sara—"that you feel now that you are a princess again."

Sara looked down and flushed a little, because she thought her pet fancy might not be easy for strangers—even nice ones—to understand at first.

"I—tried not to be anything else," she answered in a low voice—"even when I was coldest and hungriest—I tried not to be."

"Now it will not be necessary to try," said Miss Minchin, acidly, as Ram Dass salaamed her out of the room.

*　　*　　*　　*　　*　　*

She returned home and, going to her sitting room, sent at once for Miss Amelia. She sat closeted with her all the rest of the afternoon, and it must be admitted that poor Miss Amelia passed through more than one bad quarter of an hour. She shed a good many tears, and mopped her eyes a good deal. One of her unfortunate remarks almost caused her sister to snap her head entirely off, but it resulted in an unusual manner.

"I'm not as clever as you, sister," she said, "and I am always afraid to say things to you for fear of making you angry. Perhaps if I were not so timid it would be better for the school and for both of us. I must say I've often thought it would have been better if you had been less severe on Sara Crewe, and had seen that she was decently dressed and more comfortable. I know she was worked too hard for a child of her age, and I know she was only half fed—"

"How dare you say such a thing!" exclaimed Miss Minchin.

"I don't know how I dare," Miss Amelia answered, with a kind of reckless courage; "but now I've begun I may as well finish, whatever happens to me. The child was a clever child and a good child—and she would have paid you for any kindness you had shown her. But you didn't show her any. The fact was, she was too clever for you, and you always disliked her for that reason. She used to see through us both—"

"Amelia!" gasped her infuriated elder, looking as if she would box her ears and knock her cap off, as she had often done to Becky.

But Miss Amelia's disappointment had made her hysterical enough not to care what occurred next.

"She did! She did!" she cried. "She saw through us both. She saw that you were a hard-hearted, worldly woman, and that I was a weak fool, and that we were both of us vulgar and mean enough to grovel on our knees before her money, and behave ill to her because it was taken from her—though she behaved herself like a little princess even when she was a beggar. She did—she did—like a little princess!" And her hysterics got the better of the poor woman, and she began to laugh and cry both at once, and rock herself backward and forward in such a way as made Miss Minchin stare aghast.

"And now you've lost her," she cried wildly; "and some other school will get her and her money; and if she were like any other child she'd tell how she's been treated, and all our pupils would be taken away and we should be ruined. And it serves us right; but it serves you right more than it does me, for you are a hard woman, Maria Minchin—you're a hard, selfish, worldly woman!"

And she was in danger of making so much noise with her hysterical chokes and gurgles that her sister was obliged to go to her and apply salts and sal volatile to quiet her, instead of pouring forth her indignation at her audacity.

And from that time forward, it may be mentioned, the elder Miss Minchin actually began to stand a little in awe of a sister who, while she looked so foolish, was evidently not quite so foolish as she looked, and might, consequently, break out and speak truths people did not want to hear.

That evening, when the pupils were gathered together before the fire in the school-room, as was their custom before going to bed, Ermengarde came in with a letter in her hand and a queer expression on her round face. It was queer because, while it was an expression of delighted excitement, it was combined with such amazement as seemed to belong to a kind of shock just received.

"What is the matter?" cried two or three voices at once.

"Is it anything to do with the row that has been going on?" said Lavinia, eagerly. "There has been such a row in Miss Minchin's room, Miss Amelia has had something like hysterics and has had to go to bed."

Ermengarde answered them slowly as if she were half stunned.

"I have just had this letter from Sara," she said, holding it out to let them see what a long letter it was.

"From Sara!" Every voice joined in that exclamation.

"Where is she?" almost shrieked Jessie.

"Next door," said Ermengarde; "with the Indian gentleman."

"Where? Where? Has she been sent away? Does Miss Minchin know? Was the row about that? Why did she write? Tell us! Tell us!"

There was a perfect babel, and Lottie began to cry plaintively.

Ermengarde answered them slowly as if she were half plunged out into what, at the moment, seemed the most important and self-explaining thing.

"There were diamond-mines," she said stoutly; "there were!"

Open mouths and open eyes confronted her.

"They were real," she hurried on. "It was all a mistake about them. Something happened for a time, and Mr. Carrisford thought they were ruined—"

"Who is Mr. Carrisford?" shouted Jessie.

"The Indian gentleman. And Captain Crewe thought so, too—and he died; and Mr. Carrisford had brain fever and ran away, and he almost died. And he did not know where Sara was. And it turned out that there were millions and millions of diamonds in the mines; and half of them belong to Sara; and they belonged to her when she was living in the attic with no one but Melchisedec for a friend, and the cook ordering her about. And Mr. Carrisford found her this afternoon, and he has got her in his home—and she will never come back—and she will be more a princess than she ever was—a hundred and fifty thousand times more. And I am going to see her to-morrow afternoon. There!"

Even Miss Minchin herself could scarcely have controlled the uproar after this; and though she heard the noise, she did not try. She was not in the mood to face anything more than she was facing in her room, while Miss Amelia was weeping in bed. She knew that the news had penetrated the walls in some mysterious manner, and that every servant and every child would go to bed talking about it.

So until almost midnight the entire seminary, realizing somehow that all rules were laid aside, crowded round Ermengarde in the school-room and heard read and re-read the letter containing a story which was quite as wonderful as any Sara herself had ever invented, and which had the amazing charm of having happened to Sara herself and the mystic Indian gentleman in the very next house.

Becky, who had heard it also, managed to creep up-stairs earlier than usual. She wanted to get away from people and go and look at the little magic room once more. She did not know what would happen to it. It was not likely that it would be left to Miss Minchin. It would be taken away, and the attic would be bare and empty again. Glad as she was for Sara's sake, she went up the last flight of stairs with a lump in her throat and tears blurring her sight. There would be no fire to-night, and no rosy lamp; no supper, and no princess sitting in the glow reading or telling stories—no princess!

She choked down a sob as she pushed the attic door open, and then she broke into a low cry.

The lamp was flushing the room, the fire was blazing, the supper was waiting; and Ram Dass was standing smiling into her startled face.

"Missee Sahib remembered," he said. "She told the sahib all. She wished you to know the good fortune which has befallen her. Behold a letter on the tray. She has written. She did not wish that you should go to sleep unhappy. The sahib commands you to come to him to-morrow. You are to be the attendant of Missee Sahib. To-night I take these things back over the roof."

And having said this with a beaming face, he made a little salaam and slipped through the skylight with an agile silentness of movement which showed Becky how easily he had done it before.

Day 121

1. Read chapter 19 of *A Little Princess*.
2. Tell someone a summary of the book. Can you tell them what it's about without telling them everything?

ANNE

NEVER had such joy reigned in the nursery of the Large Family. Never had they dreamed of such delights as resulted from an intimate acquaintance with the little-girl-who-was-not-a-beggar. The mere fact of her sufferings and adventures made her a priceless possession. Everybody wanted to be told over and over again the things which had happened to her. When one was sitting by a warm fire in a big, glowing room, it was quite delightful to hear how cold it could be in an attic. It must be admitted that the attic was rather delighted in, and that its coldness and bareness quite sank into insignificance when Melchisedec was remembered, and one heard about the sparrows and things one could see if one climbed on the table and stuck one's head and shoulders out of the skylight.

Of course the thing loved best was the story of the banquet and the dream which was true. Sara told it for the first time the day after she had been found. Several members of the Large Family came to take tea with her, and as they sat or curled up on the hearth-rug she told the story in her own way, and the Indian gentleman listened and watched her. When she had finished she looked up at him and put her hand on his knee.

"That is my part," she said. "Now won't you tell your part of it, Uncle Tom?" He had asked her to call him always "Uncle Tom." "I don't know your part yet, and it must be beautiful."

So he told them how, when he sat alone, ill and dull and irritable, Ram Dass had tried to distract him by describing the passers-by, and there was one child who passed oftener than any one else; he had begun to be interested in her—partly perhaps because he was thinking a great deal of a little girl, and partly because Ram Dass had been able to relate the incident of his visit to the attic in chase of the monkey. He had described its cheerless look, and the bearing of the child, who seemed as if she was not of the class of those who were treated as drudges and servants. Bit by bit, Ram Dass had made discoveries concerning the wretchedness of her life. He had found out how easy a matter it was to climb across the few yards of roof to the skylight, and this fact had been the beginning of all that followed.

"Sahib," he had said one day, "I could cross the slates and make the child a fire when she is out on some errand. When she returned, wet and cold, to find it blazing, she would think a magician had done it."

The idea had been so fanciful that Mr. Carrisford's sad face had lighted with a smile, and Ram Dass had been so filled with rapture that he had enlarged upon it and explained to his master how simple it would be to accomplish numbers of other things. He had shown a childlike pleasure and invention, and the preparations for the carrying out of the plan had filled many a day with interest which would otherwise have dragged wearily. On the night of the frustrated banquet Ram Dass had kept watch, all his packages being in readiness in the attic which was his own; and the person who was to help him had waited with him, as interested as himself in the odd adventure. Ram Dass had been lying flat upon the slates, looking in at the skylight, when the banquet had come to its disastrous conclusion; he had been sure of the profoundness of Sara's wearied sleep; and then, with a dark lantern, he had crept into the room, while his companion remained outside and handed the things to him. When Sara had stirred ever so faintly, Ram Dass had closed the lantern-slide and lain flat upon the floor. These and many other exciting things the children found out by asking a thousand questions.

"I am so glad," Sara said. "I am so glad it was you who were my friend!"

There never were such friends as these two became. Somehow, they seemed to suit each other in a wonderful way. The Indian gentleman had never had a companion he liked quite as much as he liked Sara. In a month's time he was, as Mr. Carmichael had prophesied he would be, a new man. He was always amused and interested, and he began to find an actual pleasure in the possession of the wealth he had imagined that he loathed the burden of. There were so many charming things to plan for Sara. There was a little joke between them that he was a magician, and it was one of his pleasures to invent things to surprise her. She found beautiful new flowers growing in her room, whimsical little gifts tucked under pillows, and once, as they sat together in the evening, they heard the scratch of a heavy paw on the door, and when Sara went to find out what it was, there stood a great dog—a splendid Russian boarhound—with a grand silver and gold collar bearing an inscription. "I am Boris," it read; "I serve the Princess Sara."

There was nothing the Indian gentleman loved more than the recollection of the little princess in rags and tatters. The afternoons in which the Large Family, or Ermengarde and Lottie, gathered to rejoice together were very delightful. But the hours when Sara and the Indian gentleman sat alone and read or talked had a special charm of their own. During their passing many interesting things occurred.

One evening, Mr. Carrisford, looking up from his book, noticed that his companion had not stirred for some time, but sat gazing into the fire.

"What are you 'supposing,' Sara?" he asked.

Sara looked up, with a bright color on her cheek.

"I was supposing," she said; "I was remembering that hungry day, and a child I saw."

"But there were a great many hungry days," said the Indian gentleman, with rather a sad tone in his voice. "Which hungry day was it?"

"I forgot you didn't know," said Sara. "It was the day the dream came true."

Then she told him the story of the bun-shop, and the fourpence she picked up out of the sloppy mud, and the child who was hungrier than herself. She told it quite simply, and in as few words as possible; but somehow the Indian gentleman found it necessary to shade his eyes with his hand and look down at the carpet.

"And I was supposing a kind of plan," she said, when she had finished. "I was thinking I should like to do something."

"What was it?" said Mr. Carrisford, in a low tone. "You may do anything you like to do, princess."

"I was wondering," rather hesitated Sara—"you know, you say I have so much money—I was wondering if I could go to see the bun-woman, and tell her that if, when hungry children—particularly on those dreadful days—come and sit on the steps, or look in at the window, she would just call them in and give them something to eat, she might send the bills to me. Could I do that?"

"You shall do it to-morrow morning," said the Indian gentleman.

"Thank you," said Sara. "You see, I know what it is to be hungry, and it is very hard when one cannot even pretend it away."

"Yes, yes, my dear," said the Indian gentleman. "Yes, yes, it must be. Try to forget it. Come and sit on this footstool near my knee, and only remember you are a princess."

"Yes," said Sara, smiling; "and I can give buns and bread to the populace." And she went and sat on the stool, and the Indian gentleman (he used to like her to call him that, too, sometimes) drew her small dark head down on his knee and stroked her hair.

The next morning, Miss Minchin, in looking out of her window, saw the thing she perhaps least enjoyed seeing. The Indian gentleman's carriage, with its tall horses, drew up before the door of the next house, and its owner and a little figure, warm with soft, rich furs, descended the steps to get into it. The little figure was a familiar one, and reminded Miss Minchin of days in the past. It was followed by another as familiar—the sight of which she found very irritating. It was Becky, who, in the character of delighted attendant, always accompanied her young mistress to her carriage, carrying wraps and belongings. Already Becky had a pink, round face.

A little later the carriage drew up before the door of the baker's shop, and its occupants got out, oddly enough, just as the bun-woman was putting a tray of smoking-hot buns into the window.

When Sara entered the shop the woman turned and looked at her, and, leaving the buns, came and stood behind the counter. For a moment she looked at Sara very hard indeed, and then her good-natured face lighted up.

"I'm sure that I remember you, miss," she said. "And yet—"

"Yes," said Sara; "once you gave me six buns for fourpence, and—"

"And you gave five of 'em to a beggar child," the woman broke in on her. "I've always remembered it. I couldn't make it out at first." She turned round to the Indian gentleman and spoke her next words to him. "I beg your pardon, sir, but there's not many young people that notices a hungry face in that way; and I've thought of it many a time. Excuse the liberty, miss,"—to Sara—"but you look rosier and—well, better than you did that—that—"

"I am better, thank you," said Sara. "And—I am much happier—and I have come to ask you to do something for me."

"Me, miss!" exclaimed the bun-woman, smiling cheerfully. "Why, bless you! Yes, miss. What can I do?"

And then Sara, leaning on the counter, made her little proposal concerning the dreadful days and the hungry waifs and the buns.

The woman watched her, and listened with an astonished face.

"Why, bless me!" she said again when she had heard it all; "it'll be a pleasure to me to do it. I am a working-woman myself and cannot afford to do much on my own account, and there's sights of trouble on every side; but, if you'll excuse me, I'm bound to say I've given away many a bit of bread since that wet afternoon, just along o' thinking of you—an' how wet an' cold you was, an' how hungry you looked; an' yet you gave away your hot buns as if you was a princess."

The Indian gentleman smiled involuntarily at this, and Sara smiled a little, too, remembering what she had said to herself when she put the buns down on the ravenous child's ragged lap.

"She looked so hungry," she said. "She was even hungrier than I was."

"She was starving," said the woman. "Many's the time she's told me of it since—how she sat there in the wet, and felt as if a wolf was a-tearing at her poor young insides."

"Oh, have you seen her since then?" exclaimed Sara. "Do you know where she is?"

"Yes, I do," answered the woman, smiling more good-naturedly than ever. "Why, she's in that there back room, miss, an' has been for a month; an' a decent, well-meanin' girl she's goin' to turn out, an' such a help to me in the shop an' in the kitchen as you'd scarce believe, knowin' how she's lived."

She stepped to the door of the little back parlor and spoke; and the next minute a girl came out and followed her behind the counter. And actually it was the beggar-child, clean and neatly clothed, and looking as if she had not been hungry for a long time. She looked shy, but she had a nice face, now that she was no longer a savage, and the wild look had gone from her eyes. She knew Sara in an instant, and stood and looked at her as if she could never look enough.

"You see," said the woman, "I told her to come when she was hungry, and when she'd come I'd give her odd jobs to do; an' I found she was willing, and somehow I got to like her; and the end of it was, I've given her a place an' a home, and she helps me, an' behaves well, an' is as thankful as a girl can be. Her name's Anne. She has no other."

The children stood and looked at each other for a few minutes; and then Sara took her hand out of her muff and held it out across the counter, and Anne took it, and they looked straight into each other's eyes.

"I am so glad," Sara said. "And I have just thought of something. Perhaps Mrs. Brown will let you be the one to give the buns and bread to the children. Perhaps you would like to do it because you know what it is to be hungry, too.

"Yes, miss," said the girl.

And, somehow, Sara felt as if she understood her, though she said so little, and only stood still and looked and looked after her as she went out of the shop with the Indian gentleman, and they got into the carriage and drove away.

The End.

Day 122

1. Write a book report.
2. Include:
   - title and author (Frances Burnett),
   - plot, setting, and characters
   - how the main character changed from the beginning to the end
   - something you learned from this book
   - what you liked and didn't like about the book
3. You could save this in your portfolio.

Day 123

Vocabulary

1. Match the words to the definitions. Write the matching number and letter pairs on a separate sheet of paper. (Answers)

1.	sordid	A.	feeling great pleasure
2.	aperture	B.	disrespectful
3.	impudent	C.	beating, trembling
4.	dexterity	D.	to move suddenly, to happen suddenly and unexpectedly
5.	obstinate	E.	dirty
6.	rapturous	F.	unable to be comforted
7.	palpitating	G.	disrespectful
8.	reconnoiter	H.	to make observation
9.	disconsolate	I.	an opening
10.	impertinence	J.	skill
11.	incontinently	K.	without control
12.	precipitately	L.	stubborn

Day 124

1. Have fun with some more stories from *The Peterkin Papers*.
2. Tell someone about the story.

THE PETERKINS ARE OBLIGED TO MOVE.

AGAMEMNON had long felt it an impropriety to live in a house that was called a "semi-detached" house, when there was no other "semi" to it. It had always remained wholly detached, as the owner had never built the other half. Mrs. Peterkin felt this was not a sufficient reason for undertaking the terrible process of a move to another house, when they were fully satisfied with the one they were in.

But a more powerful reason forced them to go. The track of a new railroad had to be carried directly through the place, and a station was to be built on that very spot.

Mrs. Peterkin so much dreaded moving that she questioned whether they could not continue to live in the upper part of the house and give up the lower part to the station. They could then dine at the restaurant, and it would be very convenient about travelling, as there would be no danger of missing the train, if one were sure of the direction.

But when the track was actually laid by the side of the house, and the steam-engine of the construction train puffed and screamed under the dining-room windows, and the engineer calmly looked in to see what the family had for dinner, she felt, indeed, that they must move.

But where should they go? It was difficult to find a house that satisfied the whole family. One was too far off, and looked into a tan-pit; another was too much in the middle of the town, next door to a machine-shop. Elizabeth Eliza wanted a porch covered with vines, that should face the sunset; while Mr. Peterkin thought it would not be convenient to sit there looking towards the west in the late afternoon (which was his only leisure time), for the sun would shine in his face. The little boys wanted a house with a great many doors, so that they could go in and out often. But Mr. Peterkin did not like so much slamming, and felt there was more danger of burglars with so many doors. Agamemnon wanted an observatory, and Solomon John a shed for a workshop. If he could have carpenters' tools and a workbench he could build an observatory, if it were wanted.

But it was necessary to decide upon something, for they must leave their house directly. So they were obliged to take Mr. Finch's, at the Corners. It satisfied none of the family. The porch was a piazza, and was opposite a barn. There were three other doors,–too many to please Mr. Peterkin, and not enough for the little boys. There was no observatory, and nothing to observe if there were one, as the house was too low and some high trees shut out any view. Elizabeth Eliza had hoped for a view; but Mr. Peterkin consoled her by deciding it was more healthy to have to walk for a view, and Mrs. Peterkin agreed that they might get tired of the same every day.

And everybody was glad a selection was made, and the little boys carried their india-rubber boots the very first afternoon.

Elizabeth Eliza wanted to have some system in the moving, and spent the evening in drawing up a plan. It would be easy to arrange everything beforehand, so that there should not be the confusion that her mother dreaded, and the discomfort they had in their last move. Mrs. Peterkin shook her head; she did not think it possible to move with any comfort. Agamemnon said a great deal could be done with a list and a programme.

Elizabeth Eliza declared if all were well arranged a programme would make it perfectly easy. They were to have new parlor carpets, which could be put down in the new house the first thing. Then the parlor furniture could be moved in, and there would be two comfortable rooms, in which Mr. and Mrs. Peterkin could sit while the rest of the move went on. Then the old parlor carpets could be taken up for the new dining-room and the downstairs bedroom, and the family could meanwhile dine at the old house. Mr. Peterkin did not object to this, though the distance was considerable, as he felt exercise would be good for them all. Elizabeth Eliza's programme then arranged that the dining-room furniture should be moved the third day, by which time one of the old parlor carpets would be down in the new dining-room, and they could still sleep in the old house. Thus there would always be a quiet, comfortable place in one house or the other. Each night, when Mr. Peterkin came home, he would find some place for quiet thought and rest, and each day there should be moved only the furniture needed for a certain room. Great confusion would be avoided and nothing misplaced. Elizabeth Eliza wrote these last words at the head of her programme,—"Misplace nothing." And Agamemnon made a copy of the programme for each member of the family.

The first thing to be done was to buy the parlor carpets. Elizabeth Eliza had already looked at some in Boston, and the next morning she went, by an early train, with her father, Agamemnon, and Solomon John, to decide upon them.

They got home about eleven o'clock, and when they reached the house were dismayed to find two furniture wagons in front of the gate, already partly filled! Mrs. Peterkin was walking in and out of the open door, a large book in one hand, and a duster in the other, and she came to meet them in an agony of anxiety. What should they do? The furniture carts had appeared soon after the rest had left for Boston, and the men had insisted upon beginning to move the things. In vain had she shown Elizabeth Eliza's programme; in vain had she insisted they must take only the parlor furniture. They had declared they must put the heavy pieces in the bottom of the cart, and the lighter furniture on top. So she had seen them go into every room in the house, and select one piece of furniture after another, without even looking at Elizabeth Eliza's programme; she doubted if they could have read it if they had looked at it.

Mr. Peterkin had ordered the carters to come; but he had no idea they would come so early, and supposed it would take them a long time to fill the carts.

But they had taken the dining-room sideboard first,–a heavy piece of furniture,–and all its contents were now on the dining-room tables. Then, indeed, they selected the parlor book-case, but had set every book on the floor The men had told Mrs. Peterkin they would put the books in the bottom of the cart, very much in the order they were taken from the shelves. But by this time Mrs. Peterkin was considering the carters as natural enemies, and dared not trust them; besides, the books ought all to be dusted. So she was now holding one of the volumes of Agamemnon's Encyclopædia, with difficulty, in one hand, while she was dusting it with the other. Elizabeth Eliza was in dismay. At this moment four men were bringing down a large chest of drawers from her father's room, and they called to her to stand out of the way. The parlors were a scene of confusion. In dusting the books Mrs. Peterkin neglected to restore them to the careful rows in which they were left by the men, and they lay in hopeless masses in different parts of the room. Elizabeth Eliza sunk in despair upon the end of a sofa.

"It would have been better to buy the red and blue carpet," said Solomon John.

"Is not the carpet bought?" exclaimed Mrs. Peterkin. And then they were obliged to confess they had been unable to decide upon one, and had come back to consult Mrs. Peterkin.

"What shall we do?" asked Mrs. Peterkin.

Elizabeth Eliza rose from the sofa and went to the door, saying, "I shall be back in a moment."

Agamemnon slowly passed round the room, collecting the scattered volumes of his Encyclopædia. Mr. Peterkin offered a helping hand to a man lifting a wardrobe.

Elizabeth Eliza soon returned. "I did not like to go and ask her. But I felt that I must in such an emergency. I explained to her the whole matter, and she thinks we should take the carpet at Makillan's."

"Makillan's" was a store in the village, and the carpet was the only one all the family had liked without any doubt; but they had supposed they might prefer one from Boston.

The moment was a critical one. Solomon John was sent directly to Makillan's to order the carpet to be put down that very day. But where should they dine? where should they have their supper? and where was Mr. Peterkin's "quiet hour"? Elizabeth Eliza was frantic; the dining-room floor and table were covered with things.

It was decided that Mr. and Mrs. Peterkin should dine at the Bromwicks, who had been most neighborly in their offers, and the rest should get something to eat at the baker's.

Agamemnon and Elizabeth Eliza hastened away to be ready to receive the carts at the other house, and direct the furniture as they could. After all there was something exhilarating in this opening of the new house, and in deciding where things should go. Gayly Elizabeth Eliza stepped down the front garden of the new home, and across the piazza, and to the door. But it was locked, and she had no keys!

"Agamemnon, did you bring the keys?" she exclaimed.

No, he had not seen them since the morning,–when–ah!–yes, the little boys were allowed to go to the house for their india-rubber boots, as there was a threatening of rain. Perhaps they had left some door unfastened–perhaps they had put the keys under the door-mat. No, each door, each window, was solidly closed, and there was no mat!

"I shall have to go to the school to see if they took the keys with them," said Agamemnon; "or else go home to see if they left them there." The school was in a different direction from the house, and far at the other end of the town; for Mr. Peterkin had not yet changed the boys' school, as he proposed to do after their move.

"That will be the only way," said Elizabeth Eliza; for it had been arranged that the little boys should take their lunch to school, and not come home at noon.

She sat down on the steps to wait, but only for a moment, for the carts soon appeared, turning the corner. What should be done with the furniture? Of course the carters must wait for the keys, as she should need them to set the furniture up in the right places. But they could not stop for this. They put it down upon the piazza, on the steps, in the garden, and Elizabeth Eliza saw how incongruous it was! There was something from every room in the house! Even the large family chest, which had proved too heavy for them to travel with had come down from the attic, and stood against the front door.

And Solomon John appeared with the carpet woman, and a boy with a wheelbarrow, bringing the new carpet. And all stood and waited. Some opposite neighbors appeared to offer advice and look on, and Elizabeth Eliza groaned inwardly that only the shabbiest of their furniture appeared to be standing full in view.

It seemed ages before Agamemnon returned, and no wonder; for he had been to the house, then to the school, then back to the house, for one of the little boys had left the keys at home, in the pocket of his clothes. Meanwhile the carpet-woman had waited, and the boy with the wheelbarrow had waited, and when they got in they found the parlor must be swept and cleaned. So the carpet-woman went off in dudgeon, for she was sure there would not be time enough to do anything.

And one of the carts came again, and in their hurry the men set the furniture down anywhere. Elizabeth Eliza was hoping to make a little place in the dining-room, where they might have their supper, and go home to sleep. But she looked out, and there were the carters bringing the bedsteads, and proceeding to carry them upstairs.

In despair Elizabeth Eliza went back to the old house. If she had been there she might have prevented this. She found Mrs. Peterkin in an agony about the entry oil-cloth. It had been made in the house, and how could it be taken out of the house? Agamemnon made measurements; it certainly could not go out of the front door! He suggested it might be left till the house was pulled down, when it could easily be moved out of one side. But Elizabeth Eliza reminded him that the whole house was to be moved without being taken apart. Perhaps it could be cut in strips narrow enough to go out. One of the men loading the remaining cart disposed of the question by coming in and rolling up the oil-cloth and carrying it on on top of his wagon.

Elizabeth Eliza felt she must hurry back to the new house. But what should they do?–no beds here, no carpets there! The dining-room table and sideboard were at the other house, the plates, and forks, and spoons here. In vain she looked at her programme. It was all reversed; everything was misplaced. Mr. Peterkin would suppose they were to eat here and sleep here, and what had become of the little boys?

Meanwhile the man with the first cart had returned. They fell to packing the dining-room china.

They were up in the attic, they were down in the cellar. Even one suggested to take the tacks out of the parlor carpets, as they should want to take them next. Mrs. Peterkin sunk upon a kitchen chair.

"Oh, I wish we had decided to stay and be moved in the house!" she exclaimed.

Solomon John urged his mother to go to the new house, for Mr. Peterkin would be there for his "quiet hour." And when the carters at last appeared, carrying the parlor carpets on their shoulders, she sighed and said, "There is nothing left," and meekly consented to be led away.

They reached the new house to find Mr. Peterkin sitting calmly in a rocking-chair on the piazza, watching the oxen coming into the opposite barn. He was waiting for the keys, which Solomon John had taken back with him. The little boys were in a horse-chestnut tree, at the side of the house.

Agamemnon opened the door. The passages were crowded with furniture, the floors were strewn with books; the bureau was upstairs that was to stand in a lower bedroom; there was not a place to lay a table,–there was nothing to lay upon it; for the knives and plates and spoons had not come, and although the tables were there they were covered with chairs and boxes.

At this moment came a covered basket from the lady from Philadelphia. It contained a choice supper, and forks and spoons, and at the same moment appeared a pot of hot tea from an opposite neighbor. They placed all this on the back of a bookcase lying upset, and sat around it. Solomon John came rushing in from the gate.

"The last load is coming! We are all moved!" he exclaimed; and the little boys joined in a chorus, "We are moved! we are moved!"

Mrs. Peterkin looked sadly round; the kitchen utensils were lying on the parlor lounge, and an old family gun on Elizabeth Eliza's hat-box. The parlor clock stood on a barrel; some coal-scuttles had been placed on the parlor table, a bust of Washington stood in the door-way, and the looking-glasses leaned against the pillars of the piazza. But they were moved! Mrs. Peterkin felt, indeed, that they were very much moved.

Day 125

1. Read some more from *The Peterkin Papers*.
2. Tell someone about the story.

THE PETERKINS DECIDE TO LEARN THE LANGUAGES.

CERTAINLY now was the time to study the languages. The Peterkins had moved into a new house, far more convenient than their old one, where they would have a place for everything and everything in its place. Of course they would then have more time.

Elizabeth Eliza recalled the troubles of the old house, how for a long time she was obliged to sit outside of the window upon the piazza, when she wanted to play on her piano.

Mrs. Peterkin reminded them of the difficulty about the table-cloths. The upper table-cloth was kept in a trunk that had to stand in front of the door to the closet under the stairs. But the under table-cloth was kept in a drawer in the closet. So, whenever the cloths were changed, the trunk had to be pushed away under some projecting shelves to make room for opening the closet-door (as the under table-cloth must be taken out first), then the trunk was pushed back to make room for it to be opened for the upper table-cloth, and, after all, it was necessary to push the trunk away again to open the closet-door for the knife-tray. This always consumed a great deal of time.

Now that the china-closet was large enough, everything could find a place in it.

Agamemnon especially enjoyed the new library. In the old house there was no separate room for books. The dictionaries were kept upstairs, which was very inconvenient, and the volumes of the Encyclopædia could not be together. There was not room for all in one place. So from A to P were to be found downstairs, and from Q to Z were scattered in different rooms upstairs. And the worst of it was, you could never remember whether from A to P included P. "I always went upstairs after P," said Agamemnon, "and then always found it downstairs, or else it was the other way."

Of course now there were more conveniences for study. With the books all in one room, there would be no time wasted in looking for them.

Mr. Peterkin suggested they should each take a separate language. If they went abroad, this would prove a great convenience. Elizabeth Eliza could talk French with the Parisians; Agamemnon, German with the Germans; Solomon John, Italian with the Italians; Mrs. Peterkin, Spanish in Spain; and perhaps he could himself master all the Eastern Languages and Russian.

Mrs. Peterkin was uncertain about undertaking the Spanish, but all the family felt very sure they should not go to Spain (as Elizabeth Eliza dreaded the Inquisition), and Mrs. Peterkin felt more willing.

Still she had quite an objection to going abroad. She had always said she would not go till a bridge was made across the Atlantic, and she was sure it did not look like it now.

Agamemnon said there was no knowing. There was something new every day, and a bridge was surely not harder to invent than a telephone, for they had bridges in the very earliest days.

Then came up the question of the teachers. Probably these could be found in Boston. If they could all come the same day, three could be brought out in the carryall. Agamemnon could go in for them, and could learn a little on the way out and in.

Mr. Peterkin made some inquiries about the Oriental languages. He was told that Sanscrit was at the root of all. So he proposed they should all begin with Sanscrit. They would thus require but one teacher, and could branch out into the other languages afterward.

But the family preferred learning the separate languages. Elizabeth Eliza already knew something of the French. She had tried to talk it, without much success, at the Centennial Exhibition, at one of the side-stands. But she found she had been talking with a Moorish gentleman who did not understand French. Mr. Peterkin feared they might need more libraries, if all the teachers came at the same hour; but Agamemnon reminded him that they would be using different dictionaries. And Mr. Peterkin thought something might be learned by having them all at once. Each one might pick up something beside the language he was studying, and it was a great thing to learn to talk a foreign language while others were talking about you. Mrs. Peterkin was afraid it would be like the Tower of Babel, and hoped it was all right.

Agamemnon brought forward another difficulty. Of course they ought to have foreign teachers, who spoke only their native languages. But, in this case, how could they engage them to come, or explain to them about the carryall, or arrange the proposed hours? He did not understand how anybody ever began with a foreigner, because he could not even tell him what he wanted.

Elizabeth Eliza thought a great deal might be done by signs and pantomime. Solomon John and the little boys began to show how it might be done. Elizabeth Eliza explained how "langues" meant both "languages" and "tongues," and they could point to their tongues. For practice, the little boys represented the foreign teachers talking in their different languages, and Agamemnon and Solomon John went to invite them to come out, and teach the family by a series of signs.

Mr. Peterkin thought their success was admirable, and that they might almost go abroad without any study of the languages, and trust to explaining themselves by signs. Still, as the bridge was not yet made, it might be as well to wait and cultivate the languages.

Mrs. Peterkin was afraid the foreign teachers might imagine they were invited out to lunch. Solomon John had constantly pointed to his mouth as he opened it and shut it, putting out his tongue; and it looked a great deal more as if he were inviting them to eat, than asking them to teach. Agamemnon suggested that they might carry the separate dictionaries when they went to see the teachers, and that would show that they meant lessons, and not lunch.

Mrs. Peterkin was not sure but she ought to prepare a lunch for them, if they had come all that way; but she certainly did not know what they were accustomed to eat.

Mr. Peterkin thought this would be a good thing to learn of the foreigners. It would be a good preparation for going abroad, and they might get used to the dishes before starting. The little boys were delighted at the idea of having new things cooked. Agamemnon had heard that beer-soup was a favorite dish with the Germans, and he would inquire how it was made in the first lesson. Solomon John had heard they were all very fond of garlic, and thought it would be a pretty attention to have some in the house the first day, that they might be cheered by the odor.

Elizabeth Eliza wanted to surprise the lady from Philadelphia by her knowledge of French, and hoped to begin on her lessons before the Philadelphia family arrived for their annual visit.

There were still some delays. Mr. Peterkin was very anxious to obtain teachers who had been but a short time in this country. He did not want to be tempted to talk any English with them. He wanted the latest and freshest languages, and at last came home one day with a list of "brand-new foreigners."

They decided to borrow the Bromwicks' carryall to use, beside their own, for the first day, and Mr. Peterkin and Agamemnon drove into town to bring all the teachers out. One was a Russian gentleman, travelling, who came with no idea of giving lessons, but perhaps he would consent to do so. He could not yet speak English.

Mr. Peterkin had his card-case, and the cards of the several gentlemen who had recommended the different teachers, and he went with Agamemnon from hotel to hotel collecting them. He found them all very polite, and ready to come, after the explanation by signs agreed upon. The dictionaries had been forgotten, but Agamemnon had a directory, which looked the same, and seemed to satisfy the foreigners.

Mr. Peterkin was obliged to content himself with the Russian instead of one who could teach Sanscrit, as there was no new teacher of that language lately arrived.

But there was an unexpected difficulty in getting the Russian gentleman into the same carriage with the teacher of Arabic, for he was a Turk, sitting with a fez on his head, on the back seat! They glared at each other, and began to assail each other in every language they knew, none of which Mr. Peterkin could understand. It might be Russian, it might be Arabic. It was easy to understand that they would never consent to sit in the same carriage. Mr. Peterkin was in despair; he had forgotten about the Russian war! What a mistake to have invited the Turk!

Quite a crowd collected on the sidewalk in front of the hotel. But the French gentleman politely, but stiffly, invited the Russian to go with him in the first carryall. Here was another difficulty. For the German professor was quietly ensconced on the back seat! As soon as the French gentleman put his foot on the step and saw him, he addressed him in such forcible language that the German professor got out of the door the other side, and came round on the sidewalk, and took him by the collar. Certainly the German and French gentlemen could not be put together, and more crowd collected!

Agamemnon, however, had happily studied up the German word "Herr," and he applied it to the German, inviting him by signs to take a seat in the other carryall. The German consented to sit by the Turk, as they neither of them could understand the other; and at last they started, Mr. Peterkin with the Italian by his side, and the French and Russian teachers behind, vociferating to each other in languages unknown to Mr. Peterkin, while he feared they were not perfectly in harmony, so he drove home as fast as possible. Agamemnon had a silent party. The Spaniard by his side was a little moody, while the Turk and the German behind did not utter a word.

At last they reached the house, and were greeted by Mrs. Peterkin and Elizabeth Eliza, Mrs. Peterkin with her llama lace shawl over her shoulders, as a tribute to the Spanish teacher.

Mr. Peterkin was careful to take his party in first, and deposit them in a distant part of the library, far from the Turk or the German, even putting the Frenchman and Russian apart.

Solomon John found the Italian dictionary, and seated himself by his Italian; Agamemnon, with the German dictionary, by the German. The little boys took their copy of the "Arabian Nights" to the Turk. Mr. Peterkin attempted to explain to the Russian that he had no Russian dictionary, as he had hoped to learn Sanscrit of him, while Mrs. Peterkin was trying to inform her teacher that she had no books in Spanish. She got over all fears of the Inquisition, he looked so sad, and she tried to talk a little, using English words, but very slowly, and altering the accent as far as she knew how. The Spaniard bowed, looked gravely interested, and was very polite.

Elizabeth Eliza, meanwhile, was trying her grammar phrases with the Parisian. She found it easier to talk French than to understand him. But he understood perfectly her sentences. She repeated one of her vocabularies, and went on with–"J'ai le livre." "As-tu le pain?" "L'enfant a une poire." He listened with great attention, and replied slowly. Suddenly she started after making out one of his sentences, and went to her mother to whisper, "They have made the mistake you feared. They think they are invited to lunch! He has just been thanking me for our politeness in inviting them to déjeûner,–that means breakfast!"

"They have not had their breakfast!" exclaimed Mrs. Peterkin, looking at her Spaniard; "he does look hungry! What shall we do?"

Elizabeth Eliza was consulting her father. What should they do? How should they make them understand that they invited them to teach, not lunch. Elizabeth Eliza begged Agamemnon to look out "apprendre" in the dictionary. It must mean to teach. Alas, they found it means both to teach and to learn! What should they do? The foreigners were now sitting silent in their different corners. The Spaniard grew more and more sallow. What if he should faint? The Frenchman was rolling up each of his mustaches to a point as he gazed at the German. What if the Russian should fight the Turk? What if the German should be exasperated by the airs of the Parisian?

"We must give them something to eat," said Mr. Peterkin, in a low tone. "It would calm them."

"If I only knew what they were used to eating," said Mrs. Peterkin.

Solomon John suggested that none of them knew what the others were used to eating, and they might bring in anything.

Mrs. Peterkin hastened out with hospitable intents. Amanda could make good coffee. Mr. Peterkin had suggested some American dish. Solomon John sent a little boy for some olives.

It was not long before the coffee came in, and a dish of baked beans. Next, some olives and a loaf of bread, and some boiled eggs, and some bottles of beer. The effect was astonishing. Every man spoke his own tongue, and fluently. Mrs. Peterkin poured out coffee for the Spaniard, while he bowed to her. They all liked beer, they all liked olives. The Frenchman was fluent about "les moeurs Américaines." Elizabeth Eliza supposed he alluded to their not having set any table. The Turk smiled, the Russian was voluble. In the midst of the clang of the different languages, just as Mr. Peterkin was again repeating, under cover of the noise of many tongues, "How shall we make them understand that we want them to teach?"–at this very moment the door was flung open, and there came in the lady from Philadelphia, that day arrived, her first call of the season!

She started back in terror at the tumult of so many different languages! The family, with joy, rushed to meet her. All together they called upon her to explain for them. Could she help them? Could she tell the foreigners they wanted to take lessons? Lessons? They had no sooner uttered the word than their guests all started up with faces beaming with joy. It was the one English word they all knew! They had come to Boston to give lessons! The Russian traveller had hoped to learn English in this way. The thought pleased them more than the déjeûner. Yes, gladly would they give lessons. The Turk smiled at the idea. The first step was taken. The teachers knew they were expected to teach.

Day 126

    3.   Continue reading stories from *The Peterkin Papers*.
    4.   Tell someone about the story.

THE LADY WHO PUT SALT IN HER COFFEE

 THIS was Mrs. Peterkin. It was a mistake. She had poured out a delicious cup of coffee, and, just as she was helping herself to cream, she found she had put in salt instead of sugar! It tasted bad. What should she do? Of course she couldn't drink the coffee; so she called in the family, for she was sitting at a late breakfast all alone. The family came in; they all tasted, and looked, and wondered what should be done, and all sat down to think.

At last Agamemnon, who had been to college, said, "Why don't we go over and ask the advice of the chemist?" (For the chemist lived over the way, and was a very wise man.)

Mrs. Peterkin said, "Yes," and Mr. Peterkin said, "Very well," and all the children said they would go too. So the little boys put on their india-rubber boots, and over they went.

Now the chemist was just trying to find out something which should turn everything it touched into gold; and he had a large glass bottle into which he put all kinds of gold and silver, and many other valuable things, and melted them all up over the fire, till he had almost found what he wanted. He could turn things into almost gold. But just now he had used up all the gold that he had round the house, and gold was high. He had used up his wife's gold thimble and his great-grandfather's gold-bowed spectacles; and he had melted up the gold head of his great-great-grandfather's cane; and, just as the Peterkin family came in, he was down on his knees before his wife, asking her to let him have her wedding-ring to melt up with an the rest, because this time he knew he should succeed, and should be able to turn everything into gold; and then she could have a new wedding-ring of diamonds, all set in emeralds and rubies and topazes, and all the furniture could be turned into the finest of gold.

Now his wife was just consenting when the Peterkin family burst in. You can imagine how mad the chemist was! He came near throwing his crucible–that was the name of his melting-pot–at their heads. But he didn't. He listened as calmly as he could to the story of how Mrs. Peterkin had put salt in her coffee.

At first he said he couldn't do anything about it; but when Agamemnon said they would pay in gold if he would only go, he packed up his bottles in a leather case, and went back with them all.

First he looked at the coffee, and then stirred it. Then he put in a little chlorate of potassium, and the family tried it all round; but it tasted no better. Then he stirred in a little bichlorate of magnesia. But Mrs. Peterkin didn't like that. Then he added some tartaric acid and some hypersulphate of lime. But no; it was no better. "I have it!" exclaimed the chemist,–"a little ammonia is just the thing!" No, it wasn't the thing at all.

Then he tried, each in turn, some oxalic, cyanic, acetic, phosphoric, chloric, hyperchloric, sulphuric, boracic, silicic, nitric, formic, nitrous nitric, and carbonic acids. Mrs. Peterkin tasted each, and said the flavor was pleasant, but not precisely that of coffee. So then he tried a little calcium, aluminum, barium, and strontium, a little clear bitumen, and a half of a third of a sixteenth of a grain of arsenic. This gave rather a pretty color; but still Mrs. Peterkin ungratefully said it tasted of anything but coffee. The chemist was not discouraged. He put in a little belladonna and atropine, some granulated hydrogen, some potash, and a very little antimony, finishing off with a little pure carbon. But still Mrs. Peterkin was not satisfied.

The chemist said that all he had done ought to have taken out the salt. The theory remained the same, although the experiment had failed. Perhaps a little starch would have some effect. If not, that was all the time he could give. He should like to be paid, and go. They were all much obliged to him, and willing to give him $1.37 1/2 in gold. Gold was now 2.69 3/4, so Mr. Peterkin found in the newspaper. This gave Agamemnon a pretty little sum. He sat himself down to do it. But there was the coffee! All sat and thought awhile, till Elizabeth Eliza said, "Why don't we go to the herb-woman?" Elizabeth Eliza was the only daughter. She was named after her two aunts,–Elizabeth, from the sister of her father; Eliza, from her mother's sister. Now, the herb-woman was an old woman who came round to sell herbs, and knew a great deal. They all shouted with joy at the idea of asking her, and Solomon John and the younger children agreed to go and find her too. The herb-woman lived down at the very end of the street; so the boys put on their india-rubber boots again, and they set off. It was a long walk through the village, but they came at last to the herb-woman's house, at the foot of a high hill. They went through her little garden. Here she had marigolds and hollyhocks, and old maids and tall sunflowers, and all kinds of sweet-smelling herbs, so that the air was full of tansy-tea and elder-blow. Over the porch grew a hop-vine, and a brandy-cherry tree shaded the door, and a luxuriant cranberry-vine flung its delicious fruit across the window. They went into a small parlor, which smelt very spicy. All around hung little bags full of catnip, and peppermint, and all kinds of herbs; and dried stalks hung from the ceiling; and on the shelves were jars of rhubarb, senna, manna, and the like.

But there was no little old woman. She had gone up into the woods to get some more wild herbs, so they all thought they would follow her,–Elizabeth Eliza, Solomon John, and the little boys. They had to climb up over high rocks, and in among huckleberry-bushes and black berry-vines. But the little boys had their india-rubber boots. At last they discovered the little old woman. They knew her by her hat. It was steeple-crowned, without any vane. They saw her digging with her trowel round a sassafras bush. They told her their story,– how their mother had put salt in her coffee, and how the chemist had made it worse instead of better, and how their mother couldn't drink it, and wouldn't she come and see what she could do? And she said she would, and took up her little old apron, with pockets all round, all filled with everlasting and pennyroyal, and went back to her house.

There she stopped, and stuffed her huge pockets with some of all the kinds of herbs. She took some tansy and peppermint, and caraway-seed and dill, spearmint and cloves, pennyroyal and sweet marjoram, basil and rosemary, wild thyme and some of the other time,–such as you have in clocks,–sappermint and oppermint, catnip, valerian, and hop; indeed, there isn't a kind of herb you can think of that the little old woman didn't have done up in her little paper bags, that had all been dried in her little Dutch-oven. She packed these all up, and then went back with the children, taking her stick.

Meanwhile Mrs. Peterkin was getting quite impatient for her coffee.

As soon as the little old woman came she had it set over the fire, and began to stir in the different herbs. First she put in a little hop for the bitter. Mrs. Peterkin said it tasted like hop-tea, and not at all like coffee. Then she tried a little flagroot and snakeroot, then some spruce gum, and some caraway and some dill, some rue and rosemary, some sweet marjoram and sour, some oppermint and sappermint, a little spearmint and peppermint, some wild thyme, and some of the other tame time, some tansy and basil, and catnip and valerian, and sassafras, ginger, and pennyroyal. The children tasted after each mixture, but made up dreadful faces. Mrs. Peterkin tasted, and did the same. The more the old woman stirred, and the more she put in, the worse it all seemed to taste.

So the old woman shook her head, and muttered a few words, and said she must go. She believed the coffee was bewitched. She bundled up her packets of herbs, and took her trowel, and her basket, and her stick, and went back to her root of sassafras, that she had left half in the air and half out. And all she would take for pay was five cents in currency.

Then the family were in despair, and all sat and thought a great while. It was growing late in the day, and Mrs. Peterkin hadn't had her cup of coffee. At last Elizabeth Eliza said, "They say that the lady from Philadelphia, who is staying in town, is very wise. Suppose I go and ask her what is best to be done." To this they all agreed, it was a great thought, and off Elizabeth Eliza went.

She told the lady from Philadelphia the whole story,–how her mother had put salt in the coffee; how the chemist had been called in; how he tried everything but could make it no better; and how they went for the little old herb-woman, and how she had tried in vain, for her mother couldn't drink the coffee. The lady from Philadelphia listened very attentively, and then said, "Why doesn't your mother make a fresh cup of coffee?" Elizabeth Eliza started with surprise. Solomon John shouted with joy; so did Agamemnon, who had just finished his sum; so did the little boys, who had followed on. "Why didn't we think of that?" said Elizabeth Eliza; and they all went back to their mother, and she had her cup of coffee.

Day 127

1. Read chapter 6 of *The Peterkin Papers*. A "dumb-waiter" is a sort of elevator for food. The food is placed on a shelf that can be lowered or lifted from the kitchen to the dining room with a pulley system.
2. Tell someone about the story.

WHY THE PETERKINS HAD A LATE DINNER.

THE trouble was in the dumb-waiter. All had seated themselves at the dinner-table, and Amanda had gone to take out the dinner she had sent up from the kitchen on the dumb-waiter. But something was the matter; she could not pull it up. There was the dinner, but she could not reach it. All the family, in turn, went and tried; all pulled together, in vain; the dinner could not be stirred.

"No dinner!" exclaimed Agamemnon.

"I am quite hungry," said Solomon John.

At last Mr. Peterkin said, "I am not proud. I am willing to dine in the kitchen."

This room was below the dining-room. All consented to this. Each one went down, taking a napkin.

The cook laid the kitchen table, put on it her best table-cloth, and the family sat down. Amanda went to the dumb-waiter for the dinner, but she could not move it down.

The family were all in dismay. There was the dinner, half-way between the kitchen and dining-room, and there were they all hungry to eat it!

"What is there for dinner?" asked Mr. Peterkin.

"Roast turkey," said Mrs. Peterkin.

Mr. Peterkin lifted his eyes to the ceiling.

"Squash, tomato, potato, and sweet potato," Mrs. Peterkin continued.

"Sweet potato!" exclaimed both the little boys.

"I am very glad now that I did not have cranberry," said Mrs. Peterkin, anxious to find a bright point.

"Let us sit down and think about it," said Mr. Peterkin.

"I have an idea," said Agamemnon, after a while.

"Let us hear it," said Mr. Peterkin. "Let each one speak his mind."

"The turkey," said Agamemnon, "must be just above the kitchen door. If I had a ladder and an axe, I could cut away the plastering and reach it."

"That is a great idea," said Mrs. Peterkin.

"If you think you could do it," said Mr. Peterkin.

"Would it not be better to have a carpenter?" asked Elizabeth Eliza.

"A carpenter might have a ladder and an axe, and I think we have neither," said Mrs. Peterkin.

"A carpenter! A carpenter!" exclaimed the rest.

It was decided that Mr. Peterkin, Solomon John, and the little boys should go in search of a carpenter.

Agamemnon proposed that, meanwhile, he should go and borrow a book; for he had another idea.

"This affair of the turkey," he said, "reminds me of those buried cities that have been dug out,–Herculaneum, for instance."

"Oh, yes," interrupted Elizabeth Eliza, "and Pompeii."

"Yes," said Agamemnon, "they found there pots and kettles. Now, I should like to know how they did it; and I mean to borrow a book and read. I think it was done with a pickaxe."

So the party set out. But when Mr. Peterkin reached the carpenter's shop, there was no carpenter to be found there.

"He must be at his house, eating his dinner," suggested Solomon John.

"Happy man," exclaimed Mr. Peterkin, "he has a dinner to eat!"

They went to the carpenter's house, but found he had gone out of town for a day's job. But his wife told them that he always came back at night to ring the nine-o'clock bell.

"We must wait till then," said Mr. Peterkin, with an effort at cheerfulness.

At home he found Agamemnon reading his book, and all sat down to hear of Herculaneum and Pompeii.

Time passed on, and the question arose about tea. Would it do to have tea when they had had no dinner? A part of the family thought it would not do; the rest wanted tea.

"I suppose you remember the wise lady of Philadelphia, who was here not long ago," said Mr. Peterkin.

"Oh, yes," said Mrs. Peterkin.

"Let us try to think what she would advise us," said Mr. Peterkin.

"I wish she were here," said Elizabeth Eliza.

"I think," said Mr. Peterkin, "she would say, let them that want tea have it; the rest can go without."

So they had tea, and, as it proved, all sat down to it. But not much was eaten, as there had been no dinner.

When the nine-o'clock bell was heard, Agamemnon, Solomon John, and the little boys rushed to the church, and found the carpenter.

They asked him to bring a ladder, axes and pickaxe. As he felt it might be a case of fire, he brought also his fire-buckets.

When the matter was explained to him, he went into the dining-room, looked into the dumb-waiter, untwisted a cord, and arranged the weight, and pulled up the dinner.

There was a family shout.

"The trouble was in the weight," said the carpenter.

"That is why it is called a dumb-waiter," Solomon John explained to the little boys.

The dinner was put upon the table.

Mrs. Peterkin frugally suggested that they might now keep it for the next day, as to-day was almost gone, and they had had tea.

But nobody listened. All sat down to the roast turkey; and Amanda warmed over the vegetables.

"Patient waiters are no losers," said Agamemnon.

Day 128

1.   Read chapter 7 of *The Peterkin Papers*.
2.   Tell someone about the story.

THE PETERKINS' SUMMER JOURNEY.

IN fact, it was their last summer's journey—for it had been planned then; but there had been so many difficulties, it had been delayed.

The first trouble had been about trunks. The family did not own a trunk suitable for travelling.

Agamemnon had his valise, that he had used when he stayed a week at a time at the academy; and a trunk had been bought for Elizabeth Eliza when she went to the seminary. Solomon John and Mr. Peterkin, each had his patent-leather hand-bag. But all these were too small for the family. And the little boys wanted to carry their kite.

Mrs. Peterkin suggested her grandmother's trunk. This was a hair-trunk, very large and capacious. It would hold everything they would want to carry, except what would go in Elizabeth Eliza's trunk, or the valise and bags.

Everybody was delighted at this idea. It was agreed that the next day the things should be brought into Mrs. Peterkin's room, for her to see if they could all be packed.

"If we can get along," said Elizabeth Eliza, "without having to ask advice, I shall be glad!"

"Yes," said Mr. Peterkin, "It is time now for people to be coming to ask advice of us."

The next morning Mrs. Peterkin began by taking out the things that were already in the trunk. Here were last year's winter things, and not only these, but old clothes that had been put away,–Mrs. Peterkin's wedding-dress; the skirts the little boys used to wear before they put on jackets and trousers.

All day Mrs. Peterkin worked over the trunk, putting away the old things, putting in the new. She packed up all the clothes she could think of, both summer and winter ones, because you never can tell what sort of weather you will have.

Agamemnon fetched his books, and Solomon John his spy-glass. There were her own and Elizabeth Eliza's best bonnets in a bandbox; also Solomon John's hats, for he had an old one and a new one. He bought a new hat for fishing, with a very wide brim and deep crown; all of heavy straw.

Agamemnon brought down a large heavy dictionary, and an atlas still larger. This contained maps of all the countries in the world.

"I have never had a chance to look at them," he said; "but when one travels, then is the time to study geography."

Mr. Peterkin wanted to take his turning-lathe. So Mrs. Peterkin packed his tool-chest. It gave her some trouble, for it came to her just as she had packed her summer dresses. At first she thought it would help to smooth the dresses, and placed it on top; but she was forced to take all out, and set it at the bottom. This was not so much matter, as she had not yet the right dresses to put in. Both Mrs. Peterkin and Elizabeth Eliza would need new dresses for this occasion. The little boys' hoops went in; so did their india-rubber boots, in case it should not rain when they started. They each had a hoe and shovel, and some baskets, that were packed.

Mrs. Peterkin called in all the family on the evening of the second day to see how she had succeeded. Everything was packed, even the little boys' kite lay smoothly on the top.

"I like to see a thing so nicely done," said Mr. Peterkin.

The next thing was to cord up the trunk, and Mr. Peterkin tried to move it. But neither he, nor Agamemnon, nor Solomon John could lift it alone, or all together.

Here was a serious difficulty. Solomon John tried to make light of it.

"Expressmen could lift it. Expressmen were used to such things."

"But we did not plan expressing it," said Mrs. Peterkin, in a discouraged tone.

"We can take a carriage," said Solomon John.

"I am afraid the trunk would not go on the back of a carriage," said Mrs. Peterkin.

"The hackman could not lift it, either," said Mr. Peterkin.

"People do travel with a great deal of baggage," said Elizabeth Eliza.

"And with very large trunks," said Agamemnon.

"Still they are trunks that can be moved," said Mr. Peterkin, giving another try at the trunk in vain. "I am afraid we must give it up," he said; "it would be such a trouble in going from place to place."

"We would not mind if we got it to the place," said Elizabeth Eliza.

"But how to get it there?" Mr. Peterkin asked, with a sigh.

"This is our first obstacle," said Agamemnon; "we must do our best to conquer it."

"What is an obstacle?" asked the little boys.

"It is the trunk," said Solomon John.

"Suppose we look out the word in the dictionary," said Agamemnon, taking the large volume from the trunk. "Ah, here it is–" And he read:–

"OBSTACLE, an impediment."

"That is a worse word than the other," said one of the little boys.

"But listen to this," and Agamemnon continued: "Impediment is something that entangles the feet; obstacle, something that stands in the way; obstruction, something that blocks up the passage; hinderance, something that holds back."

"The trunk is all these," said Mr. Peterkin, gloomily.

"It does not entangle the feet," said Solomon John, "for it can't move."

"I wish it could," said the little boys together.

Mrs. Peterkin spent a day or two in taking the things out of the trunk and putting them away.

"At least," she said, "this has given me some experience in packing."

And the little boys felt as if they had quite been a journey.

But the family did not like to give up their plan. It was suggested that they might take the things out of the trunk, and pack it at the station; the little boys could go and come with the things. But Elizabeth Eliza thought the place too public.

Gradually the old contents of the great trunk went back again to it.

At length a friend unexpectedly offered to lend Mr. Peterkin a good-sized family trunk. But it was late in the season, and so the journey was put off from that summer.

But now the trunk was sent round to the house, and a family consultation was held about packing it. Many things would have to be left at home, it was so much smaller than the grandmother's hair-trunk. But Agamemnon had been studying the atlas through the winter, and felt familiar with the more important places, so it would not be necessary to take it. And Mr. Peterkin decided to leave his turning-lathe at home, and his tool-chest.

Again Mrs. Peterkin spent two days in accommodating the things. With great care and discretion, and by borrowing two more leather bags, it could be accomplished. Everything of importance could be packed, except the little boys' kite. What should they do about that?

The little boys proposed carrying it in their hands; but Solomon John and Elizabeth Eliza would not consent to this.

"I do think it is one of the cases where we might ask the advice of the lady from Philadelphia," said Mrs. Peterkin, at last.

"She has come on here," said Agamemnon, "and we have not been to see her this summer."

"She may think we have been neglecting her," suggested Mr. Peterkin.

The little boys begged to be allowed to go and ask her opinion about the kite. They came back in high spirits.

"She says we might leave this one at home, and make a new kite when we get there," they cried.

"What a sensible idea!" exclaimed Mr. Peterkin; "and I may have leisure to help you."

"We'll take plenty of newspapers," said Solomon John.

"And twine," said the little boys. And this matter was settled.

The question then was, "When should they go?"

Day 129

1.   Read chapter 8 of *The Peterkin Papers*.
2.   Tell someone about the story.

THE PETERKINS SNOWED-UP.

MRS. PETERKIN awoke one morning to find a heavy snow-storm raging. The wind had flung the snow against the windows, had heaped it up around the house, and thrown it into huge white drifts over the fields, covering hedges and fences.

Mrs. Peterkin went from one window to the other to look out; but nothing could be seen but the driving storm and the deep white snow. Even Mr. Bromwick's house, on the opposite side of the street, was hidden by the swift-falling flakes.

"What shall I do about it?" thought Mrs. Peterkin. "No roads cleared out! Of course there'll be no butcher and no milkman!"

The first thing to be done was to wake up all the family early; for there was enough in the house for breakfast, and there was no knowing when they would have anything more to eat.

It was best to secure the breakfast first.

So she went from one room to the other, as soon as it was light, waking the family, and before long all were dressed and downstairs.

And then all went round the house to see what had happened.

All the water-pipes that there were were frozen. The milk was frozen. They could open the door into the wood-house; but the wood-house door into the yard was banked up with snow; and the front door, and the piazza door, and the side door stuck. Nobody could get in or out!

Meanwhile, Amanda, the cook, had succeeded in making the kitchen fire, but had discovered there was no furnace coal.

"The furnace coal was to have come to-day," said Mrs. Peterkin, apologetically.

"Nothing will come to-day," said Mr. Peterkin, shivering.

But a fire could be made in a stove in the dining-room.

All were glad to sit down to breakfast and hot coffee. The little boys were much pleased to have "ice-cream" for breakfast.

"When we get a little warm," said Mr. Peterkin, "we will consider what is to be done."

"I am thankful I ordered the sausages yesterday," said Mrs. Peterkin. "I was to have had a leg of mutton to-day."

"Nothing will come to-day," said Agamemnon, gloomily.

"Are these sausages the last meat in the house?" asked Mr. Peterkin.

"Yes," said Mrs. Peterkin.

The potatoes also were gone, the barrel of apples empty, and she had meant to order more flour that very day.

"Then we are eating our last provisions," said Solomon John, helping himself to another sausage.

"I almost wish we had stayed in bed," said Agamemnon.

"I thought it best to make sure of our breakfast first," repeated Mrs. Peterkin.

"Shall we literally have nothing left to eat?" asked Mr. Peterkin.

"There's the pig!" suggested Solomon John.

Yes, happily, the pigsty was at the end of the wood-house, and could be reached under cover.

But some of the family could not eat fresh pork.

"We should have to 'corn' part of him," said Agamemnon.

"My butcher has always told me," said Mrs. Peterkin, "that if I wanted a ham I must keep a pig. Now we have the pig, but have not the ham!"

"Perhaps we could 'corn' one or two of his legs," suggested one of the little boys.

"We need not settle that now," said Mr. Peterkin. "At least the pig will keep us from starving."

The little boys looked serious; they were fond of their pig.

"If we had only decided to keep a cow," said Mrs. Peterkin.

"Alas! yes," said Mr. Peterkin, "one learns a great many things too late!"

"Then we might have had ice-cream all the time!" exclaimed the little boys.

Indeed, the little boys, in spite of the prospect of starving, were quite pleasantly excited at the idea of being snowed-up, and hurried through their breakfasts that they might go and try to shovel out a path from one of the doors.

"I ought to know more about the water-pipes," said Mr. Peterkin. "Now, I shut off the water last night in the bath-room, or else I forgot to; and I ought to have shut it off in the cellar."

The little boys came back. Such a wind at the front door, they were going to try the side door.

"Another thing I have learned to-day," said Mr. Peterkin, "is not to have all the doors on one side of the house, because the storm blows the snow against all the doors."

217

Solomon John started up.

"Let us see if we are blocked up on the east side of the house!" he exclaimed.

"Of what use," asked Mr. Peterkin, "since we have no door on the east side?"

"We could cut one," said Solomon John.

"Yes, we could cut a door," exclaimed Agamemnon.

"But how can we tell whether there is any snow there?" asked Elizabeth Eliza,–"for there is no window."

In fact, the east side of the Peterkins' house formed a blank wall. The owner had originally planned a little block of semi-detached houses. He had completed only one, very semi and very detached.

"It is not necessary to see," said Agamemnon, profoundly; "of course, if the storm blows against this side of the house, the house itself must keep the snow from the other side."

"Yes," said Solomon John, "there must be a space clear of snow on the east side of the house, and if we could open a way to that "–

"We could open a way to the butcher," said Mr. Peterkin, promptly.

Agamemnon went for his pick-axe. He had kept one in the house ever since the adventure of the dumb-waiter.

"What part of the wall had we better attack?" asked Mr. Peterkin.

Mrs. Peterkin was alarmed.

"What will Mr. Mudge, the owner of the house, think of it?" she exclaimed. "Have we a right to injure the wall of the house?"

"It is right to preserve ourselves from starving," said Mr. Peterkin. "The drowning man must snatch at a straw!"

"It is better that he should find his house chopped a little when the thaw comes," said Elizabeth Eliza, "than that he should find us lying about the house, dead of hunger, upon the floor."

Mrs. Peterkin was partially convinced.

The little boys came in to warm their hands. They had not succeeded in opening the side door, and were planning trying to open the door from the wood-house to the garden.

"That would be of no use," said Mrs. Peterkin, "the butcher cannot get into the garden."

"But we might shovel off the snow," suggested one of the little boys, "and dig down to some of last year's onions."

Meanwhile, Mr. Peterkin, Agamemnon, and Solomon John had been bringing together their carpenter's tools, and Elizabeth Eliza proposed using a gouge, if they would choose the right spot to begin.

The little boys were delighted with the plan, and hastened to find,—one, a little hatchet, and the other a gimlet. Even Amanda armed herself with a poker.

"It would be better to begin on the ground floor," said Mr. Peterkin.

"Except that we may meet with a stone foundation," said Solomon John.

"If the wall is thinner upstairs," said Agamemnon, "it will do as well to cut a window as a door, and haul up anything the butcher may bring below in his cart."

Everybody began to pound a little on the wall to find a favorable place, and there was a great deal of noise. The little boys actually cut a bit out of the plastering with their hatchet and gimlet. Solomon John confided to Elizabeth Eliza that it reminded him of stories of prisoners who cut themselves free, through stone walls, after days and days of secret labor.

Mrs. Peterkin, even, had come with a pair of tongs in her hand. She was interrupted by a voice behind her.

"Here's your leg of mutton, marm!"

It was the butcher. How had he got in?

"Excuse me, marm, for coming in at the side door, but the back gate is kinder blocked up. You were making such a pounding I could not make anybody hear me knock at the side door."

"But how did you make a path to the door?" asked Mr. Peterkin. "You must have been working at it a long time. It must be near noon now."

"I'm about on regular time," answered the butcher. "The town team has cleared out the high road, and the wind has been down the last half-hour. The storm is over."

True enough! The Peterkins had been so busy inside the house they had not noticed the ceasing of the storm outside.

"And we were all up an hour earlier than usual," said Mr. Peterkin, when the butcher left. He had not explained to the butcher why he had a pickaxe in his hand.

"If we had lain abed till the usual time," said Solomon John, "we should have been all right."

"For here is the milkman!" said Elizabeth Eliza, as a knock was now heard at the side door.

"It is a good thing to learn" said Mr. Peterkin, "not to get up any earlier than is necessary."

Day 130

1.   Read chapter 9 of *The Peterkin Papers*.
2.   Tell someone about the story.

THE PETERKINS DECIDE TO KEEP A COW.

NOT that they were fond of drinking milk, nor that they drank very much. But for that reason Mr. Peterkin thought it would be well to have a cow, to encourage the family to drink more, as he felt it would be so healthy.

Mrs. Peterkin recalled the troubles of the last cold winter, and how near they came to starving, when they were shut up in a severe snow-storm, and the water-pipes burst, and the milk was frozen. If the cow-shed could open out of the wood-shed, such trouble might be prevented.

Tony Larkin was to come over and milk the cow every morning, and Agamemnon and Solomon John agreed to learn how to milk, in case Tony should be "snowed up," or have the whooping-cough in the course of the winter. The little boys thought they knew how already.

But if they were to have three or four pailfuls of milk every day, it was important to know where to keep it.

"One way will be," said Mrs. Peterkin, "to use a great deal every day. We will make butter."

"That will be admirable," thought Mr. Peterkin.

"And custards," suggested Solomon John.

"And syllabub," said Elizabeth Eliza.

"And cocoa-nut cakes," exclaimed the little boys.

"We don't need the milk for cocoa-nut cakes," said Mrs. Peterkin.

The little boys thought they might have a cocoa-nut tree instead of a cow. You could have the milk from the cocoa-nuts, and it would be pleasant climbing the tree, and you would not have to feed it.

"Yes," said Mr. Peterkin, "we shall have to feed the cow."

"Where shall we pasture her?" asked Agamemnon.

"Up on the hills, up on the hills," exclaimed the little boys, "where there are a great many bars to take down, and huckleberry-bushes!"

Mr. Peterkin had been thinking of their own little lot behind the house.

"But I don't know," he said, "but the cow might eat off all the grass in one day, and there would not be any left for to-morrow, unless the grass grew fast enough every night."

Agamemnon said it would depend upon the season. In a rainy season the grass would come up very fast, in a drought it might not grow at all.

"I suppose," said Mrs. Peterkin, "that is the worst of having a cow,–there might be a drought."

Mr. Peterkin thought they might make some calculation from the quantity of grass in the lot.

Solomon John suggested that measurements might be made by seeing how much grass the Bromwicks' cow, opposite them, eat up in a day.

The little boys agreed to go over and spend the day on the Bromwicks' fence, and take an observation.

"The trouble would be," said Elizabeth Eliza, "that cows walk about so, and the Bromwicks' yard is very large. Now she would be eating in one place, and then she would walk to another. She would not be eating all the time, a part of the time she would be chewing."

The little boys thought they should like nothing better than to have some sticks, and keep the cow in one corner of the yard till the calculations were made.

But Elizabeth Eliza was afraid the Bromwicks would not like it.

"Of course, it would bring all the boys in the school about the place, and very likely they would make the cow angry."

Agamemnon recalled that Mr. Bromwick once wanted to hire Mr. Peterkin's lot for his cow.

Mr. Peterkin started up.

"That is true; and of course Mr. Bromwick must have known there was feed enough for one cow."

"And the reason you didn't let him have it," said Solomon John, "was that Elizabeth Eliza was afraid of cows."

"I did not like the idea," said Elizabeth Eliza, "of their cow's looking at me over the top of the fence, perhaps, when I should be planting the sweet peas in the garden. I hope our cow would be a quiet one. I should not like her jumping over the fence into the flower-beds."

Mr. Peterkin declared that he should buy a cow of the quietest kind.

"I should think something might be done about covering her horns," said Mrs. Peterkin; "that seems the most dangerous part. Perhaps they might be padded with cotton."

Elizabeth Eliza said cows were built so large and clumsy, that if they came at you they could not help knocking you over.

The little boys would prefer having the pasture a great way off. Half the fun of having a cow would be going up on the hills after her.

Agamemnon thought the feed was not so good on the hills.

"The cow would like it ever so much better," the little boys declared, "on account of the variety. If she did not like the rocks and the bushes, she could walk round and find the grassy places."

"I am not sure," said Elizabeth Eliza, "but it would be less dangerous to keep the cow in the lot behind the house, because she would not be coming and going, morning and night, in that jerky way the Larkins' cows come home. They don't mind which gate they rush in at. I should hate to have our cow dash into our front yard just as I was coming home of an afternoon."

"That is true," said Mr. Peterkin; "we can have the door of the cow-house open directly into the pasture, and save the coming and going."

The little boys were quite disappointed. The cow would miss the exercise, and they would lose a great pleasure.

Solomon John suggested that they might sit on the fence and watch the cow.

It was decided to keep the cow in their own pasture; and as they were to put on an end kitchen, it would be perfectly easy to build a dairy.

The cow proved a quiet one. She was a little excited when all the family stood round at the first milking, and watched her slowly walking into the shed.

Elizabeth Eliza had her scarlet sack dyed brown a fortnight before. It was the one she did her gardening in, and it might have infuriated the cow. And she kept out of the garden the first day or two.

Mrs. Peterkin and Elizabeth Eliza bought the best kind of milk-pans, of every size.

But there was a little disappointment about the taste of the milk.

The little boys liked it, and drank large mugs of it. Elizabeth Eliza said she could never learn to love milk warm from the cow, though she would like to do her best to patronize the cow.

Mrs. Peterkin was afraid Amanda did not understand about taking care of the milk; yet she had been down to overlook her, and she was sure the pans and the closet were all clean.

"Suppose we send a pitcher of cream over to the lady from Philadelphia to try," said Elizabeth Eliza; "it will be a pretty attention before she goes."

"It might be awkward if she didn't like it," said Solomon John. "Perhaps something is the matter with the grass."

"I gave the cow an apple to eat yesterday," said one of the little boys, remorsefully.

Elizabeth Eliza went over, and Mrs. Peterkin too, and explained all to the lady from Philadelphia, asking her to taste the milk.

The lady from Philadelphia tasted, and said the truth was that the milk was sour!

"I was afraid it was so," said Mrs. Peterkin; "but I didn't know what to expect from these new kinds of cows."

The lady from Philadelphia asked where the milk was kept.

"In the new dairy," answered Elizabeth Eliza.

"Is that in a cool place?" asked the lady from Philadelphia.

Elizabeth Eliza explained it was close by the new kitchen.

"Is it near the chimney?" inquired the lady from Philadelphia.

"It is directly back of the chimney and the new kitchen-range," replied Elizabeth Eliza. "I suppose it is too hot!"

"Well, well!" said Mrs. Peterkin, "that is it! Last winter the milk froze, and now we have gone to the other extreme! Where shall we put our dairy?"

Day 131

1.   Read chapter 10 of *The Peterkin Papers*.
2.   Tell someone about the story.

THE PETERKINS' CHRISTMAS-TREE.

EARLY in the autumn the Peterkins began to prepare for their Christmas-tree. Everything was done in great privacy, as it was to be a surprise to the neighbors, as well as to the rest of the family. Mr. Peterkin had been up to Mr. Bromwick's wood-lot, and, with his consent, selected the tree. Agamemnon went to look at it occasionally after dark, and Solomon John made frequent visits to it mornings, just after sunrise. Mr. Peterkin drove Elizabeth Eliza and her mother that way, and pointed furtively to it with his whip; but none of them ever spoke of it aloud to each other. It was suspected that the little boys had been to see it Wednesday and Saturday afternoons. But they came home with their pockets full of chestnuts, and said nothing about it.

At length Mr. Peterkin had it cut down and brought secretly into the Larkin's barn. A week or two before Christmas a measurement was made of it with Elizabeth Eliza's yard-measure. To Mr. Peterkin's great dismay it was discovered that it was too high to stand in the back parlor.

This fact was brought out at a secret council of Mr. and Mrs. Peterkin, Elizabeth Eliza, and Agamemnon.

Agamemnon suggested that it might be set up slanting; but Mrs. Peterkin was very sure it would make her dizzy, and the candles would drip.

But a brilliant idea came to Mr. Peterkin. He proposed that the ceiling of the parlor should be raised to make room for the top of the tree.

Elizabeth Eliza thought the space would need to be quite large. It must not be like a small box, or you could not see the tree.

"Yes," said Mr. Peterkin, "I should have the ceiling lifted all across the room; the effect would be finer."

Elizabeth Eliza objected to having the whole ceiling raised, because her room was over the back parlor, and she would have no floor while the alteration was going on, which would be very awkward. Besides, her room was not very high now, and, if the floor were raised, perhaps she could not walk in it upright.

Mr. Peterkin explained that he didn't propose altering the whole ceiling, but to life up a ridge across the room at the back part where the tree was to stand. This would make a hump, to be sure, in Elizabeth Eliza's room; but it would go across the whole room.

Elizabeth Eliza said she would not mind that. It would be like the cuddy thing that comes up on the deck of a ship, that you sit against, only here you would not have the sea-sickness. She thought she should like it, for a rarity. She might use it for a divan.

Mrs. Peterkin thought it would come in the worn place of the carpet, and might be a convenience in making the carpet over.

Agamemnon was afraid there would be trouble in keeping the matter secret, for it would be a long piece of work for a carpenter; but Mr. Peterkin proposed having the carpenter for a day or two, for a number of other jobs.

One of them was to make all the chairs in the house of the same height, for Mrs. Peterkin had nearly broken her spine by sitting down in a chair that she had supposed was her own rocking-chair, and it had proved to be two inches lower. The little boys were now large enough to sit in any chair; so a medium was fixed upon to satisfy all the family, and the chairs were made uniformly of the same height.

On consulting the carpenter, however, he insisted that the tree could be cut off at the lower end to suit the height of the parlor, and demurred at so great a change as altering the ceiling. But Mr. Peterkin had set his mind upon the improvement, and Elizabeth Eliza had cut her carpet in preparation for it.

So the folding-doors into the back parlor were closed, and for nearly a fortnight before Christmas there was great litter of fallen plastering, and laths, and chips, and shavings; and Elizabeth Eliza's carpet was taken up, and the furniture had to be changed, and one night she had to sleep at the Bromwicks', for there was a long hole in her floor that might be dangerous.

All this delighted the little boys. They could not understand what was going on. Perhaps they suspected a Christmas-tree, but they did not know why a Christmas-tree should have so many chips, and were still more astonished at the hump that appeared in Elizabeth Eliza's room. It must be a Christmas present, or else the tree in a box.

Some aunts and uncles, too, arrived a day or two before Christmas, with some small cousins. These cousins occupied the attention of the little boys, and there was a great deal of whispering and mystery, behind doors, and under the stairs, and in the corners of the entry.

Solomon John was busy, privately making some candles for the tree. He had been collecting some bayberries, as he understood they made very nice candles, so that it would not be necessary to buy any.

The elders of the family never all went into the back parlor together, and all tried not to see what was going on. Mrs. Peterkin would go in with Solomon John, or Mr. Peterkin with Elizabeth Eliza, or Elizabeth Eliza and Agamemnon and Solomon John. The little boys and the small cousins were never allowed even to look inside the room.

Elizabeth Eliza meanwhile went into town a number of times. She wanted to consult Amanda as to how much ice-cream they should need, and whether they could make it at home, as they had cream and ice. She was pretty busy in her own room; the furniture had to be changed, and the carpet altered. The "hump" was higher than she expected. There was danger of bumping her own head whenever she crossed it. She had to nail some padding on the ceiling for fear of accidents.

The afternoon before Christmas, Elizabeth Eliza, Solomon John, and their father collected in the back parlor for a council. The carpenters had done their work, and the tree stood at its full height at the back of the room, the top stretching up into the space arranged for it. All the chips and shavings were cleared away, and it stood on a neat box.

But what were they to put upon the tree?

Solomon John had brought in his supply of candles; but they proved to be very "stringy" and very few of them. It was strange how many bayberries it took to make a few candles! The little boys had helped him, and he had gathered as much as a bushel of bayberries. He had put them in water, and skimmed off the wax, according to the directions; but there was so little wax!

Solomon John had given the little boys some of the bits sawed off from the legs of the chairs. He had suggested that they should cover them with gilt paper, to answer for gilt apples, without telling them what they were for.

These apples, a little blunt at the end, and the candles were all they had for the tree!

After all her trips into town Elizabeth Eliza had forgotten to bring anything for it.

"I thought of candies and sugar-plums," she said; "but I concluded if we made caramels ourselves we should not need them. But, then, we have not made caramels. The fact is, that day my head was full of my carpet. I had bumped it pretty badly, too."

Mr. Peterkin wished he had taken, instead of a fir-tree, an apple-tree he had seen in October, full of red fruit.

"But the leaves would have fallen off by this time," said Elizabeth Eliza.

"And the apples, too," said Solomon John.

"It is odd I should have forgotten, that day I went in on purpose to get the things," said Elizabeth Eliza, musingly. "But I went from shop to shop, and didn't know exactly what to get. I saw a great many gilt things for Christmas-trees; but I knew the little boys were making the gilt apples; there were plenty of candles in the shops, but I knew Solomon John was making the candles."

Mr. Peterkin thought it was quite natural.

Solomon John wondered if it were too late for them to go into town now.

Elizabeth Eliza could not go in the next morning, for there was to be a grand Christmas dinner, and Mr. Peterkin could not be spared, and Solomon John was sure he and Agamemnon would not know what to buy. Besides, they would want to try the candles to-night.

Mr. Peterkin asked if the presents everybody had been preparing would not answer. But Elizabeth Eliza knew they would be too heavy.

A gloom came over the room. There was only a flickering gleam from one of Solomon John's candles that he had lighted by way of trial.

Solomon John again proposed going into town. He lighted a match to examine the newspaper about the trains. There were plenty of trains coming out at that hour, but none going in except a very late one. That would not leave time to do anything and come back.

"We could go in, Elizabeth Eliza and I," said Solomon John, "but we should not have time to buy anything."

Agamemnon was summoned in. Mrs. Peterkin was entertaining the uncles and aunts in the front parlor. Agamemnon wished there was time to study up something about electric lights. If they could only have a calcium light! Solomon John's candle sputtered and went out.

At this moment there was a loud knocking at the front door. The little boys, and the small cousins, and the uncles and aunts, and Mrs. Peterkin, hastened to see what was the matter.

The uncles and aunts thought somebody's house must be on fire. The door was opened, and there was a man, white with flakes, for it was beginning to snow, and he was pulling in a large box.

Mrs. Peterkin supposed it contained some of Elizabeth Eliza's purchases, so she ordered it to be pushed into the back parlor, and hastily called back her guests and the little boys into the other room. The little boys and the small cousins were sure they had seen Santa Claus himself.

Mr. Peterkin lighted the gas. The box was addressed to Elizabeth Eliza. It was from the lady from Philadelphia! She had gathered a hint from Elizabeth Eliza's letters that there was to be a Christmas-tree, and had filled this box with all that would be needed.

It was opened directly. There was every kind of gilt hanging-thing, from gilt pea-pods to butterflies on springs. There were shining flags and lanterns, and birdcages, and nests with birds sitting on them, baskets of fruit, gilt apples and bunches of grapes, and, at the bottom of the whole, a large box of candles and a box of Philadelphia bonbons!

Elizabeth Eliza and Solomon John could scarcely keep from screaming. The little boys and the small cousins knocked on the folding-doors to ask what was the matter.

Hastily Mr. Peterkin and the rest took out the things and hung them on the tree, and put on the candles.

When all was done, it looked so well that Mr. Peterkin exclaimed:–

"Let us light the candles now, and send to invite all the neighbors to-night, and have the tree on Christmas Eve!"

And so it was that the Peterkins had their Christmas-tree the day before, and on Christmas night could go and visit their neighbors.

Day 132

1.　　　　Read chapter 11 of *The Peterkin Papers*.
2.　　　　Tell someone about the story.

MRS. PETERKIN'S TEA-PARTY.

TWAS important to have a tea-party, as they had all been invited by everybody,–the Bromwicks, the Tremletts, and the Gibbonses. It would be such a good chance to pay off some of their old debts, now that the lady from Philadelphia was back again, and her two daughters, who would be sure to make it all go off well.

But as soon as they began to make out the list, they saw there were too many to have at once, for there were but twelve cups and saucers in the best set.

"There are seven of us, to begin with," said Mr. Peterkin.

"We need not all drink tea," said Mrs. Peterkin.

"I never do," said Solomon John. The little boys never did.

"And we could have coffee, too," suggested Elizabeth Eliza.

"That would take as many cups," objected Agamemnon.

"We could use the every-day set for the coffee," answered Elizabeth Eliza; "they are the right shape. Besides," she went on, "they would not all come. Mr. and Mrs. Bromwick, for instance; they never go out."

"There are but six cups in the every-day set," said Mrs. Peterkin.

The little boys said there were plenty of saucers; and Mr. Peterkin agreed with Elizabeth Eliza that all would not come. Old Mr. Jeffers never went out.

"There are three of the Tremletts," said Elizabeth Eliza; "they never go out together. One of them, if not two, will be sure to have the headache. Ann Maria Bromwick would come, and the three Gibbons boys, and their sister Juliana; but the other sisters are out West, and there is but one Osborne."

It really did seem safe to ask "everybody." They would be sorry, after it was over, that they had not asked more.

"We have the cow," said Mrs. Peterkin, "so there will be as much cream and milk as we shall need."

"And our own pig," said Agamemnon. "I am glad we had it salted; so we can have plenty of sandwiches."

"I will buy a chest of tea," exclaimed Mr. Peterkin. "I have been thinking of a chest for some time."

Mrs. Peterkin thought a whole chest would not be needed: it was as well to buy the tea and coffee by the pound. But Mr. Peterkin determined on a chest of tea and a bag of coffee.

So they decided to give the invitations to all. It might be a stormy evening and some would be prevented.

The lady from Philadelphia and her daughters accepted.

And it turned out a fair day, and more came than were expected. Ann Maria Bromwick had a friend staying with her, and brought her over, for the Bromwicks were opposite neighbors. And the Tremletts had a niece, and Mary Osborne an aunt, that they took the liberty to bring.

The little boys were at the door, to show in the guests, and as each set came to the front gate, they ran back to tell their mother that more were coming. Mrs. Peterkin had grown dizzy with counting those who had come, and trying to calculate how many were to come, and wondering why there were always more and never less, and whether the cups would go round.

The three Tremletts all came, with their niece. They all had had their headaches the day before, and were having that banged feeling you always have after a headache; so they all sat at the same side of the room on the long sofa.

All the Jefferses came, though they had sent uncertain answers. Old Mr. Jeffers had to be helped in, with his cane, by Mr. Peterkin.

The Gibbons boys came, and would stand just outside the parlor door. And Juliana appeared afterward, with the two other sisters, unexpectedly home from the West.

"Got home this morning!" they said. "And so glad to be in time to see everybody,–a little tired, to be sure, after forty-eight hours in a sleeping-car!"

"Forty-eight!" repeated Mrs. Peterkin; and wondered if there were forty-eight people, and why they were all so glad to come, and whether all could sit down.

Old Mr. and Mrs. Bromwick came. They thought it would not be neighborly to stay away. They insisted on getting into the most uncomfortable seats.

Yet there seemed to be seats enough while the Gibbons boys preferred to stand. But they never could sit round a tea-table. Elizabeth Eliza had thought they all might have room at the table, and Solomon John and the little boys could help in the waiting.

It was a great moment when the lady from Philadelphia arrived with her daughters. Mr. Peterkin was talking to Mr. Bromwick, who was a little deaf. The Gibbons boys retreated a little farther behind the parlor door. Mrs. Peterkin hastened forward to shake hands with the lady from Philadelphia, saying:–

"Four Gibbons girls and Mary Osborne's aunt,–that makes nineteen; and now"–

It made no difference what she said; for there was such a murmuring of talk that any words suited. And the lady from Philadelphia wanted to be introduced to the Bromwicks.

It was delightful for the little boys. They came to Elizabeth Eliza, and asked:–

"Can't we go and ask more? Can't we fetch the Larkins?"

"Oh, dear, no!" answered Elizabeth Eliza. "I can't even count them."

Mrs. Peterkin found time to meet Elizabeth Eliza in the side entry, to ask if there were going to be cups enough.

"I have set Agamemnon in the front entry to count," said Elizabeth Eliza, putting her hand to her head.

The little boys came to say that the Maberlys were coming.

"The Maberlys!" exclaimed Elizabeth Eliza. "I never asked them."

"It is your father's doing," cried Mrs. Peterkin. "I do believe he asked everybody he saw!" And she hurried back to her guests.

"What if father really has asked everybody?" Elizabeth Eliza said to herself, pressing her head again with her hand.

There were the cow and the pig. But if they all took tea or coffee, or both, the cups could not go round.

Agamemnon returned in the midst of her agony.

He had not been able to count the guests, they moved about so, they talked so; and it would not look well to appear to count.

"What shall we do?" exclaimed Elizabeth Eliza.

"We are not a family for an emergency," said Agamemnon.

"What do you suppose they did in Philadelphia at the Exhibition, when there were more people than cups and saucers?" asked Elizabeth Eliza. "Could not you go and inquire? I know the lady from Philadelphia is talking about the Exhibition, and telling how she stayed at home to receive friends. And they must have had trouble there! Could not you go in and ask, just as if you wanted to know?"

Agamemnon looked into the room, but there were too many talking with the lady from Philadelphia.

"If we could only look into some book," he said,–"the encyclopaedia or the dictionary, they are such a help sometimes!"

At this moment he thought of his "Great Triumphs of Great Men," that he was reading just now. He had not reached the lives of the Stephensons, or any of the men of modern times. He might skip over to them,–he knew they were men for emergencies.

He ran up to his room, and met Solomon John coming down with chairs.

"That is a good thought," said Agamemnon. "I will bring down more upstairs chairs."

"No," said Solomon John; "here are all that can come down; the rest of the bedroom chairs match bureaus, and they never will do!"

Agamemnon kept on to his own room, to consult his books. If only he could invent something on the spur of the moment,–a set of bedroom furniture, that in an emergency could be turned into parlor chairs! It seemed an idea; and he sat himself down to his table and pencils, when he was interrupted by the little boys, who came to tell him that Elizabeth Eliza wanted him.

The little boys had been busy thinking. They proposed that the tea-table, with all the things on, should be pushed into the front room, where the company were; and those could take cups who could find cups.

But Elizabeth Eliza feared it would not be safe to push so large a table; it might upset, and break what china they had.

Agamemnon came down to find her pouring out tea, in the back room. She called to him:–

"Agamemnon, you must bring Mary Osborne to help, and perhaps one of the Gibbons boys would carry round some of the cups."

And so she began to pour out and to send round the sandwiches, and the tea, and the coffee. Let things go as far as they would!

The little boys took the sugar and cream.

"As soon as they have done drinking bring back the cups and saucers to be washed," she said to the Gibbons boys and the little boys.

This was an idea of Mary Osborne's.

But what was their surprise, that the more they poured out, the more cups they seemed to have! Elizabeth Eliza took the coffee, and Mary Osborne the tea. Amanda brought fresh cups from the kitchen.

"I can't understand it," Elizabeth Eliza said to Amanda. "Do they come back to you, round through the piazza? Surely there are more cups than there were!"

Her surprise was greater when some of them proved to be coffee-cups that matched the set! And they never had had coffee-cups.

Solomon John came in at this moment, breathless with triumph.

"Solomon John!" Elizabeth Eliza exclaimed; "I cannot understand the cups!"

"It is my doing," said Solomon John, with an elevated air. "I went to the lady from Philadelphia, in the midst of her talk 'What do you do in Philadelphia, when you haven't enough cups?' 'Borrow of my neighbors,' she answered, as quick as she could."

"She must have guessed," interrupted Elizabeth Eliza.

"That may be," said Solomon John. "But I whispered to Ann Maria Bromwick,–she was standing by,–and she took me straight over into their closet, and old Mr. Bromwick bought this set just where we bought ours. And they had a coffee-set, too"–

"You mean where our father and mother bought them. We were not born," said Elizabeth Eliza.

"It is all the same," said Solomon John. "They match exactly."

So they did, and more and more came in.

Elizabeth Eliza exclaimed:

"And Agamemnon says we are not a family for emergencies!"

"Ann Maria was very good about it," said Solomon John; "and quick, too. And old Mrs. Bromwick has kept all her set of two dozen coffee and tea cups!"

Elizabeth Eliza was ready to faint with delight and relief. She told the Gibbons boys, by mistake, instead of Agamemnon, and the little boys. She almost let fall the cups and saucers she took in her hand.

"No trouble now!"

She thought of the cow, and she thought of the pig, and she poured on.

No trouble, except about the chairs. She looked into the room; all seemed to be sitting down, even her mother. No, her father was standing, talking to Mr. Jeffers. But he was drinking coffee, and the Gibbons boys were handing things around.

The daughters of the lady from Philadelphia were sitting on shawls on the edge of the window that opened upon the piazza. It was a soft, warm evening, and some of the young people were on the piazza. Everybody was talking and laughing, except those who were listening.

Mr. Peterkin broke away, to bring back his cup and another for more coffee.

"It's a great success, Elizabeth Eliza," he whispered. "The coffee is admirable, and plenty of cups. We asked none too many. I should not mind having a tea-party every week."

Elizabeth Eliza sighed with relief as she filled his cup. It was going off well. There were cups enough, but she was not sure she could live over another such hour of anxiety; and what was to be done after tea?

Day 133

1.   Read chapter 12 of *The Peterkin Papers*. This is a play they are putting on.
Vocabulary

1.   A synonym is a word with similar meaning.
2.   Write down a synonym for each word. (There can be more than one correct answer.) (Answers)
   - fight, consequence, happiness, sneaky, frightful, worry, jealousy, ask, distress, argument, covered

THE PETERKINS TOO LATE FOR THE EXHIBITION.

Dramatis Personæ. –Amanda (friend of Elizabeth Eliza), Amanda's mother, girls of the graduating class, Mrs. Peterkin, Elizabeth Eliza.

AMANDA [coming in with a few graduates] Mother, the exhibition is over, and I have brought the whole class home to the collation.

MOTHER.– The whole class! I But I only expected a few.

AMANDA.– The rest are coming. I brought Julie, and Clara, and Sophie with me. [A voice is heard.] Here are the rest.

MOTHER.– Why, no. It is Mrs. Peterkin and Elizabeth Eliza!

AMANDA.– Too late for the exhibition. Such a shame! But in time for the collation.

MOTHER [to herself].– If the ice-cream will go round.

AMANDA.– But what made you so late? Did you miss the train? This is Elizabeth Eliza, girls–you have heard me speak of her. What a pity you were too late!

MRS. PETERKIN.– We tried to come; we did our best.

MOTHER.– Did you miss the train? Didn't you get my postal-card?

MRS. PETERKIN.– We had nothing to do with the train.

AMANDA.– You don't mean you walked?

MRS. PETERKIN.– O no, indeed!

ELIZABETH ELIZA.– We came in a horse and carryall.

JULIA.– I always wondered how anybody could come in a horse!

AMANDA.– You are too foolish, Julia. They came in the carryall part. But didn't you start in time?

MRS. PETERKIN.– It all comes from the carryall being so hard to turn. I told Mr. Peterkin we should get into trouble with one of those carryalls that don't turn easy.

ELIZABETH ELIZA.– They turn easy enough in the stable, so you can't tell.

MRS. PETERKIN.– Yes; we started with the little boys and Solomon John on the back seat, and Elizabeth Eliza on the front. She was to drive, and I was to see to the driving. But the horse was not faced toward Boston.

MOTHER.– And you tipped over in turning round! Oh, what an accident!

AMANDA.– And the little boys–where are they? Are they killed?

ELIZABETH ELIZA.– The little boys are all safe. We left them at the Pringles', with Solomon John.

MOTHER.– But what did happen?

MRS. PETERKIN.– We started the wrong way.

MOTHER.– You lost your way, after all?

ELIZABETH ELIZA.– No; we knew the way well enough.

AMANDA.– It's as plain as a pikestaff!

MRS. PETERKIN.– No; we had the horse faced in the wrong direction,–toward Providence.

ELIZABETH ELIZA.– And mother was afraid to have me turn, and we kept on and on till we should reach a wide place.

MRS. PETERKIN.– I thought we should come to a road that would veer off to the right or left, and bring us back to the right direction.

MOTHER.– Could not you all get out and turn the thing round?

MRS. PETERKIN.– Why, no; if it had broken down we should not have been in anything, and could not have gone anywhere.

ELIZABETH ELIZA.– Yes, I have always heard it was best to stay in the carriage, whatever happens.

JULIA.– But nothing seemed to happen.

MRS. PETERKIN.– O yes; we met one man after another, and we asked the way to Boston.

ELIZABETH ELIZA.– And all they would say was, "Turn right round–you are on the road to Providence."

MRS. PETERKIN.– As if we could turn right round! That was just what we couldn't.

MOTHER.– You don't mean you kept on all the way to Providence?

ELIZABETH ELIZA.– O dear, no! We kept on and on, till we met a man with a black hand-bag–black leather I should say.

JULIA.– He must have been a book-agent.

MRS. PETERKIN.– I dare say he was; his bag seemed heavy. He set it on a stone.

MOTHER.– I dare say it was the same one that came here the other day. He wanted me to buy the "History of the Aborigines, Brought up from Earliest Times to the Present Date," in four volumes. I told him I hadn't time to read so much. He said that was no matter, few did, and it wasn't much worth it–they bought books for the look of the thing.

AMANDA.– Now, that was illiterate; he never could have graduated. I hope, Elizabeth Eliza, you had nothing to do with that man.

ELIZABETH ELIZA.– Very likely it was not the same one.

MOTHER.– Did he have a kind of pepper-and-salt suit, with one of the buttons worn?

MRS. PETERKIN.– I noticed one of the buttons was off.

AMANDA.– We're off the subject. Did you buy his book?

ELIZABETH ELIZA.– He never offered us his book.

MRS. PETERKIN.– He told us the same story,–we were going to Providence; if we wanted to go to Boston, we must turn directly round.

ELIZABETH ELIZA.– I told him I couldn't; but he took the horse's head, and the first thing I knew–

AMANDA.– He had yanked you round!

MRS. PETERKIN.– I screamed; I couldn't help it!

ELIZABETH ELIZA.– I was glad when it was over!

MOTHER.– Well, well; it shows the disadvantage of starting wrong.

MRS. PETERKIN.– Yes, we came straight enough when the horse was headed right; but we lost time.

ELIZABETH ELIZA.– I am sorry enough I lost the exhibition, and seeing you take the diploma, Amanda. I never got the diploma myself. I came near it.

MRS. PETERKIN.– Somehow, Elizabeth Eliza never succeeded. I think there was partiality about the promotions.

ELIZABETH ELIZA.– I never was good about remembering things. I studied well enough, but, when I came to say off my lesson, I couldn't think what it was. Yet I could have answered some of the other girls' questions.

JULIA.– It's odd how the other girls always have the easiest questions.

ELIZABETH ELIZA.– I never could remember poetry. There was only one thing I could repeat.

AMANDA.– Oh, do let us have it now; and then we'll recite to you some of our exhibition pieces.

ELIZABETH ELIZA.– I'll try.

MRS. PETERKIN.– Yes, Elizabeth Eliza, do what you can to help entertain Amanda's friends.

[All stand looking at ELIZABETH ELIZA, who remains silent and thoughtful.]

ELIZABETH ELIZA.– I'm trying to think what it is about. You all know it. You remember, Amanda,–the name is rather long.

AMANDA.– It can't be Nebuchadnezzar, can it?–that is one of the longest names I know.

ELIZABETH ELIZA.– O dear, no!

JULIA.– Perhaps it's Cleopatra.

ELIZABETH ELIZA.– It does begin with a "C"–only he was a boy.

AMANDA.– That's a pity, for it might be "We are seven," only that is a girl. Some of them were boys.

ELIZABETH ELIZA.– It begins about a boy–if I could only think where he was. I can't remember.

AMANDA.– Perhaps he "stood upon the burning deck?"

ELIZABETH ELIZA.– That's just it; I knew he stood somewhere.

AMANDA.– Casabianca! Now begin–go ahead.

ELIZABETH ELIZA.–

"The boy stood on the burning deck,

  When–When–"

I can't think who stood there with him

JULIA.– If the deck was burning, it must have been on fire. I guess the rest ran away, or jumped into boats.

AMANDA.– That's just it:–

"Whence all but him had fled."

ELIZABETH ELIZA.– I think I can say it now.

"The boy stood on the burning deck,

  Whence all but him had fled–"

[She hesitates.] Then I think he went–

JULIA.– Of course, he fled after the rest.

AMANDA.– Dear, no! That's the point. He didn't.

"The flames rolled on, he would not go

  Without his father's word."

ELIZABETH ELIZA.– O yes. Now I can say it.

"The boy stood on the burning deck,

  Whence all but him had fled;

The flames rolled on, he would not go

  Without his father's word."

But it used to rhyme. I don't know what has happened to it.

MRS. PETERKIN.– Elizabeth Eliza is very particular about the rhymes.

ELIZABETH ELIZA.– It must be "without his father's head," or, perhaps, "without his father said" he should.

JULIA.– I think you must have omitted something.

AMANDA.– She has left out ever so much!

MOTHER.– Perhaps it's as well to omit some, for the ice-cream has come, and you must all come down.

AMANDA.– And here are the rest of the girls; and let us all unite in a song!

[Exeunt omnes, singing.]

Day 134

> 1.   Read chapter 13 of *The Peterkin Papers.*
> 2.   Tell someone about the story.

THE PETERKINS CELEBRATE THE FOURTH OF JULY.

THE day began early.

A compact had been made with the little boys the evening before.

They were to be allowed to usher in the glorious day by the blowing of horns exactly at sunrise. But they were to blow them for precisely five minutes only, and no sound of the horns should be heard afterward till the family were downstairs.

It was thought that a peace might thus be bought by a short, though crowded, period of noise.

The morning came. Even before the morning, at half-past three o'clock, a terrible blast of the horns aroused the whole family.

Mrs. Peterkin clasped her hands to her head and exclaimed: "I am thankful the lady from Philadelphia is not here!" For she had been invited to stay a week, but had declined to come before the Fourth of July, as she was not well, and her doctor had prescribed quiet.

And the number of the horns was most remarkable! It was as though every cow in the place had arisen and was blowing through both her own horns!

"How many little boys are there? How many have we?" exclaimed Mr. Peterkin, going over their names one by one mechanically, thinking he would do it, as he might count imaginary sheep jumping over a fence, to put himself to sleep. Alas! the counting could not put him to sleep now, in such a din.

And how unexpectedly long the five minutes seemed! Elizabeth Eliza was to take out her watch and give the signal for the end of the five minutes, and the ceasing of the horns. Why did not the signal come? Why did not Elizabeth Eliza stop them?

And certainly it was long before sunrise; there was no dawn to be seen!

"We will not try this plan again," said Mrs. Peterkin.

"If we live to another Fourth," added Mr. Peterkin, hastening to the door to inquire into the state of affairs.

Alas! Amanda, by mistake, had waked up the little boys an hour too early. And by another mistake the little boys had invited three or four of their friends to spend the night with them. Mrs. Peterkin had given them permission to have the boys for the whole day, and they understood the day as beginning when they went to bed the night before. This accounted for the number of horns.

It would have been impossible to hear any explanation; but the five minutes were over, and the horns had ceased, and there remained only the noise of a singular leaping of feet, explained perhaps by a possible pillow-fight, that kept the family below partially awake until the bells and cannon made known the dawning of the glorious day,–the sunrise, or "the rising of the sons," as Mr. Peterkin jocosely called it when they heard the little boys and their friends clattering down the stairs to begin the outside festivities.

They were bound first for the swamp, for Elizabeth Eliza, at the suggestion of the lady from Philadelphia, had advised them to hang some flags around the pillars of the piazza. Now the little boys knew of a place in the swamp where they had been in the habit of digging for "flag-root," and where they might find plenty of flag flowers. They did bring away all they could, but they were a little out of bloom. The boys were in the midst of nailing up all they had on the pillars of the piazza when the procession of the Antiques and Horribles passed along. As the procession saw the festive arrangements on the piazza, and the crowd of boys, who cheered them loudly, it stopped to salute the house with some especial strains of greeting.

Poor Mrs. Peterkin! They were directly under her windows! In a few moments of quiet, during the boys' absence from the house on their visit to the swamp, she had been trying to find out whether she had a sick-headache, or whether it was all the noise, and she was just deciding it was the sick headache, but was falling into a light slumber, when the fresh noise outside began.

There were the imitations of the crowing of cocks, and braying of donkeys, and the sound of horns, encored and increased by the cheers of the boys. Then began the torpedoes, and the Antiques and Horribles had Chinese crackers also.

And, in despair of sleep, the family came down to breakfast.

Mrs. Peterkin had always been much afraid of fire-works, and had never allowed the boys to bring gunpowder into the house. She was even afraid of torpedoes; they looked so much like sugar-plums she was sure some the children would swallow them, and explode before anybody knew it.

She was very timid about other things. She was not sure even about pea-nuts. Everybody exclaimed over this: "Surely there was no danger in pea-nuts!" But Mrs. Peterkin declared she had been very much alarmed at the Centennial Exhibition, and in the crowded corners of the streets in Boston, at the pea-nut stands, where they had machines to roast the pea-nuts. She did not think it was safe. They might go off any time, in the midst of a crowd of people, too!

Mr. Peterkin thought there actually was no danger, and he should be sorry to give up the pea-nut. He thought it an American institution, something really belonging to the Fourth of July. He even confessed to a quiet pleasure in crushing the empty shells with his feet on the sidewalks as he went along the streets.

Agamemnon thought it a simple joy.

In consideration, however, of the fact that they had had no real celebration of the Fourth the last year, Mrs. Peterkin had consented to give over the day, this year, to the amusement of the family as a Centennial celebration. She would prepare herself for a terrible noise,– only she did not want any gunpowder brought into the house.

The little boys had begun by firing some torpedoes a few days beforehand, that their mother might be used to the sound, and had selected their horns some weeks before.

Solomon John had been very busy in inventing some fireworks. As Mrs. Peterkin objected to the use of gunpowder, he found out from the dictionary what the different parts of gunpowder are,–saltpetre, charcoal, and sulphur. Charcoal, he discovered, they had in the wood-house; saltpetre they would find in the cellar, in the beef barrel; and sulphur they could buy at the apothecary's. He explained to his mother that these materials had never yet exploded in the house, and she was quieted.

Agamemnon, meanwhile, remembered a recipe he had read somewhere for making a "fulminating paste" of iron-filings and powder of brimstone. He had written it down on a piece of paper in his pocket-book. But the iron filings must be finely powdered. This they began upon a day or two before, and the very afternoon before laid out some of the paste on the piazza.

Pin-wheels and rockets were contributed by Mr. Peterkin for the evening. According to a programme drawn up by Agamemnon and Solomon John, the reading of the Declaration of Independence was to take place in the morning, on the piazza, under the flags.

The Bromwicks brought over their flag to hang over the door.

"That is what the lady from Philadelphia meant," explained Elizabeth Eliza.

"She said the flags of our country," said the little boys. "We thought she meant 'in the country.'"

Quite a company assembled; but it seemed nobody had a copy of the Declaration of Independence.

Elizabeth Eliza said she could say one line, if they each could add as much. But it proved they all knew the same line that she did, as they began:–

"When, in the course of–when, in the course of–when, in the course of human–when in the course of human events–when, in the course of human events, it becomes–when, in the course of human events, it becomes necessary–when, in the course of human events it becomes necessary for one people"–

They could not get any farther. Some of the party decided that "one people" was a good place to stop, and the little boys sent off some fresh torpedoes in honor of the people. But Mr. Peterkin was not satisfied. He invited the assembled party to stay until sunset, and meanwhile he would find a copy, and torpedoes were to be saved to be fired off at the close of every sentence.

And now the noon bells rang and the noon bells ceased.

Mrs. Peterkin wanted to ask everybody to dinner. She should have some cold beef. She had let Amanda go, because it was the Fourth, and everybody ought to be free that one day; so she could not have much of a dinner. But when she went to cut her beef she found Solomon had taken it to soak, on account of the saltpetre, for the fireworks!

Well, they had a pig; so she took a ham, and the boys had bought tamarinds and buns and a cocoa-nut. So the company stayed on, and when the Antiques and Horribles passed again they were treated to pea-nuts and lemonade.

They sung patriotic songs, they told stories, they fired torpedoes, they frightened the cats with them. It was a warm afternoon; the red poppies were out wide, and the hot sun poured down on the alley-ways in the garden. There was a seething sound of a hot day in the buzzing of insects, in the steaming heat that came up from the ground. Some neighboring boys were firing a toy cannon. Every time it went off Mrs. Peterkin started, and looked to see if one of the little boys was gone. Mr. Peterkin had set out to find a copy of the "Declaration." Agamemnon had disappeared. She had not a moment to decide about her headache. She asked Ann Maria if she were not anxious about the fireworks, and if rockets were not dangerous. They went up, but you were never sure where they came down.

And then came a fresh tumult! All the fire-engines in town rushed toward them, clanging with bells, men and boys yelling! They were out for a practice and for a Fourth-of-July show.

Mrs. Peterkin thought the house was on fire, and so did some of the guests. There was great rushing hither and thither. Some thought they would better go home; some thought they would better stay. Mrs. Peterkin hastened into the house to save herself, or see what she could save. Elizabeth Eliza followed her, first proceeding to collect all the pokers and tongs she could find, because they could be thrown out of the window without breaking. She had read of people who had flung looking-glasses out of the window by mistake, in the excitement of the house being on fire, and had carried the pokers and tongs carefully into the garden. There was nothing like being prepared. She had always determined to do the reverse. So with calmness she told Solomon John to take down the looking-glasses. But she met with a difficulty,—there were no pokers and tongs, as they did not use them. They had no open fires; Mrs. Peterkin had been afraid of them. So Elizabeth Eliza took all the pots and kettles up to the upper windows, ready to be thrown out.

But where was Mrs. Peterkin? Solomon John found she had fled to the attic in terror. He persuaded her to come down, assuring her it was the most unsafe place; but she insisted upon stopping to collect some bags of old pieces, that nobody would think of saving from the general wreck, she said, unless she did. Alas! this was the result of fireworks on Fourth of July! As they came downstairs they heard the voices of all the company declaring there was no fire; the danger was past. It was long before Mrs. Peterkin could believe it. They told her the fire company was only out for show, and to celebrate the Fourth of July. She thought it already too much celebrated.

Elizabeth Eliza's kettles and pans had come down through the windows with a crash, that had only added to the festivities, the little boys thought.

Mr. Peterkin had been roaming about all this time in search of a copy of the Declaration of Independence. The public library was shut, and he had to go from house to house; but now, as the sunset bells and cannon began, he returned with a copy, and read it, to the pealing of the bells and sounding of the cannon. Torpedoes and crackers were fired at every pause. Some sweet-marjoram pots, tin cans filled with crackers which were lighted, went off with great explosions.

At the most exciting moment, near the close of the reading, Agamemnon, with an expression of terror, pulled Solomon John aside.

"I have suddenly remembered where I read about the 'fulminating paste' we made. It was in the preface to 'Woodstock,' and I have been round to borrow the book to read the directions over again, because I was afraid about the 'paste' going off. READ THIS QUICKLY! and tell me, Where is the fulminating paste? "

Solomon John was busy winding some covers of paper over a little parcel. It contained chlorate of potash and sulphur mixed. A friend had told him of the composition. The more thicknesses of paper you put round it the louder it would go off. You must pound it with a hammer. Solomon John felt it must be perfectly safe, as his mother had taken potash for a medicine.

He still held the parcel as he read from Agamemnon's book: "This paste, when it has lain together about twenty-six hours, will of itself take fire, and burn all the sulphur away with a blue flame and a bad smell."

"Where is the paste?" repeated Solomon John, in terror.

"We made it just twenty-six hours ago," said Agamemnon.

"We put it on the piazza," exclaimed Solomon John, rapidly recalling the facts, "and it is in front of our mother's feet!"

 He hastened to snatch the paste away before it should take fire, flinging aside the packet in his hurry. Agamemnon, jumping upon the piazza at the same moment, trod upon the paper parcel, which exploded at once with the shock, and he fell to the ground, while at the same moment the paste "fulminated" into a blue flame directly in front of Mrs. Peterkin!

It was a moment of great confusion. There were cries and screams. The bells were still ringing, the cannon firing, and Mr. Peterkin had just reached the closing words: "Our lives, our fortunes, and our sacred honor."

"We are all blown up, as I feared we should be," Mrs. Peterkin at length ventured to say, finding herself in a lilac-bush by the side of the piazza. She scarcely dared to open her eyes to see the scattered limbs about her.

It was so with all. Even Ann Maria Bromwick clutched a pillar of the piazza, with closed eyes.

At length Mr. Peterkin said, calmly, "Is anybody killed?"

There was no reply. Nobody could tell whether it was because everybody was killed, or because they were too wounded to answer. It was a great while before Mrs. Peterkin ventured to move.

But the little boys soon shouted with joy, and cheered the success of Solomon John's fireworks, and hoped he had some more. One of them had his face blackened by an unexpected cracker, and Elizabeth Eliza's muslin dress was burned here and there. But no one was hurt; no one had lost any limbs, though Mrs. Peterkin was sure she had seen some flying in the air. Nobody could understand how, as she had kept her eyes firmly shut.

No greater accident had occurred than the singeing of the tip of Solomon John's nose. But there was an unpleasant and terrible odor from the "fulminating paste."

Mrs. Peterkin was extricated from the lilac-bush. No one knew how she got there. Indeed, the thundering noise had stunned everybody. It had roused the neighborhood even more than before. Answering explosions came on every side, and, though the sunset light had not faded away, the little boys hastened to send off rockets under cover of the confusion. Solomon John's other fireworks would not go. But all felt he had done enough.

Mrs. Peterkin retreated into the parlor, deciding she really did have a headache. At times she had to come out when a rocket went off, to see if it was one of the little boys. She was exhausted by the adventures of the day, and almost thought it could not have been worse if the boys had been allowed gunpowder. The distracted lady was thankful there was likely to be but one Centennial Fourth in her lifetime, and declared she should never more keep anything in the house as dangerous as saltpetred beef, and she should never venture to take another spoonful of potash.

Day 135

    1.   Read chapter 14 of *The Peterkin Papers.*
    2.   Tell someone about the story.

THE PETERKINS' PICNIC.

THERE was some doubt about the weather. Solomon John looked at the "Probabilities;" there were to be "areas" of rain in the New England States.

Agamemnon thought if they could only know where the areas of rain were to be they might go to the others. Mr. Peterkin proposed walking round the house in a procession, to examine the sky. As they returned they met Ann Maria Bromwick, who was to go, much surprised not to find them ready.

Mr. and Mrs. Peterkin were to go in the carryall, and take up the lady from Philadelphia, and Ann Maria, with the rest, was to follow in a wagon, and to stop for the daughters of the lady from Philadelphia. The wagon arrived, and so Mr. Peterkin had the horse put into the carryall.

A basket had been kept on the back piazza for some days, where anybody could put anything that would be needed for the picnic as soon as it was thought of. Agamemnon had already decided to take a thermometer; somebody was always complaining of being too hot or too cold at a picnic, and it would be a great convenience to see if she really were so. He thought now he might take a barometer, as "Probabilities" was so uncertain. Then, if it went down in a threatening way, they could all come back.

The little boys had tied their kites to the basket. They had never tried them at home; it might be a good chance on the hills. Solomon John had put in some fishing-poles; Elizabeth Eliza, a book of poetry. Mr. Peterkin did not like sitting on the ground, and proposed taking two chairs, one for himself and one for anybody else. The little boys were perfectly happy; they jumped in and out of the wagon a dozen times, with new india-rubber boots, bought for the occasion.

Before they started, Mrs. Peterkin began to think she had already had enough of the picnic, what with going and coming, and trying to remember things. So many mistakes were made. The things that were to go in the wagon were put in the carryall, and the things in the carryall had to be taken out for the wagon! Elizabeth Eliza forgot her water-proof, and had to go back for her veil, and Mr. Peterkin came near forgetting his umbrella.

Mrs. Peterkin sat on the piazza and tried to think. She felt as if she must have forgotten something; she knew she must. Why could not she think of it now, before it was too late? It seems hard any day to think what to have for dinner, but how much easier now it would be to stay at home quietly and order the dinner,–and there was the butcher's cart! But now they must think of everything.

At last she was put into the carryall, and Mr. Peterkin in front to drive. Twice they started, and twice they found something was left behind,–the loaf of fresh brown bread on the back piazza, and a basket of sandwiches on the front porch. And just as the wagon was leaving, the little boys shrieked, "The basket of things was left behind!"

Everybody got out of the wagon. Agamemnon went back into the house, to see if anything else were left. He looked into the closets; he shut the front door, and was so busy that he forgot to get into the wagon himself. It started off and went down the street without him!

He was wondering what he should do if he were left behind (why had they not thought to arrange a telegraph wire to the back wheel of the wagon, so that he might have sent a message in such a case!), when the Bromwicks drove out of their yard in their buggy, and took him in.

They joined the rest of the party at Tatham Corners, where they were all to meet and consult where they were to go. Mrs. Peterkin called to Agamemnon, as soon as he appeared. She had been holding the barometer and the thermometer, and they waggled so that it troubled her. It was hard keeping the thermometer out of the sun, which would make it so warm. It really took away her pleasure, holding the things. Agamemnon decided to get into the carryall, on the seat with his father, and take the barometer and thermometer.

The consultation went on. Should they go to Cherry Swamp, or Lonetown Hill? You had the view if you went to Lonetown Hill, but maybe the drive to Cherry Swamp was prettier.

Somebody suggested asking the lady from Philadelphia, as the picnic was got up for her.

But where was she?

"I declare," said Mr. Peterkin, "I forgot to stop for her!" The whole picnic there, and no lady from Philadelphia!

It seemed the horse had twitched his head in a threatening manner as they passed the house, and Mr. Peterkin had forgotten to stop, and Mrs. Peterkin had been so busy managing the thermometers that she had not noticed, and the wagon had followed on behind.

Mrs. Peterkin was in despair. She knew they had forgotten something! She did not like to have Mr. Peterkin make a short turn, and it was getting late, and what would the lady from Philadelphia think of it, and had they not better give it all up?

But everybody said "No!" and Mr. Peterkin said he could make a wide turn round the Lovejoy barn. So they made the turn, and took up the lady from Philadelphia, and the wagon followed behind and took up their daughters, for there was a driver in the wagon besides Solomon John.

Ann Maria Bromwick said it was so late by this time, they might as well stop and have the picnic on the Common! But the question was put again, Where should they go?

The lady from Philadelphia decided for Strawberry Nook–it sounded inviting. There were no strawberries, and there was no nook, it was said, but there was a good place to tie the horses.

Mrs. Peterkin was feeling a little nervous, for she did not know what the lady from Philadelphia would think of their having forgotten her, and the more she tried to explain it, the worse it seemed to make it. She supposed they never did such things in Philadelphia; she knew they had invited all the world to a party, but she was sure she would never want to invite anybody again. There was no fun about it till it was all over. Such a mistake–to have a party for a person, and then go without her; but she knew they would forget something! She wished they had not called it their picnic.

There was another bother! Mr. Peterkin stopped. "Was anything broke?" exclaimed Mrs. Peterkin. "Was something forgotten?" asked the lady from Philadelphia.

No! But Mr. Peterkin didn't know the way; and here he was leading all the party, and a long row of carriages following.

They stopped, and it seemed nobody knew the way to Strawberry Nook, unless it was the Gibbons boys, who were far behind. They were made to drive up, and said that Strawberry Nook was in quite a different direction, but they could bring the party round to it through the meadows.

The lady from Philadelphia thought they might stop anywhere, such a pleasant day, but Mr. Peterkin said they were started for Strawberry Nook, and had better keep on,

So they kept on. It proved to be an excellent place, where they could tie the horses to a fence. Mrs. Peterkin did not like their all heading different ways; it seemed as if any of them might come at her, and tear up the fence, especially as the little boys had their kites flapping round. The Tremletts insisted upon the whole party going up the hill; it was too damp below. So the Gibbons boys, and the little boys and Agamemnon, and Solomon John, and all the party had to carry everything up to the rocks. The large basket of "things" was very heavy. It had been difficult to lift it into the wagon, and it was harder to take it out. But with the help of the driver, and Mr. Peterkin, and old Mr. Bromwick, it was got up the hill.

And at last all was arranged. Mr. Peterkin was seated in his chair. The other was offered to the lady from Philadelphia, but she preferred the carriage cushions; so did old Mr. Bromwick. And the table-cloth was spread,—for they did bring a table-cloth,—and the baskets were opened, and the picnic really began. The pickles had tumbled into the butter, and the spoons had been forgotten, and the Tremletts' basket had been left on their front door-step. But nobody seemed to mind. Everybody was hungry, and everything they ate seemed of the best. The little boys were perfectly happy, and ate of all the kinds of cake. Two of the Tremletts would stand while they were eating, because they were afraid of the ants and the spiders that seemed to be crawling round. And Elizabeth Eliza had to keep poking with a fern leaf to drive the insects out of the plates. The lady from Philadelphia was made comfortable with the cushions and shawls, leaning against a rock. Mrs. Peterkin wondered if she forgot she had been forgotten.

John Osborne said it was time for conundrums, and asked: "Why is a pastoral musical play better than the music we have here? Because one is a grasshopper, and the other is a grass-opera!"

247

Elizabeth Eliza said she knew a conundrum, a very funny one, one of her friends in Boston had told her. It was, "Why is–" It began, "Why is something like–" –no, "Why are they different?" It was something about an old woman, or else it was something about a young one. It was very funny, if she could only think what it was about, or whether it was alike or different.

The lady from Philadelphia was proposing they should guess Elizabeth Eliza's conundrum, first the question, and then the answer, when one of the Tremletts came running down the hill, and declared she had just discovered a very threatening cloud, and she was sure it was going to rain down directly. Everybody started up, though no cloud was to be seen.

There was a great looking for umbrellas and water-proofs. Then it appeared that Elizabeth Eliza had left hers, after all, though she had gone back for it twice. Mr. Peterkin knew he had not forgotten his umbrella, because he had put the whole umbrella-stand into the wagon, and it had been brought up the hill, but it proved to hold only the family canes!

There was a great cry for the "emergency basket," that had not been opened yet. Mrs. Peterkin explained how for days the family had been putting into it what might be needed, as soon as anything was thought of. Everybody stopped to see its contents. It was carefully covered with newspapers. First came out a backgammon-board. "That would be useful," said Ann Maria, "if we have to spend the afternoon in anybody's barn." Next, a pair of andirons. "What were they for?" "In case of needing a fire in the woods," explained Solomon John. Then came a volume of the Encyclopædia. But it was the first volume, Agamemnon now regretted, and contained only A and a part of B, and nothing about rain or showers. Next, a bag of pea-nuts, put in by the little boys, and Elizabeth Eliza's book of poetry, and a change of boots for Mr. Peterkin; a small foot-rug in case the ground should be damp; some paint-boxes of the little boys'; a box of fish-hooks for Solomon John; an ink-bottle, carefully done up in a great deal of newspaper, which was fortunate, as the ink was oozing out; some old magazines, and a blacking-bottle; and at the bottom, a sun-dial. It was all very entertaining, and there seemed to be something for every occasion but the present. Old Mr. Bromwick did not wonder the basket was so heavy. It was all so interesting that nobody but the Tremletts went down to the carriages.

The sun was shining brighter than ever, and Ann Maria insisted on setting up the sun-dial. Certainly there was no danger of a shower, and they might as well go on with the picnic. But when Solomon John and Ann Maria had arranged the sun-dial, they asked everybody to look at their watches, so that they might see if it was right. And then came a great exclamation at the hour: "It was time they were all going home!"

The lady from Philadelphia had been wrapping her shawl about her, as she felt the sun was low. But nobody had any idea it was so late! Well, they had left late, and went back a great many times, had stopped sometimes to consult, and had been long on the road, and it had taken a long time to fetch up the things, so it was no wonder it was time to go away. But it had been a delightful picnic, after all.

Day 136

1.   Read chapter 15 of *The Peterkin Papers.*
2.   Tell someone about the story.

THE PETERKINS' CHARADES.

EVER since the picnic the Peterkins had been wanting to have "something" at their house in the way of entertainment. The little boys wanted to get up a "great Exposition," to show to the people of the place. But Mr. Peterkin thought it too great an effort to send to foreign countries for "exhibits," and it was given up.

There was, however, a new water-trough needed on the town common, and the ladies of the place thought it ought to be something handsome,–something more than a common trough,–and they ought to work for it.

Elizabeth Eliza had heard at Philadelphia how much women had done, and she felt they ought to contribute to such a cause. She had an idea, but she would not speak of it at first, not until after she had written to the lady from Philadelphia. She had often thought, in many cases, if they had asked her advice first, they might have saved trouble.

Still, how could they ask advice before they themselves knew what they wanted? It was very easy to ask advice, but you must first know what to ask about. And again: Elizabeth Eliza felt you might have ideas, but you could not always put them together. There was this idea of the water-trough, and then this idea of getting some money for it. So she began with writing to the lady from Philadelphia. The little boys believed she spent enough for it in postage-stamps before it all came out.

But it did come out at last that the Peterkins were to have some charades at their own house for the benefit of the needed water-trough,–tickets sold only to especial friends. Ann Maria Bromwick was to help act, because she could bring some old bonnets and gowns that had been worn by an aged aunt years ago, and which they had always kept. Elizabeth Eliza said that Solomon John would have to be a Turk, and they must borrow all the red things and cashmere scarfs in the place. She knew people would be willing to lend things.

Agamemnon thought you ought to get in something about the Hindoos, they were such an odd people. Elizabeth Eliza said you must not have it too odd, or people would not understand it, and she did not want anything to frighten her mother. She had one word suggested by the lady from Philadelphia in her letters,—the one that had "Turk" in it,—but they ought to have two words

"Oh, yes," Ann Maria said, "you must have two words; if the people paid for their tickets they would want to get their money's worth."

Solomon John thought you might have "Hindoos"; the little boys could color their faces brown, to look like Hindoos. You could have the first scene an Irishman catching a hen, and then paying the water-taxes for "dues," and then have the little boys for Hindoos.

A great many other words were talked of, but nothing seemed to suit. There was a curtain, too, to be thought of, because the folding-doors stuck when you tried to open and shut them. Agamemnon said that the Pan-Elocutionists had a curtain they would probably lend John Osborne, and so it was decided to ask John Osborne to help.

If they had a curtain they ought to have a stage. Solomon John said he was sure he had boards and nails enough, and it would be easy to make a stage if John Osborne would help put it up.

All this talk was the day before the charades. In the midst of it Ann Maria went over for her old bonnets and dresses and umbrellas, and they spent the evening in trying on the various things,—such odd caps and remarkable bonnets! Solomon John said they ought to have plenty of bandboxes; if you only had bandboxes enough a charade was sure to go off well; he had seen charades in Boston. Mrs. Peterkin said there were plenty in their attic, and the little boys brought down piles of them, and the back parlor was filled with costumes.

Ann Maria said she could bring over more things if she only knew what they were going to act. Elizabeth Eliza told her to bring anything she had,—it would all come of use.

The morning came, and the boards were collected for the stage. Agamemnon and Solomon John gave themselves to the work, and John Osborne helped zealously. He said the Pan-Elocutionists would lend a scene also. There was a great clatter of bandboxes, and piles of shawls in corners, and such a piece of work in getting up the curtain! In the midst of it came in the little boys, shouting, "All the tickets are sold, at ten cents each!"

"Seventy tickets sold!" exclaimed Agamemnon.

"Seven dollars for the water-trough!" said Elizabeth Eliza.

"And we do not know yet what we are going to act!" exclaimed Ann Maria.

But everybody's attention had to be given to the scene that was going up in the background, borrowed from the Pan-Elocutionists. It was magnificent, and represented a forest.

"Where are we going to put seventy people?" exclaimed Mrs. Peterkin, venturing, dismayed, into the heaps of shavings, and boards, and litter.

The little boys exclaimed that a large part of the audience consisted of boys, who would not take up much room. But how much clearing and sweeping and moving of chairs was necessary before all could be made ready! It was late, and some of the people had already come to secure good seats, even before the actors had assembled.

"What are we going to act?" asked Ann Maria.

"I have been so torn with one thing and another," said Elizabeth Eliza, "I haven't had time to think!"

"Haven't you the word yet?" asked John Osborne, for the audience was flocking in, and the seats were filling up rapidly.

"I have got one word in my pocket," said Elizabeth Eliza, "in the letter from the lady from Philadelphia. She sent me the parts of the word. Solomon John is to be a Turk, but I don't yet understand the whole of the word."

"You don't know the word, and the people are all here!" said John Osborne, impatiently.

"Elizabeth Eliza!" exclaimed Ann Maria, "Solomon John says I'm to be a Turkish slave, and I'll have to wear a veil. Do you know where the veils are? You know I brought them over last night."

"Elizabeth Eliza! Solomon John wants you to send him the large cashmere scarf!" exclaimed one of the little boys, coming in.

"Elizabeth Eliza! you must tell us what kind of faces to make up!" cried another of the boys.

And the audience were heard meanwhile taking the seats on the other side of the thin curtain.

"You sit in front, Mrs. Bromwick; you are a little hard of hearing; sit where you can hear."

"And let Julia Fitch come where she can see," said another voice.

"And we have not any words for them to hear or see!" exclaimed John Osborne, behind the curtain.

"Oh, I wish we'd never determined to have charades!" exclaimed Elizabeth Eliza. "Can't we return the money?"

"They are all here; we must give them something!" said John Osborne, heroically.

"And Solomon John is almost dressed," reported Ann Maria, winding a veil around her head.

"Why don't we take Solomon John's word 'Hindoos' for the first?" said Agamemnon.

John Osborne agreed to go in the first, hunting the "hin," or anything, and one of the little boys took the part of the hen, with the help of a feather duster. The bell rang, and the first scene began.

It was a great success. John Osborne's Irish was perfect. Nobody guessed the word, for the hen crowed by mistake; but it received great applause.

Mr. Peterkin came on in the second scene to receive the water-rates, and made a long speech on taxation. He was interrupted by Ann Maria as an old woman in a huge bonnet. She persisted in turning her back to the audience, speaking so low nobody heard her; and Elizabeth Eliza, who appeared in a more remarkable bonnet, was so alarmed she went directly back, saying she had forgotten something But this was supposed to be the effect intended, and it was loudly cheered.

Then came a long delay, for the little boys brought out a number of their friends to be browned for Hindoos. Ann Maria played on the piano till the scene was ready. The curtain rose upon five brown boys done up in blankets and turbans.

"I am thankful that is over," said Elizabeth Eliza, "for now we can act my word. Only I don't myself know the whole."

"Never mind, let us act it," said John Osborne, "and the audience can guess the whole."

"The first syllable must be the letter P," said Elizabeth Eliza, "and we must have a school."

Agamemnon was master, and the little boys and their friends went on as scholars. All the boys talked and shouted at once, acting their idea of a school by flinging pea-nuts about, and scoffing at the master.

"They'll guess that to be 'row,'" said John Osborne in despair; "they'll never guess 'P'!"

The next scene was gorgeous. Solomon John, as a Turk, reclined on John Osborne's army-blanket. He had on a turban, and a long beard, and all the family shawls. Ann Maria and Elizabeth Eliza were brought in to him, veiled, by the little boys in their Hindoo costumes.

This was considered the great scene of the evening, though Elizabeth Eliza was sure she did not know what to do,–whether to kneel or sit down; she did not know whether Turkish women did sit down, and she could not help laughing whenever she looked at Solomon John. He, however, kept his solemnity. "I suppose I need not say much," he had said, "for I shall be the 'Turk who was dreaming of the hour.'" But he did order the little boys to bring sherbet, and when they brought it without ice insisted they must have their heads cut off, and Ann Maria fainted, and the scene closed.

"What are we to do now?" asked John Osborne, warming up to the occasion.

"We must have an 'inn' scene," said Elizabeth Eliza, consulting her letter; "two inns, if we can."

"We will have some travellers disgusted with one inn, and going to another," said John Osborne.

"Now is the time for the bandboxes," said Solomon John, who, since his Turk scene was over, could give his attention to the rest of the charade.

Elizabeth Eliza and Ann Maria went on as rival hostesses, trying to draw Solomon John, Agamemnon, and John Osborne into their several inns. The little boys carried valises, hand-bags, umbrellas, and bandboxes. Bandbox after bandbox appeared, and when Agamemnon sat down upon his the applause was immense. At last the curtain fell.

"Now for the whole," said John Osborne, as he made his way off the stage over a heap of umbrellas.

"I can't think why the lady from Philadelphia did not send me the whole," said Elizabeth Eliza, musing over the letter.

"Listen, they are guessing," said John Osborne. "'D-ice-box.' I don't wonder they get it wrong."

"But we know it can't be that!" exclaimed Elizabeth Eliza, in agony. "How can we act the whole if we don't know it ourselves?"

"Oh, I see it!" said Ann Maria, clapping her hands. "Get your whole family in for the last scene."

Mr. and Mrs. Peterkin were summoned to the stage, and formed the background, standing on stools; in front were Agamemnon and Solomon John, leaving room for Elizabeth Eliza between; a little in advance, and in front of all, half kneeling, were the little boys, in their india-rubber boots.

The audience rose to an exclamation of delight, "The Peterkins !" "P-Turk-Inns!"

It was not until this moment that Elizabeth Eliza guessed the whole.

"What a tableau!" exclaimed Mr. Bromwick; "the Peterkin family guessing their own charade."

Day 137

1. Read chapter 1 of *The Story Book of Science*.
2. All year you have been reading fiction, made-up stories. This is a factual book.
3. Tell someone what this chapter was about.

CHAPTER I THE SIX

ONE evening, at twilight, they were assembled in a group, all six of them. Uncle Paul was reading in a large book. He always reads to rest himself from his labors, finding that after work nothing refreshes so much as communion with a book that teaches us the best that others have done, said, and thought. He has in his room, well arranged on pine shelves, books of all kinds. There are large and small ones, with and without pictures, bound and unbound, and even gilt-edged ones. When he shuts himself up in his room it takes something very serious to divert him from his reading. And so they say that Uncle Paul knows any number of stories. He investigates, he observes for himself. When he walks in his garden he is seen now and then to stop before the hive, around which the bees are humming, or under the elder bush, from which the little flowers fall softly, like flakes of snow; sometimes he stoops to the ground for a better view of a little crawling insect, or a blade of grass just pushing into view. What does he see? What does he observe? Who knows? They say, however, that there comes to his beaming face a holy joy, as if he had just found himself face to face with some secret of the wonders of God. It makes us feel better when we hear stories that he tells at these moments; we feel better, and furthermore we learn a number of things that some day may be very useful to us.

Uncle Paul is an excellent, God-fearing man, obliging to every one, and, as "good as bread." The village has the greatest esteem for him, so much so that they call him Maître Paul, on account of his learning, which is at the service of all.

To help him in his field work—for I must tell you that Uncle Paul knows how to handle a plow as well as a book, and cultivates his little estate with success—he has Jacques, the old husband of old Ambroisine. Mother Ambroisine has the care of the house, Jacques looks after the animals and fields. They are better than two servants; they are two friends in whom Uncle Paul has every confidence. They saw Paul born and have been in the house a long, long time. How often has Jacques made whistles from the bark of a willow to console little Paul when he was unhappy!

How many times Ambroisine, to encourage him to go to school without crying, has put a hard-boiled new-laid egg in his lunch basket! So Paul has a great veneration for his father's two old servants. His house is their house. You should see, too, how Jacques and Mother Ambroisine love their master! For him, if it were necessary, they would let themselves be quartered.

Uncle Paul has no family, he is alone; yet he is never happier than when with children, children who chatter, who ask this, that, and the other, with the adorable ingenuousness of an awakening mind. He has prevailed upon his brother to let his children spend a part of the year with their uncle. There are three: Emile, Jules, and Claire.

Claire is the oldest. When the first cherries come she will be twelve years old. Little Claire is industrious, obedient, gentle, a little timid, but not in the least vain. She knits stockings, hems handkerchiefs, studies her lessons, without thinking of what dress she shall wear Sunday. When her uncle, or Mother Ambroisine, who is almost a mother to her, tells her to do a certain thing, she does it at once, even with pleasure, happy in being able to render some little service. It is a very good quality.

Jules is two years younger. He is a rather thin little body, lively, all fire and flame. When he is preoccupied about something, he does not sleep. He has an insatiable appetite for knowledge. Everything interests and takes possession of him. An ant drawing a straw, a sparrow chirping on the roof, are sufficient to engross his attention. He then turns to his uncle with his interminable questions: Why is this? Why is that? His uncle has great faith in this curiosity, which, properly guided, may lead to good results. But there is one thing about Jules that his uncle does not like. As we must be honest, we will own that Jules has a little fault which would become a grave one if not guarded against: he has a temper. If he is opposed he cries, gets angry, makes big eyes, and spitefully throws away his cap. But it is like the boiling over of milk soup: a trifle will calm him. Uncle Paul hopes to be able to bring him round by gentle reprimands, for Jules has a good heart.

Emile, the youngest of the three, is a complete madcap; his age permits it. If any one gets a face smeared with berries, a bump on the forehead, or a thorn in the finger, it is sure to be he. As much as Jules and Claire enjoy a new book, he enjoys a visit to his box of playthings. And what has he not in the way of playthings? Now it is a spinning-top that makes a loud hum, then blue and red lead soldiers, a Noah's Ark with all sorts of animals, a trumpet which his uncle has forbidden him to blow because it makes too much noise, then— But he is the only one that knows what there is in that famous box. Let us say at once, before we forget it, Emile is already asking questions of his uncle. His attention is awakening. He begins to understand that in this world a good top is not everything. If one of these days he should forget his box of playthings for a story, no one would be surprised.

Day 138

1.	Read chapter 2 of *The Story Book of Science*.
2.	Pay attention to how she gets across the information. How does she present it? (Answers)

CHAPTER II THE FAIRY TALE AND THE TRUE STORY

THE six of them were gathered together. Uncle Paul was reading in a big book, Jacques braiding a wicker basket, Mother Ambroisine plying her distaff, Claire marking linen with red thread, Emile and Jules playing with the Noah's Ark. And when they had lined up the horse after the camel, the dog after the horse, then the sheep, donkey, ox, lion, elephant, bear, gazelle, and a great many others,—when they had them all arranged in a long procession leading to the ark, Emile and Jules, tired of playing, said to Mother Ambroisine: "Tell us a story, Mother Ambroisine—one that will amuse us."

And with the simplicity of old age Mother Ambroisine spoke as follows, at the same time twirling her spindle:

"Once upon a time a grasshopper went to the fair with an ant. The river was all frozen. Then the grasshopper gave a jump and landed on the other side of the ice, but the ant could not do this; and it said to the grasshopper: 'Take me on your shoulders; I weigh so little.' But the grasshopper said: 'Do as I do; give a spring, and jump.' The ant gave a spring, but slipped and broke its leg.

"Ice, ice, the strong should be kind; but you are wicked, to have broken the ant's leg—poor little leg.

"Then the ice said: 'The sun is stronger than I, and it melts me.'

"Sun, sun, the strong should be kind; but you are wicked, to melt the ice; and you, ice, to have broken the ant's leg—poor little leg.

"Then the sun said: 'The clouds are stronger than I; they hide me.'

"Clouds, clouds, the strong should be kind; but you are wicked, to hide the sun; you, sun, to melt the ice; and you, ice, to have broken the ant's leg—poor little leg.

"Then the clouds said: 'The wind is stronger than we; it drives us away.'

"Wind, wind, the strong should be kind; but you are wicked, to drive away the clouds; you, clouds, to hide the sun; you, sun, to melt the ice; and you, ice, to have broken the ant's leg—poor little leg.

"Then the wind said: 'The walls are stronger than I; they stop me.'

"Walls, walls, the strong should be kind; but you are wicked, to stop the wind; you, wind, to drive away the clouds; you, clouds, to hide the sun; you, sun, to melt the ice; and you, ice, to have broken the ant's leg—poor little leg.

"Then the walls said: 'The rat is stronger than we; it bores holes through us.'

"Rat, rat, the strong—"

"But it is all the same thing, over and over again, Mother Ambroisine," exclaimed Jules impatiently.

"Not quite, my child. After the rat comes the cat that eats the rat, then the broom that strikes the cat, then the fire that burns the broom, then the water that puts out the fire, then the ox that quenches his thirst with the water, then the fly that stings the ox, then the swallow that snaps up the fly, then the snare that catches the swallow, then—"

"And does it go on very long like that?" asked Emile.

"As long as you please," replied Mother Ambroisine, "for however strong one may be, there are always others stronger still."

"Really, Mother Ambroisine," said Emile, "that story tires me."

"Then listen to this one: Once upon a time there lived a woodchopper and his wife, and they were very poor. They had seven children, the youngest so very, very small that a wooden shoe answered for its bed."

"I know that story," again interposed Emile. "The seven children are going to get lost in the woods. Little Hop-o'-my-Thumb marks the way at first with white pebbles, then with bread crumbs. Birds eat the crumbs. The children get lost. Hop-o'-my-Thumb, from the top of a tree, sees a light in the distance. They run to it: rat-tat-tat! It is the dwelling of an ogre!"

"There is no truth in that," declared Jules, "nor in Puss-in-Boots, nor Cinderella, nor Bluebeard. They are fairy tales, not true stories. For my part, I want stories that are really and truly so."

At the words, true stories, Uncle Paul raised his head and closed his big book. A fine opportunity offered for turning the conversation to more useful and interesting subjects than Mother Ambroisine's old tales.

"I approve of your wanting true stories," said he. "You will find in them at the same time the marvelous, which pleases so much at your age, and also the useful, with which even at your age you must concern yourselves, in preparation for after life. Believe me, a true story is much more interesting than a tale in which ogres smell fresh blood and fairies change pumpkins into carriages and lizards into lackeys. And could it be otherwise? Compared with truth, fiction is but a pitiful trifle; for the former is the work of God, the latter the dream of man. Mother Ambroisine could not interest you with the ant that broke its leg in trying to cross the ice. Shall I be more fortunate? Who wants to hear a true story of real ants?"

"I! I!" cried Emile, Jules, and Claire all together.

Day 139

1.   Read chapter 3 of *The Story Book of Science.*
2.   Tell someone what this story was about.

CHAPTER III THE BUILDING OF THE CITY

"THEY are noble workers," began Uncle Paul, "Many a time, when the morning sun begins to warm up, I have taken pleasure in observing the activity that reigns around their little mounds of earth, each with its summit pierced by a hole for exit and entrance.

"There are some that come from the bottom of this hole. Others follow them, and still more, on and on. They carry between their teeth a tiny grain of earth, an enormous weight for them. Arrived at the top of the mound, they let their burden fall, and it rolls over the slope, and they immediately descend again into their well. They do not play on the way, or stop with their companions to rest a while. Oh! no: the work is urgent, and they have so much to do! Each one arrives, serious, with its grain of earth, deposits it, and descends in search of another. What are they so busy about?

"They are building a subterranean town, with streets, squares, dormitories, storehouses; they are hollowing out a dwelling-place for themselves and their family. At a depth where rain cannot penetrate they dig the earth and pierce it with galleries, which lengthen into long communicating streets, sub-divided into short ones, crossing one another here and there, sometimes ascending, sometimes descending, and opening into large halls. These immense works are executed grain by grain, drawn by strength of the jaws. If any one could see that black army of miners at work under the ground, he would be filled with astonishment.

"They are there by the thousands, scratching, biting, drawing, pulling, in the deepest darkness. What patience! What efforts! And when the grain of sand has at last given way, how they go off, head held high and proud, carrying it triumphantly above! I have seen ants, whose heads tottered under the tremendous load, exhaust themselves in getting to the top of the mound. In jostling their companions, they seemed to say: See how I work! And nobody could blame them, for the pride of work is a noble pride. Little by little, at the gate of the town, that is to say at the edge of the hole, this little mound of earth is piled up, formed by excavated material from the city that is being built. The larger the mound, the larger the subterranean dwelling, it is plain.

"Hollowing out these galleries in the ground is not all; they must also prevent landslides, fortify weak places, uphold the vaults with pillars, make partitions. These miners are then seconded by carpenters. The first carry the earth out of the ant-hill, the second bring the building materials. What are these materials? They are pieces of timber-work, beams, and small joists, suitable for the edifice. A tiny little bit of straw is a solid beam for a ceiling, the stem of a dry leaf can become a strong column. The carpenters explore the neighboring forests, that is to say, the tufts of grass, to choose their pieces.

"Good! see this covering of an oat-grain. It is very thin, dry, and solid. It will make an excellent plank for the partition they are constructing below. But it is heavy, enormously heavy. The ant that has made the discovery draws backward and makes itself rigid on its six feet. No success: the heavy mass does not move. It tries again, all its little body trembling with energy. The oat-husk just moves a tiny bit. The ant recognizes its powerlessness. It goes off. Will it abandon the piece? Oh! no. When one is an ant, one has the perseverance that commands success. Here it is coming back with two helpers. One seizes the oat in front, the others hitch themselves to the side, and behold! it rolls, it advances; it will get there. There are difficult steps, but the ants they meet along the route will give them a shoulder.

"They have succeeded, not without trouble. The oat is at the entrance to the underground city. Now things become complicated; the piece gets awry; leaning against the edge of the hole, it cannot enter. Helpers hasten up. Ten, twenty unite their efforts without success. Two or three of them, engineers perhaps, detach themselves from the band, and seek the cause of this insurmountable resistance. The difficulty is soon solved: they must put the piece with the point at the bottom. The oat is drawn back a little, so that one end overhangs the hole. One ant seizes this end while the others lift the end that is on the ground, and the piece, turning a somersault, falls into the well, but is prudently held on to by the carpenters clinging to the sides. You may perhaps think, my children that the miners mounting with their grain of earth would stop from curiosity before this mechanical prodigy? Not at all, they have not time. They pass with their loads of excavated material, without a glance at the carpenters' work. In their ardor they are even bold enough to slide under the moving beams, at the risk of being crippled. Let them look out! That is their affair.

"One must eat when one works so hard. Nothing creates an appetite like violent exercise. Milkmaid ants go through the ranks; they have just milked the cows and are now distributing the milk to the workers."

Here Emile burst out laughing. "But that is not really and truly so?" said he to his uncle. "Milkmaid ants, cows, milk! It is a fairy tale like Mother Ambroisine's."

Emile was not the only one to be surprised at the peculiar expressions Uncle Paul had used. Mother Ambroisine no longer turned her spindle, Jacques did not plait his wickers, Jules and Claire stared with wide-open eyes. All thought it a jest.

"No, my dears," said Uncle Paul. "I am not jesting; no. I have not exchanged the truth for a fairy tale. It is true there are milkmaid ants and cows. But as that demands some explanation, we will put off the continuation of the story until to-morrow."

Emile drew Jules off into a corner, and said to him in confidence: "Uncle's true stories are very amusing, much more so than Mother Ambroisine's tales. To hear the rest about those wonderful cows I would willingly leave my Noah's Ark."

Day 140

1. Read chapter 4 of *The Story Book of Science*.
2. Tell someone what this story was about.

CHAPTER IV THE COWS

THE next day Emile, when only half awake, began to think of the ants' cows. "We must beg uncle," said he to Jules, "to tell us the rest of his story this morning."

No sooner said than done: they went to look for their uncle.

"Aha!" cried he upon hearing their request, "the ants' cows are interesting you. I will do better than tell you about them, I will show them to you. First of all call Claire."

Claire came in haste. Their uncle took them under the elder bush in the garden, and this is what they saw:

The bush is white with flowers. Bees, flies, beetles, butterflies, fly from one flower to another with a drowsy murmur. On the trunk of the elder, amongst the ridges of the bark, numbers of ants are crawling, some ascending, some descending. Those ascending are the more eager. They sometimes stop the others on the way and appear to consult them as to what is going on above. Being informed, they begin climbing again with even more ardor, proof that the news is good. Those descending go in a leisurely manner, with short steps. Willingly they halt to rest or to give advice to those who consult them. One can easily guess the cause of the difference in eagerness of those ascending and those descending. The descending ants have their stomachs swollen, heavy, deformed, so full are they; those ascending have their stomachs thin, folded up, crying hunger. You cannot mistake them: the descending ants are coming back from a feast and, well fed, are returning home with the slowness that a heavy paunch demands; the ascending ants are running to the same feast and put into the assault of the bush the eagerness of an empty stomach.

"What do they find on the elder to fill their stomachs?" asked Jules. "Here are some that can hardly drag along. Oh, the gluttons!"

"Gluttons! no," Uncle Paul corrected him; "for they have a worthy motive for gorging themselves. There is above, on the elder, an immense number of the cows. The descending ants have just milked them, and it is in their paunch that they carry the milk for the common nourishment of the ant-hill colony. Let us look at the cows and the way of milking them. Don't expect, I warn you, herds like ours. One leaf serves them for pasturage."

Uncle Paul drew down to the children's level the top of a branch, and all looked at it attentively. Innumerable black velvety lice, immobile and so close together as to touch one another, cover the under side of the leaves and the still tender wood. With a sucker more delicate than a hair plunged into the bark, they fill themselves peacefully with the sap of the elder without changing their position. At the end of their back, they have two short and hollow hairs, two tubes from which, if you look attentively, you can see a little drop of sugary liquid escape from time to time. These black lice are called plant-lice. They are the ants' cows. The two tubes are the udders, and the liquor which drips from their extremity is the milk.

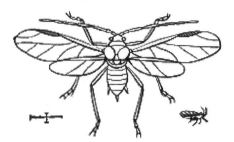

In the midst of the herd, on the herd, even, when the cattle are too close together, the famished ants come and go from one louse to another, watching for the delicious little drop. The one who sees it runs, drinks, enjoys it, and seems to say on raising its little head: Oh, how good, oh, how good it is! Then it goes on its way looking for another mouthful of milk. But plant-lice are stingy with their milk; they are not always disposed to let it run through their tubes. Then the ant, like a milkmaid ready to milk her cow, lavishes the most endearing caresses on the plant-louse. With its antennæ, that is to say, with its little delicate flexible horns, it gently pats the stomach and tickles the milk-tubes. The ant nearly always succeeds. What cannot gentleness accomplish! The plant-louse lets itself be conquered; a drop appears which is immediately licked up. Oh, how good, how good! As the little paunch is not full, the ant goes to other plant-lice trying the same caresses.

Uncle Paul let go the branch, which sprang back into its natural position. Milkmaids, cattle, and pasture were at once at the top of the elder bush.

"That is wonderful, Uncle," cried Claire.

"Wonderful, my dear child. The elder is not the only bush that nourishes milk herds for the ants. Plant-lice can be found on many other forms of vegetation. Those on the rosebush and cabbage are green; on the elder, bean, poppy, nettle, willow, poplar, black; on the oak and thistle, bronze color; on the oleander and nut, yellow. All have the two tubes from which oozes the sugary liquor; all vie with one another in feasting the ants."

Claire and her uncle went in-doors. Emile and Jules, enraptured by what they had just seen, began to look for lice on other plants. In less than an hour they had found four different kinds, all receiving visits of no disinterested sort from the ants.

Day 141

1.	Read chapter 5 of *The Story Book of Science*.
2.	Tell someone what this story was about.

CHAPTER V THE SHEEPFOLD

IN the evening Uncle Paul resumed the story of the ants. At that hour Jacques was in the habit of going the round of the stables to see if the oxen were eating their fodder and if the well-fed lambs were sleeping peacefully beside their mothers. Under the pretense of giving the finishing touches to his wicker basket, Jacques stayed where he was. The real reason was that the ants' cows were on his mind. Uncle Paul related in detail what they had seen in the morning on the elder: how the plant-lice let the sugary drops ooze from their tubes, how the ants drank this delicious liquid and knew how, if necessary, to obtain it by caresses.

"What you are telling us, Master," said Jacques, "puts warmth into my old veins. I see once more how God takes care of His creatures, He who gives the plant-louse to the ant as He gives the cow to man."

"Yes, my good Jacques," returned Uncle Paul, "these things are done to increase our faith in Providence, whose all-seeing eye nothing can escape. To a thoughtful person, the beetle that drinks from the depths of a flower, the tuft of moss that receives the raindrop on the burning tile, bear witness to the divine goodness.

"To return to my story. If our cows wandered at will in the country, if we were obliged to take troublesome journeys to go and milk them in distant pastures, uncertain whether we should find them or not, it would be hard work for us, and very often impossible. How do we manage then? We keep them close at hand, in inclosures and in stables. This also is sometimes done by the ants with the plant-lice. To avoid tiresome journeys, sometimes useless, they put their herds in a park. Not all have this admirable foresight, however. Besides, if they had, it would be impossible to construct a park large enough for such innumerable cattle and their pasturage. How, for example, could they inclose in walls the willow that we saw this morning with its population of black lice? It is necessary to have conditions that are not beyond the forces available. Given a tuft of grass whose base is covered with a few plant-lice, the park is practicable.

"Ants that have found a little herd plan how to build a sheepfold, a summer châlet, where the plant-lice can be inclosed, sheltered from the too bright rays of the sun. They too will stay at the châlet for some time, so as to have the cows within reach and to milk them at leisure. To this end, they begin by removing a little of the earth at the base of the tuft so as to uncover the upper part of the root. This exposed part forms a sort of natural frame on which the building can rest. Now grains of damp earth are piled up one by one and shaped into a large vault, which rests on the frame of the roots and surrounds the stem above the point occupied by the plant-lice. Openings are made for the service of the sheepfold. The châlet is finished. Its inmates enjoy cool and quiet, with an assured supply of provisions. What more is needed for happiness? The cows are there, very peaceful, at their rack, that is to say, fixed by their stickers to the bark. Without leaving home the ants can drink to satiety that sweet milk from the tubes.

"Let us say, then, that the sheepfold made of clay is a building of not much importance, raised with little expense and hastily. One could overturn it by blowing hard. Why lavish such pains on so temporary a shelter? Does the shepherd in the high mountains take more care of his hut of pine branches, which must serve him for one or two months?

"It is said that ants are not satisfied with inclosing small herds of plant-lice found at the base of a tuft of grass, but that they also bring into the sheepfold plant-lice encountered at a distance. They thus make a herd for themselves when they do not find one already made. This mark of great foresight would not surprise me; but I dare not certify it, never having had the chance to prove it myself. What I have seen with my own eyes is the sheepfold of the plant-lice. If Jules looks carefully he will find some this summer, when the days are warmest, at the base of various potted plants."

"You may be sure, Uncle," said Jules, "I shall look for them. I want to see those strange ants' châlets. You have not yet told us why ants gorge themselves so, when they have the good luck to find a herd of plant-lice. You said those descending the elder with their big stomachs were going to distribute the food in the ant-hill."

"A foraging ant does not fail to regale itself on its own account if the occasion offers; and it is only fair. Before working for others must one not take care of one's own strength? But as soon as it has fed itself, it thinks of the other hungry ones. Among men, my child, it does not always happen so. There are people who, well fed themselves, think everybody else has dined. They are called egoists. God forbid your ever bearing that sorry name, of which the ant, paltry little creature, would be ashamed! As soon as it is satisfied, then, the ant remembers the hungry ones, and consequently fills the only vessel it has for carrying liquid food home; that is to say, its paunch.

"Now see it returning, with its swollen stomach. Oh! how it has stuffed so that others may eat! Miners, carpenters, and all the workers occupied in building the city await it so as to resume their work heartily, for pressing occupations do not permit them to go and seek the plant-lice themselves. It meets a carpenter, who for an instant drops his straw. The two ants meet mouth to mouth, as if to kiss. The milk-carrying ant disgorges a tiny little bit of the contents of its paunch, and the other one drinks the drop with avidity. Delicious! Oh! now how courageously it will work! The carpenter goes back to his straw again, the milk-carrier continues his delivery route. Another hungry one is met. Another kiss, another drop disgorged and passed from mouth to mouth. And so on with all the ants that present themselves, until the paunch is emptied. The milk-ant then departs to fill up its can again.

"Now, you can imagine that, to feed by the beakful a crowd of workers who cannot go themselves for victuals, one milk-ant is not enough; there must be a host of them. And then, under the ground, in the warm dormitories, there is another population of hungry ones. They are the young ants, the family, the hope of the city. I must tell you that ants, as well as other insects, hatch from an egg, like birds."

"One day," interposed Emile, "I lifted up a stone and saw a lot of little white grains that the ants hastened to carry away under the ground."

"Those white grains were eggs," said Uncle Paul, "which the ants had brought up from the bottom of their dwelling to expose them under the stone to the heat of the sun and facilitate their hatching. They hurried to descend again, when the stone was raised, so as to put them in a safe place, sheltered from danger.

"On coming out from the egg, the ant has not the form that you know. It is a little white worm, without feet, and quite powerless, not even able to move. There are in an ant-hill thousands of those little worms. Without stop or rest, the ants go from one to another, distributing a beakful, so that they begin to grow and change in one day into ants. I leave you to think how much they must work and how many plant-lice must be milked, merely to nurse the little ones that fill the dormitories."

Day 142

1. Read chapter 6 of *The Story Book of Science*.
2. Tell someone what this story was about.

CHAPTER VI THE WILY DERVISH

"THERE are ant-hills everywhere, large or small," observed Jules. "Even in the garden I could have counted a dozen. From some the ants are so numerous they blacken the road when they come out. It must take a great many plant-lice to nourish all that little colony."

"Numerous though they be," his uncle assured him, "they will never lack cows, as plant-lice are still more numerous. There are so many that they often seriously menace our harvests. The miserable louse declares war against us. To understand it, listen to this story:

"There was once a king of India who was much bored. To entertain him, a dervish invented the game of chess. You do not know this game. Well, on a board something like a checkerboard two adversaries range, in battle array, one white, the other black, pieces of different values: pawns, knights, bishops, castles, queen and king. The action begins.

The pawns, simple foot-soldiers, are destined as always to receive the first of the glory on the battlefield. The king looks on at their extermination, guarded by his grandeur far from the fray. Now the cavalry charge, slashing with their swords right and left; even the bishops fight with hot-headed enthusiasm, and the ambulating castles go here and there, protecting the flanks of the army. Victory is decided. Of the blacks, the queen is a prisoner; the king has lost his castles; one knight and one bishop do wonderful deeds to procure his flight. They succumb. The king is checkmated. The game is lost.

"This clever game, image of war, pleased the bored king very much, and he asked the dervish what reward he desired for his invention.

"'Light of the faithful,' answered the inventor, 'a poor dervish is easily satisfied. You shall give me one grain of wheat for the first square of the chessboard, two for the second, four for the third, eight for the fourth, and you will double thus the number of grains, to the last square, which is the sixty-fourth. I shall be satisfied with that. My blue pigeons will have enough grain for some days.'

"'This man is a fool,' said the king to himself; 'he might have had great riches and he asks me for a few handfuls of wheat.' Then, turning to his minister:—'Count out ten purses of a thousand sequins for this man, and have a sack of wheat given him. He will have a hundred times the amount of grain he asks of me.'

"'Commander of the faithful,' answered the dervish, 'keep the purses of sequins, useless to my blue pigeons, and give me the wheat as I wish.'

"'Very well. Instead of one sack, you shall have a hundred.'

"'It is not enough, Sun of Justice.'

"'You shall have a thousand.'

"'Not enough, Terror of the unfaithful. The squares of my chessboard would not have their proper amount.'

"In the meantime the courtiers whispered among themselves, astonished at the singular pretensions of the dervish, who, in the contents of a thousand sacks, would not find his grain of wheat doubled sixty-four times. Out of patience, the king convoked the learned men to hold a meeting and calculate the grains of wheat demanded. The dervish smiled maliciously in his beard, and modestly moved aside while awaiting the end of the calculation.

"And behold, under the pen of the calculators, the figure grew larger and larger. The work finished, the head one rose.

"'Sublime Commander,' said he, 'arithmetic has decided. To satisfy the dervish's demand, there is not enough wheat in your granaries. There is not enough in the town, in the kingdom, or in the whole world. For the quantity of grain demanded, the whole earth, sea and continents together, would be covered with a continuous bed to the depth of a finger.'

"The king angrily bit his mustache and, unable to count out to him his grains of wheat, named the inventor of chess prime vizier. That is what the wily dervish wanted."

"Like the king, I should have fallen into the dervish's snare," said Jules. "I should have thought that doubling a grain sixty-four times would only give a few handfuls of wheat."

"Henceforth," returned Uncle Paul, "you will know that a number, even very small, when multiplied a number of times by the same figure, is like a snow-ball which grows in rolling, and soon becomes an enormous ball which all our efforts cannot move."

"Your dervish was very crafty," remarked Emile. "He modestly contented himself with one grain of wheat for his blue pigeons, on condition that they doubled the number on each square. Apparently, he asked next to nothing; in reality, he asked more than the king possessed. What is a dervish, Uncle?"

"In the religions of the East they call by that name those who renounce the world to give themselves up to prayer and contemplation."

"You say the king made him prime vizier. Is that a high office?"

"Prime vizier means prime minister. The dervish then became the greatest dignitary of the State, after the king."

"I am no longer surprised that he refused the ten purses of a thousand sequins. He was waiting for something better. The ten purses, however, would make a good sum?"

"A sequin is a gold piece worth about twelve francs. At that rate, the king offered the dervish a sum of one hundred and twenty thousand francs, besides the sacks of wheat.

"And the dervish preferred the grain sixty-four times doubled.

"In comparison what was offered him was nothing."

"And the plant-lice?" asked Jules.

"The story of the dervish is bringing us to that directly," his uncle assured him.

Day 143

1. Read chapter 7 of *The Story Book of Science*.
2. Tell someone what this story was about.
3. The author uses pictures sometimes to help her get across information. When you present non-fiction, pictures or charts and graphs can help convey your meaning.

CHAPTER VII A NUMEROUS FAMILY

"A PLANT-LOUSE, we will suppose," resumed Uncle Paul, "has just established itself on the tender shoot of a rosebush. It is alone, all alone. A few days after, young plant-lice surround it: they are its sons. How many are there? Ten, twenty, a hundred? Let us say ten. Is that enough to assure the preservation of the species? Don't laugh at my question. I know well that if the plant-lice were missing from the rosebushes, the order of things would not be sensibly changed."

"The ants would be the most to be pitied," said Emile.

"The round earth would continue to turn just the same, even when the last plant-louse was dying on its leaf; but it is not, in truth, an idle question to ask if ten plant-lice suffice to preserve the race; for science has no higher object than the quest of providential means for maintaining everything in a just measure of prosperity.

"Well, ten plant-lice coming from one would be far too many if we did not have to take account of destructive agencies. One replacing one, the population remains the same; ten replacing one, in a short time the number increases beyond all possible limits. Think of the dervish's grain of wheat doubled sixty-four times, so that it becomes a bed of wheat of a finger's depth over the whole earth. What would it be if it had been multiplied ten times instead of doubled! In like manner, after a few years, the descendants of a first plant-louse, continually multiplied tenfold, would be in straitened circumstances in this world. But there is the great reaper, death, which puts an invincible obstacle to overcrowding, counterbalances life in its overgrowing fecundity, and, in partnership with it, keeps all things in a perpetual youth. On a rosebush apparently most peaceful there is death every minute. But the small, the humble, and weak, are the habitual pasture, the daily bread, of the large eaters. To how many dangers is not the plant-louse exposed, so tiny, so weak, and without any means of defense! No sooner does a little bird, hardly out of the shell, discover with its piercing eyes a spot haunted by the plant-lice, than, merely as an appetizer, it will swallow hundreds. And if a worm, far more rapacious, a horrible worm expressly created and put into the world to eat you alive, joins in, ah! my poor plant-lice, may God, the good God of little creatures, protect you; for your race is indeed in peril.

"This devourer is of a delicate green with a white stripe on its back. It is tapering in front, swollen at the back. When it doubles itself up it takes the shape of a tear-drop. They call it the ants' lion because of the ravages it makes in the stupid herd. It establishes itself among them. With its pointed mouth, it seizes one, the biggest, the plumpest; it sucks it and throws away the skin, which is too hard for it. Its pointed head is lowered again, a second plant-louse seized, raised from the leaf, and sucked. Then another and another, a twentieth, a hundredth. The foolish herd, whose ranks are thinning, do not even seem to perceive what is going on. The trapped plant-louse kicks between the lion's fangs; the others, as if nothing were happening, continue to feed peacefully. It would take a good deal more than that to spoil their appetite! They eat while they are waiting to be eaten. The lion has had enough. He squats amidst the herd to digest at his ease. But digestion is soon over and already the greedy worm has its eye on those that he will soon crunch. After two weeks of continual feasting, after having browsed as it were on whole herds of plant-lice, the worm turns into an elegant little dragon-fly with eyes as bright as gold, and known as the hemerobius.

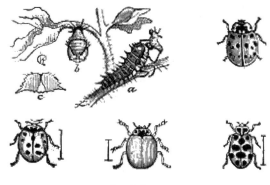

Ladybug

"Is that all? Oh, no. Here is the lady-bug, the good God's bug. It is round and red, with black spots. It is very pleasing; it has an innocent air. Who would take it also to be a devourer, filling its stomach with plant-lice! Look at it closely on the rosebush, and you will see it at its ferocious feasting. It is very pretty and innocent-looking; but it is a glutton, there is no denying the fact, so fond is it of plant-lice.

268

"Is that all? Oh, no. Those poor plant-lice are manna, the regular diet of all sorts of ravagers. Young birds eat them, the hemerobius eats them, lady-birds eat them, gluttons of all kinds eat them; and still there are always plant-lice. Ah! that is where, in the fight between fecundity which repairs and the rough battle of life which destroys, the weak excel by opposing legions and legions to the chances of annihilation. In vain the devourers come from all sides and pounce upon their prey; the devoured survive by sacrificing a million to preserve one. The weaker they are, the more fruitful they are.

"The herring, cod, and sardine are given over as pasturage for the devourers of the sea, earth and sky. When they undertake long voyages to graze in favorable spots, their extermination is imminent. The hungry ones of the sea surround the school of fish; the famished ones of the sky hover over their route; those of the earth await them on the shore. Man hastens to lend a strong hand to the killing and to take his share of the sea food. He equips fleets, goes to the fish with naval armies in which all nations are represented; he dries in the sun, salts, smokes, packs. But there is no perceptible diminution in the supply; for him the weak are infinite in number. One cod lays nine million eggs! Where are the devourers that will see the end of such a family?"

"Nine million eggs!" exclaimed Emile. "Is that a great many?"

"Just to count them, one by one, would take nearly a year of ten working hours each day."

"Whoever counted them had lots of patience," was Emile's comment.

"They are not counted," replied Uncle Paul; "they are weighed, which is quickly done; and from the weight the number is deduced.

"Like the cod in the sea, the plant-lice are exposed on their rosebushes and alders to numerous chances of destruction. I have told you that they are the daily bread of a multitude of eaters. So, to increase their legions, they have rapid means that are not found in other insects. Instead of laying eggs, very slow in developing, they bring forth living plant-lice, which all, absolutely all, in two weeks have obtained their growth and begin to produce another generation. This is repeated all through the season, that is to say at least half the year, so that the number of generations succeeding one another during this period cannot be less than a dozen. Let us say that one plant-louse produces ten, which is certainly below the actual number. Each of these ten plant-lice borne by the first one bears ten more, making one hundred in all; each of these hundred bears ten, in all one thousand; each of the thousand bears ten, in all ten thousand; and so on, multiplying always by ten, eleven times. Here is the same calculation as the dervish's grain of wheat, which grew with such astonishing rapidity when they multiplied it by two. For the family of the plant-lice the increase is much more rapid, as the multiplication is made by ten. It is true that the calculation stops at the twelfth instead of going on to the sixty-fourth. No matter, the result would stupefy you; it is equal to a hundred thousand millions. To count a cod's eggs, one

269

by one, would take nearly a year; to count the descendants of one plant-louse for six months would take ten thousand years! Where are the devourers that would see the end of the miserable louse? Guess how much space these plant-lice would cover, as closely packed as they are on the elder branch."

"Perhaps as large a place as our garden," suggested Claire.

"More than that; the garden is a hundred meters long and the same in width. Well, the family of that one plant-louse would cover a surface ten times larger; that is to say, ten hectares. What do you say to that? Is it not necessary that the young birds, little lady-bugs, and the dragon-fly with the golden eyes should work hard in the extermination of the louse, which if unhindered would in a few years overrun the world?

"In spite of the hungry ones which devour them, the plant-lice seriously alarm mankind. Winged plant-lice have been seen flying in clouds thick enough to obscure the daylight. Their black legions went from one canton to another, alighted on the fruit trees, and ravaged them. Ah! when God wishes to try us, the elements are not always unchained. He sends against us in our pride the paltriest of creatures. The invisible mower, the feeble plant-louse, comes, and man is filled with fear; for the good things of the earth are in great peril.

"Man, so powerful, can do nothing against these little creatures, invincible in their multitude."

Uncle Paul finished the story of the ants and their cows. Several times since, Emile, Jules, and Claire have talked of the prodigious families of the plant-louse and the cod, but rather lost themselves in the millions and thousand millions. Their uncle was right: his stories interested them much more than Mother Ambroisine's tales.

Day 144

1.   Read chapter 8 of *The Story Book of Science*.
2.   Tell someone what this story was about.

CHAPTER VIII THE OLD PEAR TREE

UNCLE PAUL had just cut down a pear-tree in the garden. The tree was old, its trunk ravaged by worms, and for several years it had not borne any fruit. It was to be replaced by another. The children found their Uncle Paul seated on the trunk of the pear-tree. He was looking attentively at something. "One, two, three, four, five," said he, tapping with his finger upon the cross-section of the felled tree. What was he counting?

"Come quick," he called, "come; the pear-tree is waiting to tell you its story. It seems to have some curious things to tell you."

The children burst out laughing.

"And what does the old pear-tree wish to tell us?" asked Jules.

"Look here, at the cut which I was careful to make very clean with the ax. Don't you see some rings in the wood, rings which begin around the marrow and keep getting larger and larger until they reach the bark?"

"I see them," Jules replied; "they are rings fitted one inside another."

"It looks a little like the circles that come just after throwing a stone into the water," remarked Claire.

"I see them too by looking closely," chimed in Emile.

"I must tell you," continued Uncle Paul, "that those circles are called annual layers. Why annual, if you please? Because one is formed every year; one only, understand, neither more nor less. The learned who spend their lives studying plants, and who are called botanists, tell us that no doubt is possible on that point. From the moment the little tree springs from the seed to the time when the old tree dies, every year there is formed a ring, a layer of wood. This understood, let us count the layers of our pear-tree."

Uncle Paul took a pin to guide his counting; Emile, Jules, and Claire looked on attentively. One, two, three, four, five—They counted thus up to forty-five, from the marrow to the bark.

"The trunk has forty-five layers of wood," announced Uncle Paul. "Who can tell me what that signifies? How old is the pear-tree?"

"That is not very hard," answered Jules, "after what you have just told us. As it makes one ring every year, and we have counted forty-five, the pear-tree must be forty-five years old."

"Eh! Eh! what did I tell you?" cried Uncle Paul, in triumph. "Has not the pear-tree talked? It has begun its history by telling us its age. Truly, the tree is forty-five years old."

"What a singular thing!" Jules exclaimed. "You can know the age of a tree as if you saw its birth. You count the layers of wood; so many layers, so many years. One must be with you, Uncle, to learn those things. And the other trees, oak, beech, chestnut, do they do the same?"

"Absolutely the same. In our country every tree counts one year for each layer. Count its layers and you have its age."

"Oh! how sorry I am I did not know that the other day," put in Emile, "when they cut down the big beech which was in the way on the edge of the road. Oh, my! What a fine tree! It covered a whole field with its branches. It must have been very old."

"Not very," said Uncle Paul. "I counted its layers; it had one hundred and seventy."

"One hundred and seventy, Uncle Paul! Honest and truly?"

"Honest and truly, my little friend, one hundred and seventy."

"Then the beech was a hundred and seventy years old," said Jules. "Is it possible? A tree to grow so old! And no doubt it would have lived many years longer if the road-mender had not had it cut down to widen the road."

"For us, a hundred and seventy years would certainly be a great age," assented his uncle; "no one lives so long. For a tree it is very little. Let us sit down in the shade. I have more to tell you about the age of trees."

Day 145

1.   Read chapter 9 of *The Story Book of Science*.
2.   Tell someone what this story was about.

CHAPTER IX THE AGE OF TREES

"THEY used to tell of a chestnut of Sancerre whose trunk was more than four meters round. According to the most moderate estimate its age must have been three or four hundred years. Don't cry out at the age of this chestnut. My story is just beginning, and you may be sure that, as a narrator who stimulates the curiosity of his audience, I reserve the oldest for the end.

"Much larger chestnuts are known; for example, that of Neuve-Celle, on the borders of the Lake of Geneva, and that of Esaü, in the neighborhood of Montélimar. The first is thirteen meters round at the base of the trunk. From the year 1408 it sheltered a hermitage; the story has been testified to. Since then four centuries and half have passed, adding to its age, and lightning has struck it at different times. No matter, it is still vigorous and full of leaves. The second is a majestic ruin. Its high branches are despoiled; its trunk, eleven meters round, is plowed with deep crevices, the wrinkles of old age. To tell the age of these two giants is hardly possible. Perhaps it might be reckoned at a thousand years, and still the two old trees bear fruit; they will not die."

"A thousand years! If Uncle had not said it, I should not believe it." This from Jules.

"Sh! You must listen to the end without saying anything," cautioned his uncle.

"The largest tree in the world is a chestnut on the slopes of Etna, in Sicily. Look at the map: you will see down there, at the extreme end of Italy, opposite the toe of that beautiful country which has the shape of a boot, a large island with three corners. That is Sicily. On that island is a celebrated mountain which throws up burning matter—a volcano, in short.

It is called Etna. To come back to our chestnut, I must tell you that they call it 'the chestnut of a hundred horses,' because Jane, Queen of Aragon, visiting the volcano one day and, overtaken by a storm, took refuge under it with her escort of a hundred horsemen. Under its forest of leaves both riders and horses found shelter. To surround the giant, thirty people extending their arms and joining hands would not be enough. The trunk is more than fifty meters round. Judged by its size, it is less a tree-trunk than a fortress, a tower. An opening large enough to permit two carriages to pass abreast goes through the base of the chestnut and gives access into the cavity of the trunk, which is fitted up for the use of those who go to gather chestnuts; for the old colossus still has young sap and seldom fails to bear fruit. It is impossible to estimate the age of this giant by its size, for one suspects that a trunk as large as that comes from several chestnuts, originally distinct, but so near together that they have become welded into one.

"Neustadt, in Württemberg, has a linden whose branches, overburdened by years, are held up by a hundred pillars of masonry. The branches cover all together a space 130 meters in circumference. In 1229 this tree was already old, for writers of that time call it 'the big linden.' Its probable age today is seven or eight hundred years.

"There was in France, at the beginning of this century, an older tree than the veteran of Neustadt. In 1804 could be seen at the castle of Chaillé, in the Deux-Sèvres, a linden 15 meters round. It had six main branches propped with numerous pillars. If it still exists it cannot be less than eleven centuries old.

White Oak

"The cemetery of Allouville, in Normandy, is shaded by one of the oldest oaks in France. The dust of the dead, into which it has thrust its roots, seems to have given it an exceptional vigor. Its trunk measures ten meters in circumference at the base. A hermit's chamber surmounted by a little steeple rises in the midst of its enormous branches. The base of the trunk, partly hollow, is fitted up as a chapel dedicated to Our Lady of Peace. The greatest personages have esteemed it an honor to go and pray in this rustic sanctuary and meditate a moment under the shade of the old tree which has seen so many graves open and shut. According to its size, they consider this oak to be about nine hundred years old. The acorn that produced it must, then, have germinated about the year 1000. To-day the old oak carries its monstrous branches without effort. Glorified by men and ravaged by lightning, it peacefully follows the course of ages, perhaps having before it a future equal to its past.

"Much older oaks are known. In 1824 a wood-cutter of Ardennes felled a gigantic oak in whose trunk were found sacrificial vases and antique coins. The old oak had had fifteen or sixteen centuries of existence.

"After the Allouville oak I will tell you of some more companions of the dead; for it is above all in these fields of repose, where the sanctity of the place protects them against the injuries of man, that the trees attain such an advanced age. Two yews in the cemetery of Haie-de-Routot, department of Eure, merit attention above all. In 1832 they shaded with their foliage the whole of the field of the dead and a part of the church, without having experienced serious damage, when an extremely violent windstorm threw a part of their branches to the ground. In spite of this mutilation these two yews are still majestic old trees. Their trunks, entirely hollow, measure each of them nine meters in circumference. Their age is estimated at fourteen hundred years.

"That, however, is not more than half the age that some other trees of the same kind have attained. A yew in a Scotch cemetery measured twenty-nine meters around. Its probable age was two thousand five hundred years. Another yew, also in a cemetery in the same country, was, in 1660, so prodigious that the whole country was talking about it. They reckoned its age then at two thousand eight hundred and twenty-four years. If it is still standing, this patriarch of European trees bears the weight of more than thirty centuries.

"Enough for the present. Now it is your turn to talk."

"I like better to be silent, Uncle Paul," said Jules. "You have upset my mind with your trees that will not die."

"I am thinking of the old yew in the Scotch cemetery. Did you say three thousand years?" asked Claire.

"Three thousand years, my dear child; and we might go still further back, if I were to tell you of certain trees in foreign countries. Some are known to be almost as old as the world."

Day 146

1.　　　Read chapter 10 of *The Story Book of Science*.
2.　　　Tell someone what this story was about.

CHAPTER X THE LENGTH OF ANIMAL LIFE

JULES and Claire could not get over the astonishment caused by their uncle's story of the old trees to which centuries are less than years are to us. Emile, with his usual restlessness, led the conversation to another subject:

"And animals, Uncle," asked he, "how long do they live?"

"Domestic animals," was the reply, "seldom attain the age that nature allows them. We grudge them their nourishment, overtire them, and do not give them proper shelter. And then, we take from them their milk, fleece, hide, flesh, in fact everything. How can you ever grow old when the butcher is waiting for you at the stable door with his knife? Useless to speak of these poor victims of our need: to give us long life, they do not live out their time. Supposing that an animal is well treated, that it suffers neither hunger nor cold, that it lives in peace without excessive fatigue, without fear of knacker or butcher; under these good conditions, how many years will it live?

"Let us begin with the ox. Here is a robust one, I hope. What chest and shoulders! And then that big square forehead, with its vigorous horns around which the strap of the yoke goes; those eyes shining with the serene majesty of strength. If old age is the portion of the strong, the ox ought to live for centuries."

"I should think so too," assented Jules.

"Quite wrong, my dear children; the ox, so big, strong, massive, is old, very old, at twenty or thirty years. What to us would be verdant youth is for it decrepit old age.

"Let us pass on to the horse. You see I do not take my examples from among the weak; I choose the most vigorous. Well, the horse, as well as its modest companion, the ass, scarcely reaches more than thirty or thirty-five years."

"How mistaken I was!" Jules exclaimed. "I thought the horse and ox strong enough to live at least a century. They are so big, they take up so much room!"

"I do not know, my little friend, whether you can understand me, but I want to inform you that to take up a great deal of room in this world is not the way to live in peace and to enjoy a long life. There are people who take up a lot of space, not in the body—they are no bigger than we—but in their pretensions and their ambitious manœuvers. Do they live in peace, are they preparing for themselves a venerable old age? It is very doubtful. Let us remain small; that is to say, let us content ourselves with the little that God has given us; let us beware of the temptations of envy, the foolish counsels of pride; let us be full of activity, of work, and not of ambition. That is the only way we are permitted to hope for length of days.

"Let us return without delay to our animals. Our other domestic animals live a still shorter time. A dog, at twenty or twenty-five years, can no longer drag himself along; a pig is a tottering veteran at twenty; at fifteen at the most, a cat no longer chases mice, it says good-by to the joys of the roof and retires to some corner of a granary to die in peace; the goat and sheep, at ten or fifteen, touch extreme old age, the rabbit is at the end of its skein at eight or ten; and the miserable rat, if it lives four years, is looked upon among its own kind as a prodigy of longevity.

"Would you like me to tell you about birds? Very well. The pigeon may live from six to ten years; the guinea fowl, hen, and turkey, twelve. A goose lives longer; it is true that in its quality of goose it does not worry. The goose attains twenty-five years, and even a good deal more.

"But here is something better. The goldfinch, sparrow, birds free from care, always singing, always frisking, happy as possible with a ray of sunlight in the foliage and a grain of hemp-seed, live as long as the gluttonous goose, and longer than the stupid turkey. These very happy little birds live from twenty to twenty-five years, the age of an ox. As I told you, taking up a lot of room in this world is not the way to prepare oneself for a long life.

"As to man, if he leads a regular life, he often lives to eighty or ninety. Sometimes he reaches a hundred or even more. But should he attain only the ordinary age, the average age, as they say, that is about forty, then he is to be considered a privileged creature as to length of life; the foregoing facts show it. And besides, for man, my dear children, length of life is not measured exactly according to the number of years. He lives most who works most. When God calls us to Him, let us take with us the sincere esteem of others and the consciousness of having done our duty to the end; and, whatever our age, we shall have lived long enough."

Day 147

1.   Read chapter 11 of *The Story Book of Science*.
2.   Tell someone what this story was about.

CHAPTER XI THE KETTLE

NOW, that day, Mother Ambroisine was very tired. She had taken down from their shelves kettles, saucepans, lamps, candlesticks, casseroles, pans, and lids. After having rubbed them with fine sand and ashes, then washed them well, she had put the utensils in the sun to dry them thoroughly. They all shone like a mirror. The kettles particularly were superb with their rosy reflections; one might have said that tongues of fire were shining inside them. The candlesticks were a dazzling yellow. Emile and Jules were lost in admiration.

"I should like to know what they make kettles of, they shine so," remarked Emile. "They are very ugly outside, all black, daubed with soot; but inside, how beautiful they are!"

"You must ask Uncle," replied his brother.

"Yes," assented Emile.

No sooner said than done: they went in search of their uncle. He did not have to be entreated; he was happy whenever there was an opportunity to teach them something.

"Kettles are made of copper," he began.

"And copper?" asked Jules.

"Copper is not made. In certain countries, it is found already made, mixed with stone. It is one of the substances that it is not in the power of man to make. We use these substances as God has deposited them in the bosom of the earth for purposes of human industry; but all our knowledge and all our skill could not produce them.

"In the bosom of mountains where copper is found, they hollow out galleries which go down deep into the earth. There workmen called miners, with lamps to light them, attack the rock with great blows of the pick, while others carry the detached blocks outside. These blocks of stone in which copper is found are called ore. In furnaces made for the purpose they heat the ore to a very high temperature. The heat of our stove, when it is red-hot, is nothing in comparison. The copper melts, runs, and is separated from the rest. Then, with hammers of enormous weight, set in motion by a wheel turned by water, they strike the mass of copper which, little by little, becomes thin and is hollowed into a large basin.

"The coppersmith continues the work. He takes the shapeless basin and, with little strokes of the hammer, fashions it on the anvil to give it a regular shape."

"That is why coppersmiths tap all day with their hammers," commented Jules. "I had often wondered, when passing their shops, why they made so much noise, always tapping, without any stop. They were thinning the copper; shaping it into saucepans and kettles."

Here Emile asked: "When a kettle is old, has holes in it and can't be used, what do they do with it? I heard Mother Ambroisine speak of selling a worn-out kettle."

"It is melted, and another new kettle made out of the copper," replied Uncle Paul.

"Then the copper does not wear away?"

"It wears away too much, my friend: some of it is lost when they rub it with sand to make it shine; some is lost, too, by the continual action of the fire; but what is left is still good."

"Mother Ambroisine also spoke of recasting a lamp which had lost a foot. What are lamps made of?"

"They are of tin, another substance that we find ready-made in the bosom of the earth, without the power of producing it ourselves."

Day 148

1. Read chapter 12 of *The Story Book of Science*.
2. Tell someone about it.

CHAPTER XII METALS

"COPPER and tin are called metals," continued Uncle Paul. "They are heavy, shining substances, which bear the blows of the hammer without breaking. They flatten, but do not break. There are still other substances which possess the considerable weight of copper and tin, as well as their brilliancy and resistance to blows. All these substances are called metals."

"Then lead, which is so heavy, is a metal too?" asked Emile.

"Iron also, silver and gold?" queried his brother.

"Yes, these substances and still others are metals. All have a peculiar brilliancy called metallic luster, but the color varies. Copper is red; gold, yellow; silver, iron, lead, tin, white, with a very slightly different shade one from another."

"The candlesticks Mother Ambroisine is drying in the sun," said Emile, "are a magnificent yellow and so shiny they dazzle. Are they gold?"

"No, my dear child; your uncle does not possess such riches. They are brass. To vary the colors and other properties of the metals, instead of always using them separately, they often mix two or three together, or even more. They melt them together, and the whole constitutes a sort of new metal, different from those which enter into its composition. Thus, in melting together copper and a kind of white metal called zinc, the same as the garden watering pots are made of, they obtain brass, which has not the red of copper, nor the white of zinc, but the yellow of gold. The material of the candlesticks is, then, made of copper and zinc together; in a word, it is brass, and not gold, in spite of its luster and yellow color. Gold is yellow and glitters; but all that is yellow and glitters is not gold. At the last village fair they sold magnificent rings whose brilliancy deceived you. In gold, they would have cost a fine sum. The merchant sold them for a sou. They were brass."

278

"How can they tell gold from brass, since the color and luster are almost the same?" asked Jules.

"By the weight, chiefly. Gold is much heavier than brass; it is indeed the heaviest metal in frequent use. After it comes lead, then silver, copper, iron, tin, and finally zinc, the lightest of all."

"You told us that to melt copper," put in Emile, "they needed a fire so intense, that the heat of a red-hot stove would be nothing in comparison. All metals do not resist like that, for I remember very well in what a sorry way the first leaden soldiers you gave me came to their end. Last winter, I had lined them up on the luke-warm stove. Just when I was not watching, the troop tottered, sank down, and ran in little streams of melted lead. I had only time to save half a dozen grenadiers, and their feet were missing."

"And when Mother Ambroisine thoughtlessly put the lamp on the stove," added Jules, "oh! it was soon done for: a finger's breadth of tin had disappeared."

"Tin and lead melt very easily," explained Uncle Paul. "The heat of our hearth is enough to make them run. Zinc also melts without much trouble; but silver, then copper, then gold, and finally iron, need fires of an intensity unknown in our houses. Iron, above all, has excessive resistance, very valuable to us.

"Shovels, tongs, grates, stoves, are iron. These various objects, always in contact with the fire, do not melt, however; do not even soften. To soften iron, so as to shape it easily on the anvil by blows from the hammer, the smith needs all the heat of his forge. In vain would he blow and put on coal; he would never succeed in melting it. Iron, however, can be melted, but you must use the most intense heat that human skill can produce."

Day 149

1.   Read chapter 13 of *The Story Book of Science*.
2.   Tell someone what this story was about.

CHAPTER XIII METAL PLATING

IN the morning some wandering coppersmiths were passing. Mother Ambroisine had sold them the old kettle. Besides the sale, they were to make over the lamp whose foot had melted on the stove, and replate two saucepans. So the smiths lighted a fire in the open air, set up their bellows on the ground, and in a large round iron spoon melted the old lamp, adding a little tin to replace what had been lost. The melted metal was run into a mold, from which it came out in the shape of a lamp. This lamp, still pretty large, was fixed on the lathe which a little boy set in motion; and while it turned, the master touched it with the edge of a steel tool. The tin thus planed off fell in thin shavings, rolled up like curl-papers. The lamp was visibly becoming perfect: it took the proper polish and shape.

Afterward they busied themselves plating the copper saucepans. They cleaned them thoroughly inside with sand, put them on the fire, and, when they were very hot, went over the whole of their surface with a tow pad and a little melted tin. Wherever the pad rubbed, the tin stuck to the copper. In a few moments the inside of the saucepan, red before, was now shiny white.

Emile and Jules, while eating their little lunch of apples and bread, looked on at this curious work without saying a word. They promised themselves to ask their uncle the reason for whitening the inside of the copper saucepans with tin. In the evening, accordingly, they spoke of the tinning and plating.

"Highly cleaned and polished iron is very brilliant," explained their uncle. "The blade of a new knife, Claire's scissors, carefully kept in their case, are examples. But, if exposed to damp air, iron tarnishes quickly and covers itself with an earthy and red crust called—"

"Rust," interposed Claire.

"Yes, it is called rust."

"The big nails that hold the iron wires where the bell-flowers climb up the garden wall are covered with that red crust," remarked Jules; and Emile added:

"This old knife I found in the ground is covered with it too."

"Those large nails and the old knife are encrusted with rust because they have remained for a long time exposed to the air and dampness. Damp air corrodes iron; it becomes incorporated with the metal and makes it unrecognizable. When rusty, iron no longer has the properties that make it so useful to us; it is a kind of red or yellow earth, in which, without looking attentively, it would be impossible to suspect a metal."

"I can well believe it," said Jules. "For my part, I should never have taken rust for iron with which air and moisture had become incorporated."

"Many other metals rust like iron; that is to say, they are converted into earthy matter by contact with damp air. The color of rust varies according to the metal. Iron rust is yellow or red, that of copper is green, lead and zinc white."

"Then the green rust of old pennies is copper rust," said Jules.

"The white matter that covers the nozzle of the pump must be lead rust?" queried Claire.

"Exactly. The prime difficulty with rust is that it makes metals ugly: they lose their brilliance and polish; but it works still greater injury. There are harmless rusts which might get mixed with our food without danger: such is iron rust. On the contrary, copper and lead rusts are deadly poisons. If, by mischance, these rusts should get into our food, we might die, or at least we should experience cruel suffering. We will speak only of copper, for lead, on account of its quick melting, cannot go on the fire and is not used for kitchen utensils. Copper rust, I say, is a mortal poison; and yet they prepare food in copper vessels. Ask Mother Ambroisine."

"Very true," said she, "but I always have my eye on my saucepans: I keep them very clean and from time to time have them replated."

"I don't understand," put in Jules, "how the work that the tinsmith did this morning could prevent the copper rust being a poison."

"The smith's work will not make the copper rust cease to be a poison," replied Uncle Paul, "but it will prevent the rust's forming. Of the common metals tin rusts the least. Exposed to the air a long time, it scarcely tarnishes. And then the rust, which forms in small quantities, is innocuous, like iron rust. To prevent copper from covering itself with poisonous green spots, to preserve it from rust, it must be kept from contact with damp air and also with certain alimentary substances such as vinegar, oil, grease—substances that provoke the rapid formation of rust. For this reason the copper saucepan is coated over with tin inside. Under the thin bed of tin which covers it, the copper cannot rust, because it is no longer in contact with the air. The tin remains; but this metal changes with difficulty, and, besides, its rust, if it forms any, is harmless. So they plate copper, that is to say they cover it with a thin bed of tin, to prevent its rusting, and thus to prevent the formation of the dangerous poison that might, some day or other, be mixed with our food.

"They also tin iron, not to prevent the formation of poison, for the rust of this metal is harmless, but simply to preserve it from changing and covering itself with ugly red spots. This tinned iron is called tin-plate. Lids, coffee-pots, dripping-pans, graters, lanterns, and innumerable other things, are of tin-plate; that is to say, thin sheets of iron covered on both sides with a coating of tin."

Day 150

    1.   Read chapter 14 of *The Story Book of Science*.
    2.   Tell someone what this story was about.

CHAPTER XIV GOLD AND IRON

"SOME metals never rust; such a one is gold. Ancient gold pieces found in the earth after centuries are as bright as the day they were coined. No dross, no rust covers their effigy and inscription. Time, fire, humidity, air, cannot harm this admirable metal. Therefore gold, on account of its unchangeable luster and its rarity, is preeminently the material for ornaments and coins.

"Furthermore, gold is the first metal that man became acquainted with, long before iron, lead, tin, and the others. The reason why man's attention was called to gold, long centuries before iron, is not hard to understand. Gold never rusts; iron rusts with such grievous facility that in a short time, if we are not careful, it is converted into a red earth. I have just told you that gold objects, however old they may be, have come to us intact, even after having been in the dampest ground. As for objects of iron, not one has reached us that was not in an unrecognizable state. Corroded with rust, they have become a shapeless earthy crust. Now I will ask Jules if the iron ore that is extracted from the bowels of the earth can be real, pure iron, such as we use."

"It seems to me not, Uncle; for if iron at any given moment is pure, it must rust with time and change to earthy matter, as does the blade of a knife buried in the ground."

"My brother seems to reason correctly; I agree with him," said Claire.

"And gold?" Uncle Paul asked her.

"It is different with gold," she replied. "As that metal never rusts, is not changed by time, air, and dampness, it must be pure."

"Exactly so. In the rocks where it is disseminated in small scales, gold is as brilliant as in jewelers' boxes. Claire's earrings have not more luster than the particles set by nature in the rock. On the contrary, what a pitiful appearance iron makes when it is found! It is an earthy crust, a reddish stone, in which only after long research can one suspect the presence of a metal; it is, in fact, rust, mixed more or less with other substances. And then, it is not enough to perceive that this rusty stone contains a metal; a way must still be found to decompose the ore and bring the iron back to its metallic state. How many efforts were necessary to attain this result, one of the most difficult to achieve! How many fruitless attempts, how many painful trials! Iron, then, was the last to become of use to us, long after gold and other metals, like copper and silver, which are sometimes, but not always, found pure. That most useful of metals was the last; but with it an immense advance was made in human industry. From the moment man was in possession of iron, he found himself master of the earth.

"At the head of substances that resist shock, iron must be placed; and it is precisely its enormous resistance to rupture that makes this metal so precious to us. Never would a gold, copper, marble, or stone anvil resist the blows of the smith's hammer as an iron one does. The hammer itself, of what substance other than iron could it be made? If of copper, silver, or gold, it would flatten, crush, and become useless in a short time; for these metals lack hardness. If of stone, it would break at the first rather hard blow. For these implements nothing can take the place of iron. Nor can it for axes, saws, knives, the mason's chisel, the quarry-man's pick, the plowshare, and a number of other implements which cut, hew, pierce, plane, file, give or receive violent blows. Iron alone has the hardness that can cut most other substances, and the resistance that sets blows at defiance. In this respect iron is, of all mineral substances, the handsomest present that Providence has given to man. It is preëminently the material for tools, indispensable in every art and industry."

"Claire and I read one day," said Jules, "that when the Spaniards discovered America, the savages of that new country had gold axes, which they very willingly exchanged for iron ones. I laughed at their innocence, which made them give such a costly price for a piece of very common metal. I think I see now that the exchange was to their advantage."

"Yes, decidedly to their advantage; for with an iron ax they could fell trees to make their dug-out canoes and their huts; they could better defend themselves against wild animals and attack the game in their hunts. This piece of iron gave them an assurance of food, a substantial boat, a warm dwelling, a redoubtable weapon. In comparison, a gold ax was only a useless plaything."

"If iron came last, what did men do before they knew of it?" asked Jules.

"They made their weapons and tools of copper; for, like gold, this metal is sometimes in a pure state so that it can be utilized just as nature gives it to us. But a copper implement, having little hardness, is of much less value than an iron one. Thus, in those far-off days of copper axes, man was indeed a wretched creature.

"He was still more so before knowing copper. He cut a flint into a point, or split it, and fastened it to the end of a stick; and that was his only weapon.

"With this stone he had to procure food, clothing, a hut, and to defend himself from wild beasts. His clothing was a skin thrown over his back, his dwelling a hut made of twisted branches and mud; his food a piece of flesh, produce of the chase. Domestic animals were unknown, the earth uncultivated, and industry lacking."

"And where was that?" asked Claire.

"Everywhere, my dear child; here, even in places where to-day are our most flourishing towns. Oh! how forlorn man was before attaining, by the help of iron, the well-being that we enjoy to-day; how forlorn was man and what a great present Providence made him in giving him this metal!"

Just as Uncle Paul finished, Jacques knocked discreetly at the door; Jules ran to open it. They whispered a few words to each other. It was about an important affair for the next day.

Day 151

1.   Read chapter 15 of *The Story Book of Science*.
2.   Tell someone what this story was about.

CHAPTER XV THE FLEECE

AS was agreed upon the day before, Jacques made ready for the performance. To keep the patients from moving, they were obliged to make them lie down, their feet tied, between the two inclined planks of a rack. Steel knives shone on the ground. As for them, innocent victims of the needs of man, they were already bound and lying on their sides. With gentle resignation they awaited their sad fate. Were they going to be slain? Oh, no: they were to be shorn. Jacques took a sheep by its feet, placed it between the two planks of the rack, and, with large scissors, began, cra-cra-cra, to cut off the wool. Little by little, the fleece fell all in one piece. When the sheep had been despoiled, it ran free to one side, ashamed and chilly. It had just given its covering to clothe man. Jacques put another one on the rack, and the scissors began to move.

"Tell me, Jacques," said Jules, "are not the sheep very cold when they have had their wool cut off? See how that one trembles that you have just shorn."

"Never mind that: I have chosen a fine day for it. The sun is warm. By to-morrow they won't feel the need of their wool. And besides, ought not the sheep to suffer a little cold so that we may be warm?"

"We warm? How?"

"You astonish me. You do not know that, you who read so many books? Well, with this wool they will make you stockings and knitted things for this winter; they will even make cloth, fine cloth for clothes."

"Peuh!" exclaimed Emile. "This wool is too dirty and ugly to make stockings, knitted things, and cloth."

"Dirty at present," Jacques agreed, "but it will be washed in the river, and when it has become very white Mother Ambroisine will work it on her spinning-wheel and make yarn of it. This yarn knitted with needles will become stockings that one is very glad to have on one's feet when obliged to run in the snow."

"I have never seen red, green, blue sheep; and yet there are red, green, blue, and other colored wools," said Emile.

"They dye the white wool that the sheep gives us; they put it into boiling water with drugs and coloring matter, and it comes out of that water with a color that stays."

"And cloth?"

"And cloth is made with threads of wool like those of stockings; but in order to weave these threads, make them cross each other regularly, and convert them into fabric, you must have complicated machines, weaving looms that cannot be had in our houses. These are only found in large factories used for manufacturing woolen goods."

"Then these trousers that I have on come from the sheep; this vest; my cravat, stockings too. I am dressed in the spoils of the sheep?" This from Jules.

"Yes, to defend ourselves from the cold, we take the sheep's wool. The poor beast furnishes its fleece for our clothes, its milk and flesh for our nourishment, its skin for our gloves. We live on the life of our domestic animals. The ox gives us his strength, flesh, hide; the cow, besides, gives us milk. The donkey, mule, horse, work for us. As soon as they are dead they leave us their skin, of which we make leather for our shoes. The hen gives us eggs, the dog puts his intelligence at our service. And yet there are people who, without any motive, maltreat these animals without which we should be so poor; who let them suffer hunger and beat them unmercifully! Never imitate those heartless ones; it would be an insult to God, who has given us the donkey, ox, sheep, and other animals. When I think that these valuable creatures give us all, even to their very life, I would share my last crust with them." And the shears meanwhile continued their cra-cra-cra; and the fleece fell.

Day 152

1.   Read chapter 16 of *The Story Book of Science*.
2.   Tell someone what this story was about.

CHAPTER XVI FLAX AND HEMP

WHILE listening to what Jacques was saying about wool, Emile examined his handkerchief attentively. He turned it over and over, felt it, then looked through it. Jacques foresaw the question Emile was getting ready to ask him, and he said:

"Handkerchiefs and linens are not woolen. Certain plants, cotton, hemp, flax, and not sheep, furnish them; for, you see, I don't know much about those things myself. I have heard tell of the cotton plant, but have never seen it. And, besides, I am afraid talking to you will make me cut the sheep's skin."

In the evening, at Jules's request, they took up the history of the materials with which we clothe ourselves, and Uncle Paul explained their nature.

"The outside of hemp and flax is composed of long threads, very fine, supple, and tenacious, from which we manufacture our fabrics. We clothe ourselves with the spoils of the sheep, we make ourselves fine with the bark of the plant. The fabrics of luxury, cambric, tulle, gauze, point-lace, Mechlin lace, are made from flax; the stronger ones, even to coarse sacking, are of hemp. The cotton plant gives us the fabrics made of cotton.

Flax

"Flax is a slender plant with little delicate blue flowers, and is sown and harvested every year. It is much cultivated in Northern France, Belgium, and Holland. It is the first plant used by man for woven fabrics. Mummies of Egypt, the old land of Moses and the patriarchs, mummies which have lain buried four thousand years and more, are swathed in bands of linen."

"Mummies, did you say?" interposed Jules. "I don't know what they are."

"I will tell you, my dear child. Respect for the dead is found among all people and in all ages. Man regards as sacred what was the seat of a soul made in the image of God; he honors the dead, but the honors rendered differ according to time, place, customs. We inter the dead and put over the burial place a tombstone with an inscription, or at least a humble cross, divine emblem of life eternal. The ancients burned them on a funeral pile; they piously gathered the bones bleached by the fire and inclosed them in priceless vases. In Egypt, to preserve the cherished remains for the family, they embalmed the dead; that is to say, they impregnated them with aromatics and swathed them in linen to prevent decomposition. These pious duties were so delicately performed that, after centuries and centuries, we find intact in their chests of sweet-smelling wood, but dried and blackened by years, contemporaries of the ancient kings of Egypt or the Pharaohs. These are what are called mummies.

"Hemp has been cultivated all over Europe for many centuries. It is an annual, of a strong, nauseous odor, with little, green, dull-looking flowers, whose stem, of the thickness of a quill pen, rises to about two meters. It is cultivated, like flax, both for its bark and for its grain, called hemp-seed."

"That is the grain, I think," said Emile, "we give the goldfinch, which it cracks with its beak when it breaks the shell to get out the little kernel."

"Yes, hemp-seed is the feast of little birds.

"The bark of the hemp has not the fineness of flax. The fibers of this latter plant are so fine that twenty-five grams of tow spun on the spinning wheel furnishes a thread almost a league long. The spider's web alone can rival in delicacy certain linen fabrics.

"When hemp and flax reach maturity, they are harvested, and the seeds are separated by thrashing. The next operation, retting, then takes place, its purpose being to render the filaments of the bark, or the fibers, as they are called, easily separable from the wood. These fibers, in fact, are pasted to the stem and stuck together by a gummy substance that is very resistant and prevents separation until it is destroyed by rot. They sometimes do this retting by spreading the plants in the fields for a couple of weeks and turning them over now and then, until the tow detaches itself from the woody part or hemp-stalk.

But the quickest way is to tie the flax and hemp in bundles and keep them submerged in a pond. There soon follows a rot which gives out intolerable smells; the bark decays, and the fiber, endowed with exceptional resistance, is freed.

"Then the bundles are dried; after that they crush them between the jaws of an instrument called a brake, to crush the stems into small pieces and separate the tow. Finally, to purge the tow of all woody refuse and to divide it into the finest threads, they pass it between the iron teeth of a sort of big comb called a heckle. In this state, the fiber is spun either by hand or by machine. The thread obtained is ready for weaving.

"On a loom they place in order, side by side, numerous threads composing what they call the warp. By turns, impelled by a pedal on which the operator's foot presses, one half of these threads descends while the other half ascends. At the same time the operator passes a transverse thread in a shuttle through the two halves of the warp, from left to right, then from right to left. From this inter-crossing comes the woven fabric. And it is finished; the garb of the plant has changed masters; the bark of the hemp has become cloth, that of flax a princely lace worth some hundreds of francs by the piece."

Day 153

1.   Read chapter 17 of *The Story Book of Science*.
2.   Tell someone what this story was about.

CHAPTER XVII COTTON

"COTTON the most important of the materials used for our woven fabrics, is furnished by a semi-tropical plant called the cotton plant.

Cotton Plant and Cotton Boll

It is an herb or even a shrub from one to two meters high, and its large yellow flowers are followed by an abundant fruitage of bolls, each as large as an egg, filled with a silky flock, sometimes brilliantly white, sometimes a pale yellowish shade, according to the kind of cotton. In the middle of this flock are the seeds."

"It seems to me I have seen flock of that kind fall in flakes in the spring from the top of poplars and willows," said Claire.

"The comparison is very good. Willows and poplars have for their fruit tiny little long and pointed bolls three or four time as large as a pin's head. In the month of May these bolls are ripe. They open and set free a very fine white down, in the middle of which are the seeds. If the air is calm, this down piles up at the foot of the tree in a bed of cotton wool, as white as snow; but at the least breath of wind the flakes are borne long distances, carrying with them the seeds, which thus find unoccupied places where they can germinate and become trees. Many other seeds are provided with soft aigrettes, silky plumes, which keep them up in the air a long time and permit them distant journeys in order to disseminate the plant. For example, who is not familiar with the seeds of thistles and dandelions, those beautiful silky plumed seeds that you take pleasure in blowing into the air?"

"Can the flock of poplar bolls be put to the same use as cotton?" Jules asked.

"By no means. There is too little of it, and it would be too difficult to gather. Besides, it is so short it might not be possible to spin it. But if we ourselves cannot make use of it, others find it very useful. This flock is the little birds' cotton; many gather it to line their nests. The goldfinch, among others, is one of the cleverest of the clever. Its house of cotton is a masterpiece of elegance and solidity. In the fork of several little branches, with the cottony flock of the willow and poplar, with bits of wool that hedge thorns pull out from sheep as they pass, with the plumy aigrettes of thistle seeds, it makes for its young a cup-shaped mattress, so soft and warm and wadded that no little prince in his swaddling-clothes ever had the like.

"To build their nests, birds find materials near at hand; they only have to set to work. When spring comes, the goldfinch does not have to think of the materials for its nest; it is sure that the osier-beds, thistles, and roadside hedges will furnish in abundance all that it needs. And it ought to be thus, for a bird has not the intelligence to prepare a long time in advance, by careful and wise industry, the things that it will need. Man, whose noble prerogative it is to acquire everything by work and reflection, procures cotton from distant countries; a bird finds its cotton on the poplars of its grove.

"At maturity the cotton bolls open wide, and their flock bursts out in soft flakes that are gathered by hand, boll by boll. The flock, well dried in the sun on screens, is beaten with flails or, better, submitted to the action of certain machines. It is thus freed from all seeds and husks. Without any other preparation, cotton comes to us in large bales to be converted into fabrics in our manufactories. The countries that furnish the most of it are India, Egypt, Brazil, and, above all, the United States of North America.

"In a single year the European manufactories work up nearly eight hundred million kilograms of cotton. This enormous weight is not too much, for the whole world clothes itself with the precious flock, turned into print, percale, calico. Thus human activity has no greater field than the cotton trade. How many workmen, how many delicate operations, what long voyages, all for a simple piece of print costing a few centimes! A handful of cotton is gathered, we will suppose, two or three thousand leagues from here. This cotton crosses the ocean, goes a quarter round the globe, and comes to France or England to be manufactured. Then it is spun, woven, ornamented with colored designs, and, converted into print, crosses the seas again, to go perhaps to the other end of the world to serve as head-dress for some woolly-haired negro. What a multiplicity of interests are brought into play! It was necessary to sow the plant; then, for a good half of the year, to cultivate it. Out of a handful of flock, then, provision must be made for the remuneration of those who have cultivated and harvested. Next come the dealer who buys and the mariner who transports it. To each of them is due a part of the handful of flock. Then follow the spinner, weaver, dyer, all of whom the cotton must indemnify for their work. It is far from being finished. Now come other dealers who buy the fabrics, other mariners who carry them to all parts of the world, and finally merchants who sell them at retail. How can the handful of flock pay all these interested ones without itself acquiring an exorbitant price?

"To accomplish this wonder two industrial powers intervene: work on a large scale and the aid of machinery. You have seen how Ambroisine spins wool on the wheel. The carded wool is first divided into long locks. One of these locks is applied to a hook which turns rapidly. The hook seizes the wool and in its rotation twists the fibers into one thread, which lengthens little by little at the expense of the lock held and regulated by the fingers. When the thread attains a certain length, Mother Ambroisine rolls it on the spindle by a suitable movement of the wheel; then she continues twisting the wool again.

"Strictly speaking, cotton could be spun in the same way; but, however clever Mother Ambroisine may be, the fabrics made from the thread of her wheel would cost an enormous price on account of the time spent. What, then, is to be done? A machine is made to spin the cotton. In rooms larger than the biggest church are placed, by hundreds of thousands, the nicely adjusted machines proper for spinning, with hooks, spindles, and bobbins. And all turn at the same time with a precision and rapidity that defy watching. The work goes on with noise enough to deafen you. The flock of cotton is seized by thousands and thousands of hooks; the endless threads come and go from one bobbin to another, and roll themselves on the spindles. In a few hours a mountain of cotton is converted into thread, the length of which would go several times around the whole earth. What have they spent for work which would have exhausted the strength of an army of spinners as clever as Mother Ambroisine? Some shovelfuls of coal to heat the water, the steam of which starts the machine that sets everything going. Weaving, the printing of the colored designs,—in short, the various operations that the flock undergoes to become cloth are executed by means quite as expeditious, quite as economical. And it is thus that the planter, broker, mariner, spinner, weaver, dyer, and merchant can all have their share in the handful of cotton flock which has become a piece of calico and is sold for four sous."

Day 154

1. Read chapter 18 of *The Story Book of Science*.
2. Tell someone what this story was about.

CHAPTER XVIII PAPER

MOTHER AMBROISINE called Claire. A friend had just come to see her to learn about an embroidery stitch that troubled her. At the request of Jules and Emile, however, Uncle Paul continued. He knew Jules would take pleasure in repeating the conversation to his sister.

"Flax, linen, and cotton, especially the last-named, have still another use of great importance. First they clothe us; then, when too ragged to use any more, they serve to make paper."

"Paper!" exclaimed Emile.

"Paper, real paper, that on which we write, of which we make books. The beautiful white sheets of your copybooks, the leaves of a book, even the costliest, gilt-edged and enriched with magnificent pictures, come to us from miserable rags.

"Despicable tatters are collected: some of them are picked up from the filth of the street, some are unspeakably filthy. They are sorted over, these for fine paper, those for coarse. They are thoroughly washed, for they need it. Now machines take them in hand. Scissors cut them, steel claws tear them, wheels make pulp of them and reduce them to shreds. Mill-stones take them and grind them still more, then triturate them in water, and convert them into a sort of soup. The pulp is gray, it must be whitened. Then recourse is had to powerful drugs, which attack everything they touch, and in less than no time make it white as snow. Behold the pulpy mass thoroughly purified. Other machines spread it in thin layers on sieves. Water drips through, and the rag soup forms into felt. Cylinders press this felt, others dry it, others give it a polish. The paper is finished.

"Before it became paper, the first material was rags, or cloth too tattered to use. How many uses has not this cloth served, and what energetic treatments has it not undergone before being cast out as rubbish! Washing with corrosive ashes, contact with acrid soup, pounding with a beetle, exposure to the sun, air, and rain. What is then this material which, in spite of its delicacy, resists the brutalities of washing, soap, sun, and air; which remains intact in the bosom of rottenness; which braves the machines and drugs of paper-making, and always comes out of these ordeals more supple and whiter, to become at last a sheet of paper, beautiful satiny paper, the confidant of our thoughts? You know now, my little friends, this admirable material, source of so much intellectual progress, comes to us from the flock of the cotton plant and the bark of hemp and flax."

"I am certainly going to surprise Claire," said Jules, "when I tell her that her beautiful prayer-book with the silver clasp was made from horrid rags, perhaps from ragged handkerchiefs thrown away for rubbish, or from tatters picked up from the mud of the street."

"Claire will be interested to learn the nature of paper; but, I am sure, the lowly origin of her prayer-book will not lessen the value of it in her mind. Skill performs a marvel in transforming despicable rags into a book, depository of noble thoughts. God, my dear child, does incomparably more in the miracle of vegetation. The filth of the dung-hill, when buried in the soil, becomes transformed into the most pleasing things in the world; for it becomes the rose, the lily, and other flowers. As for us, let us be like Claire's book and the flowers of the good God: let us try to have real value in ourselves, and let us never blush at our humble extraction. There is only one true greatness, only one true nobility: greatness and nobility of the soul. If we possess them, the merit is all the greater by reason of our lowly origin."

Day 155

1.   Read chapter 19 of *The Story Book of Science*.
2.   Tell the main idea of what you read about today.

CHAPTER XIX THE BOOK

"NOW that I know what paper is made of," said Jules, "I should like to know how they make books."

"I could listen all day without getting tired," Emile asserted. "For a story I would leave my top and my soldiers."

"To make a book, my children, there is double work: first the labor of the one who thinks and writes it, then the labor of the one who prints it. To think a book and write it under the sole dictation of one's mind is a difficult and serious business. Brain-work exhausts our strength much more quickly than manual labor, for we must put the best of ourselves into it, our soul. I tell you these things that you may see what gratitude you owe those who, solicitous for your future, think and write in order to teach you to think for yourselves and to free you from the miseries of ignorance."

"I am quite convinced," returned Jules, "of the difficulties to be overcome in order to compose a book under the sole dictation of one's mind; for when I want to write a letter of half a page to wish you a Happy New Year, I come to a full stop at the first word. How hard it is to find the first word! My head is heavy, my face flushes, and I can't see straight. I shall do better when I know my grammar well."

"I am sorry, my dear child, but I must undeceive you. Grammar cannot teach one to write. It teaches us to make a verb agree with its subject, an adjective with a substantive, and other things of that kind. It is very useful, I admit, for nothing is more displeasing than to violate the rules of language; but that does not impart the gift of writing. There are people whose memories are crammed with rules of grammar, who, like you, stop short at the first word.

"Language is in some sort the clothing of thought. We cannot clothe what does not exist; we cannot speak or write what we do not find in our minds. Thought dictates and the pen writes. When the head is furnished with ideas, and usage, still more than grammar, has taught us the rules of language, we have all that is necessary to write excellent things correctly. But, again, if ideas are wanting, if there is nothing in the head, what can you write? How are these ideas to be acquired? By study, reading, and conversation with people better instructed than we."

"Then, in listening to all these fine things you tell us, I am no doubt learning to write," said Jules.

"Why, certainly, my little friend. Is it not true, for example, that if it had been proposed to you, a few days ago, to write only two lines about the origin of paper, you would not have been able to do it? What was wanting? Ideas and not grammar, although you know very little of that yet."

"It is true, I was entirely ignorant what paper comes from. To-day I know that cotton is a flock found in the bolls of a shrub called the cotton plant: I know that with this flock they make thread; then, after the thread, cloth; I know that when the cloth gets old with use, it is reduced to pulp by machines, and that this pulp, stretched in very thin layers and pressed, finally becomes a sheet of paper. I know these things well, and yet I should find it very hard to write them."

"You are mistaken, for all you need do is to put in writing exactly what you have just told me."

"You write then just as you talk?" asked the boy, incredulously.

"Yes, provided that speech is corrected, if necessary, on reflection, since writing gives time for it, whereas talking does not."

"In that case, I should soon have my five lines on paper. I should write: 'Cotton is the flock that is found in the bolls of a shrub called the cotton plant. With this flock they make thread; and with this thread, cloth. When the cloth is worn out, machines tear it into little pieces, and mill-stones grind it with water to make it into a pulp. This pulp is stretched in thin layers which are pressed and dried. Then it is paper.' There! Is that right, Uncle?"

"As well as one could wish from one of your age," his uncle assured him.

"But that could not be put into a book."

"And why not? I promise you that shall be in a book some day. It has been said to me that our talks might be useful to many other little boys as desirous to learn as you, and I propose to collect them in all their simplicity and make a book of them."

"A book where I could read at leisure the stories that you tell us? Oh, how pleased I am, Uncle, and how I love you! You won't put my ignorant questions in that book?"

"I shall put them all in. You know next to nothing now, my dear child, but you ardently desire to learn. That is a fine quality, and a very becoming one."

"Are you at least sure that the little boys who read this book will not laugh at me?"

"I am sure."

"Tell them then that I love them well and embrace them all."

"Tell them I wish them as good a top and as fine lead soldiers as those you gave me," put in Emile.

"Take care, Emile," cautioned his brother. "Uncle may put your lead soldier's in the book."

"They will be there, they are there."

Day 156

1. Read chapter 20 of *The Story Book of Science*.
2. Tell the main idea of what you read about today.

CHAPTER XX PRINTING

"AFTER a book is written, the author sends his work, his manuscript, to the printer, who is to reproduce it in printed letters and in as many copies as are desired.

"Picture to yourself fine and short metal sticks, on the end of each of which is carved in relief a letter of the alphabet. One of these sticks has an A on the end, another a B, another a C, etc. There are others which have a full-stop, a comma, a semi-colon; in fact, there are as many distinct kinds of these little metal pieces as there are letters and orthographic signs in our written language. Besides, each letter and each sign are represented a great many times. Let us take note, too, that all these characters are carved wrong side before; you will soon see the reason.

"A workman called a compositor has before him a stand of cases, of which each compartment is occupied by a single letter of the alphabet, or by an orthographic sign. The a's are in such a compartment, the b's in a second, the c's in a third, and so on. The letters, furthermore, are not arranged in the case alphabetically. To shorten the work, they put in the compartments near to hand the letters that occur most frequently, such as the e's, r's, i's, a's; and they place in the more distant compartments the letters less often used, such as x's and y's.

"The compositor has before him a manuscript, and at his left hand a little flanged iron ruler called a composing-stick. As he reads, his right hand, guided by long habit, searches in the case the desired letter and places it in the composing-stick, upright and in a row with the others. He separates the words by means of a metal stick like those of the letters, but the end of which remains depressed and does not bear any carving. The first line finished, the compositor begins another by setting a new row of little metal pieces next to the row already finished. Finally, when the composing-stick is full, the workman cautiously places the contents in an iron frame, which keeps the delicate combination from going to pieces; and he continues thus until the frame is quite full and we have what is called the printing-bed. This plate is composed of a multitude of little metal sticks, simply placed side by side. There are as many of these as there are letters, orthographic signs, and spaces separating the words. The arrangement of these numerous bits of metal is a masterpiece that a false movement might ruin. It is held firm in its iron frame by means of wedges, so that the whole thing seems made of a single block of metal. The bed is then ready for printing.

"A roller impregnated with a thick ink made of oil and lampblack is passed over the plate. The letters and orthographic signs, which alone stand out in relief, become covered with ink; the rest does not take it because its surface is lower. A sheet of paper is placed on the inked plate; it is covered with a pad to protect it, then pressed hard. The ink of the characters is deposited on the paper, and the sheet is found printed on one side. To print the other, the operation is repeated with a second plate. The metal letters are, as I said, carved wrong side before, as the letters of a book appear when you look at them in a mirror. The inky imprint left by them on the paper reproduces them in a reversed position, and consequently in the right way.

"The first sheet is followed immediately by a second. With the roller the plate is inked again, a sheet of paper is applied, pressure is exerted, and it is done. Then comes a third sheet, a hundredth, a thousandth, indefinitely. All that is needed each time is to ink the plate, cover it with paper, then press. All this is done with such rapidity that in a short time we have a great pile of printed sheets, each of which it would take a whole day to write by hand.

"Before the invention of this marvelous art, which enables us to reproduce the works of the mind very rapidly and in as great numbers as may be desired, we were restricted to hand-made copies. These manuscript books required years of work, and hence were very rare and high-priced. Large fortunes were necessary to acquire a library of several volumes. To-day books find their way everywhere, spreading in profusion, even among the lowest classes, the sacred bread of intelligence. Printing has been known for four hundred years: its invention is due to Gutenberg."

"That is a name I shall never forget," said Jules.

"It deserves, above all, to be remembered, for with the printed book Gutenberg rendered impossible henceforth the ignorant times through which man has miserably passed. Our intellectual treasures, resources for the future, are better than engraved on stone or metal; they are inscribed on sheets of paper, in copies too numerous to be all destroyed."

Day 157

1. Read chapter 21 of *The Story Book of Science*.
2. Tell someone what this story was about.

CHAPTER XXI BUTTERFLIES

OH, how beautiful! Oh, my goodness, how beautiful they are! There are some whose wings are barred with red on a garnet background; some bright blue with black circles; others are sulphur-yellow with orange spots; again others are white fringed with gold-color. They have on the forehead two fine horns, two antennæ, sometimes fringed like an aigrette, sometimes cut off like a tuft of feathers. Under the head they have a proboscis, a sucker as fine as a hair and twisted into a spiral. When they approach a flower, they untwist the proboscis and plunge it to the bottom of the corolla to drink a drop of honeyed liquor. Oh, how beautiful they are! Oh, my goodness, how beautiful they are! But if one manages to touch them, their wings tarnish and leave between the fingers a fine dust like that of precious metals.

Now their uncle told the children the names of the butterflies that flew on the flowers in the garden. "This one," said he, "whose wings are white with a black border and three black spots, is called the cabbage butterfly. This larger one, whose yellow wings barred with black terminate in a long tail, at the base of which are found a large rust colored eye and blue spots, is called the swallow-tail. This tiny one, sky-blue above, silver-gray underneath, sprinkled with black eyes in white circles, with a line of reddish spots bordering the wings, is called the Argus."

And Uncle Paul continued thus, naming the butterflies that a bright sun had drawn to the flowers.

"The Argus ought to be difficult to catch," observed Emile. "He sees everywhere; his wings are covered with eyes."

"The pretty round spots that a great many butterflies have on their wings are not really eyes, although they are called by that name; they are ornaments, nothing more. Real eyes, eyes for seeing, are in the head. The Argus has two, neither more nor fewer than the other butterflies."

"Claire tells me," said Jules, "that butterflies come from caterpillars. Is it true, Uncle?"

"Yes, my child. Every butterfly, before becoming the graceful creature which flies from flower to flower with magnificent wings, is an ugly caterpillar that creeps with effort. Thus the cabbage butterfly which I have just shown you, is first a green caterpillar, which stays on the cabbages and gnaws the leaves. Jacques will tell you how much pains he takes to protect his cabbage patch from the voracious insect; for, you see, caterpillars have a terrible appetite. You will soon learn the reason.

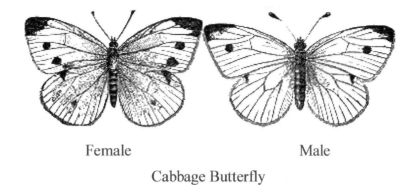

Female   Male

Cabbage Butterfly

"Most insects behave like caterpillars. On coming out of the egg, they have a provisional form that they must replace later by another. They are, as it were, born twice: first imperfect, dull, voracious, ugly: then perfect, agile, abstemious, and often of an admirable richness and elegance. Under its first form, the insect is a worm called by the general name of larva.

"You remember the lion of the plant-lice, the grub that eats the lice of the rosebush and, for weeks, without being able to satisfy itself, continues night and day its ferocious feasting. Well, this grub is a larva, that will change itself into a little lace-winged fly, the hemerobius, whose wings are of gauze and eyes of gold. Before becoming the pretty red lady-bird with black spots, this pretty insect, which, in spite of its innocent air, crunches the plant-lice, is a very ugly worm, a slate-colored larva, covered with little points, and itself very fond of plant-lice. The June bug, the silly June bug, which, if its leg is held by a thread, awkwardly puffs out its wings, makes all preparations, and starts out to the tune of 'Fly, fly, fly!' is at first a white worm, a plump larva, fat as bacon, which lives underground, attacks the roots of plants, and destroys our crops. The big stag-beetle, whose head is armed with menacing mandibles shaped like the stag's horns, is at first a large worm that lives in old tree-trunks. It is the same with the capricorn, so peculiar for its long antennæ. And the worm found in our ripe cherries, which is so repugnant to us, what does it become? It becomes a beautiful fly, its wings adorned with four bands of black velvet. And so on with others.

"Well, this initial state of the insect, this worm, first form of youth, is called the larva. The wonderful change which transforms the larva into a perfect insect is called metamorphosis. Caterpillars are larvæ.

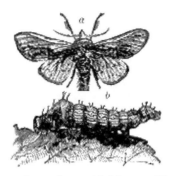

By metamorphosis they turn into those beautiful butterflies whose wings, decorated with the richest colors, fill us with admiration. The Argus, now so beautiful with its celestial blue wings, was first a poor hairy caterpillar; the splendid swallowtail began by being a green caterpillar with black stripes across it and red spots on its sides. Out of these despicable vermin metamorphosis has made those delightful creatures which only the flowers can rival in elegance.

"You all know the tale of Cinderella. The sisters have left for the ball, very proud, very smart. Cinderella, her heart full, is watching the kettle. The godmother arrives. 'Go,' says she, 'to the garden and get a pumpkin.' And behold, the scooped-out pumpkin changes under the godmother's wand, into a gilded carriage. 'Cinderella,' says she again, 'open the mouse-trap.' Six mice run out of it, and are no sooner touched by the magic wand than they turn into six beautiful dappled-gray horses. A bearded rat becomes a big coachman with a commanding mustache. Six lizards sleeping behind the watering pot become green bedizened footmen, who immediately jump up behind the carriage. Finally the poor girl's shabby clothes are changed to gold and silver ones sprinkled with precious stones. Cinderella starts for the ball, in glass slippers. You, apparently, know the rest of it better than I.

"These powerful godmothers for whom it is play to change mice into horses, lizards into footmen, ugly clothes into sumptuous ones, these gracious fairies who astonish you with their fabulous prodigies, what are they, my dear children, in comparison with reality, the great fairy of the good God, who, out of a dirty worm, object of disgust, knows how to make a creature of ravishing beauty! He touches with his divine wand a miserable hairy caterpillar, an abject worm that slobbers in rotten wood, and the miracle is accomplished: the disgusting larva has turned into a beetle all shining with gold, a butterfly whose azure wings would have outshone Cinderella's fine toilette."

Day 158

1.　　　Read chapter 22 of *The Story Book of Science.*
2.　　　Tell someone about what you read.

CHAPTER XXII THE BIG EATERS

"INSECTS propagate themselves by eggs, which they lay, with admirable foresight, where the young will be sure to find nourishment. The little creature that comes from the egg is a larva, a feeble grub, which, most often, has to shift for itself, procure at its own risk food and shelter—the most difficult thing in this world. In these painful beginnings it cannot expect any help from its mother, dead some time before; for in insect life the parents generally die before the hatching of the eggs that produce the young. Without delay the little larva sets to work. It eats. It is its sole business, and a serious one, on which its future depends. It eats, not only to keep up its strength from day to day, but above all to acquire the plumpness necessary for its future metamorphosis. I must tell you—and this perhaps will surprise you—that an insect ceases to grow after attaining its final perfect form. It is known, too, that there are insects—among others, the butterfly of the silkworm—that do not take any nourishment at all.

"A cat is at first a tiny little pink-nosed creature, so small that it could rest in the hollow of the hand. In one or two months it is a pretty kitten that amuses itself at a mere nothing, and with its nimble paw whips the wisp of paper that one throws before it. Another year, and it is a tom-cat that patiently watches for mice or joins battle with its rivals on the roof. But, whether a tiny creature hardly able to open its little blue eyes, or a pretty playful kitten, or a big quarrelsome tom-cat, it has always the form of a cat.

"It is otherwise with insects. The swallow-tail, under its form of butterfly, is not first small, then medium, then large. When, for the first time, it opens its wings and takes flight, it is as large as it ever will be. When it comes out from under-ground, where it lived as a grub, when for the first time it appears in the daylight, the June bug is such as you know it. There are little cats, but no little swallow-tails nor little June hugs. After the metamorphosis, an insect is what it will be to the end."

"But I have seen small June bugs flying round the willows in the evening," objected Jules.

"Those little June bugs are of a different kind. They will always remain the same. Never will they grow and become common June bugs, any more than a cat would grow into a tiger, which it resembles so much.

"The grub alone grows. At first very small on coming out of the egg, little by little it acquires a size in conformity with the future insect. It gathers the materials that the metamorphosis will use,—materials for the wings, antennæ, legs, and all those things that the larva does not have, but that the insect must have. Out of what will the big green worm that lives in dead wood, and must some day become a stag-beetle, make the enormous branched mandibles and the robust horny covering of the perfect insect? Of what will the larva make the long antennæ of the capricorn? Of what will the caterpillar make the large wings of the swallowtail? Of that which the caterpillar, larva, and worm amass now, with thrifty hoarding of life-supporting matter.

"If the little pink-nosed cat were born without ears, paws, tail, fur, mustaches, if it were simply a little ball of flesh, and should some day have to acquire all at once, while asleep, ears, paws, tail, fur, mustaches, and many other things, is it not true that this work of life would necessitate materials gathered together beforehand and held in reserve in the fatty tissues of the animal? No thing can be made from nothing; the smallest hair of the cat's mustache shoots forth at the expense of the substance of the animal, substance which it acquires by eating.

"The larva is in precisely this case: it has nothing, or next to nothing, that the perfect insects must have. It must therefore amass, in view of future changes, materials for the change; it must eat for two: for itself first, and then for the insect that will come from its substance, transformed and, in a sense, recast. So the larvæ are endowed with an incomparable appetite. As I have said, to eat is their sole business. They eat night and day, often without stopping, without taking breath. To lose a mouthful, what imprudence! The future butterfly would perhaps have one scale less to its wings. So they eat gluttonously, take on a stomach, become big, fat, plump. It is the duty of larvæ.

"Some attack plants; they browse on the leaves, chew the flowers, bite the flesh of fruit. Others have a stomach strong enough to digest wood; they hollow out galleries in the tree-trunks, file off, grate, pulverize the hardest oak, as well as the tender willow. Others, again, prefer decomposed animal matter; they haunt infected corpses, fill their stomachs with rottenness. Still others seek excrement and feast on filth. They are all scavengers on whom has developed the high mission of cleansing the earth of its pollution. You would sicken at the mere thought of these worms that swarm in pus; yet one of the most important services, a providential service, is rendered by these disgusting eaters which clear away infection and give back its constituent elements to life. As if to make amends for its filthy needs, one of these larvæ will later be a magnificent fly, rivaling polished bronze in its brilliancy; another, a beetle perfumed with musk, its rich coat vying with gold and precious stones in splendor.

"But these larvæ devoted to the work of general sanitation cannot make us forget other eaters, of whom we are victims. The grubs of the June bug alone sometimes multiply so rapidly in the ground that immense tracts are denuded of vegetation, which is gnawed at the roots.

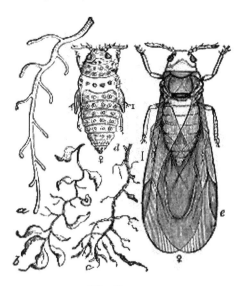

Phylloxera

The forester's shrubs, the farmer's harvests, the gardener's plants, just when everything seems prosperous, some fine morning, hang withered, smitten to death. The worm has passed that way, and all is lost. Fire could not have committed more frightful ravages. A miserable yellow louse, hardly visible, lives under ground, where it attacks the roots of the grape vine. It is called phylloxera. Its calamitous breed threatens to destroy all our vineyards. Some grubs, small enough to lodge in a grain of wheat, ravage the wheat in our granaries and leave only the bran. Others browse the lucerne so that the mower finds nothing left. Others, for years, gnaw at the heart of the wood of the oak, poplar, pine, and divers other large trees. Others, which turn into those little white butterflies flying around the lamp in the evening and called moths, eat our cloth stuffs bit by bit, and finish by reducing them to rags. Others attack wainscoting, old furniture, and reduce them to powder. Others—But I should never get through if I were to tell you all. This little people to which we often disdain to pay the slightest attention, this little race of insects, is so powerful on account of the robust appetite of its larvæ, that man ought seriously to reckon with it. If a certain grub succeeds in multiplying beyond measure, whole provinces are threatened with the tragic fate of starvation. And we are left in perfect ignorance on the subject of these devourers! How can you defend yourself if the enemy is unknown to you? Ah, if I only had the management of these things! As for you, my dear children, while waiting for our talks to be resumed with more detail concerning these ravagers, remember this: the larvæ of insects are the great eaters of this world, the providential demolishers that finish the work of death and thus prepare for the work of life, since everything or nearly everything passes through their stomach."

Day 159

1.   Read chapter 23 of *The Story Book of Science*.
2.   Tell someone about what you read.

CHAPTER XXIII SILK

"SOONER or later, according to its species, a day comes when the larva feels itself strong enough to face the perils of metamorphosis. It has valiantly done its duty, since to stuff its paunch is the duty of a worm; it has eaten for two, itself and the matured insect. Now it is advisable to renounce feasting, retire from the world, and prepare itself a quiet shelter for the death-like sleep during which its second birth takes place. A thousand methods are employed for the preparation of this lodging.

"Certain larvæ simply bury themselves in the ground, others hollow out round niches with polished sides. There are some that make themselves a case out of dry leaves; there are others that know how to glue together a hollow ball out of grains of sand or rotten wood or loam. Those that live in tree-trunks stop up with plugs of sawdust both ends of the galleries they have hollowed out; those that live in wheat gnaw all the farinaceous part of the grain, scrupulously leaving untouched the outside, or bran, which is to serve them as cradle. Others, with less precaution, shelter themselves in some crack of the bark or of a wall, and fasten themselves there by a string which goes round their body. To this number belong the caterpillars of the cabbage butterfly and the swallow tail. But especially in the making of the silk cell called cocoon is the highest skill of the larvæ shown.

"An ashy white caterpillar, the size of the little finger, is raised in large numbers for its cocoon, with which silk stuffs are made. It is called the silkworm. In very clean rooms are placed reed screens, on which they put mulberry leaves, and the young caterpillars come from eggs hatched in the house. The mulberry is a large tree cultivated on purpose to nourish these caterpillars; it has no value except for its leaves, the sole food of silkworms. Large tracts are devoted to its cultivation, so precious is the handiwork of the worm. The caterpillars eat the ration of leaves that is frequently renewed on the screens, and from time to time change their skin, according to their rate of growth. Their appetite is such that the clicking of their jaws is like the noise of a shower falling during a calm on the foliage of the trees. It is true that the room contains thousands and thousands of worms. The caterpillar gets its growth in four or five weeks. Then the screens are set with sprigs of heather, on which the worms climb when the time comes for them to spin their cocoons. They settle themselves one by one amid the sprigs and fasten here and there a multitude of very fine threads, so as to make a kind of network which will hold them suspended and serve them as scaffolding for the great work of the cocoon.

"The silk thread comes out of the under lip, through a hole called the spinneret. In the body of the caterpillar the silk material is a very thick, sticky liquid, resembling gum. In coming through the opening of the lip, this liquid is drawn out into a thread, which glues itself to the preceding threads and immediately hardens. The silk matter is not entirely contained in the mulberry leaf that the worm eats, any more than is milk in the grass that the cow browses. The caterpillar makes it out of the materials of its food, just as the cow makes milk of the constituents of her forage. Without the caterpillar's help man could never extract from the mulberry leaves the material for his costliest fabrics. Our most beautiful silk stuffs really take birth in the worm that drivels them into a thread.

"Let us return to the caterpillar suspended in the midst of its net. Now it is working at the cocoon. Its head is in continual motion. It advances, retires, ascends, descends, goes to right and left, while letting escape from its lip a tiny thread, which rolls itself loosely around the animal, sticks itself to the thread already in place, and finishes by forming a continuous envelope the size of a pigeon's egg. The silken structure is at first transparent enough to permit one to see the caterpillar at work; but as it grows thicker what passes within is soon hidden from view. What follows can easily be guessed. For three or four days the caterpillar continues to thicken the walls of the cocoon until it has exhausted its store of liquid silk. Here it is at last, retired from the world, isolated, tranquil, ready for the transfiguration so soon to take place. Its whole life, its long life of a month, it has worked in anticipation of the metamorphosis; it has crammed itself with mulberry leaves, has extenuated itself to make the silk for its cocoon, but thus it is going to become a butterfly. What a solemn moment for the caterpillar!

"Ah! my children, I had almost forgotten man's part in all this. Hardly is the work of the cocoon finished when he runs to the heather sprig, lays violent hands on the cocoons and sells them to the manufacturer. The latter, without delay, puts them into an oven and subjects them to the action of burning vapor to kill the future butterfly, whose tender flesh is beginning to form. If he delayed, the butterfly would pierce the cocoon, which, no longer capable of being unwound on account of its broken threads, would lose its value. This precaution taken, the rest is done at leisure. The cocoons are unwound in factories called spinning mills. They are put into a pan of boiling water to dissolve the gum which holds the successive windings together. A work-woman armed with a little heather broom stirs them in the water, in order to find and seize the end of the thread, which she puts on a revolving reel. Under the action of the machine the thread of silk unwinds while the cocoon jumps about in the hot water like a ball of wool when one pulls the yarn.

"In the center of the threadbare cocoon is the chrysalis, scorched and killed by the fire. Later the silk undergoes divers operations which give it more suppleness and luster; it passes into the dyer's vats where it takes any color desired; finally it is woven and converted into fabric."

Day 160

1. Read chapter 24 of *The Story Book of Science*.
2. Tell someone about what you read.

CHAPTER XXIV THE METAMORPHOSIS

"ONCE enclosed in its cocoon, the caterpillar withers and shrivels up, as if dying. First, the skin splits on the back; then, by repeated convulsions that pull it this way and that, the worm with much difficulty tears off its skin. With the skin comes everything: the case of the skull, jaws, eyes, legs, stomach and the rest. It is a general tearing-off. The ragged covering of the old body is finally pushed into a corner of the cocoon.

"What do they find then in the cells of silk? Another caterpillar, a butterfly? Neither. They find an almond shaped body, rounded at one end, pointed at the other, of a leathery appearance, and called a chrysalis. It is an intermediate state between the caterpillar and the butterfly. There can be seen certain projections which already indicate the shape of the future insect: at the large end can be distinguished the antennæ and the wings tightly folded crosswise on the chrysalis.

"The larvæ of the June bug, capricorn, stag-beetle, and other beetles pass through a similar state, but with more accentuated forms. The different parts of the head, wings, legs delicately folded at their sides, are very recognizable. But all is immobile, soft, white, or even transparent as crystal. This insect in outline is called a nymph. The name of chrysalis used for butterflies and that of nymph used for the other insects signify the same thing under somewhat different appearances. Both the chrysalis and the nymph are insects in process of formation—insects closely wrapped in swaddling clothes, under which is finished the mysterious operation that will change their first structure front top to bottom.

"In a couple of weeks, if the temperature is favorable, the chrysalis of the silkworm opens like a ripe fruit, and from its burst shell the butterfly escapes, all ragged, moist, scarcely able to stand on its trembling legs. Open air is necessary for it to gain strength, to spread and dry its wings. It must get out of the cocoon. But how? The caterpillar has made the cocoon so solid and the butterfly is so weak! Will it perish in its prison, the poor little thing! It would not be worth the trouble of going through so much to stifle miserably in the close cell, just as the end is attained!"

"Could it not tear the cocoon open with its teeth?" asked Emile.

"But, my innocent child, it has none, nor anything like them. It has only a proboscis, incapable of the slightest effort."

"With its claws then?" suggested Jules.

"Yes, if it had any strong enough. The trouble is, it is not provided with any."

"But it must be able to get out," persisted Jules.

"Doubtless it will get out. Has not every creature resources in the difficult moments of life! To break the hen's egg that imprisons it, the tiny little chicken has at the end of its beak a little hard point made on purpose; and the butterfly is to have nothing to open its cocoon? Oh, yes! But you would never guess the singular tool that it will use. It will use its eyes—"

"Its eyes!" interrupted Claire in amazement.

"Yes. Insects' eyes are covered with a cap of transparent horn, hard and cut in facets. A magnifying glass is needed in order to distinguish these facets, they are so fine; but, fine as they are, they have sharp bones which all together can, in time of need, be used as a grater. The butterfly begins then by moistening with a drop of saliva the point of the cocoon it wishes to attack, and then applying an eye to the spot thus softened, it writhes, knocks, scratches, files. One by one the threads of silk succumb to the rasping. The hole is made, the butterfly comes out. What do you think about it? Do not animals sometimes have intelligence enough for four? Which of us would have thought of forcing the prison walls by striking them with the eye?"

"The butterfly must have studied a long time to think of that ingenious way?" queried Emile.

"The butterfly does not study, does not reflect; it knows at once what to do and how to do well whatever concerns it. Another has reflected for it."

"Who?"

"God himself! God, the great wise one. The silkworm butterfly is not pretty. It is whitish, tun-bellied, heavy. It does not fly like the others from flower to flower, for it takes no nourishment. As soon as it is out of the cocoon, it sets to work laying eggs; then it dies. Silkworm eggs are commonly called seed, a very good term, for the egg is the seed of the animal as the seed is the egg of the plant. Egg and seed correspond. They do not stifle all the cocoons in the vapor to wind them afterwards; they keep out a certain number so as to obtain butterflies and consequently eggs or seeds. These are the seeds which, the following year, produce the fresh brood of worms.

"All insects that are metamorphosed pass through the four states that I have just told you about: egg, larva, chrysalis or nymph, perfect insect. The perfect insect lays its eggs, and the series of transformations begins again."

Day 161

1. Read chapter 25 of *The Story Book of Science*.
2. Tell someone about what you read.

CHAPTER XXV SPIDERS

ONE morning, Mother Ambroisine was chopping herbs and cooked apples for a brood of little chickens hatched not long before. A large gray spider, letting itself slide the length of its thread, descended from the ceiling to the good woman's shoulders. At sight of the creature with long velvety legs, Mother Ambroisine could not suppress a cry of fear, and, shaking her shoulder, made the insect fall, and crushed it under her foot. "Spider in the morning stands for mourning," said she to herself. At this instant Uncle Paul and Claire entered.

"No, sir, it is not right," said Mother Ambroisine, "that we poor mortals should have so much useless trouble. Twelve little chickens are hatched out for us, bright as gold; and just as I am preparing them something to eat, a villainous spider falls on my shoulder."

And Mother Ambroisine pointed with her finger at the crushed insect with its legs still trembling.

"I do not see that those little chickens have anything to fear from the spider," remarked Uncle Paul.

"Oh! nothing, sir: the horrid creature is dead. But you know the proverb: 'Spider in the morning, mourning; spider at night, delight.' Everybody knows that a spider seen in the morning is a sign of bad luck. Our little chickens are in danger; the cats will claw them. You'll see, sir, you'll see."

Tears of emotion came to Mother Ambroisine's eyes.

"Put the little chickens in a safe place, watch the cats, and I will answer for the rest. The proverb of the spider is only a foolish prejudice," said Uncle Paul.

Mother Ambroisine did not utter another word. She knew that Maître Paul found a reason for everything, and on occasion was capable of pronouncing a eulogy on the spider. Claire, who saw this eulogy coming, ventured a question.

"I know: in your eyes all animals, however hideous they may be, have excellent excuses to plead: all merit consideration; all play a part ordained by Providence; all are interesting to observe and to study. You are the advocate of the good God's creatures; you would plead for the toad. But permit your niece to see there only an impulse of your kind heart, and not the real truth. What could you say in praise of the spider, horrid beast, which is poisonous and disfigures the ceiling with its webs?"

"What could I say? Much, my dear child, much. In the meantime, feed your little chickens and beware of cats if you want to prove the spider proverb false."

In the evening Mother Ambroisine, her large round spectacles on her nose, was knitting stockings. On her knees the cat slept and mingled its purring with the tick-tack of the needles. The children were waiting for the story of the spider. Their uncle began.

"Which of you three can tell me what spiders do with their webs, those fine webs stretched in the corners of the granary or between two shrubs in the garden?"

Emile spoke first. "It is their nest, Uncle, their house, their hiding-place."

"Hiding place!" exclaimed Jules; "yes, I think it is more than that. One day I heard, between the lilac branches, a little shrill noise—he-e-e-e! A blue fly was entangled in a cobweb and trying to escape. It was the fly that was making the noise with its fluttering. A spider ran from the bottom of the silken funnel, seized the fly, and carried it off to its hole, doubtless to eat it. Since then I have thought spiders' webs were hunting nets."

"That is even so," said his uncle. "All spiders live on live prey; they make continual war on flies, gnats, and other insects. If you fear mosquitoes, those insufferable little insects that sting us at night until they bring blood, you must bless the spider, for it does its best to rid us of them. To catch game, a net is necessary. Now, the net to catch flies in their flight is a cloth woven with silk, which the spider itself produces.

"In the body of the insect the silky matter is, as with caterpillars, a sticky liquid resembling glue or gum. As soon as it comes in contact with the air, this matter congeals, hardens, and becomes a thread on which water has no effect. When the spider wants to spin, the silk liquid flows from four nipples, called spinnerets, placed at the end of the stomach. These nipples are pierced at their extremity by a number of holes, like the sprinkler of a watering-pot. The number of these holes for all the nipples is roughly reckoned as a thousand. Each one lets its tiny little jet of liquid flow, which hardens and becomes thread; and from a thousand threads stuck together into one results the final thread employed by the spider. To designate something very fine there is no better term of comparison than the spider's thread. It is so delicate, in fact, that it can only just be seen. Our silk threads, those of the finest textures, are cables in comparison, cables of two, three, four strands, while this one, in its unequaled tenuity, contains a thousand. How many spiders' threads are required to make a strand of the thickness of a hair? Not far from ten. And how many elementary threads, such as issue from the separate holes of the spinneret? Ten thousand. To what a degree of tenuity then this silky matter can be reduced that stretches out in threads of which it takes ten thousand to equal the size of one hair! What marvels, my children, and only to catch a fly that is to serve for the spider's dinner!"

Day 162

1.   Read chapter 26 of *The Story Book of Science*.
2.   Tell someone about what you read.

CHAPTER XXVI THE EPEIRA'S BRIDGE

HERE Uncle Paul caught Claire looking at him thoughtfully. It was evident that some change was taking place in her mind: the spider was no longer a repulsive creature, unworthy of our regard. Uncle Paul continued:

"With its legs, armed with sharp-toothed little claws like combs, the spider draws the thread from its spinnerets as it has need. If it wishes to descend, like the one this morning that came down from the ceiling on to Mother Ambroisine's shoulder, it glues the end of the thread to the point of departure and lets itself fall perpendicularly. The thread is drawn from the spinnerets by the weight of the spider, and the latter, softly suspended, descends to any depth it wishes, and as slowly as it pleases. In order to ascend again, it climbs up the thread by folding it gradually into a skein between its legs. For a second descent, the spider has only to let its skein of silk unwind little by little.

"To weave its web, each kind of spider has its own method of procedure, according to the kind of game it is going to hunt, the places it frequents, and according to its particular inclinations, tastes, and instincts. I will merely tell you a few words about the epeiræ, large spiders magnificently speckled with yellow, black, and silvery white. They are hunters of big game,—of green or blue damsel-flies that frequent the water-courses, of butterflies, and large flies. They stretch their web vertically between two trees and even from one bank of a stream to the other. Let us examine this last case.

"An epeira has found a good place for hunting: the dragon-flies, or blue and green damsel-flies, come and go from one tuft of reeds to another, sometimes going up, sometimes down the stream. Along its course are butterflies also, and horse-flies, or large flies that suck blood from cattle. The site is a good one. Now, then, to work! The epeira climbs to the top of a willow at the water's edge. There it matures its plan, an audacious one, the execution of which seems impossible. A suspension bridge, a cable which serves as support for the future web, must be stretched from one bank to the other. And observe, children, that the spider cannot cross the stream by swimming; it would perish by drowning if it ventured into the water. It must stretch its cable, its bridge, from the top of its branch without changing place. Never has an engineer found himself in such difficulties. What will the little creature do? Put your heads together, children; I am waiting for your ideas."

"Build a bridge from one side to the other, without crossing the water or moving away from its place? If the spider can do that it is cleverer than I am." Thus spoke Jules.

"Than I, too," chimed in his brother.

"If I did not already know," said Claire, "since you have just told us, that the spider does accomplish it, I should say that its bridge is impossible."

Mother Ambroisine said nothing, but by the slackening of the tick-tack of her needles, every one could see that she was much interested in the spider's bridge.

"Animals often have more intelligence than we," continued Uncle Paul; "the epeira will prove it to us. With its hind legs it draws a thread from its spinnerets. The thread lengthens and lengthens; it floats from the top of the branch. The spider draws out more and more; finally, it stops. Is the thread long enough? Is it too short? That is what must be looked after. If too long, it would be wasting the precious silky liquid; if too short, it would not fulfil the given conditions. A glance is thrown at the distance to be crossed, an exact glance, you may be sure. The thread is found too short. The spider lengthens it by drawing out a little more. Now all goes well: the thread has the wished-for length, and the work is done. The epeira waits at the top of its branch: the rest will be accomplished without help. From time to time it bears with its legs on the thread to see if it resists. Ah! it resists; the bridge is fixed! The spider crosses the stream on its suspension bridge! What has happened, then? This: The thread floated from the top of the willow. A breath of air blew the free end of the thread into the branches on the opposite bank. This end got entangled there: behold the mystery. The epeira has only to draw the thread to itself, to stretch it properly and make a suspension bridge of it."

"Oh, how simple!" cried Jules. "And yet not one of us would have thought of it."

"Yes, my friend, it is very simple, but at the same time very ingenious. It is thus with all work: simplicity in the means employed is a sign of excellence. To simplify is to have knowledge; to complicate is to be ignorant. The epeira, in its kind of construction, is science perfected."

"Where does it get that science, Uncle?" asked Claire. "Animals have not reason. Then who teaches the epeira to build its suspension bridges?"

"No one, my dear child; it is born with this knowledge. It has it by instinct, the infallible inspiration of the Father of all things, who creates in the least of His creatures, for their preservation, ways of acting before which our reason is often confounded. When the epeira, from the top of the willow, gets ready to spin its web, what inspires it with the audacious project of the bridge; what gives it patience to wait for the floating end of the thread to entwine in the branches of the other bank; what assures it of the success of a labor that it is performing perhaps for the first time, and has never seen done? It is the universal Reason that watches over creation, and takes among men the thrice-holy name of Providence."

Uncle Paul had won his case: in the eyes of all, even of Mother Ambroisine, spiders were no longer frightful creatures.

Day 163

1. Read chapter 27 of *The Story Book of Science*.
2. Tell someone about what you read.

CHAPTER XXVII THE SPIDER'S WEB

THE next day the little chickens were all hatched and doing well. The hen had led them to the courtyard, and, scratching the soil and clucking, she dug up small seeds which the little ones came and took from their mother's beak. At the slightest approach of danger, the hen called the brood, and all ran to snuggle under her outspread wings. The boldest soon put their heads out, their pretty little yellow heads framed in their mother's black feathers. The alarm over, the hen began clucking and scratching again, and the little ones went trotting around her once more. Completely reassured, Mother Ambroisine forever renounced her proverb of the spider. In the evening Uncle Paul continued the story of the epeira.

"Since it must serve as a support to the silken network, the first thread stretched from one bank to the other must be of exceptional firmness. The epeira begins, therefore, by fixing both ends well; then, going and coming on the thread from one extremity to the other, always spinning, it doubles and trebles the strands and sticks them together in a common cable. A second similar cable is necessary, placed beneath the first in an almost parallel direction. It is between the two that the web must be spun.

"For this purpose, from one of the ends of the cable already constructed the epeira lets itself fall perpendicularly, hanging by the thread that escapes from its spinnerets. It reaches a lower branch, fastens the thread firmly to it, and ascends to the communicating bridge by the vertical thread it used for descending. The spider then reaches the other bank, still spinning, but without gluing this new strand of silk to the cable. Arrived at the other side, it lets itself slide on to a branch conveniently placed, and there fastens the end of the thread that it has spun on its way from one bank to the other. This second chief piece of the framework becomes a cable by the addition of new threads. Finally the two parallel cables are made firm at each end by divers threads starting from it in every direction and attaching themselves to the branches. Other threads go out from this point and that, from one cable to the other, leaving between them, in the middle of the construction, a large open space, almost circular, destined for the net.

"Thus far the epeira has only constructed the framework of its building, a rough but solid frame-work; now begins the work of fine precision. The net must be spun. Across the open circular space that the divers threads of the framework leave between them, a first thread is stretched. The epeira stations itself right in the middle of this thread, central point of the web to be constructed. From this center numerous threads must start at equal distances from one another and be fastened to the circumference by the other end. They are called radiating lines. Accordingly the epeira glues a thread to the center and, ascending by the transverse thread already stretched, fixes the end of the line to the circumference. That done, it returns to the center by the line that it has just stretched; there it glues a second thread and immediately regains the circumference, where it fastens the end of the second line a short distance from the first one. Going thus alternately from the center to the circumference and from the circumference to the center by way of the last thread just stretched, the spider fills the circular space with radiating lines so regularly spaced that you would say they were traced with rule and compass by an expert hand.

"When the radiating lines are finished, the most delicate work of all is still left for the spider. Each of these lines must be bound by a thread that, starting at the circumference, twists and turns in a spiral line around the center, where it terminates. The epeira starts from the top of the web and, unwinding its thread, stretches it from one radiating line to another, keeping always at an equal distance from the outside thread. By thus circling about, always at the same distance from the preceding thread, the spider ends at the center of the radiating lines. The network is then finished.

"Now there must be arranged a little ambuscade from which the epeira can survey its web, a resting-room where it finds shelter from the coolness of the night and the heat of the day. In a little bunch of leaves close together the spider builds itself a silk den, a sort of funnel of close texture. That is its usual abiding place. If the weather is favorable and the passage of game abundant, morning and evening especially, the epeira leaves its den and posts itself, motionless, in the center of the web, to watch events more closely and run to the game quickly enough to prevent its escape. The spider is at its post, in the middle of the network, its eight legs spread out wide. It does not move, pretends to be dead. No hunter on the watch would have such patience. Let us copy its example and await the coming of the game."

The children were disappointed: at the moment when the story became the most interesting, Uncle Paul broke off his narrative.

"The epeira has interested me very much, Uncle," said Jules. "The bridge over the stream, the cobweb with its regular radiating lines, and the thread that twists and turns, getting nearer and nearer to the center, the room for ambush and rest—all that is very astonishing in a creature that does these wonderful things without having to learn how. Catching the game ought to be still more curious."

"Very curious indeed. Therefore, instead of telling you about the hunt, I prefer to show it to you. Yesterday, in crossing the field, I saw an epeira constructing its web between two trees on the little stream where such fine crayfish are caught. Let us get up early in the morning and go and see the chase."

Day 164

1.   Read chapter 28 of *The Story Book of Science*.
2.   Tell someone about what you read.

CHAPTER XXVIII THE CHASE

UNCLE PAUL had said: "Let us get up early in the morning." No one had to be called. One sleeps little when one is going to see an epeira hunt. About seven o'clock, with the sun shining bright, they were at the border of the stream. The cobweb was finished. Some dewdrops hanging to the threads shone like pearls. Hence the spider was not yet in the center of the net; no doubt it was waiting, before descending from its room, for the sun to dissipate the morning dampness. The party sat down on the grass for breakfast, at the very foot of the alder-tree to which were fastened the cables of the net. Blue damsel-flies flew from one tuft of rushes to another and chased each other playfully. Beware, you giddy ones, who will not know how to avoid the web by passing over and under it! Ah! it has happened; so much the worse for the victim. When one plays foolishly with one's companions, one must at least look where one is going. A dragon-fly is caught in the meshes of the web. With one wing free it struggles to escape. It shakes the web, but the cables hold in spite of the shaking. Threads in communication with the resting-room warn the epeira, by their agitation, of the important things taking place in the net. The spider hastily descends, but it does not get there in time. With a desperate stroke of its wing the dragon-fly frees itself and escapes, tearing a large hole in the web.

"Oh! how well it got out!" cried Jules. "A little more and the poor thing would have been eaten alive. Did you see, Emile, how quickly the spider ran down from its hiding place when it felt the web move! The hunt begins badly; the game escapes and the net is torn."

"Yes, but the spider is going to mend it," his uncle reassured him.

And, in fact, as soon as it had recovered from its misadventure, the epeira renewed the broken threads with delicate dexterity. The darning finished, the damage could hardly be detected. The spider now takes its place in the center of the network: the right moment for the chase has come, apparently, and it is advisable for it to pounce upon the game as quickly as possible, to avoid other misadventures. It spreads its eight feet in a circle, to receive the slightest movement that may come at any point of the web, and it waits, completely motionless.

The dragon-flies continue their evolutions. Not one is caught: the recent alarm has rendered them circumspect; they fly around the web to pass beyond it. Oh! oh! what is that coming so giddily and striking its head against the network? It is a little bumble-bee, all velvety and black, with a red stomach. It is caught. The epeira runs. But the captive is vigorous and formidable; perhaps it has a sting. The spider mistrusts it. It draws a thread from its spinneret and passes it quickly over the bee. A second silk string, a third, a fourth, soon subdue the captive's desperate efforts. Here is the bee strangled but still full of life, and menacing. To seize it in that state would be great imprudence: the epeira's life would be at stake. What must be done so as to leave nothing to fear from this dangerous prey? The spider possesses, folded under its head, two sharp-pointed fangs, which let flow a little drop of poison through a hole in their extremities. That is its hunting weapon. The epeira approaches cautiously, opens its fangs, stings the bee, and immediately moves aside. In the twinkling of an eye it is all over. The poison acts instantly: the bee trembles, its legs stiffen, it is dead. The spider carries it off to its silken chamber to suck it at leisure. When nothing but the skin is left, the spider will throw the remains of the bee far from its domicile, so as not to soil its web with a corpse that might frighten other game.

"It was done so quickly," complained Jules, "I did not see the spider's poisonous fangs. If we were to wait a little longer, another bumble-bee might perhaps come and then I should see it better."

"It is not necessary to wait," replied Uncle Paul. "If we proceed skilfully we can make the spider recommence its hunting manœuvers. All of you look attentively."

Uncle Paul searched among the field flowers for a moment and caught a large fly; then, holding it by one wing, put it near the web. The insect, beating about, gets entangled in the threads. The web shakes, the spider leaves its bee and runs, delighted with the fortunate chance that brings him prey again so quickly. The same manœuvers begin again. The fly is first strangled; the epeira opens its pointed fangs, stings the fly a little, and all is over. The victim trembles, stretches itself out, and ceases to move.

"Ah! that time I saw it," said Jules, satisfied at last.

"Claire, did you notice the fineness of the spider's fangs?" asked Emile. "I am sure that in your needle-case you haven't any such fine-pointed needles."

"I dare say not. As for me, what surprises me the most is not the fineness of the spider's fangs, but the quickness of the victim's death. It seems to me that a fly as large as this one ought not to die so quickly even from the coarser pricks of our needles."

"Very true," assented her uncle. "An insect transfixed by a pin still lives a long time; but if it is only pricked by the fine point of the spider's fangs, it dies almost instantly. But then, the spider takes care to poison its weapon. Its fangs are venomous; they are perforated by a minute canal through which the spider lets flow at will a scarcely visible little drop of liquid called venom, which the creature makes as it makes the silk liquid. The venom is held in reserve in a slender pocket placed in the interior of the fangs. When the spider pricks its prey, it makes a little of this liquid pass into the wound, and that suffices to bring speedy death to the wounded insect. The victim dies, not from the prick itself, but from the dreadful ravages wrought by the venom discharged into the wound."

Here Uncle Paul, in order to give his hearers a better view of the poisonous fangs, took the epeira with the tips of his fingers. Claire uttered a cry of fear, but her uncle soon calmed her.

"Don't be uneasy, my dear child: the poison that kills a fly will have no effect on Uncle Paul's hard skin."

And with the aid of a pin he opened the creature's fangs to show them in detail to the children, who were quite reassured.

"You must not be too frightened," he continued, "at the quick death of the fly and of the bumble-bee, and so look on spiders as creatures to be feared by us. The fangs of most of them would have great difficulty in piercing our skin. Courageous observers have let themselves be bitten by the various spiders of our country. The sting has never produced any serious results; nothing more than a redness less painful than that produced by the sting of a mosquito. At the same time, persons with a delicate skin ought to beware of the large kinds, were it only to spare themselves a passing pain. Without any excessive alarm we avoid the wasp's sting, which is very painful; let us avoid the spider's fangs in the same way without uttering loud cries at the sight of one of these creatures. We will resume the subject of the venomous insects. But it is late; let us go."

Day 165

1.   Read chapter 29 of *The Story Book of Science*.
2.   Tell someone about it.

CHAPTER XXIX VENOMOUS INSECTS

"YOU have heard that certain creatures emit poison, that is to say, shoot from a distance into the face and on to the hands of those who approach a liquid capable of causing death, or at least of blinding or otherwise injuring them. Last week Jules found on the leaves of the potato-vines a large caterpillar armed with a curved horn."

"I know, I know," put in Jules. "It is the caterpillar, you told me, that turns into a magnificent butterfly called the sphinx Atropos. This butterfly, large as my hand, has on its back a white spot that frightens many people, for it has a vague resemblance to a death's-head. And besides, its eyes shine in the dark. You added that it was a harmless creature of which it would be unreasonable to be afraid."

"Jacques, who was weeding the potatoes," continued Uncle Paul, "knocked the sphinx caterpillar out of Jules's hands, and hastened to crush it with his big wooden shoe. 'What you are doing is very dangerous,' said the good Jacques. 'Handling poisonous creatures— of all things! Do you see that green venom? Don't get too close; the silly thing is not quite

314

dead; it might yet throw some poison on you.' The worthy man took the green entrails of the crushed caterpillar for poison. Those entrails did not contain anything dangerous; they were green because they were swollen with the juice of the leaves that the poor thing had just eaten.

"Many persons are of the same opinion as Jacques: they are afraid of a caterpillar and the green of its entrails. They think that certain creatures poison everything they touch and throw out venom.

"Well, my dear children, you must bear this in mind, for it is a very important thing and frees us from foolish fears, while it puts us on guard against real danger: no animal of any kind, absolutely none, shoots venom and can harm us from a distance. To be convinced of this it suffices to know what venom really is. Divers creatures, large or small, are endowed with a poisoned weapon that serves them either as defense or to attack their prey. The bee is our best known venomous creature."

"What!" exclaimed Emile, "a bee is poisonous, the bee that makes honey for us?"

"Yes, the bee; the bee without which we could not have those honey cakes that Mother Ambroisine hands round when you are good. You don't think then of the stings that made you cry so?"

Emile blushed: his uncle had just revived unpleasant memories. From pure heedlessness he tried one day to see what the bees were doing. They say he even thrust a stick through the little door of the hive. The bees became incensed at this indiscretion. Three or four stung the poor boy on the cheeks and hands. He cried out most piteously, and thought himself done for. His uncle had much difficulty in consoling him. Compresses of cold water finally soothed his smarting pains.

"The bee is venomous," repeated Uncle Paul; "Emile could tell you that."

"The wasp too, then?" asked Jules. "One stung me once when I tried to drive it from a bunch of grapes. I did not say anything, but all the same I was not very comfortable. To think that such a tiny thing can hurt one so! It seemed as if my hands were on fire."

"Certainly, the wasp is venomous; more so than the bee, in the sense that its sting causes greater pain. Bumble-bees are, too, as well as hornets, those large reddish wasps, an inch long, which sometimes come and gnaw the pears in the orchard. You must beware especially of hornets, my little friends. One sting from them, one only, would give you hours of horrible pain.

"All these insects have, for their defense, a poisoned weapon constructed in the same way. It is called the sting. It is a small, hard, and very pointed blade, a kind of dagger finer than the finest needle. The sting is placed at the end of the creature's stomach. When in repose, it is not seen; it is hidden in a scabbard that goes into its stomach. To defend itself, the insect draws it out of its sheath and plunges the point into the imprudent finger found within reach.

American Hornet

"Now it is not exactly the wound made by the sting that causes the smarting pain that you are familiar with. This wound is so slight, so minute, we cannot see it. We should hardly feel it were it made with a needle or a thorn as fine as the sting. But the sting communicates with a pocket of venom lodged in the creature's body, and, by means of a hollowed-out canal, it carries to the bottom of the wound a little drop of the formidable liquid. The sting is then drawn back. As to the venom, it stays in the wound and it is that, that alone, which causes those shooting pains that Emile could, if necessary, tell us about."

At this second attack from Uncle Paul, who dwelt on this misadventure in order to blame him for his heedless treatment of the bees, Emile blew his nose, although he did not need to. It was a way of hiding his confusion. His uncle did not appear to notice it, and continued:

"Scholars who have made a study of this curious question tell us of the following experiment, to make clear that it is really the venomous liquid introduced into the wound, and not the wound itself, that causes the pain. When one pricks oneself with a very fine needle, the hurt is very slight and soon passes off. I am sure Claire is not much frightened when she pricks her finger in sewing."

"Oh! no," said she. "That is so soon over, even if blood comes."

"Well, the prick of a needle, insignificant in itself can cause sharp pains if the little wound is poisoned with the venom of the bee or wasp. The scholars I am telling you of dip the point of the needle into the bee's pocket of venom, and with this point thus wet with the venomous liquid give themselves a slight sting. The pain is now sharp and of long duration, more so than if the insect itself had stung the experimenter. This increase of pain is due to the fact that the comparatively large needle introduces into the wound more venom than could the bee's slender sting. You understand it now, I hope: it is the introduction of the venom into the wound that causes all the trouble."

"That is plain," said Jules. "But tell me, Uncle, why these scholars amuse themselves by pricking themselves with needles dipped in the bee's venom? It is a queer amusement, to hurt oneself for nothing."

"For nothing, Mr. Harum-scarum? Do you count as nothing what I have just told you? If I know it, must not others have taught me? Who are these others? They are the valiant investigators who learn about everything, observe and study everything, in order to alleviate our suffering. When they voluntarily prick themselves with poison, they propose to study in themselves, at their own risk and peril, the action of the venom, to teach us to combat its effects, which are sometimes so formidable. Let a viper or a scorpion sting us, and our life is in peril. Ah, then it is important to know exactly how the venom acts and what must be done to arrest its ravages; it is then that the scholars' researches are appreciated, researches that Jules looks upon as merely a queer amusement. Science, my little friend, has sacred enthusiasms that do not shrink from any test that may enlarge the sphere of our knowledge and diminish human suffering."

Jules, confused by his unfortunate remark, lowered his head and said not a word. Uncle Paul was on the point of getting vexed, but peace was soon restored and he continued the account of venomous creatures.

Day 166

1.   Read chapter 30 of *The Story Book of Science*.
2.   Tell someone about it.

CHAPTER XXX VENOM

"ALL venomous creatures act in the same way as the bee, wasp, and hornet. With a special weapon—needle, fang, sting, lancet—placed sometimes in one part of the body, sometimes in another, according to the species, they make a slight wound into which is instilled a drop of venom. The weapon has no other effect than that of opening a route for the venomous liquid, and this is what causes the injury. For the poison to act on us, it must come in contact with our blood by a wound which opens the way for it. But it has positively no effect on our skin, unless there is already a gash, a simple scratch, that permits it to penetrate into the flesh and mingle with the blood. The most terrible venom can be handled without any danger if the skin is not broken. Moreover, it can be put on the lips, on the tongue, even swallowed without any bad results. Placed on the lips, the hornet's venom produces no more effect than clear water; but if there is the slightest scratch the pain is atrocious. The viper's venom is equally harmless as long as it does not mingle with the blood. Courageous experimenters have tasted, swallowed it, and yet afterward were no worse off than before."

"Is that true, Uncle? People have had the courage to swallow a viper's venom? Ah! I should not have been so brave." This from Claire.

"It is fortunate, my girl, that others have been so for us; and we ought to be very grateful to them, for by so doing they have taught us, as you will see, the most prompt and one of the most efficacious means to employ in case of accident."

"This viper's venom, which has no effect on the hand, lips, and tongue, is it much to be feared if it mingles with the blood?"

"It is terrible, my young lady, and I was just going to tell you about it. Let us suppose that some imprudent person disturbs the formidable reptile sleeping in the sun. Suddenly the creature uncoils itself in circles one above another, unwinds with the suddenness of a spring, and, with its jaws wide open, strikes you on the hand. It is done in the twinkling of an eye. With the same rapidity the viper refolds its spiral and draws back, continuing to menace you with its head in the center of the coil. You do not wait for a second attack, you flee; but, alas! the damage is done. On the wounded hand are seen two little red points, almost insignificant, mere needle pricks. It is not very alarming; you reassure yourself if you are in ignorance of what I so earnestly desire to teach you. Delusive innocuousness! See the red spots becoming encircled with a livid ring. With dull pains the hand swells, and the swelling extends gradually to the arm. Soon come cold sweats and nausea; respiration becomes painful, sight troubled, mind torpid, a general yellowness shows itself, accompanied by convulsions. If help does not arrive in time, death may come."

Copper Head

"You give us goose-flesh, Uncle," said Jules, with a shudder. "What should we poor things do if such a misfortune happened to us away from you, away from home! They say there are vipers in the underbrush of the neighboring hills."

"May God guard you from such a mischance, my poor children! But, if it befalls you, you must bind tight the finger, hand, arm, above the wounded part to prevent the diffusion of the venom in the blood; you must make the wound bleed by pressing round it; you must suck it hard to extract the venomous liquid. I told you venom has no effect on the skin. To suck it, therefore, is harmless if the mouth has no scratch. You can see that if, by hard suction and by pressure that makes the blood flow, you succeed in extracting all the venom from the wound, the wound itself is thenceforth of no importance. For greater surety, the wound should be cauterized as soon as possible with a corrosive liquid, aqua fortis or ammonia, or even with a red-hot iron. The effect of the cauterization is to destroy the venomous matter. It is painful, I acknowledge, but one must submit to it in order to avoid a worse evil. Cauterization is the doctor's business. The initial precautions, binding to prevent the diffusion of the venom, pressure to make the poisoned blood flow, hard suction to extract the venomous liquid, concern us personally, and all that must be done instantly. The longer it is put off, the more aggravated the evil. When these precautions are taken soon enough, it is seldom that the viper's bite has injurious consequences."

"You reassure me, Uncle. Those precautions are not difficult to take, if one does not lose one's presence of mind."

"Therefore it is important that we should all acquire the habit of using our reason in time of danger, and not let ourselves be overcome by ill-regulated fears. Man master of himself is half-master of danger."

Day 167

1.   Read chapter 31 of *The Story Book of Science*.
2.   Tell someone about what you read.

CHAPTER XXXI THE VIPER AND THE SCORPION

"YOU just said," interposed Emile, "the bite of the viper, and not the sting. Then serpents bite, and do not sting. I thought it was just the other way. I have always heard they had a sting. Last Thursday lame Louis, who is not afraid of anything, caught a serpent in a hole of the old wall. He had two comrades with him. They bound the creature round the neck with a rush. I was passing, and they called me. The serpent was darting from its mouth something black, pointed, flexible, which came and went rapidly. I thought it was the sting and was much afraid of it. Louis laughed. He said what I took for a sting was the serpent's tongue; and to prove it to me, he put his hand near it."

"Louis was right," replied Uncle Paul. "All serpents dart a very flexible, forked, black filament between their lips with great swiftness.

For many purposes it is the reptile's weapon, or dart; but in reality this filament is nothing but the tongue, a quite inoffensive tongue, which the creature uses to catch insects and to express in its peculiar manner the passions that agitate it by darting it quickly from between the lips. All serpents, without any exception, have one; but in our countries the viper alone possesses the terrible venomous apparatus.

Forked Tongue

"This apparatus is composed, first, of two hooks, or teeth, long and pointed, placed in the upper jaw. At the will of the creature they stand up erect for the attack or lie down in a groove of the gum, and hold themselves there as inoffensive as a stiletto in its sheath. In that way the reptile runs no danger of wounding itself. These fangs are hollow and pierced toward the point by a small opening through which the venom is injected into the wound. Finally, at the base of each fang is a little pocket full of venomous liquid. It is an innocent-looking humor, odorless, tasteless; one would almost think it was water. When the viper strikes with its fangs, the venomous pocket drives a drop of its contents into the canal of the tooth, and the terrible liquid is instilled into the wound.

"By preference the viper inhabits warm and rocky hills; it keeps under stones and thickets of brush. It is brown or reddish in color. On the back it has a somber zigzag band, and on each side a row of spots. Its stomach is slate-gray. Its head is a little triangular, larger than the neck, obtuse and as if cut off in front. The viper is timid and fearful; it attacks man only in self-defense. Its movements are brusk, irregular, and sluggish.

"The other serpents of our countries, serpents designated by the general name of snakes, have not the venomous fangs of the viper. Their bite therefore is not of importance, and the repugnance they inspire in us is really groundless.

"Next to the viper there is in France no venomous creature more to be feared than the scorpion. It is very ugly and walks on eight feet. In front it has two pincers like those of the crayfish, and behind a knotty, curled tail ending in a sting. The pincers are inoffensive, despite their menacing aspect; it is the sting with which the end of the tail is armed that is venomous. The scorpion makes use of it in self-defense and to kill the insects on which it feeds. In the southern departments of France are found two different kinds of scorpions. One, of a greenish black, frequents dark and cool places and even establishes itself in houses. It leaves its retreat only at night. It can be seen then running on the damp and cracked walls, seeking wood-lice and spiders, its customary prey. The other, much larger, is pale yellow. It keeps under warm and sandy stones. The black scorpion's sting does not cause serious injury; that of the yellow may be mortal. When one of these creatures is irritated, a little drop of liquid can be seen forming into a pearl at the extremity of the sting, which is all ready to strike. It is the drop of venom that the scorpion injects into the wound.

"There are many other important things I could tell you about the venomous creatures of foreign countries, about divers serpents whose bite causes a dreadful death; but I hear Mother Ambroisine calling us to dinner. Let us go over rapidly what I have just told you. No creature, however ugly it may be, shoots venom or can do us any harm from a distance. All venomous species act in the same way: with a special weapon a slight wound is made; and into this wound a drop of venom is introduced. The wound, by itself, is nothing; it is the injected liquid that makes it painful and sometimes mortal. The venomous weapon serves the creature for hunting and for defense. It is placed in a part of the body that varies according to the species. Spiders have a double fang folded at the entrance of the mouth; bees, wasps, hornets, bumble-bees, have a sting at the end of the stomach and kept invisible in its sheath when in repose; the viper and all venomous serpents have two long hollowed-out teeth on the upper jaw; the scorpion carries a sting at the end of its tail."

"I am very sorry," said Jules, "that Jacques did not hear your account of venomous creatures; he would have understood that caterpillars' green entrails are not venom. I will tell him all these things; and if I find another beautiful sphinx caterpillar I will not crush it."

Day 168

1.   Read chapter 32 of *The Story Book of Science*.
2.   Tell someone about what you read.

CHAPTER XXXII THE NETTLE

AFTER dinner, while their uncle read under the chestnut tree, the children scattered in the garden. Claire attended to her cuttings, Jules watered his vases, and Emile—Ah, giddy-pate, what should happen to him but another misfortune! A large butterfly was flying over the weeds that grow at the foot of the wall. Oh, what a magnificent butterfly! On the upper side its wings are red, fringed with black, with big blue eyes; underneath they are brown with wavy lines. It alights. Good. Emile makes himself small, approaches softly on tip-toe, puts out his hand, and, all at once, the butterfly is gone. But mark what follows. Emile draws his hand back quickly; it smarts, is red. The pain increases and becomes so bad that the poor boy runs to his uncle, his eyes swollen with tears.

"A venomous creature has stung me!" he cries. "See my hand, Uncle! It smarts—oh, how it smarts! Some viper has bitten me!"

At this word viper, Uncle Paul started. He rose and looked at the injured hand. A smile came to his lips.

"Impossible, my little friend; there is no viper in the garden. What foolishness have you been committing? Where have you been?"

"I ran after a butterfly, and when I put out my hand to catch it on the weeds at the foot of the wall, something stung me. See!"

"It is nothing, my poor Emile; go and dip your hand into the cool water of the fountain, and the pain will go away."

Quarter of an hour later they were talking of Emile's accident, he being quite recovered from his misadventure.

"Now that the pain is gone, does not Emile want to know what stung him?" asked his uncle.

"I certainly ought to know, so as not to be caught another time."

"Well, it is a plant called nettle. Its leaves, stems, slightest branches are covered with a multitude of bristles, stiff, hollow, and filled with a venomous liquid. When one of these bristles penetrates the skin, the point breaks, the little vial of venom opens and spills its contents into the wound. From that comes a smarting but not dangerous pain. You see, the nettle's bristles act like the weapons of venomous creatures. It is always a hollow point that makes a fine wound in the skin, and passes a drop of liquid into it, the cause of all the ill. The nettle is thus a venomous plant.

"I will also tell Emile that the beautiful butterfly for which he thoughtlessly thrust his hand into the tuft of nettles is called the Vanessa Io. Its caterpillar is velvety black with white spots. It also bristles with thorns. It does not make a cocoon. Its chrysalis, ornamented with bands that shine like gold, is suspended in the air by the end of its tail. The caterpillar lives on the nettle, of which it eats the leaves, notwithstanding their venomous bristles."

"In browsing on the venomous plant, how does the caterpillar manage so as not to poison itself?" Claire inquired.

"My dear child, you confound venomous with poisonous. Venomous is said of a substance that, introduced into the blood by any kind of a wound, causes injury in the manner of the viper's venom. Poisonous is said of a substance that, swallowed or introduced into the stomach, may cause death. Fatal drugs are poisonous: they kill if eaten or drunk. The liquid that flows from the viper's fangs and the scorpion's sting is venomous: it kills when it mixes with the blood; but it is not poisonous, for it can be swallowed with impunity. It is the same with the nettle's venom. So Mother Ambroisine gives the poultry chopped nettles, and the caterpillar of the Vanessa feeds without danger on the plant which, a little while ago, made Emile cry with pain. Of venomous plants we have in our country only nettles; but we have many poisonous plants that, when eaten, cause illness and even death, I must certainly tell you about them some day, so as to teach you to avoid them.

Nettle

"The nettle's bristles remind me of the caterpillar's hairs. Many caterpillars have the skin quite bare. They are then perfectly inoffensive. They can be handled without any danger, however large they may be, even those that have horn at the end of the back. They are no more to be feared than the silkworm. Others have bodies all bristly with hairs, sometimes very sharp and barbed, which can lodge in the skin, leave their points there, and thus produce lively itchings or even painful swellings. It is well then to mistrust velvety caterpillars, particularly those living in companies on oaks and pines, in large silk nests, and called processionary caterpillars. But here we have a word that calls for another story."

Day 169

1. Read chapter 33 of *The Story Book of Science*.
2. Tell someone about what you read.

CHAPTER XXXIII PROCESSIONARY CATERPILLARS

"WE frequently see, at the ends of pine branches, voluminous bags of white silk intermixed with leaves. These bags are, generally, puffed out at the top and narrow at the bottom, pear-shaped. They are sometimes as large as a person's head. They are nests where live together a kind of very velvety caterpillars with red hairs. A family of caterpillars, coming from the eggs laid by one butterfly, construct a silk lodging in common. All take part in the work, all spin and weave in the general interest. The interior of the nest is divided by thin silk partitions into a number of compartments. At the large end, sometimes elsewhere, is seen a wide funnel-shaped opening; it is the large door for entering and departing. Other doors, smaller, are distributed here and there. The caterpillars pass the winter in their nest, well sheltered from bad weather. In summer they take refuge there at night and during the great heat.

"As soon as it is day, they set out to spread themselves on the pine and eat the leaves. After eating their fill they reënter their silk dwelling, sheltered from the heat of the sun. Now, when they are out on a campaign, be it on the tree that bears the nest, or on the ground passing from one pine to another, these caterpillars march in a singular fashion, which has given them the name of processionaries, because, in fact, they defile in a procession, one after the other, and in the finest order.

"One, the first come—for amongst them there is perfect equality—starts on the way and serves as head of the expedition. A second follows, without a space between; a third follows the second in the same way; always thus, as many as there are caterpillars in the nest. The procession, numbering several hundreds, is now on the march. It defiles in one line, sometimes straight, sometimes winding, but always continuous, for each caterpillar that follows touches with its head the rear end of the preceding caterpillar. The procession describes on the ground a long and pleasing garland, which undulates to the right and left with unceasing variation. When several nests are near together and their processions happen to meet, the spectacle attains its highest interest. Then the different living garlands cross each other, get entangled and disentangled, knotted up and unknotted, forming the most capricious figures. The encounter does not lead to confusion. All the caterpillars of the same file march with a uniform and almost grave step; not one hastens to get before the others, not one remains behind, not one makes a mistake in the procession. Each one keeps its rank and scrupulously regulates its march by the one that precedes it. The file-leader of the troop directs the evolutions. When it turns to the right, all the caterpillars of the same line, one after the other, turn to the right; when it turns to the left, all, one after the other, turn to the left. If it stops, the whole procession stops, but not simultaneously; the second caterpillar first, then the third, fourth, fifth, and so on until the last. They would be called well-trained troops that, when defiling in order, stop at the word of command and close their ranks.

"The expedition, simply a promenade, or a journey in search of provisions, is now finished. They have gone far away from their nest. It is time to go home. How can they find it, through the grass and underbrush, and over all the obstacles of the road they have just traveled? Will they let themselves be guided by sight, obstructed though it be by every little tuft of grass; by the sense of smell, which wafted odors of every sort may put at fault? No, no; processionary caterpillars have for their guidance in traveling something better than sight or smell. They have instinct, which inspires them with infallible resources. Without taking account of what they do, they call to their service means that seem dictated by reason. Without doubt, they do not reason, but they obey the secret impulse of the eternal Reason, in whom and through whom all live.

"Now, this is what the processionary caterpillars do in order not to lose their way home again after a distant expedition. We pave our roads with crushed stone; caterpillars are more luxurious in their highways: they spread on their road a carpet of silk, they walk on nothing but silk. They spin continually on the journey and glue their silk all along the road. In fact, each caterpillar of the procession can be seen lowering and raising its head alternately. In the first movement, the spinneret, situated in the lower lip, glues the thread to the road that the procession is following; in the second, the spinneret lets the thread run out while the caterpillar is taking several steps. Then the head is lowered and lifted again, and a second length of thread is put in place. Each caterpillar that follows walks on the threads left by the preceding ones and adds its own thread to the silk, so that in all its length the road passed over is carpeted with a silky ribbon. It is by following this ribbon conductor that the processionaries get back to their home without ever losing their way, however tortuous the road may be.

"If one wishes to embarrass the procession, it suffices to pass the finger over the track so as to cut the silk road. The procession stops before the cut with every indication of fear and mistrust. Shall they go on? Shall they not go on? The heads rise and fall in anxious quest of the conductor threads. At last, one caterpillar bolder than the others, or perhaps more impatient, crosses the bad place and stretches its thread from one end of the cut to the other. A second, without hesitating, passes over on the thread left by the first, and in passing adds its own thread to the bridge. The others in turn all do the same. Soon the broken road is repaired and the defile of the procession continues.

"The processionary caterpillar of the oak marches in another way. It is covered with white hairs turned back and very long. One nest contains from seven to eight hundred individuals. When an expedition is decided on, a caterpillar leaves the nest and pauses at a certain distance to give the others time to arrange themselves in rank and file and form a battalion. This first caterpillar has to start the march. Following it, others place themselves, not one after another, like the processionaries of the pine, but in rows of two, three, four, and more. The troop, completed, begins to move in obedience to the evolutions of its file-leader, which always marches alone at the head of the legion, while the other caterpillars advance several abreast, dressing their ranks in perfect order. The first ranks of the army corps are always arranged in wedge formation, because of the gradual increase in the number of caterpillars composing it; the remainder are more or less expanded in different places. There are sometimes rows of from fifteen to twenty caterpillars marching in step, like well-trained soldiers, so that the head of one is never beyond the head of another. Of course the troop carpets its road with silk as it marches, so as to find its way back to its nest.

"The processionaries, especially those of the oak, retire to their nests to slough their skins, and these nests finally become filled with a fine dust of broken hairs. When you touch these nests, the dust of the hairs sticks to your hands and face, and causes an inflammation that lasts several days if the skin is delicate. One has only to stand at the foot of an oak where the processionaries have established themselves, to receive the irritating dust blown by the wind, and to feel a smart itching."

"What a pity the processionaries have those detestable hairs!" Jules exclaimed. "If they hadn't—"

"If they hadn't Jules would much like to see the caterpillars' procession. Never mind; after all, the danger is not so great. And then, if one had to scratch one's self a little, it would not be a serious matter. Besides, we will turn our attention to the processionary of the pine, less to be feared than that of the oak. At the warmest part of the day we will go and look for a caterpillars' nest in the pine wood; but Jules and I will go alone. It would be too hot for Emile and Claire."

Day 170

1.   Read chapter 34 of *The Story Book of Science*.
2.   Tell someone about what you read.

CHAPTER XXXIV THE STORM

AND, in fact, it was very hot when Uncle Paul and Jules started out. With a burning sun, they were sure to find the caterpillars in their silk bag, where they do not fail to take refuge to shelter themselves from a light that is too glaring for them; at an earlier or later hour, the nests might be empty, and the journey a fruitless one.

His heart full of the naïve joys proper to his age, his mind preoccupied by the caterpillars and their processions, Jules walked at a good pace, forgetting heat and fatigue. He had untied his cravat and thrown his blouse back on his shoulders. A holly stick, cut by his uncle from the hedge, served him as a third leg.

In the meantime the crickets chirped louder than usual; frogs croaked in the ponds; flies became teasing and persistent; sometimes a breath of air all at once blew along the road and raised a whirling column of dust. Jules did not notice these signs, but his uncle did, and from time to time looked up at the sky. Masses of reddish mist in the south seemed to give him some concern. "Perhaps we shall have rain," said he; "we must hurry."

About three o'clock they were at the pine wood. Uncle Paul cut a branch bearing a magnificent nest. He had guessed right: all the caterpillars had returned to their lodging, perhaps in prevision of bad weather. Then they sat in the shade of a group of pines, to rest a little before returning. Naturally they talked about caterpillars.

"The processionaries, you told me," said Jules, "leave their nests to scatter over the pines and eat the leaves. There are, in fact, a great many branches almost reduced to sticks of dry wood. Look at that pine I am pointing at; it is half stripped of leaves, as if fire had passed over it. I like the way the processionaries travel, but I can't help pitying those fine trees that wither under the miserable caterpillar's teeth."

"If the owner of these pines understood his interests better," returned Uncle Paul, "he would, in the winter, when the caterpillars are assembled in their silk bags, have the nests collected and burn them, in order to destroy the detestable breed that will gnaw the young shoots, browse the buds, and arrest the tree's development. The harm is much greater in our orchards. Various caterpillars live in companies on our fruit trees and spin nests in the same way as the processionaries. When summer comes, the starveling vermin scatter all over the trees, destroying leaves, buds, shoots. In a few hours the orchard is shorn and the crop is destroyed in its budding. So it is necessary to keep a careful lookout for caterpillar nests, remove them from the tree before spring, and burn them, so that nothing can escape; the future of the crop depends on it. It is fortunate that several kinds of creatures, little birds especially, come to our aid in this war to the death between man and the caterpillar; otherwise the worm, stronger than man on account of its infinite number, would ravage our crops. But we will talk of the little birds another time; the weather is threatening, we must go."

See how the reddish mist in the south, thicker and darker every moment, has become a large black cloud visibly invading the still clear part of the sky. Wind precedes it, bending the tops of the pines like a field of grain. There rises from the soil that odor of dust which the dry earth gives forth at the beginning of a storm.

"We must not think of starting now," cautioned Uncle Paul. "The storm is coming; it will be upon us in a few minutes. Let us hurry and find shelter."

Rain forms in the distance like a dim curtain extending clear across the sky. The sheet of water advances rapidly; it would beat the fastest racing horse. It is coming, it has come. Violent flashes of lightning furrow it, thunder roars in its depths.

At a clap of thunder heavier than the others Jules starts. "Let us stay here, Uncle," says the frightened child; "let us stay under this big bushy pine. It doesn't rain here under cover."

"No, my child," replies his uncle, who perceives that they are in the very heart of the storm; "let us get away from this dangerous tree."

And, taking Jules by the hand, he leads him hastily through the hail and rain. Beyond the wood Uncle Paul knows of an excavation hollowed out in the rock. They arrive there just as the storm breaks with all its force.

They had been there a quarter of an hour, silent before the solemn spectacle of the tempest, when a flash of fire, of dazzling brightness, rent the dark cloud in a zigzag line and struck a pine with a frightful detonation that had no reverberation or echo, but was so violent that one would have said the sky was falling. The fearful spectacle was over in the twinkling of an eye. Wild with terror, Jules had let himself fall on his knees, with clasped hands. He was crying and praying. His uncle's serenity was undisturbed.

"Take courage, my poor child," said Uncle Paul as soon as the first fright had passed. "Let us embrace each other and thank God for having kept us safe. We have just escaped a great danger; the thunderbolt struck the pine under which we were going to take shelter."

"Oh, what a scare I had, Uncle!" cried the boy. "I thought I should die of it. When you insisted on hurrying away in spite of the rain, did you know that the bolt would strike that tree?"

"No, my dear, I knew nothing about it, nor could any one know; only certain reasons made me fear the neighborhood of the big branching pine, and prudence dictated the search for a less dangerous shelter. If I yielded to my fears, if I listened to the voice of prudence, let us give thanks to God, who gave me presence of mind at that moment."

"You will tell me what made you avoid the dangerous shelter of the tree, will you not?"

"Very willingly; but when we are all together, so that each one may profit by it. No one ought to ignore the danger one runs in taking shelter under a tree during a storm."

In the meantime the rain-cloud with its lightnings and thunders had moved on into the distance. On one side, the sun was setting radiant; on the opposite side, in the wake of the storm, the rainbow bent its immense bright arch of all colors. Uncle Paul and Jules started on their way, without forgetting the famous caterpillars' nest which might have cost them so dear.

Day 171

1. Read chapter 35 of *The Story Book of Science*.
2. Tell someone about it.

CHAPTER XXXVI ELECTRICITY

JULES gave a lengthy account of the day to his brother and sister. At the part relating to the thunderbolt Claire trembled like a leaf. "I should have died of fright," said she, "if I had seen the lightning strike the pine." After the deeper emotion came curiosity, and they all agreed to beg their uncle for a talk on the subject of thunder. And so the next day Jules, Emile, and Claire gathered around their Uncle Paul to hear him tell them all about it. Jules broached the subject.

"Now that I am no longer afraid, will you please tell us, Uncle, why we should not take refuge under trees during a storm? Emile, I am sure, would like to know."

"I should first of all like to know what thunder is," said Emile.

"I too," said Claire. "When we know a little what thunder is, it will be much easier to understand the danger from trees."

"Quite right," commented their uncle, approvingly. "First let us see whether any one of you knows anything about thunder."

"When I was very small," Emile volunteered, "I used to think it was produced by rolling a large ball of iron made of resounding metal over the vault of the sky. If the vault broke anywhere, the ball was dashed to the ground and the thunder fell. But I don't believe that now. I am too big."

"Too big—a little fellow not so high as the first button on my vest! Say rather that your little reasoning powers are awakening and that the simple explanation of the iron ball no longer satisfies them."

Then Claire spoke. "I am not satisfied either with the explanations I used to give myself a while ago. With me, thunder was a wagon heavily loaded with old iron. It rolled on top of a sonorous vault. Sometimes a spark would flash out from under the wheels, the same as from a horse's hoof when it strikes a stone: that was the lightning. The vault was slippery and bordered with precipices. If the wagon happened to tip over, the load of old iron would fall to the ground, crushing people, trees, and houses. I laughed yesterday at my explanation, but I am no farther advanced now: I still know nothing at all about thunder."

"Your two thunders, varying to suit your infant imaginations, are based on the same idea, the idea of a sonorous vault. Well, know once for all that the blue vault of the sky is only an appearance due to the air which envelops us, and which, owing to the thickness of the envelope, has a beautiful blue color. Around us there is no vault, only a thick layer of air; and beyond that there is nothing for a vast distance until you come to the region of the stars."

"We will give up the blue vault," said Jules. "Emile, Claire, and I are persuaded there isn't any. Please go on."

"Go on? Here is where difficulty begins. Do you know, my children, that your questions are sometimes very embarrassing? 'Go on' is soon said; and, filled with unbounded faith in your Uncle Paul's knowledge, you expect an answer which, you feel sure, will satisfy your curiosity. You must, however, understand that there are innumerable things beyond your intelligence, and before you can grasp them you must attain to riper reason. With age and study many things will become clear that now are dark to you. In this number is the cause of thunder. I am very willing to tell you something about it; but if you do not understand all that I say you must blame your own premature curiosity. It is a difficult subject for you, very difficult."

"Only tell us about it," Jules persisted; "we will listen attentively."

"So be it. Air is not visible, one cannot take hold of it; if it were always at rest you would not, perhaps, suspect its existence. But when a violent wind bends tall poplars and scatters the leaves in eddies, when it uproots trees and carries off the roofs of buildings, who can doubt the existence of air? For wind is only air streaming irresistibly from place to place. Air, so subtle, so invisible, so peaceful in repose, is therefore in very truth a material substance, even a very brutal one when in violent motion. That is to say, a substance can exist, although at times nothing betrays its presence. We do not see it or touch it, are not sensible of it, and yet it is there, all about us; we are surrounded by it, live in the midst of it.

"Well, there is something still more hidden than air, more invisible, more difficult to detect. It is everywhere, absolutely everywhere, even in us; but it keeps itself so quiet that until now you have never heard of it."

Emile, Claire, and Jules exchanged glances full of meaning, trying to guess what it could be that was found everywhere and that they did not yet know of. They were a hundred leagues from guessing what their uncle meant.

"You might seek in vain by yourselves all day, all the year, perhaps all your life; you would not find it. The thing I am speaking of, you understand, is singularly well hidden; scholars had to make very delicate researches to learn anything about it. Let us make use of the means they have taught us to bring it to light."

Uncle Paul took from his desk a stick of sealing-wax and rubbed it rapidly over his cloth sleeve; then he put it near a small piece of paper. The children were all eyes. Behold, the paper flies up and sticks to the sealing-wax. The experiment is repeated several times. Each time the paper rises unaided, starts off, and fastens on to the stick.

"The piece of sealing-wax, which formerly did not attract the paper, now does. The rubbing on the cloth has, then, developed in it something that cannot be seen, for the stick has not changed in appearance; and this invisible thing is nevertheless very real, since it can lift up the paper, draw it to the wax, and hold it glued there. This thing is called electricity. You can easily produce it by rubbing on cloth either a piece of glass or a stick of sulphur, resin, or sealing-wax. All these substances, when rubbed, will acquire the property of drawing to themselves very light objects, like small pieces of straw, little bits of paper, or particles of dust. This evening the cat shall teach us more about it, if it will be good."

Day 172

1. Read chapter 36 of *The Story Book of Science*.
2. Tell someone about what you read.

CHAPTER XXXVI THE EXPERIMENT WITH THE CAT

THE wind blew cold and dry. The storm of the day before had brought it on. Uncle Paul took this pretext to have the kitchen stove lighted in spite of Mother Ambroisine's remarks, who cried out at the unseasonableness of making a fire.

"Light up the stove in summer!" said she; "did one ever see the like? No one but our master would have such a notion. We shall be roasted."

Uncle Paul let her talk; he had his own idea. They sat down at the table. After eating its supper the big cat, never too warm, settled itself on a chair by the side of the stove, and soon, with its back turned to the warm sheet-iron, began to purr with happiness. All was going as desired; Uncle Paul's projects were taking an excellent turn. There was some complaint of the heat, but he took no notice.

"Ah! do you think it is for you the stove is lighted?" said he to the children. "Undeceive yourselves, my little friends: it is for the cat, the cat alone. It is so chilly, poor thing; see how happy it is on its chair."

Emile was on the point of laughing at his uncle's kindly attentions to the tom-cat, but Claire, who suspected serious designs, nudged him with her elbow. Claire's suspicious were well founded. When they had finished supper they resumed the subject of thunder. Uncle Paul began:

"This morning I promised to show you, with the cat's help, some very curious things. The time has come for keeping my word, provided Puss is agreeable."

He look the cat, whose hair was burning hot, and put it on his knees. The children drew near.

"Jules, put out the lamp; we must be in the dark."

The lamp put out, Uncle Paul passed and repassed his hand over the tom-cat's back. Oh! oh! wonderful! The beast's hair is streaming with bright beads; little flashes of white light appear, crackle, and disappear as the hand rubs; you would have said that sparks of fireworks were bursting out from the fur. All looked on in wonder at the tom-cat's splendor.

"That puts the finishing touch! Here is our cat making fire!" cried Mother Ambroisine.

"Does that fire burn, Uncle?" asked Jules. "The cat does not cry out, and you stroke him without being afraid."

"Those sparks are not fire," replied Uncle Paul. "You all remember the stick of sealing wax which, after being rubbed on cloth, attracts little pieces of straw and paper. I told you that electricity, aroused by friction, is what makes the paper draw to the wax. Well, in rubbing the cat's back with my hand I produce electricity, but in greater abundance, so much so that it becomes visible where it was at first invisible, and bursts forth in sparks."

"If it doesn't burn, let me try," pleaded Jules.

Jules passed his hand over the cat's fur. The bright beads and their cracklings began again still stronger. Emile and Claire did the same. Mother Ambroisine was afraid. The worthy woman perhaps saw some witchcraft in the bright sparkles from her cat. The cat was then let loose. Besides, the experiment was beginning to give annoyance, and if Uncle Paul had not held the animal fast perhaps it would have begun to scratch.

Day 173

1.   Read chapter 37 of *The Story Book of Science*.
2.   Tell someone about what you read.

CHAPTER XXXVII THE EXPERIMENT WITH PAPER

"SINCE the cat threatens to get cross, we will have recourse to another way of producing electricity.

"You fold lengthwise a good sheet of ordinary paper; then take hold of the double strip by each end. Next, you heat it just to the scorching point over a stove or in front of a hot fire. The greater the heat, the more electricity will be developed. Finally, still holding the strip by the ends alone, you rub it quickly, as soon as it is hot, on a piece of woolen cloth previously warmed and stretched over the knee. It can be rubbed on the trousers if they are woolen. The friction must be rapid and lengthwise of the paper. After a short rubbing the band is quickly raised with one hand, with great care not to let the paper touch against anything; if it did the electricity would be dissipated. Then without delay you bring up the knuckles of your free hand, or, better, the end of a key, near to the middle of the strip of paper; and you will see a bright spark dart from the paper to the key with a slight crackling. To get another spark you must go through the same operations again, for at the approach of the finger or key the sheet of paper loses all its electricity.

"Instead of making a spark, you can hold the electrified sheet flat above little pieces of paper, straw, or feathers. These light bodies are attracted and repelled in turn; they come and go rapidly from the electrified strip to the object which serves them as support, and from this to the strip."

Adding example to precept, Uncle Paul took a sheet of paper, folded it in a strip to give it more resistance, warmed it, rubbed it on his knee, and finally made a spark fly from it on the approach of his finger-joint. The children were full of wonder at the lightning that sprang from the paper with a crackle. The cat's beads were more numerous, but less strong and brilliant.

They say that Mother Ambroisine had much trouble that evening in getting Jules to go to bed; for, once master of the process, he did not tire of warming and rubbing. His uncle's intervention was necessary to put an end to the electric experiments.

Day 174

1. Read chapter 41 of *The Story Book of Science*. (If you noticed, I skipped some.)
2. Tell someone about what you read.

CHAPTER XLI CLOUDS

TO finish his talk on lightning, the next morning Uncle Paul told them about clouds. The occasion, moreover, was very favorable. In one part of the sky great white clouds like mountains of cotton were piled up. The eye was delighted with the soft outlines of that celestial wadding.

"You remember," he began, "all those fogs that on damp autumn and winter mornings cover the earth with a veil of gray smoke, hide the sun, and prevent our seeing a few steps in front of us?"

"Looking into the air, you could see something like fine dust of water floating," said Claire; and Jules added:

"We played hide and seek with Emile in that kind of damp smoke. We could not see each other a few steps away."

"Well," resumed Uncle Paul, "clouds and fog are the same thing; only fog spreads about us and shows for what it is, gray, damp, cold; while clouds keep more or less above us and take on, with distance, a rich appearance. There are some of dazzling whiteness, like those you see over there; others of a red color, or golden-hued, or like fire; still others of the color of ashes, and others that are black. The color changes, too, from moment to moment. At sunset you will see a cloud begin with being white, then turn scarlet, then shine like a pile of embers, or like a lake of melted gold, and finally become dull and turn gray or black, according as the sun's rays strike it less and less. All that is a matter of illumination by the sun. In reality, clouds, however splendid in appearance, are formed of a damp vapor like that of fog. We can assure ourselves of this by a near approach."

"People can then mount as high as the clouds, Uncle?" Emile asked.

"Certainly. All one needs is a pair of legs stout enough to climb to the top of a mountain. Often then clouds are under one's feet."

"And you have seen clouds underneath you?"

"Sometimes."

"That must be a very beautiful sight."

"So beautiful that words cannot express it. But it is not exactly a pleasure if the clouds mount and envelop you. You can be very much embarrassed by the obscurity of the fog alone. You lose your way; you become confused, without suspecting any danger in the most dangerous places, at the risk of falling into some abyss; you lose sight of the guides, who alone know the way and could save you from a false step. No, all is not roses up among the clouds. You will perhaps learn that some day to your cost. Meanwhile let us transport ourselves in imagination to the top of a cloud-capped mountain. If circumstances are favorable, here is what we shall see:

"Above our heads the sky, perfectly clear, presents no unusual appearance; the sun shines there in all its brilliancy. Down there at our feet, almost in the plains, white clouds spread themselves out. The wind sweeps them before it and drives them toward the summit. There they are, rolling and mounting up the side of the mountain. One would think they were immense flocks of cotton pushed up the slope by some invisible hand. Now and then a ray of sunlight penetrates their depths and gives them the brilliancy of gold and fire. The beautiful clouds behind which the sun disappears at its setting are not richer. What brilliant tints, what soft suppleness! They mount higher and higher. Now they roll up like a shining white band around the top of the mountain, and hide the view of the plain from us. Only the point where we are projects above the cloud-curtain, like an islet above the sea. At last this point is invaded, we are in the bosom of the clouds. Warm tints, soft outlines, striking views—all have disappeared. It is now only a dark fog that saturates with moisture and makes us feel depressed. Ah, if some breath of wind would make haste and sweep away these disagreeable clouds!

"That, my little friends, is what one does not fail to wish when one is in the clouds, which, so beautiful at a distance, are nothing but gloomy fog when close at hand. The spectacle of the clouds should be seen from afar. When in our curiosity we wish to examine certain appearances too closely, we sometimes find them deceptive; but we also find that, under a secondary brilliancy, which serves to adorn the earth, they hide realities of the first importance. The marvels of the clouds are only an appearance, an illusion of light; but under this illusion are concealed the reservoirs of rain, source of the earth's fecundity. God, by whom the smallest details of creation have been ordered, willed that the most common but also most necessary substances should serve as an ornament to the earth in spite of their really humble aspect; and he clothes them with a prestige dependent on the distance from which we are to contemplate them. The gray vapor of the clouds gives us rain. That is its chief utility. The sun illuminates it, and that suffices to transform it into a celestial tapestry in which the astonished eye finds the splendor of purple, gold and fire. That is its ornamental function.

"The height maintained by clouds is very variable and is generally less than you might suppose. There are clouds that lazily trail along the ground; they are the fogs. There are others that cling to the sides of moderately high mountains, and still others that crown the summits. The region where they are commonly found is at a height varying from 500 to 1500 meters. In some rather rare instances they rise to nearly four leagues. Beyond that eternal serenity reigns; clouds never mount there, thunder never rumbles, and snow, hail, and rain never form.

"Those clouds are called 'cirrus' that look sometimes like light flocks of curly wool, sometimes like drawn-out-filaments of dazzling whiteness, sharply contrasting with the deep blue of the sky. They are the highest of all the clouds. They are often a league high. When cirrus clouds are small and rounded and closely grouped in large numbers, so as to look like the backs of a flock of sheep, the sky thus covered is said to be dappled. It is usually a sign that the weather is going to change.

"The name 'cumulus' is given to those large white clouds with round outlines which pile up, during the heat of summer, like immense mountains of cotton-wool. Their appearance presages a storm."

"Then the clouds we see over there next to the mountains," queried Jules, "are cumulus? They look like piles of cotton. Will they bring us a storm?"

"I think not. The wind is driving them in another direction. The storm always takes place in their neighborhood. There! Hear that?"

A sudden light had just flashed through the flocks of the cumulus. After rather a long wait the noise of the thunder reached them, but greatly weakened by distance. Questions came quickly from Jules's and Emile's lips: "Why does it rain over there, and not here? Why does the noise of the thunder come after the lightning? Why—"

"We are going to talk about all that," said Uncle Paul; "but first let us learn the other forms of clouds. 'Stratus' is applied to clouds disposed in irregular bands placed in tiers on the horizon at sunrise or sunset. They are clouds that, in the fading daylight, especially in autumn, take the glowing tints of melted metals and of flame. The red stratus of the morning are followed by rain or wind.

"Finally, we give the name 'nimbus' to a mass of dark clouds of a uniform gray, so crowded together that it is impossible to distinguish one cloud from another. These clouds generally dissolve into rain. Seen from a distance, they often look like broad stripes extending in a straight line from heaven to earth. They are trails of rain.

"Now, Emile may ask his questions."

Day 175

1.   Read chapter 42 of *The Story Book of Science*.
2.   Tell someone about what you read.

CHAPTER XLII THE VELOCITY OF SOUND

"UNDER that big white cloud that you call cumulus," said Emile, "there is at this very moment a storm. We have just seen the lightning and heard the thunder. Here, on the contrary, the sky is blue. So it does not rain everywhere at the same time. When rain is falling in one country, it is fine in others. And yet, when it rains here the whole sky is covered with clouds."

"You need only put your hand over your eyes to hide the sky," his uncle explained. "A cloud much farther off, but also much larger, produces the same effect: it veils what is surrounding us and makes it all cloudy. But that is only in appearance; beyond the region covered by the cloud the sky may be serene and the weather magnificent. Under the cumulus where the thunder is growling now, it rains, you may be sure, and the sky looks black. To the people in that region the surroundings present only a rainy appearance, because they are wrapped in clouds; if they were to go elsewhere, beyond the clouds, they would find the sky as serene as we have it here."

"With a fast horse they could, then," suggested Emile, "get from under the clouds, leave the rain, and come into fine weather; as also they could leave the sunshine and get into the rain under the clouds."

"Sometimes that would be possible, but more often not, because clouds can cover large areas. Besides, they travel, they go from one country to another, with such speed that the best horseman could not follow them in their course. You have all seen the shadow of the clouds run over the ground when the wind blows. Hills, valleys, plains, water-courses, all are crossed in less than no time. The shadow of a cloud passes over you at the moment you reach the top of a hill. Before you have taken three steps to descend into the valley, the shadow, with giant strides, is mounting the opposite slopes. Who could flatter himself that he could follow the cloud and keep under its cover?

"If rain sometimes falls over great stretches of country, it is never general, absolutely. If it should rain at one time over a whole province, what is that compared with the earth? A clod compared with a large field. Chased by the wind, clouds run hither and thither in the vast spaces of the atmosphere. They travel, and on their way throw a shadow or precipitate rain. Where they pass there is rain; everywhere else, no. In the same place there can even be both rain and fine weather, according as one is below or above the clouds. You know that on a mountain-top the clouds are sometimes beneath one. The plain under the clouds may receive a hard shower, while on the summit the sun shines without a single drop of rain."

"All that is easily understood," said Jules. "It is my turn now, Uncle, to ask you a question. From the storm-cloud that we see from here, there first came a flash of lightning; then, after waiting some time, the sound of the thunder was heard. Why do not the sound and the lightning come together?"

"Two things tell us of the thunderbolt: light and noise. The light is the flash of the lightning, the noise is thunder. Likewise in the discharge of fire-arms there is the light produced by the ignition of the powder and the noise resulting therefrom. At the scene of the explosion light and noise are coincident; but for persons at a distance the light, which travels at an incomparably greater velocity, arrives before the sound, which moves more slowly. If you note the discharge of a gun a considerable distance away, you see first the flash and smoke of the explosion, and do not hear the report until some time after; the more distant the explosion, the longer the time. Light travels an immense distance in an exceedingly short time. The flash of the explosion, therefore, reaches the eye at the very instant of its occurrence. If the sound does not arrive until after, it is because it travels much less rapidly and, in order to cover a considerable distance, requires considerable time, which is easily measured.

"Suppose ten seconds pass between the flash of a cannon's discharge and the arrival of the sound. The distance is measured between the place where the explosion occurred and that where it was heard. It is found to be 3400 meters. Sound, therefore, moves through the air, in a single second, a distance of 3400 meters. That is a good rate of speed, comparable with that of the cannon-ball, but nothing, after all, in comparison with the inconceivable velocity of light.

"The unequal rapidity with which sound and light travel accounts for the following fact. From a distance a wood-cutter is seen chopping wood, or a mason cutting stone. We see the ax strike the wood, the mallet tap the stone, and some time after we hear the sound."

"One Sunday before church," interposed Jules, "I was watching from a distance the ringing of the bell. I saw the tongue strike and the sound did not come until later. Now I see the reason."

"If you count the number of seconds between the appearance of the flash and the instant the thunder begins to be heard, you can tell what distance you are from the storm-cloud."

"Is a second very long?" Emile asked.

"It is about the length of one beat of the pulse. All we have to do, then, is to count, one, two, three, four, etc., without haste, but not too slowly, to have about the number of seconds. Note the instant the flash lights up the stormy cumulus, and count slowly until you hear the thunder."

With watchful eye and attentive ear all began the observation. Finally a flash was seen. They counted, the uncle beating time. One—two—three—four—five— At twelve came the thunder, but so faint that they could only just hear it.

"It took twelve seconds for the sound of the thunder to reach us," said Uncle Paul. "From what distance does it come, if sound travels 340 meters a second?"

"You must multiply 340 by twelve," replied Claire.

"Well, Miss, do it."

Claire made the calculation. The result was 4080 meters.

"The flash of lightning was 4080 meters away; we are more than a league from the storm-cloud," said her uncle.

"How easy that is!" exclaimed Emile. "You count one, two, three, four, and without moving you know how far away the thunderbolt has just fallen."

"The longer the time between the flash and the noise, the farther away is the cloud. When the report comes at the same time as the flash, the explosion is quite near. Jules knows that well since the day of the storm in the pine woods."

"I have heard that there is no longer any danger after the lightning is seen," said Claire.

"A thunderbolt is as rapid as light. An electric explosion is, therefore, ended as soon as the flash appears, and all danger is then passed; for the thunder, however loud it may be, can do no harm."

Day 176

1.   We'll finish off with some more stories from *The Peterkin Papers*.
2.   Tell someone about the story.

MODERN IMPROVEMENTS AT THE PETERKINS'.

AGAMEMNON felt that it became necessary for him to choose a profession. It was important on account of the little boys. If he should make a trial of several different professions he could find out which would be the most likely to be successful, and it would then be easy to bring up the little boys in the right direction.

Elizabeth Eliza agreed with this. She thought the family occasionally made mistakes, and had come near disgracing themselves. Now was their chance to avoid this in future by giving the little boys a proper education.

Solomon John was almost determined to become a doctor. From earliest childhood he had practiced writing recipes on little slips of paper. Mrs. Peterkin, to be sure, was afraid of infection. She could not bear the idea of his bringing one disease after the other into the family circle. Solomon John, too, did not like sick people. He thought he might manage it if he should not have to see his patients while they were sick. If he could only visit them when they were recovering, and when the danger of infection was over, he would really enjoy making calls.

He should have a comfortable doctor's chaise, and take one of the little boys to hold his horse while he went in, and he thought he could get through the conversational part very well, and feeling the pulse, perhaps looking at the tongue. He should take and read all the newspapers, and so be thoroughly acquainted with the news of the day to talk of. But he should not like to be waked up at night to visit. Mr. Peterkin thought that would not be necessary. He had seen signs on doors of "Night Doctor," and certainly it would be as convenient to have a sign of "Not a Night Doctor."

Solomon John thought he might write his advice to those of his patients who were dangerously ill, from whom there was danger of infection. And then Elizabeth Eliza agreed that his prescriptions would probably be so satisfactory that they would keep his patients well,–not too well to do without a doctor, but needing his recipes.

Agamemnon was delayed, however, in his choice of a profession, by a desire he had to become a famous inventor. If he could only invent something important, and get out a patent, he would make himself known all over the country. If he could get out a patent he would be set up for life, or at least as long as the patent lasted, and it would be well to be sure to arrange it to last through his natural life.

Indeed, he had gone so far as to make his invention. It had been suggested by their trouble with a key, in their late moving to their new house. He had studied the matter over a great deal. He looked it up in the Encyclopædia, and had spent a day or two in the Public Library, in reading about Chubb's Lock and other patent locks.

But his plan was more simple. It was this: that all keys should be made alike! He wondered it had not been thought of before; but so it was, Solomon John said, with all inventions, with Christopher Columbus, and everybody. Nobody knew the invention till it was invented, and then it looked very simple. With Agamemnon's plan you need have but one key, that should fit everything! It should be a medium-sized key, not too large to carry. It ought to answer for a house door, but you might open a portmanteau with it. How much less danger there would be of losing one's keys if there were only one to lose!

Mrs. Peterkin thought it would be inconvenient if their father were out, and she wanted to open the jam-closet for the little boys. But Agamemnon explained that he did not mean there should be but one key in the family, or in a town,–you might have as many as you pleased, only they should all be alike.

Elizabeth Eliza felt it would be a great convenience,–they could keep the front door always locked, yet she could open it with the key of her upper drawer; that she was sure to have with her. And Mrs. Peterkin felt it might be a convenience if they had one on each story, so that they need not go up and down for it.

Mr. Peterkin studied all the papers and advertisements, to decide about the lawyer whom they should consult, and at last, one morning, they went into town to visit a patent-agent.

Elizabeth Eliza took the occasion to make a call upon the lady from Philadelphia, but she came back hurriedly to her mother.

"I have had a delightful call," she said; "but–perhaps I was wrong–I could not help, in conversation, speaking of Agamemnon's proposed patent. I ought not to have mentioned it, as such things are kept profound secrets; they say women always do tell things; I suppose that is the reason."

"But where is the harm?" asked Mrs. Peterkin. "I'm sure you can trust the lady from Philadelphia."

Elizabeth Eliza then explained that the lady from Philadelphia had questioned the plan a little when it was told her, and had suggested that "if everybody had the same key there would be no particular use in a lock."

"Did you explain to her," said Mrs. Peterkin, "that we were not all to have the same keys?"

"I couldn't quite understand her," said Elizabeth Eliza, "but she seemed to think that burglars and other people might come in if the keys were the same."

"Agamemnon would not sell his patent to burglars!" said Mrs. Peterkin, indignantly.

"But about other people," said Elizabeth Eliza; "there is my upper drawer; the little boys might open it at Christmas-time,–and their presents in it!"

"And I am not sure that I could trust Amanda," said Mrs. Peterkin, considering.

Both she and Elizabeth Eliza felt that Mr. Peterkin ought to know what the lady from Philadelphia had suggested. Elizabeth Eliza then proposed going into town, but it would take so long she might not reach them in time. A telegram would be better, and she ventured to suggest using the Telegraph Alarm.

For, on moving into their new house, they had discovered it was provided with all the modern improvements. This had been a disappointment to Mrs. Peterkin, for she was afraid of them, since their experience the last winter, when their water-pipes were frozen up. She had been originally attracted to the house by an old pump at the side, which had led her to believe there were no modern improvements. It had pleased the little boys, too. They liked to pump the handle up and down, and agreed to pump all the water needed, and bring it into the house.

There was an old well, with a picturesque well-sweep, in a corner by the barn. Mrs. Peterkin was frightened by this at first. She was afraid the little boys would be falling in every day. And they showed great fondness for pulling the bucket up and down. It proved, however, that the well was dry. There was no water in it; so she had some moss thrown down, and an old feather-bed, for safety, and the old well was a favorite place of amusement.

The house, it had proved, was well furnished with bath-rooms, and "set-waters" everywhere. Water-pipes and gas-pipes all over the house; and a hack-, telegraph-, and fire-alarm, with a little knob for each.

Mrs. Peterkin was very anxious. She feared the little boys would be summoning somebody all the time, and it was decided to conceal from them the use of the knobs, and the card of directions at the side was destroyed. Agamemnon had made one of his first inventions to help this. He had arranged a number of similar knobs to be put in rows in different parts of the house, to appear as if they were intended for ornament, and had added some to the original knobs. Mrs. Peterkin felt more secure, and Agamemnon thought of taking out a patent for this invention.

It was, therefore, with some doubt that Elizabeth Eliza proposed sending a telegram to her father. Mrs. Peterkin, however, was pleased with the idea. Solomon John was out, and the little boys were at school, and she herself would touch the knob, while Elizabeth Eliza should write the telegram.

"I think it is the fourth knob from the beginning," she said, looking at one of the rows of knobs.

Elizabeth Eliza was sure of this. Agamemnon, she believed, had put three extra knobs at each end.

"But which is the end, and which is the beginning,—the top or the bottom?" Mrs. Peterkin asked hopelessly.

Still she bravely selected a knob, and Elizabeth Eliza hastened with her to look out for the messenger. How soon should they see the telegraph boy?

They seemed to have scarcely reached the window, when a terrible noise was heard, and down the shady street the white horses of the fire-brigade were seen rushing at a fatal speed!

It was a terrific moment!

"I have touched the fire-alarm," Mrs. Peterkin exclaimed.

Both rushed to open the front door in agony. By this time the fire-engines were approaching.

"Do not be alarmed," said the chief engineer; "the furniture shall be carefully covered, and we will move all that is necessary."

"Move again!" exclaimed Mrs. Peterkin, in agony.

Elizabeth Eliza strove to explain that she was only sending a telegram to her father, who was in Boston.

"It is not important," said the head engineer; "the fire will all be out before it could reach him."

And he ran upstairs, for the engines were beginning to play upon the roof.

Mrs. Peterkin rushed to the knobs again hurriedly; there was more necessity for summoning Mr. Peterkin home.

"Write a telegram to your father," she said to Elizabeth Eliza, "to 'come home directly.'"

"That will take but three words," said Elizabeth Eliza, with presence of mind, "and we need ten. I was just trying to make them out."

"What has come now?" exclaimed Mrs. Peterkin, and they hurried again to the window, to see a row of carriages coming down the street.

"I must have touched the carriage-knob," cried Mrs. Peterkin, "and I pushed it half-a-dozen times I felt so anxious!"

Six hacks stood before the door. All the village boys were assembling. Even their own little boys had returned from school, and were showing the firemen the way to the well.

Again Mrs. Peterkin rushed to the knobs, and a fearful sound arose. She had touched the burglar-alarm!

The former owner of the house, who had a great fear of burglars, had invented a machine of his own, which he had connected with a knob. A wire attached to the knob moved a spring that could put in motion a number of watchmen's rattles, hidden under the eaves of the piazza.

All these were now set a-going, and their terrible din roused those of the neighborhood who had not before assembled around the house. At this moment Elizabeth Eliza met the chief engineer.

"You need not send for more help," he said; "we have all the engines in town here, and have stirred up all the towns in the neighborhood; there's no use in springing any more alarms. I can't find the fire yet, but we have water pouring all over the house."

Elizabeth Eliza waved her telegram in the air.

"We are only trying to send a telegram to my father and brother, who are in town," she endeavored to explain.

"If it is necessary," said the chief engineer, "you might send it down in one of the hackney carriages. I see a number standing before the door. We'd better begin to move the heavier furniture, and some of you women might fill the carriages with smaller things."

Mrs. Peterkin was ready to fall into hysterics. She controlled herself with a supreme power, and hastened to touch another knob.

Elizabeth Eliza corrected her telegram, and decided to take the advice of the chief engineer and went to the door to give her message to one of the hackmen, when she saw a telegraph boy appear. Her mother had touched the right knob. It was the fourth from the beginning; but the beginning was at the other end!

She went out to meet the boy, when, to her joy, she saw behind him her father and Agamemnon. She clutched her telegram, and hurried toward them.

Mr. Peterkin was bewildered. Was the house on fire? If so, where were the flames?

He saw the row of carriages. Was there a funeral, or a wedding? Who was dead? Who was to be married?

He seized the telegram that Elizabeth Eliza reached to him, and read it aloud.

"Come to us directly–the house is NOT on fire!"

The chief engineer was standing on the steps.

"The house not on fire!" he exclaimed. "What are we all summoned for?"

"It is a mistake," cried Elizabeth Eliza, wringing her hands. "We touched the wrong knob; we wanted the telegraph boy!"

"We touched all the wrong knobs," exclaimed Mrs. Peterkin, from the house.

The chief engineer turned directly to give counter-directions, with a few exclamations of disgust, as the bells of distant fire-engines were heard approaching.

Solomon John appeared at this moment, and proposed taking one of the carriages, and going for a doctor for his mother, for she was now nearly ready to fall into hysterics, and Agamemnon thought to send a telegram down by the boy, for the evening papers, to announce that the Peterkins' house had not been on fire.

The crisis of the commotion had reached its height. The beds of flowers, bordered with dark-colored leaves, were trodden down by the feet of the crowd that had assembled.

The chief engineer grew more and more indignant, as he sent his men to order back the fire-engines from the neighboring towns. The collection of boys followed the procession as it went away. The fire-brigade hastily removed covers from some of the furniture, restored the rest to their places, and took away their ladders. Many neighbors remained, but Mr. Peterkin hastened into the house to attend to Mrs. Peterkin.

Elizabeth Eliza took an opportunity to question her father, before he went in, as to the success of their visit to town.

"We saw all the patent-agents," answered Mr. Peterkin, in a hollow whisper. "Not one of them will touch the patent, or have anything to do with it."

Elizabeth Eliza looked at Agamemnon, as he walked silently into the house. She would not now speak to him of the patent; but she recalled some words of Solomon John. When they were discussing the patent he had said that many an inventor had grown gray before his discovery was acknowledged by the public. Others might reap the harvest, but it came, perhaps, only when he was going to his grave.

Elizabeth Eliza looked at Agamemnon reverently, and followed him silently into the house.

Day 177

1.   Read *The Peterkin Papers*, chapter 19
2.   Tell someone about the story.

AGAMEMNON'S CAREER.

THERE had apparently been some mistake in Agamemnon's education. He had been to a number of colleges, indeed, but he had never completed his course in any one. He had continually fallen into some difficulty with the authorities. It was singular, for he was of an inquiring mind, and had always tried to find out what would be expected of him, but had never hit upon the right thing.

Solomon John thought the trouble might be in what they called the elective system, where you were to choose what study you might take. This had always bewildered Agamemnon a good deal.

"And how was a feller to tell," Solomon John had asked, "whether he wanted to study a thing before he tried it? It might turn out awful hard!"

Agamemnon had always been fond of reading, from his childhood up. He was at his book all day long. Mrs Peterkin had imagined he would come out a great scholar, because she could never get him away from his books.

And so it was in his colleges; he was always to be found in the library, reading and reading. But they were always the wrong books.

For instance: the class were required to prepare themselves on the Spartan war. This turned Agamemnon's attention to the Fenians, and to study the subject he read up on "Charles O'Malley," and "Harry Lorrequer," and some later novels of that sort, which did not help him on the subject required, yet took up all his time, so that he found himself unfitted for anything else when the examinations came. In consequence he was requested to leave.

Agamemnon always missed in his recitations, for the same reason that Elizabeth Eliza did not get on in school, because he was always asked the questions he did not know. It seemed provoking; if the professors had only asked something else! But they always hit upon the very things he had not studied up.

Mrs. Peterkin felt this was encouraging, for Agamemnon knew the things they did not know in colleges. In colleges they were willing to take for students only those who already knew certain things. She thought Agamemnon might be a professor in a college for those students who didn't know those things.

"I suppose these professors could not have known a great deal," she added, "or they would not have asked you so many questions; they would have told you something."

Agamemnon had left another college on account of a mistake he had made with some of his classmates. They had taken a great deal of trouble to bring some wood from a distant wood-pile to make a bonfire with, under one of the professors' windows. Agamemnon had felt it would be a compliment to the professor.

It was with bonfires that heroes had been greeted on their return from successful wars. In this way beacon-lights had been kindled upon lofty heights, that had inspired mariners seeking their homes after distant adventures. As he plodded back and forward he imagined himself some hero of antiquity. He was reading "Plutarch's Lives" with deep interest. This had been recommended at a former college, and he was now taking it up in the midst of his French course. He fancied, even, that some future Plutarch was growing up in Lynn, perhaps, who would write of this night of suffering, and glorify its heroes.

For himself he took a severe cold and suffered from chilblains, in consequence of going back and forward through the snow, carrying the wood.

But the flames of the bonfire caught the blinds of the professor's room, and set fire to the building, and came near burning up the whole institution. Agamemnon regretted the result as much as his predecessor, who gave him his name, must have regretted that other bonfire, on the shores of Aulis, that deprived him of a daughter.

The result for Agamemnon was that he was requested to leave, after having been in the institution but a few months.

He left another college in consequence of a misunderstanding about the hour for morning prayers. He went every day regularly at ten o'clock, but found, afterward, that he should have gone at half-past six. This hour seemed to him and to Mrs. Peterkin unseasonable, at a time of year when the sun was not up, and he would have been obliged to go to the expense of candles.

Agamemnon was always willing to try another college, wherever he could be admitted. He wanted to attain knowledge, however it might be found. But, after going to five, and leaving each before the year was out, he gave it up.

He determined to lay out the money that would have been expended in a collegiate education in buying an Encyclopædia, the most complete that he could find, and to spend his life studying it systematically. He would not content himself with merely reading it, but he would study into each subject as it came up, and perfect himself in that subject. By the time, then, that he had finished the Encyclopædia he should have embraced all knowledge, and have experienced much of it.

The family were much interested in this plan of making practice of every subject that came up.

He did not, of course, get on very fast in this way. In the second column of the very first page he met with A as a note in music. This led him to the study of music. He bought a flute, and took some lessons, and attempted to accompany Elizabeth Eliza on the piano. This, of course, distracted him from his work on the Encyclopædia. But he did not wish to return to A until he felt perfect in music. This required a long time.

Then in this same paragraph a reference was made; in it he was requested to "see Keys." It was necessary, then, to turn to "Keys." This was about the time the family were moving, which we have mentioned, when the difficult subject of keys came up, that suggested to him his own simple invention, and the hope of getting a patent for it. This led him astray, as inventions before have done with master-minds, so that he was drawn aside from his regular study.

The family, however, were perfectly satisfied with the career Agamemnon had chosen. It would help them all, in any path of life, if he should master the Encyclopædia in a thorough way.

Mr. Peterkin agreed it would in the end be not as expensive as a college course, even if Agamemnon should buy all the different Encyclopædias that appeared. There would be no "spreads" involved; no expense of receiving friends at entertainments in college; he could live at home, so that it would not be necessary to fit up another room, as at college. At all the times of his leaving he had sold out favorably to other occupants.

Solomon John's destiny was more uncertain. He was looking forward to being a doctor some time, but he had not decided whether to be allopathic or homeopathic, or whether he could not better invent his own pills. And he could not understand how to obtain his doctor's degree.

For a few weeks he acted as clerk in a druggist's store. But he could serve only in the toothbrush and soap department, because it was found he was not familiar enough with the Latin language to compound the drugs. He agreed to spend his evenings in studying the Latin grammar; but his course was interrupted by his being dismissed for treating the little boys too frequently to soda.

The little boys were going through the schools regularly. The family had been much exercised with regard to their education. Elizabeth Eliza felt that everything should be expected from them; they ought to take advantage from the family mistakes. Every new method that came up was tried upon the little boys. They had been taught spelling by all the different systems, and were just able to read, when Mr. Peterkin learned that it was now considered best that children should not be taught to read till they were ten years old.

Mrs. Peterkin was in despair. Perhaps, if their books were taken from them even then, they might forget what they had learned. But no, the evil was done; the brain had received certain impressions that could not be blurred over.

This was long ago, however. The little boys had since entered the public schools. They went also to a gymnasium, and a whittling school, and joined a class in music, and another in dancing; they went to some afternoon lectures for children, when there was no other school, and belonged to a walking-club. Still Mr. Peterkin was dissatisfied by the slowness of their progress. He visited the schools himself, and found that they did not lead their classes. It seemed to him a great deal of time was spent in things that were not instructive, such as putting on and taking off their india-rubber boots.

Elizabeth Eliza proposed that they should be taken from school and taught by Agamemnon from the Encyclopædia. The rest of the family might help in the education at all hours of the day. Solomon John could take up the Latin grammar, and she could give lessons in French.

The little boys were enchanted with the plan, only they did not want to have the study-hours all the time.

Mr. Peterkin, however, had a magnificent idea, that they should make their life one grand Object Lesson. They should begin at breakfast, and study everything put upon the table,– the material of which it was made, and where it came from. In the study of the letter A, Agamemnon had embraced the study of music, and from one meal they might gain instruction enough for a day.

"We shall have the assistance," said Mr. Peterkin, "of Agamemnon, with his Encyclopædia."

Agamemnon modestly suggested that he had not yet got out of A, and in their first breakfast everything would therefore have to begin with A.

"That would not be impossible," said Mr. Peterkin. "There is Amanda, who will wait on table, to start with–"

"We could have 'am-and-eggs," suggested Solomon John

Mrs. Peterkin was distressed. It was hard enough to think of anything for breakfast, and impossible, if it all had to begin with one letter.

Elizabeth Eliza thought it would not be necessary. All they were to do was to ask questions, as in examination papers, and find their answers as they could. They could still apply to the Encyclopædia, even if it were not in Agamemnon's alphabetical course.

Mr. Peterkin suggested a great variety. One day they would study the botany of the breakfast-table, another day, its natural history. The study of butter would include that of the cow. Even that of the butter-dish would bring in geology. The little boys were charmed at the idea of learning pottery from the cream-jug, and they were promised a potter's wheel directly.

"You see, my dear," said Mr. Peterkin to his wife, "before many weeks, we shall be drinking our milk from jugs made by our children."

Elizabeth Eliza hoped for a thorough study.

"Yes," said Mr. Peterkin, "we might begin with botany. That would be near to Agamemnon alphabetically. We ought to find out the botany of butter. On what does the cow feed?"

The little boys were eager to go out and see.

"If she eats clover," said Mr. Peterkin, "we shall expect the botany of clover."

The little boys insisted that they were to begin the next day; that very evening they should go out and study the cow.

Mrs. Peterkin sighed, and decided she would order a simple breakfast. The little boys took their note-books and pencils, and clambered upon the fence, where they seated themselves in a row.

For there were three little boys. So it was now supposed. They were always coming in or going out, and it had been difficult to count them, and nobody was very sure how many there were.

There they sat, however, on the fence, looking at the cow. She looked at them with large eyes.

"She won't eat," they cried, "while we are looking at her!"

So they turned about, and pretended to look into the street, and seated themselves that way, turning their heads back, from time to time, to see the cow.

"Now she is nibbling a clover."

"No, that is a bit of sorrel."

"It's a whole handful of grass."

"What kind of grass?" they exclaimed.

It was very hard, sitting with their backs to the cow, and pretending to the cow that they were looking into the street, and yet to be looking at the cow all the time, and finding out what she was eating; and the upper rail of the fence was narrow and a little sharp. It was very high, too, for some additional rails had been put on to prevent the cow from jumping into the garden or street.

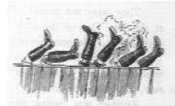

Suddenly, looking out into the hazy twilight, Elizabeth Eliza saw six legs and six india-rubber boots in the air, and the little boys disappeared!

"They are tossed by the cow! The little boys are tossed by the cow!"

Mrs. Peterkin rushed for the window, but fainted on the way. Solomon John and Elizabeth Eliza were hurrying to the door, but stopped, not knowing what to do next. Mrs. Peterkin recovered herself with a supreme effort, and sent them out to the rescue.

But what could they do? The fence had been made so high, to keep the cow out, that nobody could get in. The boy that did the milking had gone off with the key of the outer gate, and perhaps with the key of the shed door. Even if that were not locked, before Agamemnon could get round by the wood-shed and cow-shed, the little boys might be gored through and through!

Elizabeth Eliza ran to the neighbors, Solomon John to the druggist's for plasters, while Agamemnon made his way through the dining-room to the wood-shed and outer-shed door. Mr. Peterkin mounted the outside of the fence, while Mrs. Peterkin begged him not to put himself in danger. He climbed high enough to view the scene. He held to the corner post and reported what he saw.

They were not gored. The cow was at the other end of the lot. One of the little boys were lying in a bunch of dark leaves. He was moving.

The cow glared, but did not stir. Another little boy was pulling his india-rubber boots out of the mud. The cow still looked at him.

Another was feeling the top of his head. The cow began to crop the grass, still looking at him.

Agamemnon had reached and opened the shed-door. The little boys were next seen running toward it.

A crowd of neighbors, with pitchforks, had returned meanwhile with Elizabeth Eliza. Solomon John had brought four druggists. But, by the time they had reached the house, the three little boys were safe in the arms of their mother!

"This is too dangerous a form of education," she cried; "I had rather they went to school."

"No!" they bravely cried. They were still willing to try the other way.

Day 178

1. Read *The Peterkin Papers*, chapter 20
2. Tell someone about the story.

THE EDUCATIONAL BREAKFAST.

MRS. PETERKIN'S nerves were so shaken by the excitement of the fall of the three little boys into the enclosure where the cow was kept that the educational breakfast was long postponed. The little boys continued at school, as before, and the conversation dwelt as little as possible upon the subject of education.

Mrs. Peterkin's spirits, however, gradually recovered. The little boys were allowed to watch the cow at her feed. A series of strings were arranged by Agamemnon and Solomon John, by which the little boys could be pulled up, if they should again fall down into the enclosure. These were planned something like curtain-cords, and Solomon John frequently amused himself by pulling one of the little boys up or letting him down.

Some conversation did again fall upon the old difficulty of questions. Elizabeth Eliza declared that it was not always necessary to answer; that many who could did not answer questions,–the conductors of the railroads, for instance, who probably knew the names of all the stations on a road, but were seldom able to tell them.

"Yes," said Agamemnon, "one might be a conductor without even knowing the names of the stations, because you can't understand them when they do tell them!"

"I never know," said Elizabeth Eliza, "whether it is ignorance in them, or unwillingness, that prevents them from telling you how soon one station is coming, or how long you are to stop, even if one asks ever so many times. It would be useful if they would tell."

Mrs. Peterkin thought this was carried too far in the horse-cars in Boston. The conductors had always left you as far as possible from the place where you wanted to stop; but it seemed a little too much to have the aldermen take it up, and put a notice in the cars, ordering the conductors "to stop at the farthest crossing."

Mrs. Peterkin was, indeed, recovering her spirits. She had been carrying on a brisk correspondence with Philadelphia, that she had imparted to no one, and at last she announced, as its result, that she was ready for a breakfast on educational principles.

A breakfast indeed, when it appeared! Mrs. Peterkin had mistaken the alphabetical suggestion, and had grasped the idea that the whole alphabet must be represented in one breakfast.

This, therefore, was the bill of fare: Apple-sauce, Bread, Butter, Coffee, Cream, Doughnuts, Eggs, Fish-balls, Griddles, Ham, Ice (on butter), Jam, Krout (sour), Lamb-chops, Morning Newspapers, Oatmeal, Pepper, Quince-marmalade, Rolls, Salt, Tea Urn, Veal-pie, Waffles, Yeast-biscuit.

Mr. Peterkin was proud and astonished. "Excellent!" he cried. "Every letter represented except Z." Mrs. Peterkin drew from her pocket a letter from the lady from Philadelphia. "She thought you would call it X-cellent for X, and she tells us," she read, "that if you come with a zest, you will bring the Z."

Mr. Peterkin was enchanted. He only felt that he ought to invite the children in the primary schools to such a breakfast; what a zest, indeed, it would give to the study of their letters!

It was decided to begin with Apple-sauce.

"How happy," exclaimed Mr. Peterkin, "that this should come first of all! A child might be brought up on apple-sauce till he had mastered the first letter of the alphabet, and could go on to the more involved subjects hidden in bread, butter, baked beans, etc."

Agamemnon thought his father hardly knew how much was hidden in the apple. There was all the story of William Tell and the Swiss independence. The little boys were wild to act William Tell, but Mrs. Peterkin was afraid of the arrows. Mrs. Peterkin proposed they should begin by eating the apple-sauce, then discussing it, first botanically, next historically; or perhaps first historically, beginning with Adam and Eve, and the first apple.

Mrs. Peterkin feared the coffee would be getting cold, and the griddles were waiting. For herself, she declared she felt more at home on the marmalade, because the quinces came from grandfather's, and she had seen them planted; she remembered all about it, and now the bush came up to the sitting-room window. She seemed to have heard him tell that the town of Quincy, where the granite came from, was named from them, and she never quite recollected why, except they were so hard, as hard as stone, and it took you almost the whole day to stew them, and then you might as well set them on again.

Mr. Peterkin was glad to be reminded of the old place at grandfather's. In order to know thoroughly about apples, they ought to understand the making of cider. Now, they might some time drive up to grandfather's, scarcely twelve miles away, and see the cider made. Why, indeed, should not the family go this very day up to grandfather's, and continue the education of the breakfast?

"Why not indeed?" exclaimed the little boys. A day at grandfather's would give them the whole process of the apple, from the orchard to the cider-mill. In this way they could widen the field of study, even to follow in time the cup of coffee to Java.

It was suggested, too, that at grandfather's they might study the processes of maple-syrup as involved in the griddle-cakes.

Agamemnon pointed out the connection between the two subjects: they were both the products of trees–the apple-tree and the maple. Mr. Peterkin proposed that the lesson for the day should be considered the study of trees, and on the way they could look at other trees.

Why not, indeed, go this very day? There was no time like the present. Their breakfast had been so copious, they would scarcely be in a hurry for dinner, and would, therefore, have the whole day before them.

Mrs. Peterkin could put up the remains of the breakfast for luncheon.

But how should they go? The carryall, in spite of its name, could hardly take the whole family, though they might squeeze in six, as the little boys did not take up much room.

Elizabeth Eliza suggested that she could spend the night at grandfather's. Indeed, she had been planning a visit there, and would not object to staying some days. This would make it easier about coming home, but it did not settle the difficulty in getting there.

Why not "Ride and Tie"?

The little boys were fond of walking; so was Mr. Peterkin; and Agamemnon and Solomon John did not object to their turn. Mrs. Peterkin could sit in the carriage, when it was waiting for the pedestrians to come up; or, she said, she did not object to a little turn of walking.

Mr. Peterkin would start, with Solomon John and the little boys, before the rest, and Agamemnon should drive his mother and Elizabeth Eliza to the first stopping-place.

Then came up another question,–of Elizabeth Eliza's trunk. If she stayed a few days, she would need to carry something. It might be hot, and it might be cold. Just as soon as she carried her thin things, she would need her heaviest wraps. You never could depend upon the weather. Even "Probabilities" got you no farther than to-day.

In an inspired moment, Elizabeth Eliza bethought herself of the expressman. She would send her trunk by the express, and she left the table directly to go and pack it. Mrs. Peterkin busied herself with Amanda over the remains of the breakfast. Mr. Peterkin and Agamemnon went to order the horse and the expressman, and Solomon John and the little boys prepared themselves for a pedestrian excursion.

Elizabeth Eliza found it difficult to pack in a hurry; there were so many things she might want, and then again she might not. She must put up her music, because her grandfather had a piano; and then she bethought herself of Agamemnon's flute, and decided to pick out a volume or two of the Encyclopædia. But it was hard to decide, all by herself, whether to take G for griddle-cakes, or M for maple-syrup, or T for tree. She would take as many as she could make room for. She put up her work-box and two extra work-baskets, and she must take some French books she had never yet found time to read. This involved taking her French dictionary, as she doubted if her grandfather had one. She ought to put in a "Botany," if they were to study trees; but she could not tell which, so she would take all there were. She might as well take all her dresses, and it was no harm if one had too many wraps. When she had her trunk packed, she found it over-full; it was difficult to shut it. She had heard Solomon John set out from the front door with his father and the little boys, and Agamemnon was busy holding the horse at the side door, so there was no use in calling for help. She got upon the trunk; she jumped upon it; she sat down upon it, and, leaning over, found she could lock it! Yes, it was really locked.

But, on getting down from the trunk, she found her dress had been caught in the lid; she could not move away from it! What was worse, she was so fastened to the trunk that she could not lean forward far enough to turn the key back, to unlock the trunk and release herself! The lock had slipped easily, but she could not now get hold of the key in the right way to turn it back.

She tried to pull her dress away. No, it was caught too firmly. She called for help to her mother or Amanda, to come and open the trunk. But her door was shut. Nobody near enough to hear! She tried to pull the trunk toward the door, to open it and make herself heard; but it was so heavy that, in her constrained position, she could not stir it. In her agony, she would have been willing to have torn her dress; but it was her travelling-dress, and too stout to tear. She might cut it carefully. Alas, she had packed her scissors, and her knife she had lent to the little boys the day before! She called again. What silence there was in the house! Her voice seemed to echo through the room. At length, as she listened, she heard the sound of wheels.

Was it the carriage, rolling away from the side door? Did she hear the front door shut? She remembered then that Amanda was to "have the day." But she, Elizabeth Eliza, was to have spoken to Amanda, to explain to her to wait for the expressman. She was to have told her as she went downstairs. But she had not been able to go downstairs! And Amanda must have supposed that all the family had left, and she, too, must have gone, knowing of the expressman. Yes, she heard the wheels! She heard the front door shut!

But could they have gone without her? Then she recalled that she had proposed walking on a little way with Solomon John and her father, to be picked up by Mrs. Peterkin, if she should have finished her packing in time. Her mother must have supposed that she had done so,—that she had spoken to Amanda, and started with the rest. Well, she would soon discover her mistake. She would overtake the walking party, and, not finding Elizabeth Eliza, would return for her. Patience only was needed. She had looked around for something to read; but she had packed up all her books. She had packed her knitting. How quiet and still it was! She tried to imagine where her mother would meet the rest of the family. They were good walkers, and they might have reached the two-mile bridge. But suppose they should stop for water beneath the arch of the bridge, as they often did, and the carryall pass over it without seeing them, her mother would not know but she was with them? And suppose her mother should decide to leave the horse at the place proposed for stopping and waiting for the first pedestrian party, and herself walk on, no one would be left to tell the rest, when they should come up to the carryall. They might go on so, through the whole journey, without meeting, and she might not be missed till they should reach her grandfather's!

Horrible thought! She would be left here alone all day. The expressman would come, but the expressman would go, for he would not be able to get into the house!

She thought of the terrible story of Ginevra, of the bride who was shut up in her trunk, and forever! She was shut up on hers, and knew not when she should be released! She had acted once in the ballad of the "Mistletoe Bough." She had been one of the "guests," who had sung "Oh, the Mistletoe Bough," and had looked up at it, and she had seen at the side-scenes how the bride had laughingly stepped into the trunk. But the trunk then was only a make-believe of some boards in front of a sofa, and this was a stern reality.

It would be late now before her family would reach her grandfather's. Perhaps they would decide to spend the night. Perhaps they would fancy she was coming by express. She gave another tremendous effort to move the trunk toward the door. In vain. All was still.

Meanwhile, Mrs. Peterkin sat some time at the door, wondering why Elizabeth Eliza did not come down. Mr. Peterkin had started on with Solomon John and all the little boys.

Agamemnon had packed the things into the carriage,–a basket of lunch, a change of shoes for Mr. Peterkin, some extra wraps,–everything Mrs. Peterkin could think of, for the family comfort. Still Elizabeth Eliza did not come. "I think she must have walked on with your father," she said, at last; "you had better get in." Agamemnon now got in. "I should think she would have mentioned it," she continued; "but we may as well start on, and pick her up!" They started off. "I hope Elizabeth Eliza thought to speak to Amanda, but we must ask her when we come up with her."

But they did not come up with Elizabeth Eliza. At the turn beyond the village, they found an envelope struck up in an inviting manner against a tree. In this way, they had agreed to leave missives for each other as they passed on. This note informed them that the walking party was going to take the short cut across the meadows, and would still be in front of them. They saw the party at last, just beyond the short cut; but Mr. Peterkin was explaining the character of the oak-tree to his children as they stood around a large specimen.

"I suppose he is telling them that it is some kind of a 'Quercus,'" said Agamemnon, thoughtfully.

Mrs. Peterkin thought Mr. Peterkin would scarcely use such an expression, but she could see nothing of Elizabeth Eliza. Some of the party, however, were behind the tree, some were in front, and Elizabeth Eliza might be behind the tree. They were too far off to be shouted at. Mrs. Peterkin was calmed, and went on to the stopping-lace agreed upon, which they reached before long. This had been appointed near Farmer Gordon's barn, that there might be somebody at hand whom they knew, in case there should be any difficulty in untying the horse. The plan had been that Mrs. Peterkin should always sit in the carriage, while the others should take turns for walking; and Agamemnon tied the horse to a fence, and left her comfortably arranged with her knitting. Indeed, she had risen so early to prepare for the alphabetical breakfast, and had since been so tired with preparations, that she was quite sleepy, and would not object to a nap in the shade, by the soothing sound of the buzzing of the flies. But she called Agamemnon back, as he started off for his solitary walk, with a perplexing question:

"Suppose the rest all should arrive, how could they now be accommodated in the carryall? It would be too much for the horse! Why had Elizabeth Eliza gone with the rest without counting up? Of course, they must have expected that she–Mrs. Peterkin–would walk on to the next stopping-place!"

She decided there was no way but for her to walk on. When the rest passed her, they might make a change. So she put up knitting cheerfully. It was a little joggly in the carriage, she had already found, for the horse was restless from the flies, and she did not like being left alone.

She walked on then with Agamemnon. It was very pleasant at first, but the sun became hot, and it was not long before she was fatigued. When they reached a hay-field, she proposed going in to rest upon one of the hay-cocks. The largest and most shady was at the other end of the field, and they were seated there when the carryall passed them in the road. Mrs. Peterkin waved parasol and hat, and the party in the carryall returned their greetings, but they were too far apart to hear each other.

Mrs. Peterkin and Agamemnon slowly resumed their walk.

"Well, we shall find Elizabeth Eliza in the carryall," she said, "and that will explain all."

But it took them an hour or two to reach the carryall, with frequent stoppings for rest, and when they reached it, no one was in it. A note was pinned up in the vehicle to say they had all walked on; it was "prime fun."

In this way the parties continued to dodge each other, for Mrs. Peterkin felt that she must walk on from the next station, and the carryall missed her again while she and Agamemnon stopped in a house to rest, and for a glass of water. She reached the carryall to find again that no one was in it. The party had passed on for the last station, where it had been decided all should meet at the foot of grandfather's hill, that they might all arrive at the house together. Mrs. Peterkin and Agamemnon looked out eagerly for the party all the way, as Elizabeth Eliza must be tired by this time; but Mrs. Peterkin's last walk had been so slow, that the other party was far in advance and reached the stopping-place before them. The little boys were all rowed out on the stone fence, awaiting them, full of delight at having reached grandfather's. Mr. Peterkin came forward to meet them, and, at the same moment with Mrs. Peterkin, exclaimed: "Where is Elizabeth Eliza?" Each party looked eagerly at the other; no Elizabeth Eliza was to be seen. Where was she? What was to be done? Was she left behind? Mrs. Peterkin was convinced she must have somehow got to grandfather's. They hurried up the hill. Grandfather and all the family came out to greet them, for they had been seen approaching. There was great questioning, but no Elizabeth Eliza!

It was sunset; the view was wide and fine. Mr. and Mrs. Peterkin stood and looked out from the north to the south. Was it too late to send back for Elizabeth Eliza? Where was she?

Meanwhile the little boys had been informing the family of the object of their visit, and while Mr. and Mrs. Peterkin were looking up and down the road, and Agamemnon and Solomon John were explaining to each other the details of their journeys, they had discovered some facts.

"We shall have to go back," they exclaimed. "We are too late! The maple-syrup was all made last spring."

"We are too early; we shall have to stay two or three months,–the cider is not made till October."

The expedition was a failure! They could study the making of neither maple-syrup nor cider, and Elizabeth Eliza was lost, perhaps forever! The sun went down, and Mr. and Mrs. Peterkin still stood to look up and down the road.

*   *   *   *   *   *

Elizabeth Eliza meanwhile, had sat upon her trunk, as it seemed for ages. She recalled all the terrible stories of prisoners,–how they had watched the growth of flowers through cracks in the pavement. She wondered how long she could live without eating. How thankful she was for her abundant breakfast!

At length she heard the door-bell. But who could go to the door to answer it? In vain did she make another effort to escape; it was impossible!

How singular!–there were footsteps. Some one was going to the door; some one had opened it. "They must be burglars." Well, perhaps that was a better fate–to be gagged by burglars, and the neighbors informed–than to be forever locked on her trunk. The steps approached the door. It opened, and Amanda ushered in the expressman.

Amanda had not gone. She had gathered, while waiting at the breakfast-table, that there was to be an expressman whom she must receive.

Elizabeth Eliza explained the situation. The expressman turned the key of her trunk, and she was released!

What should she do next? So long a time had elapsed, she had given up all hope of her family returning for her. But how could she reach them?

She hastily prevailed upon the expressman to take her along until she should come up with some of the family. At least she would fall in with either the walking party or the carryall, or she would meet them if they were on their return.

She mounted the seat with the expressman, and slowly they took their way, stopping for occasional parcels as they left the village.

But much to Elizabeth Eliza's dismay, they turned off from the main road on leaving the village. She remonstrated, but the driver insisted he must go round by Millikin's to leave a bedstead. They went round by Millikin's, and then had further turns to make. Elizabeth Eliza explained that in this way it would be impossible for her to find her parents and family, and at last he proposed to take her all the way with her trunk. She remembered with a shudder that when she had first asked about her trunk, he had promised it should certainly be delivered the next morning. Suppose they should have to be out all night? Where did express-carts spend the night? She thought of herself in a lone wood, in an express-wagon! She could hardly bring herself to ask, before assenting, when he should arrive.

"He guessed he could bring up before night."

And so it happened that as Mr. and Mrs. Peterkin in the late sunset were looking down the hill, wondering what they should do about the lost Elizabeth Eliza, they saw an express wagon approaching. A female form sat upon the front seat.

"She has decided to come by express," said Mrs. Peterkin. "It is–it is–Elizabeth Eliza!"

Day 179

1. Read *The Peterkin Papers*, chapter 21
2. Tell someone about the story.

THE PETERKINS AT THE "CARNIVAL OF AUTHORS" IN BOSTON.

THE Peterkins were in quite a muddle (for them) about the carnival of authors, to be given in Boston. As soon as it was announced, their interests were excited, and they determined that all the family should go.

But they conceived a wrong idea of the entertainment, as they supposed that every one must go in costume. Elizabeth Eliza thought their lessons in the foreign languages would help them much in conversing in character.

As the carnival was announced early Solomon John thought there would be time to read up everything written by all the authors, in order to be acquainted with the characters they introduced. Mrs. Peterkin did not wish to begin too early upon the reading, for she was sure she should forget all that the different authors had written before the day came.

But Elizabeth Eliza declared that she should hardly have time enough, as it was, to be acquainted with all the authors. She had given up her French lessons, after taking six, for want of time, and had, indeed, concluded she had learned in them all she should need to know of that language. She could repeat one or two pages of phrases, and she was astonished to find how much she could understand already of what the French teacher said to her; and he assured her that when she went to Paris she could at least ask the price of gloves, or of some other things she would need, and he taught her, too, how to pronounce "garçon," in calling for more.

Agamemnon thought that different members of the family might make themselves familiar with different authors; the little boys were already acquainted with "Mother Goose." Mr. Peterkin had read the "Pickwick Papers," and Solomon John had actually seen Mr. Longfellow getting into a horse-car.

Elizabeth Eliza suggested that they might ask the Turk to give lectures upon the "Arabian Nights." Everybody else was planning something of the sort, to "raise funds" for some purpose, and she was sure they ought not to be behindhand. Mrs. Peterkin approved of this. It would be excellent if they could raise funds enough to pay for their own tickets to the carnival; then they could go every night.

Elizabeth Eliza was uncertain. She thought it was usual to use the funds for some object. Mr. Peterkin said that if they gained funds enough they might arrange a booth of their own, and sit in it, and take the carnival comfortably. But Agamemnon reminded him that none of the family were authors, and only authors had booths. Solomon John, indeed, had once started upon writing a book, but he was not able to think of anything to put in it, and nothing had occurred to him yet.

Mr. Peterkin urged him to make one more effort. If his book could come out before the carnival he could go as an author, and might have a booth of his own, and take his family.

But Agamemnon declared it would take years to become an author. You might indeed publish something, but you had to make sure that it would be read. Mrs. Peterkin, on the other hand, was certain that libraries were filled with books that never were read, yet authors had written them. For herself, she had not read half the books in their own library. And she was glad there was to be a Carnival of Authors, that she might know who they were.

Mr. Peterkin did not understand why they called them a "Carnival"; but he supposed they should find out when they went to it.

Mrs. Peterkin still felt uncertain about costumes. She proposed looking over the old trunks in the garret. They would find some suitable dresses there, and these would suggest what characters they should take. Elizabeth Eliza was pleased with this thought. She remembered an old turban of white mull muslin, in an old bandbox, and why should not her mother wear it?

Mrs. Peterkin supposed that she should then go as her own grandmother.

Agamemnon did not approve of this. Turbans are now worn in the East, and Mrs. Peterkin could go in some Eastern character. Solomon John thought she might be Cleopatra, and this was determined on. Among the treasures found were some old bonnets, of large size, with waving plumes. Elizabeth Eliza decided upon the largest of these.

She was tempted to appear as Mrs. Columbus, as Solomon John was to take the character of Christopher Columbus; but he was planning to enter upon the stage in a boat, and Elizabeth Eliza was a little afraid of sea-sickness, as he had arranged to be a great while finding the shore.

Solomon John had been led to take this character by discovering a coal-hod that would answer for a helmet; then, as Christopher Columbus was born in Genoa, he could use the phrases in Italian he had lately learned of his teacher.

As the day approached the family had their costumes prepared.

Mr. Peterkin decided to be Peter the Great. It seemed to him a happy thought, for the few words of Russian he had learned would come in play, and he was quite sure that his own family name made him kin to that of the great Czar. He studied up the life in the Encyclopædia, and decided to take the costume of a ship-builder. He visited the navy-yard and some of the docks; but none of them gave him the true idea of dress for ship-building in Holland or St. Petersburg. But he found a picture of Peter the Great, representing him in a broad-brimmed hat. So he assumed one that he found at a costumer's, and with Elizabeth Eliza's black waterproof was satisfied with his own appearance.

Elizabeth Eliza wondered if she could not go with her father in some Russian character. She would have to lay aside her large bonnet, but she had seen pictures of Russian ladies, with fur muffs on their heads, and she might wear her own muff.

Mrs. Peterkin, as Cleopatra, wore the turban, with a little row of false curls in front, and a white embroidered muslin shawl crossed over her black silk dress. The little boys thought she looked much like the picture of their great-grandmother. But doubtless Cleopatra resembled this picture, as it was all so long ago, so the rest of the family decided.

Agamemnon determined to go as Noah. The costume, as represented in one of the little boys' arks, was simple. His father's red-lined dressing gown, turned inside out, permitted it easily.

Elizabeth Eliza was now anxious to be Mrs. Shem, and make a long dress of yellow flannel, and appear with Agamemnon and the little boys. For the little boys were to represent two doves and a raven. There were feather-dusters enough in the family for their costumes, which would be then complete with their india-rubber boots.

Solomon John carried out in detail his idea of Christopher Columbus. He had a number of eggs boiled hard to take in his pocket, proposing to repeat, through the evening, the scene of setting the egg on its end. He gave up the plan of a boat, as it must be difficult to carry one into town; so he contented himself by practising the motion of landing by stepping up on a chair.

But what scene could Elizabeth Eliza carry out? If they had an ark, as Mrs. Shem she might crawl in and out of the roof constantly, if it were not too high. But Mr. Peterkin thought it as difficult to take an ark into town as Solomon John's boat.

The evening came. But with all their preparations they got to the hall late. The entrance was filled with a crowd of people, and, as they stopped at the cloakroom, to leave their wraps, they found themselves entangled with a number of people in costume coming out from a dressing-room below. Mr. Peterkin was much encouraged. They were thus joining the performers. The band was playing the "Wedding March" as they went upstairs to a door of the hall which opened upon one side of the stage. Here a procession was marching up the steps of the stage, all in costume, and entering behind the scenes.

"We are just in the right time," whispered Mr. Peterkin to his family; "they are going upon the stage; we must fall into line." The little boys had their feather-dusters ready. Some words from one of the managers made Peterkin understand the situation.

"We are going to be introduced to Mr. Dickens," he said.

"I thought he was dead!" exclaimed Mrs. Peterkin trembling.

"Authors live forever!" said Agamemnon in her ear.

At this moment they were ushered upon the stage. The stage manager glared at them, as he awaited their names for introduction, while they came up all unannounced,–a part of the programme not expected. But he uttered the words upon his lips, "Great Expectations;" and the Peterkin family swept across the stage with the rest: Mr. Peterkin costumed as Peter the Great, Mrs. Peterkin as Cleopatra, Agamemnon as Noah, Solomon John as Christopher Columbus, Elizabeth Eliza in yellow flannel as Mrs. Shem, with a large, old-fashioned bonnet on her head as Mrs. Columbus, and the little boys behind as two doves and a raven.

Across the stage, in face of all the assembled people, then following the rest down the stairs on the other side, in among the audience, they went; but into an audience not dressed in costume!

There were Ann Maria Bromwick and the Osbornes,–all the neighbors,–all as natural as though they were walking the streets at home, though Ann Maria did wear white gloves.

"I had no idea you were to appear in character," said Ann Maria to Elizabeth Eliza; "to what booth do you belong?"

"We are no particular author," said Mr. Peterkin.

"Ah, I see, a sort of varieties' booth," said Mr. Osborne.

"What is your character?" asked Ann Maria of Elizabeth Eliza.

"I have not quite decided," said Elizabeth Eliza. "I thought I should find out after I came here. The marshal called us 'Great Expectations.'"

Mrs. Peterkin was at the summit of bliss. "I have shaken hands with Dickens!" she exclaimed.

But she looked round to ask the little boys if they, too, had shaken hands with the great man, but not a little boy could she find.

They had been swept off in Mother Goose's train, which had lingered on the steps to see the Dickens reception, with which the procession of characters in costume had closed. At this moment they were dancing round the barberry bush, in a corner of the balcony in Mother Goose's quarters, their feather-dusters gayly waving in the air.

But Mrs. Peterkin, far below, could not see this, and consoled herself with the thought, they should all meet on the stage in the grand closing tableau. She was bewildered by the crowds which swept her hither and thither. At last she found herself in the Whittier Booth, and sat a long time calmly there. As Cleopatra she seemed out of place, but as her own grandmother she answered well with its New England scenery.

Solomon John wandered about, landing in America whenever he found a chance to enter a booth. Once before an admiring audience he set up his egg in the centre of the Goethe Booth, which had been deserted by its committee for the larger stage.

Agamemnon frequently stood in the background of scenes in the Arabian Nights.

It was with difficulty that the family could be repressed from going on the stage whenever the bugle sounded for the different groups represented there.

Elizabeth Eliza came near appearing in the "Dream of Fair Women," at its most culminating point.

Mr. Peterkin found himself with the "Cricket on the Hearth," in the Dickens Booth. He explained that he was Peter the Great, but always in the Russian language, which was never understood.

Elizabeth Eliza found herself, in turn, in all the booths. Every manager was puzzled by her appearance, and would send her to some other, and she passed along, always trying to explain that she had not yet decided upon her character.

Mr. Peterkin came and took Cleopatra from the Whittier Booth.

"I cannot understand," he said, "why none of our friends are dressed in costume, and why we are."

"I rather like it," said Elizabeth Eliza, "though I should be better pleased if I could form a group with some one."

The strains of the minuet began. Mrs. Peterkin was anxious to join the performers. It was the dance of her youth.

But she was delayed by one of the managers on the steps that led to the stage.

"I cannot understand this company," he said, distractedly.

"They cannot find their booth," said another.

"That is the case," said Mr. Peterkin, relieved to have it stated.

"Perhaps you had better pass into the corridor," said a polite marshal.

They did this, and, walking across, found themselves in the refreshment-room. "This is the booth for us," said Mr. Peterkin.

"Indeed it is," said Mrs. Peterkin, sinking into a chair, exhausted.

At this moment two doves and a raven appeared,–the little boys, who had been dancing eagerly in Mother Goose's establishment, and now came down for ice-cream.

"I hardly know how to sit down," said Elizabeth Eliza, "for I am sure Mrs. Shem never could. Still, as I do not know if I am Mrs. Shem, I will venture it."

Happily, seats were to be found for all, and they were soon arranged in a row, calmly eating ice-cream.

"I think the truth is," said Mr. Peterkin, "that we represent historical people, and we ought to have been fictitious characters in books. That is, I observe, what the others are. We shall know better another time."

"If we only ever get home," said Mrs. Peterkin, "I shall not wish to come again. It seems like being on the stage, sitting in a booth, and it is so bewildering, Elizabeth Eliza not knowing who she is, and going round and round in this way."

"I am afraid we shall never reach home," said Agamemnon, who had been silent for some time; "we may have to spend the night here. I find I have lost our checks for our clothes in the cloak-room!"

"Spend the night in a booth, in Cleopatra's turban!" exclaimed Mrs. Peterkin.

"We should like to come every night," cried the little boys.

"But to spend the night," repeated Mrs. Peterkin.

"I conclude the Carnival keeps up all night," said Mr. Peterkin.

"But never to recover our cloaks," said Mrs. Peterkin; "could not the little boys look round for the checks on the floors?"

She began to enumerate the many valuable things that they might never see again. She had worn her large fur cape of stone-marten,–her grandmother's,–that Elizabeth Eliza had been urging her to have made into a foot-rug. Now how she wished she had! And there were Mr. Peterkin's new overshoes, and Agamemnon had brought an umbrella, and the little boys had their mittens. Their india-rubber boots, fortunately, they had on, in the character of birds. But Solomon John had worn a fur cap, and Elizabeth Eliza a muff. Should they lose all these valuables entirely, and go home in the cold without them? No, it would be better to wait till everybody had gone, and then look carefully over the floors for the checks; if only the little boys could know where Agamemnon had been, they were willing to look. Mr. Peterkin was not sure as they would have time to reach the train. Still, they would need something to wear, and he could not tell the time. He had not brought his watch. It was a Waltham watch, and he thought it would not be in character for Peter the Great to wear it.

At this moment the strains of "Home, Sweet Home" were heard from the band, and people were seen preparing to go.

"All can go home, but we must stay," said Mrs. Peterkin, gloomily, as the well-known strains floated in from the larger hall.

A number of marshals came to the refreshment-room, looked at them, whispered to each other, as the Peterkins sat in a row.

"Can we do anything for you?" asked one at last. "Would you not like to go?" He seemed eager they should leave the room.

Mr. Peterkin explained that they could not go, as they had lost the checks for their wraps, and hoped to find their checks on the floor when everybody was gone. The marshal asked if they could not describe what they had worn, in which case the loss of the checks was not so important, as the crowds had now almost left, and it would not be difficult to identify their wraps. Mrs. Peterkin eagerly declared she could describe every article.

It was astonishing how the marshals hurried them through the quickly deserted corridors, how gladly they recovered their garments! Mrs. Peterkin, indeed, was disturbed by the eagerness of the marshals; she feared they had some pretext for getting the family out of the hall. Mrs. Peterkin was one of those who never consent to be forced to anything. She would not be compelled to go home, even with strains of music. She whispered her suspicions to Mr. Peterkin; but Agamemnon came hastily up to announce the time, which he had learned from the clock in the large hall. They must leave directly if they wished to catch the latest train, as there was barely time to reach it.

Then, indeed, was Mrs. Peterkin ready to leave. If they should miss the train! If she should have to pass the night in the streets in her turban! She was the first to lead the way, and, panting, the family followed her, just in time to take the train as it was leaving the station.

The excitement was not yet over. They found in the train many of their friends and neighbors, returning also from the Carnival; so they had many questions put to them which they were unable to answer. Still Mrs. Peterkin's turban was much admired, and indeed the whole appearance of the family; so that they felt themselves much repaid for their exertions.

But more adventures awaited them. They left the train with their friends; but as Mrs. Peterkin and Elizabeth Eliza were very tired, they walked very slowly, and Solomon John and the little boys were sent on with the pass-key to open the door. They soon returned with the startling intelligence that it was not the right key, and they could not get in. It was Mr. Peterkin's office-key; he had taken it by mistake, or he might have dropped the house-key in the cloak-room of the Carnival.

"Must we go back?" sighed Mrs. Peterkin, in an exhausted voice. More than ever did Elizabeth Eliza regret that Agamemnon's invention in keys had failed to secure a patent!

It was impossible to get into the house, for Amanda had been allowed to go and spend the night with a friend, so there was no use in ringing, though the little boys had tried it.

"We can return to the station," said Mr. Peterkin; "the rooms will be warm, on account of the midnight train. We can, at least, think what we shall do next."

At the station was one of their neighbors, proposing to take the New York midnight train, for it was now after eleven, and the train went through at half-past.

"I saw lights at the locksmith's over the way, as I passed," he said; "why do not you send over to the young man there? He can get your door open for you. I never would spend the night here."

Solomon John went over to "the young man," who agreed to go up to the house as soon as he had closed the shop, fit a key, and open the door, and come back to them on his way home. Solomon John came back to the station, for it was now cold and windy in the deserted streets. The family made themselves as comfortable as possible by the stove, sending Solomon John out occasionally to look for the young man. But somehow Solomon John missed him; the lights were out in the locksmith's shop, so he followed along to the house, hoping to find him there. But he was not there! He came back to report. Perhaps the young man had opened the door and gone on home. Solomon John and Agamemnon went back together, but they could not get in. Where was the young man? He had lately come to town, and nobody knew where he lived, for on the return of Solomon John and Agamemnon it had been proposed to go to the house of the young man. The night was wearing on. The midnight train had come and gone. The passengers who came and went looked with wonder at Mrs. Peterkin, nodding in her turban, as she sat by the stove, on a corner of a long bench. At last the station-master had to leave, for a short rest. He felt obliged to lock up the station, but he promised to return at an early hour to release them.

"Of what use," said Elizabeth Eliza, "if we cannot even then get into our own house?"

Mr. Peterkin thought the matter appeared bad, if the locksmith had left town. He feared the young man might have gone in, and helped himself to spoons, and left. Only they should have seen him if he had taken the midnight train. Solomon John thought he appeared honest. Mr. Peterkin only ventured to whisper his suspicions, as he did not wish to arouse Mrs. Peterkin, who still was nodding in the corner of the long bench.

Morning did come at last. The family decided to go to their home; perhaps by some effort in the early daylight they might make an entrance.

On the way they met with the night-policeman, returning from his beat. He stopped when he saw the family.

"Ah! that accounts," he said; "you were all out last night, and the burglars took occasion to make a raid on your house. I caught a lively young man in the very act; box of tools in his hand! If I had been a minute late he would have made his way in"–

The family then tried to interrupt–to explain–

"Where is he?" exclaimed Mr. Peterkin.

"Safe in the lock-up," answered the policeman.

"But he is the locksmith!" interrupted Solomon John.

"We have no key!" said Elizabeth Eliza; "if you have locked up the locksmith we can never get in."

The policeman looked from one to the other, smiling slightly when he understood the case.

"The locksmith!" he exclaimed; "he is a new fellow, and I did not recognize him, and arrested him! Very well, I will go and let him out, that he may let you in!" and he hurried away, surprising the Peterkin family with what seemed like insulting screams of laughter.

"It seems to me a more serious case than it appears to him," said Mr. Peterkin.

Mrs. Peterkin did not understand it at all. Had burglars entered the house? Did the policeman say they had taken spoons? And why did he appear so pleased? She was sure the old silver teapot was locked up in the closet of their room. Slowly the family walked towards the house, and, almost as soon as they, the policeman appeared with the released locksmith, and a few boys from the street, who happened to be out early.

The locksmith was not in very good humor, and took ill the jokes of the policeman. Mr. Peterkin, fearing he might not consent to open the door, pressed into his hand a large sum of money. The door flew open; the family could go in. Amanda arrived at the same moment. There was hope of breakfast. Mrs. Peterkin staggered towards the stairs. "I shall never go to another carnival!" she exclaimed.

Day 180

1.   Read *The Peterkin Papers*, chapter 22.
2.   Tell someone about the story.

THE PETERKINS AT THE FARM.

YES, at last they had reached the seaside, after much talking and deliberation, and summer after summer the journey had been constantly postponed.

But here they were at last, at the "Old Farm," so called, where seaside attractions had been praised in all the advertisements. And here they were to meet the Sylvesters, who knew all about the place, cousins of Ann Maria Bromwick. Elizabeth Eliza was astonished not to find them there, though she had not expected Ann Maria to join them till the very next day.

Their preparations had been so elaborate that at one time the whole thing had seemed hopeless; yet here they all were. Their trunks, to be sure, had not arrived; but the wagon was to be sent back for them, and, wonderful to tell, they had all their hand-baggage safe.

Agamemnon had brought his Portable Electrical Machine and Apparatus, and the volumes of the Encyclopædia that might tell him how to manage it, and Solomon John had his photograph camera. The little boys had used their india-rubber boots as portmanteaux, filling them to the brim, and carrying one in each hand,–a very convenient way for travelling they considered it; but they found on arriving (when they wanted to put their boots directly on for exploration round the house), that it was somewhat inconvenient to have to begin to unpack directly, and scarcely room enough could be found for all the contents in the small chamber allotted to them.

There was no room in the house for the electrical machine and camera. Elizabeth Eliza thought the other boarders were afraid of the machine going off; so an out-house was found for them, where Agamemnon and Solomon John could arrange them.

Mrs. Peterkin was much pleased with the old-fashioned porch and low-studded rooms, though the sleeping-rooms seemed a little stuffy at first.

Mr. Peterkin was delighted with the admirable order in which the farm was evidently kept. From the first moment he arrived he gave himself to examining the well-stocked stables and barns, and the fields and vegetable gardens, which were shown to him by a highly intelligent person, a Mr. Atwood, who devoted himself to explaining to Mr. Peterkin all the details of methods in the farming.

The rest of the family were disturbed at being so far from the sea, when they found it would take nearly all the afternoon to reach the beach. The advertisements had surely stated that the "Old Farm" was directly on the shore, and that sea-bathing would be exceedingly convenient; which was hardly the case if it took you an hour and a half to walk to it.

Mr. Peterkin declared there were always such discrepancies between the advertisements of seaside places and the actual facts; but he was more than satisfied with the farm part, and was glad to remain and admire it, while the rest of the family went to find the beach, starting off in a wagon large enough to accommodate them, Agamemnon driving the one horse.

Solomon John had depended upon taking the photographs of the family in a row on the beach; but he decided not to take his camera out the first afternoon.

This was well, as the sun was already setting when they reached the beach.

"If this wagon were not so shaky," said Mrs. Peterkin "we might drive over every morning for our bath. The road is very straight, and I suppose Agamemnon can turn on the beach."

"We should have to spend the whole day about it," said Solomon John, in a discouraged tone, "unless we can have a quicker horse."

"Perhaps we should prefer that," said Elizabeth Eliza, a little gloomily, "to staying at the house."

She had been a little disturbed to find there were not more elegant and fashionable-looking boarders at the farm, and she was disappointed that the Sylvesters had not arrived, who would understand the ways of the place. Yet, again, she was somewhat relieved, for if their trunks did not come till the next day, as was feared, she should have nothing but her travelling dress to wear, which would certainly answer for to-night.

She had been busy all the early summer in preparing her dresses for this very watering-place, and, as far as appeared, she would hardly need them, and was disappointed to have no chance to display them. But of course, when the Sylvesters and Ann Maria came, all would be different; but they would surely be wasted on the two old ladies she had seen, and on the old men who had lounged about the porch; there surely was not a gentleman among them.

Agamemnon assured her she could not tell at the seaside, as gentlemen wore their exercise dress, and took a pride in going around in shocking hats and flannel suits. Doubtless they would be dressed for dinner on their return.

On their arrival they had been shown to a room to have their meals by themselves, and could not decide whether they were eating dinner or lunch. There was a variety of meat, vegetables, and pie, that might come under either name; but Mr. and Mrs. Peterkin were well pleased.

"I had no idea we should have really farm-fare," Mrs. Peterkin said. "I have not drunk such a tumbler of milk since I was young."

Elizabeth Eliza concluded they ought not to judge from a first meal, as evidently their arrival had not been fully prepared for, in spite of the numerous letters that had been exchanged.

The little boys were, however, perfectly satisfied from the moment of their arrival, and one of them had stayed at the farm, declining to go to the beach, as he wished to admire the pigs, cows, and horses; and all the way over to the beach the other little boys were hopping in and out of the wagon, which never went too fast, to pick long mullein-stalks, for whips to urge on the reluctant horse with, or to gather huckleberries, with which they were rejoiced to find the fields were filled, although, as yet, the berries were very green.

They wanted to stay longer on the beach, when they finally reached it; but Mrs. Peterkin and Elizabeth Eliza insisted upon turning directly back, as it was not fair to be late to dinner the very first night.

On the whole the party came back cheerful, yet hungry. They found the same old men, in the same costume, standing against the porch.

"A little seedy, I should say," said Solomon John.

"Smoking pipes," said Agamemnon; "I believe that is the latest style."

"The smell of their tobacco is not very agreeable," Mrs. Peterkin was forced to say.

There seemed the same uncertainty on their arrival as to where they were to be put, and as to their meals.

Elizabeth Eliza tried to get into conversation with the old ladies, who were wandering in and out of a small sitting-room. But one of them was very deaf, and the other seemed to be a foreigner. She discovered from a moderately tidy maid, by the name of Martha, who seemed a sort of factotum, that there were other ladies in their rooms, too much of invalids to appear.

"Regular bed-ridden," Martha had described them, which Elizabeth Eliza did not consider respectful.

Mr. Peterkin appeared coming down the slope of the hill behind the house, very cheerful. He had made the tour of the farm, and found it in admirable order.

Elizabeth Eliza felt it time to ask Martha about the next meal, and ventured to call it supper, as a sort of compromise between dinner and tea. If dinner were expected she might offend by taking it for granted that it was to be "tea," and if they were unused to a late dinner they might be disturbed if they had only provided a "tea."

So she asked what was the usual hour for supper, and was surprised when Martha replied, "The lady must say," nodding to Mrs. Peterkin. "She can have it just when she wants, and just what she wants!"

This was an unexpected courtesy.

Elizabeth Eliza asked when the others had their supper.

"Oh, they took it a long time ago," Martha answered. "If the lady will go out into the kitchen she can tell what she wants."

"Bring us in what you have," said Mr. Peterkin, himself quite hungry. "If you could cook us a fresh slice of beefsteak that would be well."

"Perhaps some eggs," murmured Mrs. Peterkin.

"Scrambled," cried one of the little boys.

"Fried potatoes would not be bad," suggested Agamemnon.

"Couldn't we have some onions?" asked the little boy who had stayed at home, and had noticed the odor of onions when the others had their supper.

"A pie would come in well," said Solomon John.

"And some stewed cherries," said the other little boy.

Martha fell to laying the table, and the family was much pleased, when, in the course of time, all the dishes they had recommended appeared. Their appetites were admirable, and they pronounced the food the same.

"This is true Arab hospitality," said Mr. Peterkin, as he cut his juicy beefsteak.

"I know it," said Elizabeth Eliza, whose spirits began to rise. "We have not even seen the host and hostess."

She would, indeed, have been glad to find some one to tell her when the Sylvesters were expected, and why they had not arrived. Her room was in the wing, far from that of Mr. and Mrs. Peterkin, and near the aged deaf and foreign ladies, and she was kept awake for some time by perplexed thoughts.

She was sure the lady from Philadelphia, under such circumstances, would have written to somebody. But ought she to write to Ann Maria or the Sylvesters? And, if she did write, which had she better write to? She fully determined to write, the first thing in the morning, to both parties. But how should she address her letters? Would there be any use in sending to the Sylvesters' usual address, which she knew well by this time, merely to say they had not come? Of course the Sylvesters would know they had not come. It would be the same with Ann Maria. She might, indeed, inclose her letters to their several postmasters. Postmasters were always so obliging, and always knew where people were going to, and where to send their letters. She might, at least, write two letters, to say that they–the Peterkins–had arrived, and were disappointed not to find the Sylvesters. And she could add that their trunks had not arrived, and perhaps their friends might look out for them on their way. It really seemed a good plan to write. Yet another question came up, as to how she would get her letters to the post-office, as she had already learned it was at quite a distance, and in a different direction from the station, where they were to send the next day for their trunks.

She went over and over these same questions, kept awake by the coughing and talking of her neighbors, the other side of the thin partition.

She was scarcely sorry to be aroused from her uncomfortable sleep by the morning sounds of guinea-hens, peacocks, and every other kind of fowl.

Mrs. Peterkin expressed her satisfaction at the early breakfast, and declared she was delighted with such genuine farm sounds.

They passed the day much as the afternoon before, reaching the beach only in time to turn round to come back for their dinner, which was appointed at noon. Mrs. Peterkin was quite satisfied. "Such a straight road, and the beach such a safe place to turn round upon!"

Elizabeth Eliza was not so well pleased. A wagon had been sent to the station for their trunks, which could not be found; they were probably left at the Boston station, or, Mr. Atwood suggested, might have been switched off upon one of the White Mountain trains. There was no use to write any letters, as there was no way to send them. Elizabeth Eliza now almost hoped the Sylvesters would not come, for what should she do if the trunks did not come and all her new dresses? On her way over to the beach she had been thinking what she should do with her new foulard and cream-colored surah if the Sylvesters did not come, and if their time was spent in only driving to the beach and back. But now, she would prefer that the Sylvesters would not come till the dresses and the trunks did. All she could find out, from inquiry, on returning, was, "that another lot was expected on Saturday." The next day she suggested:–

"Suppose we take our dinner with us to the beach, and spend the day." The Sylvesters and Ann Maria then would find them on the beach, where her travelling-dress would be quite appropriate. "I am a little tired," she added, "of going back and forward over the same road; but when the rest come we can vary it."

The plan was agreed to, but Mr. Peterkin and the little boys remained to go over the farm again.

They had an excellent picnic on the beach, under the shadow of a ledge of sand. They were just putting up their things when they saw a party of people approaching from the other end of the beach.

"I am glad to see some pleasant-looking people at last," said Elizabeth Eliza, and they all turned to walk toward them.

As the other party drew near she recognized Ann Maria Bromwick! And with her were the Sylvesters,–so they proved to be, for she had never seen them before.

"What! you have come in our absence!" exclaimed Elizabeth Eliza.

"And we have been wondering what had become of you!" cried Ann Maria.

"I thought you would be at the farm before us," said Elizabeth Eliza to Mr. Sylvester, to whom she was introduced.

"We have been looking for you at the farm," he was saying to her.

"But we are at the farm," said Elizabeth Eliza.

"And so are we!" said Ann Maria.

"We have been there two days," said Mrs. Peterkin.

"And so have we, at the 'Old Farm,' just at the end of the beach," said Ann Maria.

"Our farm is old enough," said Solomon John.

"Whereabouts are you?" asked Mr. Sylvester.

Elizabeth Eliza pointed to the road they had come.

A smile came over Mr. Sylvester's face; he knew the country well.

"You mean the farm-house behind the hill, at the end of the road?" he asked.

The Peterkins all nodded affirmatively.

Ann Maria could not restrain herself, as broad smiles came over the faces of all the party.

"Why, that is the Poor-house!" she exclaimed.

"The town farm," Mr. Sylvester explained, deprecatingly.

The Peterkins were silent for a while. The Sylvesters tried not to laugh.

"There certainly were some disagreeable old men and women there!" said Elizabeth Eliza, at last.

"But we have surely been made very comfortable," Mrs. Peterkin declared.

"A very simple mistake," said Mr. Sylvester, continuing his amusement. "Your trunks arrived all right at the 'Old Farm,' two days ago."

"Let us go back directly," said Elizabeth Eliza.

"As directly as our horse will allow," said Agamemnon.

Mr. Sylvester helped them into the wagon. "Your rooms are awaiting you," he said. "Why not come with us?"

"We want to find Mr. Peterkin before we do anything else," said Mrs. Peterkin.

They rode back in silence, till Elizabeth Eliza said, "Do you suppose they took us for paupers?"

"We have not seen any 'they,'" said Solomon John, "except Mr. Atwood."

At the entrance of the farm-yard Mr. Peterkin met them.

"I have been looking for you," he said. "I have just made a discovery."

"We have made it, too," said Elizabeth Eliza; "we are in the poor-house."

"How did you find it out?" Mrs. Peterkin asked of Mr. Peterkin.

"Mr. Atwood came to me, puzzled with a telegram that had been brought to him from the station, which he ought to have got two days ago. It came from a Mr. Peters, whom they were expecting here this week, with his wife and boys, to take charge of the establishment. He telegraphed to say he cannot come till Friday. Now, Mr. Atwood had supposed we were the Peterses, whom he had sent for the day we arrived, not having received this telegram."

"Oh, I see, I see!" said Mrs. Peterkin; "and we did get into a muddle at the station!"

Mr. Atwood met them at the porch. "I beg pardon," he said. "I hope you have found it comfortable here, and shall be glad to have you stay till Mr. Peters' family comes."

At this moment wheels were heard. Mr. Sylvester had arrived, with an open wagon, to take the Peterkins to the "Old Farm."

Martha was waiting within the door, and said to Elizabeth Eliza, "Beg pardon, miss, for thinking you was one of the inmates, and putting you in that room. We thought it so kind of Mrs. Peters to take you off every day with the other gentlemen, that looked so wandering."

Elizabeth Eliza did not know whether to laugh or to cry.

Mr. Peterkin and the little boys decided to stay at the farm till Friday. But Agamemnon and Solomon John preferred to leave with Mr. Sylvester, and to take their electrical machine and camera when they came for Mr. Peterkin.

Mrs. Peterkin was tempted to stay another night, to be wakened once more by the guinea-hens. But Elizabeth Eliza bore her off. There was not much packing to be done. She shouted good-by into the ears of the deaf old lady, and waved her hand to the foreign one, and glad to bid farewell to the old men with their pipes, leaning against the porch.

"This time," she said, "it is not our trunks that were lost"–

"But we, as a family," said Mrs. Peterkin.

Congratulations on finishing EP Fourth Reader!

ANSWERS

Day 92

He is arrested for being a spy and a traitor, selling secrets to the Russians. He is convicted and sent to jail. The children think he's innocent.

Day 98

Vocabulary: conflict-dispute, consequence-result, happiness-pleasure, sneaky-crafty, frightful-terrifying, worry-anxious, jealousy-envy, ask-inquire, distress-dismay, argument-dispute, covered-clad

Day 102

yes

Day 104

She wants to know what kind of person she is. She says she doesn't know because she hasn't had any trials. It just happened to her that she is smart and rich.

Vocabulary: great-greatest, forget-forgetful, excite-excitable, annoy-annoyance, affection-affectionate, private-privacy, free-freedom, depend-dependence, lion-lioness, child-childhood

Day 106

ancient – modern antonyms, admire – respect, abundant – scarce antonyms, compromise – negotiate, dismay – distress, alert – inattentive antonyms, anticipate – expect, creative – unimaginative antonyms, clumsy – graceful antonyms, strife – conflict   The others are synonyms.

Day 115

palpitating: beating, trembling
aperture: an opening
dexterity: skill
precipitately: to move suddenly, to happen suddenly and unexpectedly
reconnoiter: to make observations

Day 118

 disconsolate: unable to be comfortable
 sordid: dirty
 obstinate: stubborn
 impertinence, impudent: disrespectful
 rapturous: feeling great pleasure

Day 123

 Vocabulary: 1.E, 2.I, 3.G or B, 4.J, 5.L, 6.A, 7.C, 8.H, 9.F, 10.B or G, 11.K, 12.D

Day 133

 fight-conflict, consequence-result, happiness-rapturous, sneaky-crafty, frightful-terrifying, worry-anxious, jealousy-envy, ask-inquire, distress-dismay, argument-dispute, covered-clad

Day 138

 through story telling

PLEASE consider passing this book along to a family in need by contacting us at allinonehomeschool@gmail.com when you are finished with it.

ABOUT THE Easy Peasy All-in-One Homeschool

The Easy Peasy All-in-One Homeschool is a free, complete online homeschool curriculum. There are 180 days of ready-to-go assignments for every level and every subject. It's created for your children to work as independently as you want them to. Preschool through high school is available as well as courses ranging from English, math, science and history to art, music, computer, thinking, physical education and health. A daily Bible lesson is offered as well. The mission of Easy Peasy is to enable those to homeschool who otherwise thought they couldn't.

Look for other books in the EP Reader Series and for more offline materials to come.